The Beginnings of the Cinema in England
1894–1901

Volume Five: 1900

The Beginnings of the Cinema in England 1894–1901

Volume Five: 1900

John Barnes

With an Introduction by
Richard Maltby

UNIVERSITY
of
EXETER
PRESS

First published in 1997 by
University of Exeter Press
Reed Hall, Streatham Drive
Exeter, Devon EX4 4QR, UK

British Library Cataloguing in Publication Data
A catalogue record for this book is
available from the British Library

ISBN 0 85989 522 X

Typeset in 10/12 pt Times New Roman
by Exe Valley Dataset Ltd, Exeter

Printed and bound in Great Britain by
Short Run Press Ltd, Exeter

Contents

Illustrations

University of Exeter Press gratefully acknowledges the generous financial support of the British Film Institute.

The series of which this is the fifth volume is published in association with the Bill Douglas Centre for the History of Cinema and Popular Culture in the University of Exeter.

Finally, the publisher would like to thank Richard Maltby: for introducing them to John Barnes' series, for editing the text and for providing the Introduction that gives the contextual background for this publication.

Introduction

RICHARD MALTBY

It is astonishing how soon one grows accustomed to new wonders. Otherwise the exhibition of animated photographs now on view at the West Street concert hall would be nothing short of sensational. As it is we have been trained within a very brief space of time to accept photographic records of events, showing all the life and movement and excitement of a scene, almost as much a matter of course as a newspaper record. The Biograph has speedily taken a place in our life as a supplemental chronicler of the more notable events of the day in all quarters of the world, and a highly interesting chronicler it is, enabling us to realise the spirit of scenes with an actuality and vividness hitherto unattainable.

Brighton Herald, 8 December 1900

This book, the fifth volume of John Barnes' *The Beginnings of the Cinema in England*, brings his archaeology of Victorian cinema to a conclusion in the final days of Queen Victoria's reign. As he shows, these early years were arguably the most inventive in the history of British cinema, as pioneers such as Robert Paul, George Albert Smith and James Williamson experimented with techniques of film narrative on some of the most innovative equipment in the world. Seldom if ever again would British filmmakers make so substantial a creative contribution to world cinema. The moment of British cinema's greatest influence coincided with the apogee of Empire itself. In 1897, William K.-L. Dickson had returned to Britain to film the celebrations of Queen Victoria's Diamond Jubilee, the height of British imperial spectacle at the moment of its greatest self-esteem. Two-and-a-half years later, Dickson sailed from Southampton to take the Biograph to battle in South Africa. The Anglo-Boer War which features so prominently in this volume became by far the largest, the most costly and the most humiliating war fought by Britain during its century of imperial pre-eminence. Despite the displays of jingoism at its outset, by the time the war ended in May 1902 it had drained the imperial enthusiasm of the British people, exposed the Empire's military vulnerability, and provoked anxieties about the 'decline of the race' and the onset of 'national decadence'. The pictorial record of the war also records, in its off-screen space, the beginnings of the decline of British international influence, cinematic and otherwise.

By 1900, Britain had ceased to be the world's largest manufacturing nation. It remained the greatest trading power in the world, but its conservative bankers and finance houses were wary of investing in new industries. Britain's economic well-being was instead coming to rest on its 'invisible' exports of insurance and banking services, and on the interest on earlier foreign investments. In the first years of the twentieth century, as Pathé Frères and the Edison Manufacturing Company began to industrialize film production in France and the United States, British companies failed to attract the investment capital needed to transform film–making in Britain from its initial cottage industry state. By 1906, Britain's growing exhibition trade was heavily reliant on imported products, and, apart from Cecil M. Hepworth, the pioneers of cinema in Britain had largely abandoned film production. In 1910, Robert Paul, the 'Father of the British Film Industry' and the central character of John Barnes' narrative in *The Beginnings of the Cinema in England* series, sold all his moving picture interests and returned to his original profession of scientific instrument making.

John Barnes' research into Victorian cinema has been one of the founding works of the resurgent study of early cinema. Since 1976, when the first volume of *The Beginnings of the Cinema in England* was published, the study of cinema has lodged itself firmly in the academy and turned slowly away from an adolescent enthusiasm for grand theory towards a recognition of the need to rewrite the history of cinema in terms other than those of the entertainment industry's publicity apparatus. Nowwhere has this 'turn to history' been more evident than in the study of early cinema, where the very strangeness of the first moving images for present-day viewers has required us to reconstruct the context of their production and projection. In this task, the sheer detail of John Barnes' pioneering research in the archives of the Patents Office, in the photographic press. *The Era* and the *London Entr'acte*, and in the magic lantern and fairground trade press, has provided an exemplary model for subsequent historians. *The Beginnings of the Cinema in England* was the first work of British film history to recognize the importance of many of these sources and to make systematic use of them. As John Fell has observed of Barnes' work, it is 'the kind of history on which others draw and which is disposed to outlive its offspring'.[1]

John Barnes' dedication to early cinema both long predates and remains aloof from the sometimes querulous disputations of the film academy. His research, conducted in partnership with his brother William, has always been precisely empirical, unencumbered by theories of ideology or spectatorship, and rooted instead in the detailed observation of the material of cinema itself; its recording and projecting equipment as much as the films themselves and contemporary accounts of their exhibition. He is, in the very best sense of the term, an *amateur*, a scholar inspired by an unqualified love for the object of his scholarship, whose work is conducted outside the institutional frameworks which now dominate academic research. It is an honourable English tradition, not least among the Victorian pioneers of British cinema.

John and William Barnes began their cinema collection in the 1930s. The brothers amassed films, equipment and publications from cinema's first decade, along with vast quantities of pre-cinema artefacts, until they had built up one of the world's greatest collections on the history of moving pictures on public display in St. Ives, Cornwall until 1986 and now held in the Archives of the Barnes Museum of Cinematography. As leading authorities in the field, they shared their expertise with collectors and researchers from all over the world with a legendary generosity. The two-volume catalogue of the Barnes Museum, long out of print and much sought-after, is a standard reference work for archivists and collectors; like the catalogue, John Barnes' history of Victorian cinema is a distillation of the joint researches of the Barnes brothers over more than sixty years.

To many of this book's readers John Barnes' work will need no introduction, but because it contains the fifth act of a narrative, some readers not familiar with the *dramatis personae* of previous volumes may find an introductory synopsis helpful. In addition to giving me the opportunity to acknowledge the importance of John Barnes' contribution to cinema history, my introduction aims to describe the cultural and political milieu in which the personnel and technology of early British film flourished, as well as to indicate some directions in which further research might develop.

The 'General Public'

> The Bradford Empire will warrant the support of all classes of society. Nothing will be seen or heard here that will raise a blush or put modesty to shame. Bring your wives and daughters.
>
>   Frank Allen, at the opening of the Bradford Empire, 30 January, 1899[2]

> Who has brought that family public to the music hall? The County Council. What is it that attracted the father, mother, cousin, sister, and aunt? It is because we have said music halls and theatres should be so decently-conducted, and that they should be so proper for the public, profitable for the employer, and because we dare to be Daniels, we dare to repress vulgarity—and to check indecency, and will not allow the music hall to resemble the ante-chamber to a brothel, or the annexe to a vulgar public-house.
>
>   George Sims, 1902.[3]

Perhaps the two principal questions a cultural historian might ask of British cinema in 1900, as indeed of any cinema, are: who made up its audience, and from what sources did the subjects of its films originate? Cinema's complexity as a cultural form emanates from its dual system of social production; while films are produced by their manufacturers—whether they be artisans, artists or oligopolies—the cinema as an occasion of social meaning is produced, and repeatedly reproduced, by its audiences. Yet we still know remarkably little about early cinema's viewers, who are too often imagined cowering under their seats trying to avoid the arrival of the train at Ciotat as if they had never before encountered the spectacle of movement projected onto a screen. The social composition of American audiences for early cinema has been a topic for discussion among film historians, but far less attention has been paid to the same question in Britain. This is curious, since Britain has always been a far more self-consciously class-based society than the United States, and distinctions among class groupings have played such a visible role in shaping British culture. Cinema adopted the aesthetic practices and preferences of the cultural milieu into which it emerged. In Britain, cinema began its commercial existence—which is to say, its social existence—in the music hall, and the content of early films provides evidence of its designed appeal to a music hall audience.

In an essay titled 'The Myth of Total Cinema', the French critic André Bazin famously argued that the invention of cinema was guided by a pervasive nineteenth-century ambition to reproduce reality mechanically, 'unburdened by the freedom of interpretation of the artist or the irreversibility of time'.[4] Dickson himself less mysteriously described cinema as 'the crown and flower of nineteenth century magic'. The two observations are less incompatible than subsequent emphases on cinema's aesthetic of realism might make them appear. Contemporary accounts of the earliest screenings single out the Lumières' *A Boat Leaving Harbour* or Robert

Paul's *Rough Sea at Dover* for particular praise. As Deac Rossell has pointed out, these films reproduce a subject familiar to audiences of magic lantern shows, which would commonly feature panoramic slipping slides of harbour scenes and other such nautical views.[5] The familiar subject matter of these screenings allowed audiences to recognize the superior illusion of cinema, conveyed by the much greater detail of movement recorded; audiences registered their astonishment at the illusion at the same time that they observed the realism of the reproduction on the screen. The subject matter of early films was chosen either because it would show off what cinema could do better than other means of projected or theatrical illusion, or because it showed things that audiences wanted to see.

Most of the audiences for early film would have been familiar with the conventions of late nineteenth century theatre as well as those of the lantern show. The sensation scenes of spectacular melodrama relied on a 'realism' conveyed through surface detail, mass and scale. The 1881 Drury Lane Theatre production of *Youth*, for instance, re-enacted a fierce engagement near the Khyber Pass in which real Gatling guns and Martini-Henry rifles were fired by the performers until the theatre was filled with smoke. The following year's spectacle, *Pluck,* featured a mob breaking bank windows made of real glass, two train crashes, a snowstorm in Piccadilly Circus and a burning building. The rest of the century saw a continuing escalation of realistic theatrical spectacle: in 1900 actor-manager Herbert Beerbohm Tree commented that, 'the public demand absolute exactitude, they delight in photographic accuracy, and are satisfied if the thing produced exactly resembles the original without stopping to think whether the original was worth reproduction'. The 1899 Drury Lane melodrama *Hearts are Trumps* featured an Alpine landslide and the Royal Academy exhibition. However, the plot reached its climax during a scene in a music hall in which a lecherous aristocratic villain is unmasked when a film of him trying to seduce the heroine is screened. According to theatre historian Michael Booth, the whole point of spectacle melodrama 'was the reproduction of emotional, physical, and social sensation and the painting of a highly selective, highly coloured portrait of modern society and modern urban life in as "realistic" a way as possible'. The cinema's enhancement of the fidelity of the visual image was not, Booth argues, 'the culmination of a teleological process in which the theatre struggled clumsily toward the divine glory of cinematic realism, but simply one of the many responses of an increasingly sophisticated entertainment technology to the demand for pictorial realism'.[6]

In the earliest venues for the exhibition of the Lumières' Cinématographe and Robert Paul's Theatrograph we can identify a tension which has to do with both the pretensions of cinema's cultural purposes and the audiences it might hope to attract. Félicien Trewey first exhibited the Cinématographe at the Polytechnic Institution in Regent Street, 'the Pioneer Institute for Technical Education', while Paul's first showings were at Finsbury Technical College and the Royal Institution. Catering to a predominantly middle-class clientele, these venues provided the education in popular science that was a feature of late Victorian bourgeois culture. In such locations, cinema emerged into a tradition of 'improving recreation' established by the illustrated lecture and lantern show. Within two years, animated photography had become a regular addition to such performances at town halls, galleries, pleasure gardens and assembly rooms throughout the country.

These first showings were, however, primarily intended for a select audience of theatrical impresarios who might be enticed into booking the equipment. For Trewey's first exhibition, 'the whole of the London press, as well as every circus, music-hall and theatre manager in London' were invited to the screening and the sumptuous banquet which followed; subsequently, he secured an exclusive engagement at the Empire Theatre of Varieties, Leicester Square.[7] Although Paul claimed to know nothing of the entertainment business, he rapidly secured simultaneous engagements at the Olympia, 'London's greatest pleasure resort' managed by the Drury Lane impresario Sir Augustus Harris, and at the Alhambra Theatre of Varieties, Leicester Square. Within a month of its first scientific screening in Britain, cinema was installed in the two most celebrated variety venues in the West End.

The Empire and the Alhambra Theatres recruited a quite different audience to the one habitually attending the Polytechnic. The Cinématographe may have first appeared on the Empire bill between the eccentric comedienne and the bicycling cockatoo, but the bill's principal attraction was the *ballet divertissement*, the chief object of which was, according to Mrs Ormiston Chant of the Britishwoman's Temperance Association, 'to show the limbs of the female performers'. In October 1894 the Empire Theatre was closed by its management during a dispute with the London County Council over the renewal of its licence. The Council sought to prohibit the drinking of alcohol in the auditorium, and to close the Empire's notorious Promenade, an area of the theatre with bars and distant views of the stage where, claimed Mrs Chant, 'young women . . . more or less painted and gorgeously dressed . . . accosted young gentlemen'. When the Empire reopened after a week, with the Promenade partitioned off from the stage, a group of young aristocratic 'heavy swells' including Winston Churchill tore down the partition in a near riot. Although the West End's night life became somewhat more subdued after the trial of Oscar Wilde in 1895, both these theatres maintained their reputation as venues for prostitutes as well as sites for variety, sensation and novelty. In another skirmish during the extended campaign to 'clean up the halls' in the 1890s, the Palace Theatre of Varieties in Shaftesbury Avenue, the future home of the Biograph and managed by the unctuously respectable 'Father of the Halls' Charles Morton, also had its licence threatened in 1894 for staging 'Living Pictures', *tableaux vivants* in which actors posed in states of undress which the Council considered 'detrimental to the best interests and moral well-being of the performers and spectators'.[8]

Paul's first Animatograph programme at the Alhambra Theatre, featuring nautch dancers, a female contortionist, a lightning cartoonist and a boxing kangaroo, was itself a music hall bill in miniature. Wherever animated photographs were exhibited, the physical constraints on the duration of early films ensured that the programme conformed to the aesthetics of the music hall and the popular press and produced a miscellaneous and ever-changing assembly of novelties, sensations and human interest enclosed within a finite space and time: 'snippets there, "turns" here . . . catching your attention for one thing and switching it on to another before you know where you are'.[9] Like the dancers, acrobats, boxers and bodybuilders of Edison's Kinetoscope films, the subject matter of Paul's first films with Birt Acres seems designed to appeal to a predominantly male audience. Their first commercial film for the Kinetoscope was the 1895 Boat Race; shortly afterwards they filmed the 1895 Derby. The following year Paul turned his filming of 'the Prince's Derby' into a performance event, as the film was rushed to London for processing and screening at the Alhambra and Canterbury music halls the day after the race. However technically unsuited these events were to the capacities of Paul's equipment, they were chosen because of their enormous popularity with the audiences who would view them.

For much of the nineteenth century, Derby Day was a carnivalesque occasion of 'violent delights' in which, as artist Gustav Doré described it in 1872, 'all classes are intermingled for a few hours on the happiest terms'. Another French observer, Hyppolyte Taine, viewed it more darkly as 'an outlet for a year of repression . . . today it is hail fellow well met; but this lasts for a day only, after the manner of the ancient saturnalia'. From the middle of the century the Boat Race had provided a similar occasion for popular bacchanalia, drawing crowds of two and three hundred thousand.[10] By 1900, these and other public gatherings—the Cup Final, the Lord Mayor's Show—were more sober and self-disciplined events, but they retained vestiges of the carnival created by the temporary suspension of class privilege and deference. West End music hall audiences recognized this promiscuous assemblage of classes in their own composition, and congratulated themselves in displays of raucously patriotic celebration; Paul's film of the 1896 Derby, won by the Prince of Wales' horse Persimmon, was viewed with 'mad enthusiasm' by the Alhambra audience, 'which demanded three repetitions of the film, and sang "God Bless the Prince of Wales"', while many stood on their seats'.[11]

Only the West End theatres drew aristocrats, army officers, students and tourists in any significant numbers, however. The mixture of classes in other London and provincial music halls was less diverse. Music hall had its origins in public house entertainments in the first half of the century; 'free and easy' gatherings in singing saloons in which local amateurs performed under the auspices of a chairman. Charles Morton opened one of the first purpose-built music halls at the Canterbury Arms, Lambeth in 1852, and thereafter the halls spread throughout the country, initially as adjuncts to pubs but increasingly after 1880 as separate establishments. The new music halls came increasingly to resemble other theatres in their architecture and organization of space, with the proscenium arch stages and fixed seating replacing the platform stage and tables of earlier auditoria. However, the content of music hall performances remained a distinctive 'bill of varieties'; a succession of single acts, each lasting ten minutes or less, with the whole four- or five-hour programme dominated by comics and singers. Like vaudeville in the United States, the music hall industry prefigured the commercial entertainment industries of the twentieth century. In the late 1890s, London's forty music halls were selling 14 million tickets annually.[12] The logic of the market ensured that the basic cost of music hall entertainment remained within the regular reach of young working people, but it evolved with its audience in its aspirations to respectability.[13]

In the last quarter of the nineteenth century, the population of Britain came to reap the benefits of its early industrialization. Living standards rose further, more generally and more conspicuously than elsewhere in Europe. Although the majority of working-class families lived on 'round about a pound a week', barely above subsistence level, social surveys conducted around the turn of the century indicate that a wide section of the working class lived in some degree of comparative comfort; their houses might be decorated with wallpaper and linoleum floors, and very occasionally there might be an upright piano in the parlour. More than half the working class participated regularly in a commercial leisure activity, and even the poorest classes now assumed that they had a right to leisure.[14] One of the most striking features of late nineteenth-century British society was its steadily diminishing rate of recorded crime, a phenomenon which distinguished Britain from other industrializing societies in the latter half of the nineteenth century. The most deprived districts of London and other large cities were no longer areas beyond the law.[15] The culture of respectability, which had led Friedrich Engels to complain that even the working class was bourgeois in this most bourgeois of nations, permeated old and new forms of popular amusement alike. The great fairs of mid-Victorian London had disappeared along with bear–baiting, cock-fighting and the gin palace. Public houses had lost many of their earlier social and economic functions; drinking hours had been restricted and drunkenness had decreased. In most trades, the irregular institution of 'St Monday' had disappeared to be replaced by four official bank holidays.

While some of these changes arose from bourgeois attempts to regulate, rationalize and improve the recreation of the lower orders, working-class leisure habits were gradually transformed not by middle-class evangelism but by the entrepreneurs of commercial entertainment, seaside resorts and professional sport, who found it more securely profitable to meet the people's respectable desires for diversion than to cater to disreputable appetites. The new leisure industries competed with equally new clothing, foodstuffs and chemical industries for the surplus income of the 'respectable' working class and the expanding membership of the lower middle classes who worked as clerks, civil servants, teachers, journalists, commercial travellers and shop assistants. These social groups were the most conspicuous beneficiaries of the sustained rise in real incomes and the fall in working hours in the last quarter of the nineteenth century. They were also the principal purchasers of the new mass-produced consumer goods—the packaged groceries of Messrs Lipton, Lever and Lyons of furniture and clothing from the multiple retailing outlets of John Jacobs, Woolworth's, Marks and Spencer; of Raleigh safety bicycles; and of the expanding world of commercial entertainment.

The transformation of the retail trade brought about by multiple outlet shops such as Home and Colonial, Boots and W.H. Smith created new categories of employment which demanded neatness, cleanliness, civility and the ability to read and write, qualities not previously required of manual workers.[16] More often than not, these jobs were taken by the sons and daughters of working-class parents, who were the beneficiaries of the mass elementary education system introduced by the 1870 Education Act and who aspired to upward social mobility. In their Sunday best clothes, these young working people looked more like their middle class equivalents than the previous generation had or when compared with workers elsewhere in Europe. On holiday, the British also 'moved up a class', exchanging their everyday habits for the clothes, food, spending patterns, resorts and recreational pursuits of the class above them.[17] A music hall song from 1900 offered this self-description of the new suburban lower middle class:

> We're none of us vulgar we're all trim and neat . . .
> We're just a bit noisy but do nothing wrong
> The week through we're working and earning the brass
> But when Saturday comes, why we try to be class.[18]

Although the niceties of class distinction grew ever more refined, two new phrases that recognized this convergence in the outward appearance and manners of the 'respectable' classes entered the language in the 1890s: journalists began to refer to 'the man in the street' as a member of a 'general public', a social grouping made up of customers and consumers, 'a clientele more passive, more predictable and more numerous than that defined by the categories of class'.[19] The cultural anxieties provoked by this new social formation were the anxieties of modernism; while middle-class reformers had worried that earlier forms of working-class entertainment had encouraged 'loose' living, the new anxiety was that the Palaces of Variety were 'seeking to provide for a new class of people a new form of entertainment', attracting middle-class youth 'to a new form of fast life' in audiences of nameless and faceless strangers eager to experiment with social styles.[20] Charles Masterman thought he was observing the emergence of a 'new race . . . the city type . . . voluble, excitable, with little ballast, stamina or endurance—seeking stimulus in drink, in betting, in any unaccustomed conflicts at home or abroad'.[21]

At least when he went to the music hall, the man in the street was most likely to behave like a 'jingo filibustering Imperialist'.[22] Partly because of the close association between Conservatism and the drink trade in opposition to evangelical reform, the music halls had an established and self-conscious tradition of Toryism. Male impersonator Vesta Tilley, who was a star of the halls from the 1880s until after the First World War and whose impresario husband became a Conservative MP, observed in 1888 that: 'Nowadays, nothing goes down better than a good patriotic song'. Every political allusion the performers made, she said, 'must be Conservative'.[23] Although the depth and tenacity of working-class support for imperialism has been a matter of debate among social historians, the sheer volume of music hall songs and sketches celebrating Britain's world position provides clear evidence of the popularity of this material with audiences. The imperialism of popular culture was undoubtedly more theatrical than theoretical; it lauded patriotic virtue rather than arguing the economic or political benefits of Empire and drew the music hall's socially mixed audience into a shared community expressing 'the superiority of Englishmen (i.e. themselves) in every respect to every nation on earth'.[24] Behaviour at the music hall did not necessarily translate into overt political action; the apathy of the majority of workers was captured in the cry heard in a Working Men's Club in 1899: 'We don't want to be bothered with politics after a hard day's work; what we want is recreation'.[25]

Incorporated so fully as it was into the forms and discourses of popular culture, imperialism—the generalized, unquestioning endorsement of 'the Imperial Ascendancy of the British Empire'—was a form of recreation, provided by national organizations such as the Primrose League and the Navy League in the form of *tableaux vivants*, exhibitions and lantern lectures. For its $1^1/_2$ million working-class members, the main attraction of the Primrose League may have been its extensive social programme, but it distributed its imperial propaganda on behalf of the Conservative Party.[26] While in the long term the most important political event of 1900 may have been the creation of the Labour Representation Committee, forerunner of the British Labour Party, it is nevertheless also true that the total active membership of the Independent Labour Party in 1900 was 6,000, equivalent to the membership of the Primrose League in Bolton, Lancashire. Attachment to Empire, monarchy and the existing order, and pride in Britain's achievements at home and overseas were more pervasive than a desire for an alternative political, social, or economic system.[27]

For the majority of Britons, the Empire was most tangible as a phenomenon of spectacle and style; the Jubilees, the imperial exhibitions and tournaments in which, as one programme exclaimed, 'the militant spirit of our empire is translated into Flesh and Blood'.[28] Those of the Queen's subjects who aspired to respectability could display their loyalty by consuming the imperialist imagery and rhetoric of popular culture. Outside the West End, jingoism as a social style was most pronounced in the music halls of the new suburbs, among a young male audience who saw themselves as sometimes raucous but never rebellious. The patriotic volume increased at moments of military excitement; the production of such 'war-warbles' such as *There'll Be a Hot Time in the Transvaal Tonight, The Boers Have Got My Daddy*, and *Cheer Up, Buller!* peaked during the Anglo-Boer War.[29] In the orgy of patriotism which greeted the relief of Mafeking, Liberal opponents of the war feared that imperialist rhetoric and display would delude the masses into acquiescing in the existing order and abandoning any interest in social reform. In *The Psychology of Jingoism*, anti-imperialist J.A. Hobson denounced the 'biased, enslaved and poisonous press' and the entertainments of the public house and the music hall for their sinister manipulation of mass emotions.[30] He believed that among the middle and working classes, the music hall was 'a more potent educator than the church, the school, the political meeting, or even the press . . . its words and melodies pass by quick magic from the Empire or the Alhambra over the length and breadth of the land, re-echoed in a thousand provincial halls, clubs, and drinking saloons, until the remotest village is familiar with air and sentiment'.[31]

The innovations in variety entertainment in the 1890s did not come from the 'imperial playgrounds' of the West End, but from the amalgamation of provincial music hall managements into theatre syndicates controlled by impresarios such as E.W. Moss, Oswald Stoll and Richard Thornton. The syndicates implemented more efficient systems of exploiting their artistes through the co-ordinated booking of acts across a circuit of theatres and the 'turns' system which made it possible for an artiste to perform in several theatres in the same area every night. During the 1890s Moss and Stoll built Empires, Hippodromes, Palaces and Olympias in almost every major city from Glasgow to Leicester and Cardiff; at the end of the decade they expanded into the London suburbs, securing their joint domination of the most valuable and prestigious tier of the nation's variety theatres and music halls. In 1899 Moss unified his holdings into one public company, capitalized at nearly 2 million, and in 1900 he opened the London Hippodrome.[32]

Earlier caterers—as music hall proprietors styled themselves—had often claimed to attract a more respectable clientele; the new syndicated 'Palaces of Variety' achieved this aim by providing an environment that would attract the middle classes as well as the traditional music hall audience. In 1887 the *Financial News* recommended the music hall to the bourgeois investors who financed the expansion of the syndicates; its audiences were growing and now included 'people of a better kind than formerly'.[33] The majority of the new theatres were designed by theatre architect Frank Matcham; their ornate façades and opulent decor provided elegant, safe and well-ventilated surroundings in which the middle class could enjoy 'healthy' variety entertainment without fear of contamination from the working class.[34] In 1900, Matcham was involved in seven theatre building and reconstruction projects, including the Palace Theatre, Leicester, which could seat 3,000 people on three tiers and which was designed with enough separate entrances and exits to permit the rapid turnover of audience required by the system of twice-nightly performances in which the Biograph featured prominently. The entrances and exits served a multiplicity of purposes: they guaranteed a high degree of safety, and in combination with the theatre's pricing structure, they maintained a rigid but unobtrusive separation of the classes by ensuring that each section of the audience was directed to its proper place, mingling only with their own kind while sharing the conviviality of a consensual entertainment.

The 'sharp but courteous businessmen' who managed these theatres were more likely to be accountants than publicans, and were more concerned to assure their shareholders of their probity than to impress their good fellowship on their customers. Their dealings with the artistes also became more formalized and saw the introduction of contracts and agents.[35] Before the days of fixed seats, music hall had relied on the rapport between the performer and the rowdy, mobile audience, in large part created by the ribald and topical patter singers interjected between the verses of their songs. But the design and size of the new theatres—one performer described playing the 3,389-seat London Coliseum as being like 'barking into a chasm'[36]— enforced a separation between artiste and audience that was furthered by manage- ment imposed restrictions on ad libbing. As early as 1879 London proprietors had petitioned the Home Secretary for the appointment of an official censor 'to protect them against their own incorrigible comics and the strictures of an amateur and capricious magistracy'.[37] When this was refused, proprietors developed house rules which required songs to be submitted in advance and restricted artistes from addressing the audience. They also employed their own songwriters as a further means of controlling material, and put on sketches or revues with several turns in them, which required more attention from the audience. Vulgarity was widely prohibited, along with material deemed topical or political. The rules for performers at Collins' theatre in 1892 included: 'No offensive allusions to be made to any Member of the Royal Family; Members of Parliament, German Princes, police authorities, or any member thereof, the London County Council, or any member of that body; no allusion whatever to religion, or any religious sect; no allusion to the administration of the law of the country'.[38]

The interests of capital and authority combined to create orderly places of popular amusement. Direct State intervention, in the form of censorship, was avoided because proprietors regulated the behaviour of their audiences and the content of the entertainment in order to safeguard their capital investments, their licences and their profits.[39] Applying what Peter Bailey has called 'the disciplines of respectability' to the reformed music hall was also more efficient. The ban on drinking in the auditorium meant that cutomers were more likely to stay in their seats for the whole of a performance, and were less likely to interrupt. Prohibiting artists from bantering with the audience not only reduced the likelihood of vulgarity but meant that performances could be scheduled more exactly, an increasingly important consideration for managers running twice-nightly shows and for artistes playing turns at several syndicated halls in an evening. In 1900, drama critic John Hollingshead described the concern of Moss, Stoll and the other syndicates to supply 'wholesome amusement for the people' as being an 'entirely commercial' one: 'Its first duty, which it strictly observes, is to conduct its business according to the rules of good citizenship; and its second duty, which it performs to the best of its ability, is to earn a satisfactory dividend for its shareholders'.[40]

Beyond their novelty appeal, animated photographs conformed almost ideally to the formal requirements of 'improved' popular entertainment. The aura of science which surrounded the screenings gave the exhibitors an appearance of respectability, while their mechanical performance enabled the content and duration to be planned and if necessary controlled in advance. Shows could be repeated, and once the initial scarcity of projection machines had been overcome, it was a relatively cheap item on the variety bill by comparison to its drawing power. Victorian film–makers were equally inclined to conform to the syndicate proprietors' requirements for material which was 'funny without vulgarity'.[41] G.A. Smith, for instance, had been a hypnotist in music hall and then the proprietor of a pleasure garden in Hove catering to a middle-class clientele before he began producing films in 1897. More generally, the pioneers of British cinema were small businessmen who possessed a good technical education; conventional members of the middle class in their aesthetics and their politics alike, innovating cinema technology within the craft tradition of the machine workshop. Whereas their developments in film technique derived from technical experiments, the unpretentious subject matter of their films was acquired from the existing spectrum of commercial culture, as catalogue descriptions of films as 'fine examples of already popular subjects' indicate.[42] Music hall acts provided one source; melodrama, pantomime, and the abundant visual culture of lantern slides, cartoons, postcards and stereographs offered overlapping opportunities for imitation and animation. Such films as *The Miller and the Sweep* (G.A. Smith 1897, Robert Paul, 1898) and *Come Along Do!* (Paul, 1898) were variations on themes regularly seen in music hall turns, jokes, cartoons and in the comic press. These familiar anecdotes from the 'socially introverted carefree world of *Ally Sloper, Judy* and *The Sporting Times*' translated effectively to the condensed form of the one-shot film, and their recurrence suggests less a direct borrowing from any individual source and rather an attempt to incorporate film into the mainstream of Victorian popular culture as fully as the formal limitations of the medium would allow.[43]

The Spread of Cinema

The first Palace Theatre Matinee of the season took place last Saturday, when there was a crowded audience. It was curious to see what a lot of young people were present. Father and mother brought their families, and looking along the stalls one would sometimes see as many as half-a-dozen youngsters in a bunch . . . When I saw such a host of young folks at the Palace last Saturday I was anxious to discover what was the item in the programme that specially attracted them and I left the building persuaded that the Biograph was, in a considerable measure, the guilty instrument.

The Entr'acte, 23 September 1897

Following on from the premières in the West End, the pioneers of English cinema toured the major syndicated variety theatres. Félicien Trewey exhibited the Cinématographe on both the Moss, Thornton and Stoll circuits in 1896; Robert Paul provided shows for the London Syndicate Halls under the control of George Adney

Payne, and acquired an agent to arrange bookings outside London. By late 1896 music hall audience tastes were influencing film content. In addition to films showing variety starts, Paul's films of the Gordon Highlanders would have stirred the patriotic emotions of the music hall audience as would the increasing number of films of royalty. By now Paul had established himself as the dominant figure in the nascent British industry and the principal supplier of projection equipment. In 1897 his company, capitalized at £60,000, declared a profit of nearly £13,000. In the next two years, as the showing of films changed from being an occasional event at the principal variety theatres to a regular or permanent item on most music hall bills, a host of other companies arose to provide for the rapidly expanding exhibition industry. (The earlier volumes of John Barnes' series provide a detailed account of these companies and the films and equipment they manufactured).

In September 1898 the *Optical Magic Lantern Journal* observed with no hint of exaggeration that, 'even in the smallest out-of-the-way villages' it would be difficult to find many people who had not seen a film of Queen Victoria's Diamond Jubilee procession.[44] Exhibition sites had multiplied to include showings at fairgrounds and pleasure parks, as well as municipal halls and the music hall circuit. Fairground exhibitions exposed poorer and younger audiences in industrial and rural areas alike to cinema's attractions. They varied in scale from grand Bioscope Shows in tents capable of holding as many as 500 spectators, to peep–show street cinématographes with eyepieces for twenty people.[45] For the fairground audiences, and their urban equivalents in the penny gaffs and shop shows set up temporarily by itinerant show-men in disused shops, the spectacle and illusion of animated photography probably provided the main attraction. The cheaper shows, certainly, used 'films bought up cheap, after having had . . . a very long life in the halls or at a travelling orthodox show', and their spectators, so low down in the exhibition chain, exerted little if any influence over the choice of subject matter.[46] In terms of earning power for the exhibitors, the music halls remained the dominant exhibition outlets.

Robert Paul's new catalogue in October 1898 stated that 'the public no longer rush to see photographs moving . . . the day is past when anything in the way of animated pictures will do for an audience'. He was arguing in favour of his own switch in production to story films, but in the process he was acknowledging the continued appeal of the 'presentation of topical scenes', such as the Jubilee, or the exhibitions sponsored by Nestlé and Lever of film of the 1897 Sydney Test Match for the Ashes. These films complemented the news coverage of the events represented, and pro-vided a visual corollary to the descriptions in the popular press. Like the panoramas, dioramas and wax museums of the late nineteenth century, they were not so much sources of news in themselves as re-presentations of current events already familiar from other sources. Recent events that still held emotional resonance for their audiences were presented as spectacles; their realism was generated as much by the familiar subject matter as by the technological illusion.

A reviewer of the Ashes film observed that, 'we do not know what further sur-prises Messrs Nestlé and Lever have in store for us, but certainly they could not have chosen a more popular subject than the inter-colonial cricket match'—particularly since England won. Both Poet Laureate Alfred Austin and the lower-middle class jingoes could have imagined only one subject closer to their shared idea of Heaven: 'news of British victories, alternately by land and by sea.'[47]

In October 1898, the first films of British military triumphs reached London from the Sudan to uproarious enthusiasm. Six months earlier, the American Biograph (which had settled into Charles Morton's Palace Theatre on an apparently permanent basis) had shown films of the Spanish-American war, but according to one review, 'there is nothing to indicate sympathy with either side in the pictures, and the crowded audience showed little inclination to make a demonstration'.[48] This audience response was in marked contrast to the reaction in the United States where the same films were eliciting strident displays of patriotic fervour. According to Charles Musser, the war gave the American film industry a new role, acting as an animated newspaper and a vehicle for propaganda: 'Moving pictures had a tangible effect on the way Americans experienced a distant war', projecting outrage at the enemy and glory in victory.[49] In Britain, these images lacked the same resonance, but in October pictures of the Guards returning home from the Sudan were shown at the Palace to prolonged applause 'breaking out as soon as the tablet announced "See the conquering heroes come! Welcome home!" '[50] With such actualities, the propaganda effect was primarily provided by the exhibition context rather than the content of the images.

The war with Spain enabled the American industry to extend its coverage of actualities by reproducing incidents in the war its equipment could not record. The Greco-Turkish war of 1897 occasioned the first such military re-enactments, in a series of films produced by Georges Méliès, which were declared by *Photograms of '97* to be 'wonderfully realistic and extremely popular', despite 'the fact that all these scenes . . . are photographed in a Parisian garden, and owe their attractiveness to good scene-painting and realistic actors'.[51] In August 1899, Méliès began work on an elaborate re-enactment of episodes in the Dreyfus affair, while Captain Dreyfus' second trial for treason was in progress. The case had attracted intense press coverage from around the world, and the scandal surrounding it had riven French society. Méliès' film contained twelve scenes staged according to the same principles that characterized the spectacular realism of the popular theatre, wax museum and panorama, combining the use of painted backdrops and special scenic effects with an attention to detail in the authenticity of costumes and the appearance of the lead figures. Its first screening provoked fights between Dreyfusards and anti-Dreyfusards in the audience; the French Government banned both it and a six-episode Pathé film on the same subject, and attempted to prevent their circulation outside France. Nevertheless, they were widely advertised in Britain, although several articles in the trade press expressed concern about the risk of the films' contentious subject matter stirring up divisive political emotions in an audience.[52]

As with the 'reformed' music hall, the issue was only in part to do with the introduction of political subject matter in an entertainment space. More importantly, the music hall auditorium was a site of consensus, described by contemporaries as a 'refuge from the world, not a place for comment on it'.[53] Its management intended that divisions within the audience—class divisions even more obviously than divisions of political opinion—should be concealed by the architecture of the auditorium and the nostalgia and escapism of the performances. Only divisive politics were, therefore, discouraged. Political subjects that encouraged the expression of consensus—a rousing chorus of *Soldiers of the Queen*, *Another Little Patch of Red*, or some other stirring imperialist anthem, or a *tableau vivant* of Britannia surrounded by exotically-costumed subjects, kangaroos, elephants and lions couchant—were completely acceptable.

The War

> It was an inflamed atmosphere, at once alarming, exciting and impressive . . . as though
> an entire nation had been indoctrinated, but in a slightly frivolous or hair-brained
> way—as though the terrific issues of war, peace and dominion had been taken over by
> actor-managers, allied perhaps with fundamentalist sectarians.[54]

The nineteenth century climaxed in sequential displays of imperial pomp, military
spectacle and gunboat diplomacy. In 1898, a year after the celebrations of Queen
Victoria's Diamond Jubilee, General Sir Herbert Kitchener's military campaign to
recover the Sudan culminated in the Battle of Omdurman, the capture of Khartoum,
and a confrontation with France for control of the Upper Nile. These spectacles of
Empire were fed to an appreciative public through a plethora of media: illustrated
magazines, children's literature and toys, the iconography of advertising and postcards, popular songs and the New Journalism of a rapidly expanding popular press,
led by the *Daily Mail*, founded by Alfred Harmsworth in 1896 and boasting a
circulation of 984,000 by 1900. Viewed with distaste by the upper classes—Lord
Salisbury, Prime Minister from 1895 to 1902, reputedly called it a paper written by
office boys for office boys—the *Daily Mail* and its imitators fostered imperialist
sentiments among its readership, whom it defined as 'the backbone of the great
purchasing public of Britain'.[55]

    For the popular press, the Empire was the greatest of all running news stories. Jan
Morris has argued that the late nineteenth century was the only truly militarist phase
of British history, 'the only brief period when the British public showed an
enthusiastic interest in guns, warships and wars'.[56] Public affection for the army, and
for the ordinary British soldier, Tommy Atkins of Rudyard Kipling's *Barrack Room
Ballads*, was without parallel in Europe. Militarism was one of a cluster of ideas
constituting a new type of racial patriotism in late Victorian society; its other
ingredients included a devotion to royalty, a hero-worshipping cult of personality,
militant Christianity and Social Darwinism. Patriots saw themselves as an 'Imperial
Race . . . vigorous and industrious and intrepid'.[57] In this perspective, the Empire
was understood as a mission, unique in scale and moral content, needed to civilize
the 'backward' world and regenerate the British through a sense of national purpose
that would reconcile class differences. Cecil Rhodes, visionary architect of an
imagined empire in Africa stretching from the Cape to Cairo, declared the British to
be 'the best people in the world, with the highest ideals of decency and justice and
liberty and peace, and the more of the world we inhabit, the better for humanity'.[58]
Such beliefs were pervasive if not universal in British society and inescapable in
popular culture. Popular and élite tastes converged; nationalist composers such as
Edward Elgar and writers such as Kipling and Sir Henry Newbolt achieved both
critical acceptance and popular acclaim.[59]

    The imperialism of popular culture exhibited its darker side not as economic
exploitation but as racial contempt and a glorification of military violence. In the
late Victorian period, argues Ben Shepherd, 'journalism was to imperialism as the
tick bird is to the rhino'. In every colonial war, the British army bore on its back war
correspondents, illustrators and professional self-promoters who would replay the
war in speaking tours across Britain on their return.[60] In a passage excised from later
editions of Kipling's first novel, *The Light that Failed*, one of his characters

denounces war correspondents as 'minister[ing] to the blind, brutal, British public's bestial thirst for blood'.[61] Describing the Battle of Omdurman, during which Kitchener's troops killed 10,000 Sudanese for the loss of twenty eight British men, war correspondent Ernest Bennett wrote of 'potting Dervishes' and eulogized 'the joy of shedding blood'.[62] In popular journalism and fiction alike, imperial warfare was most frequently represented as an adventurous game of gallant charges, heroic retreats, lucky escapes, of pluck, grit and chivalry, in which guns flashed, cannons thundered and the bayonet made short work of the enemy.[63]

By all British expectation, from the army high command to the schoolboys following troop movements in the *Boy's War News*, the South African war should have followed the predictable pattern of the colonial campaigns Britain had been fighting for the previous forty years: an initial reversal, involving the sacrifice of a few 'sons of the blood', followed by a swift retribution delivered by reinforcements from Home. The British Army of 1900 was an instrument designed and equipped for fighting the small wars described in an 1896 army textbook: campaigns 'against savages and semi-civilised races', to secure territory, 'suppress insurrection and lawlessness', 'wipe out an insult or avenge a wrong', 'overthrow a dangerous power' or destroy 'fanatics'.[64] But, however competent it had become at slaughtering indigenes, the army had not fought against Europeans since the Crimean War ended in 1856, and in the years of tension before the outbreak of war, the Boer Republics had armed themselves with German and French artillery and other military technology superior to that available to the British. In 1899, the Government anticipated the war might last three or four months, cost £10 million, and require a maximum of 75,000 troops, who would suffer, at worst, a few hundred casualties. In the event, the war cost some £230 million and involved 450,000 troops from Britain and the Empire. In the two years and eight months it lasted, more than 70,000 soldiers and civilians died.[65]

The war's origins lay in the prolonged conflict of interest between the British colonies of Natal and Cape Colony, and the Boer Republics of the Transvaal and the Orange Free State. The discovery of gold in 1886 transformed the Transvaal into a state with the resources to defend itself against Cecil Rhodes' expansionist designs in southern Africa. Rhodes' attempt to stage an armed insurrection in the Transvaal in 1895 was a fiasco, and while Britain sought to recover its political and moral position, the Transvaal government armed itself with the assistance of other European powers, especially Germany. Britain's aim was to secure the Boer Republics' cooperation in the creation of a federation of South African states in which British supremacy and interest would prevail, but Transvaal's president Paul Kruger remained resolutely hostile to any such outcome. The immediate cause of the war was Britain's insistence that Kruger concede political rights to the *Uitlanders* (foreigners), mainly British subjects working in the Rand goldfields. In the belief that Kruger would 'bluff up to the cannon's mouth' and then capitulate, Sir Alfred Milner, High Commissioner to South Africa and Governor of the Cape since 1897, made little effort at accommodation.[66] In Britain, Colonial Secretary Joseph Chamberlain devoted much effort to securing public support for his South African policy, and by the summer of 1899 the Unionist government was persuaded that the public would accept the necessity of military intervention, and that in the event of war, no European power would come to the Boers' defence. By October Kruger was convinced that Britain was intent on destroying the South African Republics by force. He issued an ultimatum demanding the removal of imperial troops from the Transvaal's borders. War began with the expiry of the ultimatum.

The Boer forces invaded the Cape and Natal with immediate success. By the time the first film footage of British troops in South Africa reached London in November, the army had already suffered a major defeat and its garrisons at Ladysmith, Kimberley and Mafeking were under siege. Such initial setbacks followed the expected course of colonial wars, but much worse was to follow when the reinforcements under General Sir Henry Redvers Buller suffered a series of traumatic and humiliating defeats, culminating in the catastrophe of 'Black Week', 10–17 December 1899, when the Boers inflicted startling defeats on all three elements of the British expeditionary force at Stormberg, Magersfontein and Colenso, killing or capturing 3,000 British troops. News of these defeats occasioned what one army chaplain described as 'a time of mental agony such as we of this generation have never known before. The shock to our national pride, the fear for the honour of our race, the anxiety lest we should prove incapable of guarding the great traditions of the past, the dull weight of personal sorrow . . . shook the heart of England'.[67]

London's theatres, music halls and restaurants were emptied, except for the Palace Theatre where 'people who were not going out to the ordinary place of entertainment went . . . for information' from the Biograph.[68] The complacencies of imperial power were shaken as never before. It was all too clear that the defeats and heavy casualities were the result of incompetent generalship. But as another contemporary chronicler noted: 'The Boers had, by their very successes, sealed their own doom.'[69] The defeats largely silenced criticism of the Government's war policy; few could envisage Britain withdrawing while being beaten. The Government appointed Lord Frederick Roberts of Kandahar as Commander-in-Chief to supersede Buller, with Kitchener—now Kitchener of Khartoum—as his Chief of Staff. Further reinforcements were ordered and calls issued for volunteers. The shibboleths of Empire, inscribed through thirty years of compulsory education in the history and geography of imperial virtues and benefits, and intensified by the enthusiastic invention of atrocity stories by the yellow press, ensured what one account called 'a magnificent outburst of loyalty and devotion to the common cause', most visible in the recruitment of the City Imperial Volunteers (CIV) and the Imperial Yeomanry.[70] Financed by London City Council, the 1,400-strong CIV was raised and equipped within three weeks, and its first contingent sailed on 13 January 1900, only three days after Roberts himself arrived in Cape Town. The volunteer units, which eventually contributed 54,000 men to the campaign, provided the middle classes with a more socially acceptable opportunity to express their patriotism than by enlisting in the regular army, whose poorly-paid ranks were largely filled by semi-skilled and unskilled workers. But while the strongest sounds of jingoism came from the lower-middle class clerks and shop assistants for whom volunteering displayed their commitment to state, nation and society, all sections of the population initially endorsed the war. With one in every seven men aged between eighteen and forty years in uniform for part of the war, few households were without some personal involvement—a cousin or a neighbour under arms.[71]

After Roberts' arrival, the course of the war began to reassert the expected pattern of a colonial war. The Boers had failed to take advantage of their initial victories; rather than pressing on into Natal and the Cape, they halted, laying ineffectual siege to the three British garrisons. While Buller, charged with the relief of Ladysmith and the reconquest of Natal, suffered a further heavy defeat at Spion Kop in late January, Roberts advanced north with his main force, relieving Kimberley in mid-February. On 27 February, the anniversary of the Boers' victory at Majuba Hill in 1881, which had resulted in the establishment of the Boer Republics, Roberts forced the surrender of the Boer general P.A. Cronjé and 4,000 troops at Paardeberg. The following day Buller's forces relieved Sir George White's garrison at Ladysmith. Two weeks later Roberts took Bloemfontein, capital of the Orange Free State. Moving northward across the Vaal River his forces entered Johannesburg on 31 May, and Pretoria, capital of the Transvaal, on 5 June. Meanwhile a separate relief column had raised the siege of Mafeking on 17 May. On 11 September Kruger left the Transvaal for exile, and in October it became a British colony, as the Orange Free State had already done. Capitalizing on the victory, the Unionist government called and won a general election in October. Roberts returned home in triumph in December, leaving Kitchener to complete military operations.

Against expectation, however, the war dragged on for another two years, robbing the eventual victory of any grandeur. The remaining Boer forces adopted guerrilla tactics, successfully harrying the British troops and cutting their communications. Kitchener required substantial reinforcements to drive the guerrillas into an ever-smaller territory. Systematically clearing great tracts of land with a scorched earth policy which burnt 30,000 farms, he interred their inhabitants in concentration camps, where 28,000 civilians, one tenth of the Boer population and more than the number of combatants killed on both sides, died in epidemics. The war 'degenerated into a messy and inglorious manhunt, soured by recriminations and reprisals, executions in the field, arson and broken oaths. . . . Kitchener's bludgeon methods had taken the fun out of following the flags'.[72] By the time the war was over in May 1902, it had exhausted the imperial enthusiasm of the British people and their government.[73]

Until victory was assured, however, the war passionately preoccupied public attention, disguising the extent to which Chamberlain's New Imperialism lacked enduring popular support.[74] Roberts' victories transformed the black depression of December into a mania of celebration, which climaxed in the hysterical reaction to the relief of Colonel Robert Baden-Powell's garrison at Mafeking. The news reached London via Reuter's at 9.20 p.m. on Friday, 18 May. By 10.00 p.m. it had been announced from the stage of every London theatre. At the Alhambra Theatre, the message was projected onto the screen used for film shows. For a few moments, according to the *Daily Mail*, cheers drowned everything else, then 'a sudden hush fell, and "God Save the Queen" was sung with all the solemnity of a hymn in a meeting-house. After this, there was a quarter of an hour of mad fits'. Similar displays of patriotic emotion took place in other theatres; the Empire was the scene of a demonstration 'absolutely unequalled in its annals'. By 11.00 p.m. London's traffic was at a standstill as groups of men, women and children danced up and down the streets arm in arm in a 'wild frenzy'. What the *Daily Mail* called 'London's Roar of Jubilation' spread rapidly to other cities, followed on the Saturday and Sunday by hastily organized official parades.[75] In their scale and intensity the five days of carnival celebration exceeded the victory celebrations of the First and Second World Wars, giving the English language a new word: 'mafficking, indulging in extravagant demonstrations of exultation'.[76]

This was more than a simple expression of joy at victory and relief that comrades in uniform were safe. The events of May 1900 were extraordinary in part because of their disproportion; the little railway town of Mafeking was of small consequence to the course of the war, but the *Daily Express* trumpeted, 'History's Most Heroic Defence Ends in Triumph . . . When Shall their Glory Fade?'[77] Baden-Powell's theatrical conduct of the town's defence, relayed in a stream of jaunty despatches to the outside world, had been a brilliantly effective exercise in self-promotion, while the presence of several members of the aristocracy in the besieged garrison was 'an assurance that British imperialism still had *class*. . . . through the days of ignominy Mafeking . . . brilliantly kept the legend of Empire alive'.[78] The relief of Mafeking celebrated, in carnivalesque mode, the survival of imperial style, in which so much had been invested; in the architecture of so many public buildings and Empire Palaces of Variety, in the Jubilee, the commemorative crockery and the biscuit tins, in the postcards and advertisements in newsagents' windows, and in the carefully hoarded cigarette card collections of the Regiments of the Queen.

What was, however, truly remarkable about May 1900 was that people of every social class participated in 'mafficking' . While the working classes were used to displaying their emotions in public, the middle classes participated with equal enthusiasm, and fraternized, according to the *Annual Register*, 'in a way so opposed to our national coldness and reserve that a foreigner might have thought that some crowning victory had been achieved'.[79] In Birmingham, 'staid citizens, whose severe respectability and decorum were usually beyond question or reproach were to be seen parading the streets, shouting patriotic songs with the full force of their lungs, dancing, jumping, screaming in a delirium of unrestrained joy'.[80] The mafficking crowds, one historian has suggested, were 'an extension of the music hall stage onto the streets', experiencing the emotional frenzy of victory in a self-conscious moment of national community and imperial identity.[81]

The War Films

> The biograph will reveal bravery as no despatch may do, and will tell the truth in all things, owing neither loyalty to chief nor submission to espirit de corps. How far this truthfulness will please the authorities remains to be seen.
>
> *Today*, 26 October 1899.[82]

> The general understanding of a 'fake' film is that of producing a film of a counterfeit representation of an actual event, such as has been practised extensively with South African war subjects, many of which were made in the suburbs of London, besides France and New Jersey, U.S.A.
>
> Charles Urban.[83]

In this climate of opinion, it was hardly surprising that so much of British film production in 1900 should be concerned with the war. Of the 480 films listed in the Appendix to this volume, ninety deal with the war itself, while a similar number show related military and naval subjects. The anecdotal evidence of reviews emphasize the great popularity of these subjects, suggesting that they may have accounted for an even larger share of exhibition time than the forty per cent of production they represented. As a stimulus to the exhibition market and an extension of cinema's cultural function, it is clear that the war had a similar role in Britain to that played two years earlier by the Spanish-American war in the United States.

Throughout 1900, audiences were saturated with a plethora of visual and verbal representations of the war, many of which deployed aspects of the theatrical aesthetic of spectacular realism. The war boosted newspaper circulation considerably, and the press covered it in enormous detail. At one stage *The Times* had twenty correspondents in South Africa. Some of the country's most celebrated authors, including Kipling and Sir Arthur Conan Doyle, travelled to the Cape as correspondents, and produced books describing their adventures. London's publishing houses produced scores of factual and fictional accounts of the war before peace was declared; the best-selling imperialist children's author G.A. Henty published two books on the war, *With Buller in Natal* and *With Roberts to Pretoria*, before his death in 1902. In many of these accounts, including newspaper reports, the boundaries between fact and fiction, reportage and propaganda, were not closely policed. The press purveyed a steady diet of atrocity stories about Boer tactics and behaviour, frequently invented without benefit of evidence. Sometimes their exaggerations stretched the tolerance of the authorities: government officials instructed Edgar Wallace, correspondent for the *Daily Mail*, to tone down his atrocious imagination.[84]

In addition to reading the newspapers, people learnt of the war from lantern lectures and theatrical re-enactments. As early as October 1899, the Canterbury music hall staged a sketch called *Briton against Boer*, featuring a 'very realistic' blowing-up of a Boer train; and in 1902, the Drury Lane spectacle, *Best of Friends*, was set in the Transvaal.[85] A host of other playlets joined the dozen or more plays staged in 1900 depicting the war, among them *A Soldier and a Man*, *One of the Best* and *Soldiers of the Queen*, an anti-Semitic drama that claimed to be 'founded on Actual Facts and Incidents that have occurred in South Africa from Majuba Hill Disaster to the Present Day'.[86] Music halls and other venues advertised the 'Latest Pictures, Recent Events in the Transvaal, Leading Generals at the Front'. In Manchester in June 1900, for example, the Free Trade Hall featured 'The War Boerograph—Life Motioned Pictures. Actual Battle scenes taken under fire'. During that summer, Mancunians could experience the war as spectacle in several forms. At Belle Vue's Zoological Gardens they could witness a 'Monster Open-Air Picture of the Siege of Ladysmith', a half-hour pyrodramatic performance which concluded with fireworks forming pictures of Generals Roberts, Buller and French, a naval officer, a colonial trooper, a 4.7 inch gun, an armoured train and the legend 'Defenders of the Empire, God save the Queen'. If they travelled to Salford football ground, they could see 'Savage South Africa', originally staged for the Greater Britain Exhibition of 1899 and now featuring as its star attraction ten Boer families, together with military equipment and other debris collected from the battle of Elandslaagte.[87]

To what extent audiences were able to differentiate among the claims to authenticity made by the various images and re-enactments of the war is, of course, uncertain, but the multiple layers of fiction and propaganda present in other representations of the war must have some bearing on our understanding of how the many 'fake' war films were perceived. In some other media, quite sophisticated conventions governed the claim to visual fidelity. Among the war artists who contributed to the illustrated magazines, the meaning of 'faking' had been quite precisely defined for some time. While the magazines' London artists would normally modify and embellish the sketches they received from the special artists at the front, they would only invent scenes *in toto* if the sketches failed to arrive. The inclusion of such images—drawings which purported to be by eye witnesses but were not in fact, as happened in the case of artist's impressions of atrocity stories—was generally condemned within the newspaper industry as 'faking', and the cinema trade press discussion of 'faked' war films may well have taken its sense of the term from this usage.[88]

The categories of fact and fiction, as understood in subsequent theories of documentary film, were clearly not demarcated either in exhibition or production practice: a 'phantom ride', for instance, might have a fiction film such as *A Kiss in the Tunnel* (G.A. Smith, 1899) cut into it.[89] Earlier reconstructions of real events, including 'reproductions' of boxing matches and Méliès' film of the Dreyfus affair, provoked several commentators at the time to question 'where this new kind of photo-faking is going to stop?'[90]. But the commentators, at least, clearly distinguished among the different types of material.

Much depended on the circumstances of exhibition, and in particular on any verbal commentary that accompanied the films. The same footage—of *Briton versus Boer* (Paul, 1900), for example—could be used to illustrate the telling of a familiar story or, equally, it could be presented as an *actual* event. Music hall bills freely intermingled different types of war films, but this does not necessarily suggest that audiences perceived 'fake' war films as actualities, regardless how they were advertised. Some films, such as Paul's *His Mother's Portrait* or Hepworth's *The Conjurer and the Boer*, were evident illusions. Others, such as the film discussed in the *Optical Magic Lantern Journal* in March 1900, could be distinguished by 'common sense': 'there is a hand-to-hand encounter between Boers and British, all realistic in its way, but the effect is somewhat spoilt by reason of the fringe of an audience appearing on the picture occasionally . . . common sense would at once pronounce the film of the sham order'.[91] While some trade pronouncements, such as those of Charles Urban's Warwick Trading Company, disparaged 'fake' films as 'counterfeit' representations of events that brought discredit on their exhibitors, this argument was clearly linked to the company's claim that 'the Warwick war films of topical events . . . are taken on the spot and are not made on Hampstead Heath, New Jersey, or in somebody's back garden'.[92]

As this book and the previous volume of *The Beginnings of the Cinema in England* detail, British film producers made three types of films dealing with the war: the actualities recorded by Dickson, Benett-Stanford, Rosenthal and the other cinematographers in the field; allegorical films such as *Wiping Something off the Slate*, which showed a British soldier obliterating the dishonour of the Boer victory at Majuba Hill in the first Anglo-Boer War of 1881; and re-enactments such as the ones advertised by Robert Paul as 'reproductions of the principal incidents of the war . . . arranged under the supervision of an experienced military officer from the front'. The re-enactments were intended 'to meet the demand for something more exciting' than the actualities of troop movements and artillery could provide.[93] Their brief narratives encapsulated British expectations of a small war; sacrifice followed by retribution. Like the press coverage, some of these films alleged Boer atrocities; just as newspaper reports played down the extent of British casualties and declined to publish photographs of the British dead at Spion Kop, considering them 'revolting Boer propaganda', so the re-enactments recorded British defiance, not British defeat. A persistent image of the war showed Tommy Atkins standing 'at the ready', bare-headed and bandaged. This was the pose of 'The Absent-Minded Beggar', Kipling's war poem set to music by Arthur Sullivan, and used by the *Daily Mail* to promote their appeal fund for the troops and their families.[94] This image appears in a number of the catalogue descriptions of war films, including *Wiping Something off the Slate*. At the Palace Theatre the Biograph's films of the war shared the bill with celebrity actress Mrs Beerbohm Tree, who recited 'The Absent-Minded Beggar' nightly, and donated her widely advertised salary of £100 a week to the *Mail*'s fund, together with any contributions from the audience. The *Era* called the Palace audience 'the most thoughtful in London', but another contemporary account, reproduced in Chapter 3, describes them as 'smug counter-jumpers, office boys, yahoos, and brainless bar-crawlers', who certainly did not receive news films of the war passively.[95]

While it is not possible to identify any cinematic contribution to the Unionist victory in the 'khaki election' of 1900, there can be little doubt that both the content of the war films and their manner of exhibition echoed the public mood that so troubled the Liberal anti-imperialists. There is equally little doubt about the political sympathies of the main British producers. One of Paul's major productions of the year was *Army Life*, released during the general election campaign and made with the co-operation of the Adjutant-General, Sir Evelyn Wood, who recognized cinema's potential as an aid to recruitment. West and Sons' 'Our Navy' performed a similar function for the senior service, accompanied, according to one review, by commentary from 'a gentleman who is an adept at this sort of thing and loses none of his opportunities to fan the patriotism of his audience into enthusiasm'.[96] Cecil Hepworth produced two series, *The British Army* and *The British Navy*, in addition to his unambiguously patriotic allegorical films; in 1905 he made a series of 'Political Pictures', which were equally unambiguous propaganda pieces supporting Conservative policies on immigration and trade in the forthcoming general election.[97] G.A. Smith's exhibition activities included the performance of a patriotic entertainment called *Our Glorious Empire*, a lantern lecture distributed through the Primrose League.[98]

The Anglo-Boer War was undoubtedly the most important single factor influencing British film in 1900. Because of the war, cinema's cultural function was extended into the realms of news and propaganda, and its role as an agent of consensus and confirmation was firmly established. In addition, as John Barnes argues in the pages that follow, the war provided a crucial incentive to the development of the techniques of fiction film in the production of re-enactments. By comparison, the other major imperial incident of the year, the Boxer rising, attracted far less public attention. Long-standing Chinese resentment at European territorial appropriations, economic exploitation and interference in religion, law and custom erupted in a national revolt. In June 1900, the Boxers laid siege to the foreign legations in Peking, provoking concerted military action by the European powers to put down the rebellion and relieve Peking in August. Although *The Times* suggested that never before had 'East and West, barbarism and civilisation, the forces of reactionary superstition and the forces of modern enlightenment, been brought into such sharp, sudden and violent collision', a theatrical trade paper reported that the public regarded the Chinese crisis with 'general indifference', and as a result it would not

feature strongly in music hall revues. The Boxer rising altered Western representations of the Chinese, however, adding to the existing stereotypes of brutality and
buffoonery the image of the Yellow Peril, ruled by an evil genius, bent on
miscegenation and world domination.[99]

While the Boxer rising provided the occasion for the most sophisticated production of the year, James Williamson's *Attack on a China Mission*, the relative lack
of seriousness with which the Chinese were represented was indicated by the
Mitchell and Kenyon film, *The Clever Correspondent*. Both films are described in the
pages which follow, and they serve as examples of how, through the thoroughness of
his empirical research in this book and its four predecessors, John Barnes has
established a great body of knowledge not only about early British films themselves,
but also by implication about the attitudes, predilections and preferences of the
audiences for whom they were designed. His work provides a model for historians in
its heroic detail, showing the way in which research of this kind not only creates a
material history of cinema, but also manages to illuminate the social world in which
it arose.

Foreword

The history of the early cinema seems to fall into three distinct periods of development. The year of its birth to the end of 1900 may be said to constitute the first period. It is characterised by the short single-shot film, the overall length of which was restricted to the footage capacity of the camera, usually from 40 to 75 feet. At the same time, the majority of machines for projecting the films were also restricted to these short lengths. Only when projectors were designed to hold longer lengths of film were producers induced to make longer films, either by increasing the capacity of the camera, or by joining two or more shots together. Films of the non-fiction class were the first to benefit in this way, whereas dramatic and comic films would seldom exceed 100 feet in length before the year 1901. This first period of the cinema's history coincided with the last six years of Queen Victoria's reign and may aptly be termed the 'Victorian Cinema.' It is this short period which is covered by the five volumes which constitute this history of the beginnings of the cinema in England.

The second period of the cinema's development spanned the years 1901 to 1907, when the story-film began to take precedence over the non-fiction film. Films also increased in length and multi-shot films became more frequent, with occasional use of camera movement and découpage, leading to a form of discontinuous narrative which was mostly dependent on a commentator for elucidation. This in turn gave way to the one reel (1000 ft) period, when a satisfactory narrative technique, supported by explanatory inter-titles, had evolved. This did away with the need for a commentator and ushered in the era of the 'nickelodeon'. In 1914, D. W. Griffith made *The Birth of a Nation*, and the primitive phase of the cinema's history drew to a close.

The present volume examines the state of the film industry in England during the last twelve months of Queen Victoria's reign. The main producers of fiction films in that year were R.W. Paul and Cecil M. Hepworth, and the South Coast film makers G.A. Smith and James Williamson. The leading producers of non-fiction films were the Warwick Trading Company under the management of Charles Urban, and the American Mutoscope & Biograph Company, which specialized in topical or news subjects. In the field of exhibition, Walter Gibbons came to the fore with his Bio-Tableaux, followed by G. West & Son, of 'Our Navy' fame, the flamboyant A.D. Thomas, and a host of lesser fry. The most important manufacturers and dealers in cinematographic equipment were J. Wrench & Son, The Prestwich Manufacturing Company, W.C. Hughes and R.W. Paul. The French firm of L. Gaumont & Cie became more conspicuous in Britain, although its future rival Pathé had not yet begun to crow. With Pathé and Gaumont, the industrial cinema would be born. In 1900, film making was still a cottage industry, but the infant cinema was on the threshold of becoming a lively art.

Please note that amendments and additions to volume 4 are detailed in Appendix 3 of this volume.

John Barnes
St Ives, Cornwall

I Three Pioneers—Paul, Acres and Hepworth

ROBERT. W. PAUL

The Boer War was the centre of attention in both public and private life during 1900, and a mad jingoism gripped practically the whole nation. It is not surprising, therefore, that many English films of this period were obsessed with the subject, sometimes to the point of absurdity, as is revealed by some of the synopses published in the appendix. The films of R.W. Paul are among the worst offenders in this respect. Perhaps the fault is more apparent today than it was at the time, because the same insane sentiments were also being expressed in other media such as music hall, newspapers and journals.

In other respects, however, Paul's films were some of the most advanced for the times. Some of his trick films were extremely ingenious; his choice of subject matter was more varied than any of his contemporaries; and his coverage of topical events, including the war in South Africa, was only matched by that of the Warwick Trading Company and the Mutoscope & Biograph Syndicate.

To achieve and maintain his position as Britain's premiere film producer, Paul built the studio at Muswell Hill, which has been described and illustrated in a previous volume of this series.[1] Now he needed more up-to-date and larger premises in which to process and print his films. On the plot of ground he had acquired for the studio, he proceeded to build a substantial brick building to house his laboratory (Plate 1). As Paul himself later recalled, 'adjacent to the studio a laboratory was erected, with a capacity for processing up to 8,000 feet of film per day'.[2] The method of handling the film was described by Frederick A. Talbot in his 1912 book: *Moving Pictures*. The negative was first wound upon a light, square wooden frame, which rested loosely on two uprights in such a way that it could revolve.

> The free end of the film was fixed to one side of the frame, and the film was then passed from one side to the other, as if being wound upon a wheel, as it was uncoiled from the spool, the inner end of the film being likewise secured to the frame. This rack was dipped first into a vertical tank to soak the film, and then was placed in a flat tank or trough to be developed in the same way as an ordinary glass plate. By this means every part of the exposed surface was developed equally. Development carried to the requisite degree, the frame was withdrawn, washed, and finally immersed in the fixing tank, which was of the same horizontal design. When the image was fixed it was placed into another tank and received a thorough washing, to remove all traces of the fixing solution, as in the ordinary developing process. This task completed, the film was uncoiled from the flat rack to be re-coiled upon a wooden drum, which was suspended from the ceiling in the drying chamber, until the film was dry and hard.[3]

After the negative had passed through these procedures it was cut to the required length and form and finally printed. The number of positive prints made depended on the estimated demand for copies.

In charge of the dark room staff was J.H. Martin, who was later to become an important producer in his own right.[4] He is perhaps remembered as a partner in the

1

(a)

(b)

Plate 1   R.W. Paul's Film Laboratory at Muswell Hill. (a) Exterior of building; note the adjacent studio at far right (b) The developing room (c) The drying drums on which the film is wound after development and washing (d) The drying room (*Barnes Collection*)

(c)

(d)

PAUL'S ANIMATOGRAPH DEPÔT.

WHOLESALE & RETAIL SHOW-ROOMS FOR THE SALE OF

Paul's New Century Animatograph, Films, Slides, Lanterns, Cameras

AND ALL ACCESSORIES FOR ANIMATED PHOTOGRAPHY.

FACTORIES: 114-15, GREAT SAFFRON HILL, E.C.
FILM WORKS & STUDIO: MUSWELL HILL, N.

TELEGRAMS: "CALIBRATE, LONDON."

68, High Holborn, W.C.

(Near Chancery Lane.) **London,** July 27th, 1900.

Dear Sir,

IMPORTANT NOTICE OF REMOVAL.

I have pleasure in informing you that owing to the rapid expansion of my business in the manufacture and sale of Animated Photographs, I have taken a lease of and fitted up the above premises, where, in future, a stock of animatographs and films will be kept, and all business transacted in this branch of my manufactures. Mr. G. H. CRICKS will continue to conduct this department, and I hope to have the pleasure of a visit from you when you are next in the neighbourhood.

An illustrated catalogue of machines and films, will shortly be issued. In the meanwhile, your kind attention to the enclosed advance particulars is requested.

Several of the new machines are already in the hands of the best professional exhibitors who are delighted with the result on the screen, which is universally acknowledged to be an immense advance on any previous machine.

The Animatograph may be seen and new films projected at the above address at any time, and I should be pleased to meet you there (by appointment) if possible.

Kindly address future communications as above, as the offices occupied by me for the last ten years, at 44, Hatton Garden, E.C., will be used in future for my scientific instrument manufactures only.

Yours faithfully,

Plate 2   Circular announcing the opening of R.W. Paul's new Animatographe Depôt at 68 High Holborn (*British Film Institute*)

pioneering firm of Cricks & Martin of Croydon. This company had formerly operated under the name of Cricks & Sharp, but when H.M. Sharp withdrew from the firm, Martin took his place in 1908 as Cricks' new partner.[5] Cricks himself had also been associated with Paul, and for some time had been responsible for the sale of films and equipment. This side of the business had initially been conducted from 44 Hatton Garden, but with the increase in business further premises were opened at 68 High Holborn, known as Paul's Animatographe Depot. On 27 July 1900, Paul circulated an 'important notice of removal': (Plate 2)

> I have pleasure in informing you that owing to the rapid expansion of my business in the manufacture and sale of animated photographs, I have taken a lease of and fitted up the above premises where, in future, a stock of animatographs and films will be kept. Mr G.H. Cricks will continue to conduct this department.[6]

Henceforth, the address at 44 Hatton Garden was to be used for scientific instrument manufacture only. The Depot in High Holborn became the showplace for Paul's new equipment, where visiting exhibitors and showmen could see the apparatus in action and have the latest films projected prior to selecting their order (Plate 3). Amongst the new equipment on view was Paul's New Century Animatographe, a greatly improved projector which combined the functions of film and slide projection. The intermittent mechanism differed from Paul's previous star-wheel *movement* and instead was composed of a small roller at the end of a revolving arm, which interacted with a slotted disc, so imparting an intermittent movement to

Plate 3   R.W. Paul's Animatograph Depôt, 68 High Holborn, London. Opened in July 1990, under the management of G.M. Cricks (*Barnes Collection*)

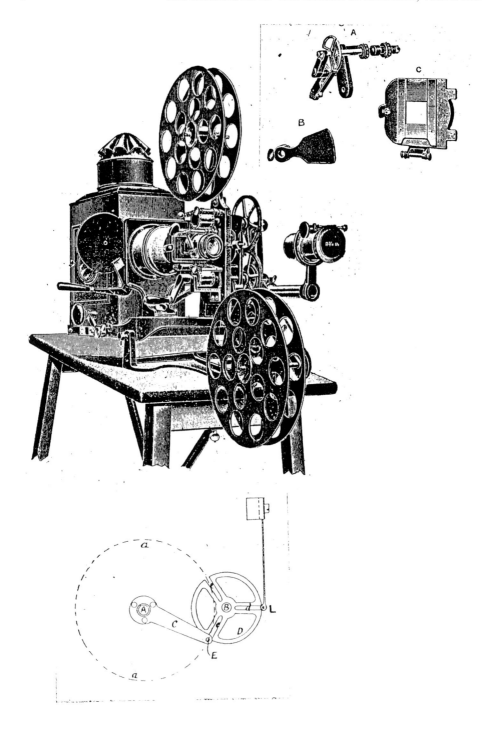

Plate 4   The New Century Animatographe 35mm film and slide projector manufactured by R.W. Paul, 44 Hatton Garden, London, 1900. Note the extra large spools to accommodate up to 2,000 feet of film. The diagram shows the intermittent mechanism and figs a, b, c, the Movement; Shutter; and Film-trap (*Barnes Collection*). *Opposite*: Two views of the Surviving mechanism in the Lester Smith Collection

the film sprocket to which it was attached (Plate 4). The period of effective motion was so short that a twenty-two-and-a-half degree shutter rendered the period of eclipse one-sixteenth of the period of illumination, with the result that, a writer in *The Optician* observed, 'certainly the absence of flicker on the screen is very noticeable'.[7]

The first theatre to be equipped with this new machine was the Alhambra Theatre, Leicester Square. An advertisement in *The Era* on 26 May announced 'Paul's New Century Animatographe now shown nightly at 10.00 o'clock'.[8] Although the first indication that a new machine of that name was in production is found as early as 14 April,[9] it was not until July that the machine was advertised for sale on the open market.[10]

With the necessary infrastructure in place, Paul embarked upon an ambitious programme of film production. Speaking about his studio at Muswell Hill to members of the British Kinematograph Society in 1936, he said: 'With the valuable aid of Walter Booth and others, hundreds of humorous, dramatic and trick films were produced in the studio.'[11] This statement has led some historians to suppose that the majority of fiction films and certainly all the trick films were the work of Walter Booth.[12] I am unable to accept this view. If Booth had been a former stage magician, as Denis Gifford and others have said,[13] then he may well have been responsible for those films which employed regular conjuring tricks or simple stop-motion substitution and double exposure techniques. But it is more than likely that Paul himself had a hand in those films which contained effects of a more complex nature, whereby the tricks were accomplished purely by mechanical means which required technical adjustments to the camera itself.

Throughout his short film career, Paul had designed and built several ciné cameras. He therefore had the knowledge and skill to adapt certain of his mechanisms to perform the effects he desired in his films. We know, for instance, that he built a camera with an adjustable moving front lens attachment whereby a witch was seen to ride upon a broomstick. Frederick A. Talbot describes how the mechanics of the effect were achieved:

> In order to get the effect of the witch riding in the sky, Paul invented a novel movement in the camera, which is now in general use in trick cinematography. The lens was arranged to be raised or lowered in relation to the area of film in the gate, but still independently of the film itself. This was done with a small gearing device whereby, when the gear handle was turned, the lens was moved upwards or downwards. The witch astride her broom stood upon the floor of the stage, which was covered with black cloth, against a background of similar material. By turning the gear handle of the lens attachment the latter was raised, until the witch riding on her broom was lifted to the upper corner of the film and there photographed. Although she simulated the action of riding through space in the traditional manner, in reality she merely moved across the black-covered floor.[14]

This effect was used in *The Magic Sword* (1901), and was described in a testimonial by J.N. Maskelyne, of the Egyptian Hall, as the finest trick subject he had yet seen.[15]

Of the trick films produced by Paul in 1900, one in particular stands out: *His Mother's Portrait* (Plates 5 and 6) which was described at the time as 'introducing an entirely new effect in animated photography'.[16] The effect takes place when the wounded soldier dreams of his mother and home. The dream appears as a 'vision' in

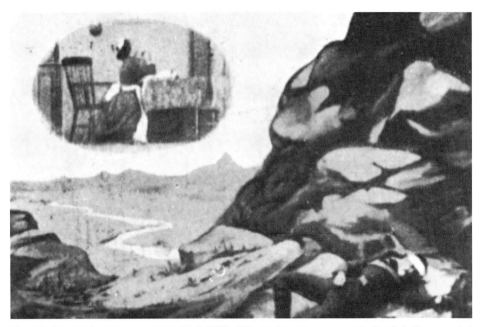

Plate 5 *His Mother's Portrait* (R.W. Paul, 1900). 'Slowly the vision appears in the sky': The wounded soldier dreams of his mother and home; a familiar Victorian image depicted in popular prints and magic lantern slides (*Barnes Collection*)

Plate 6 The *Soldier's Dream*. Engraved by Edmund Evans, after a painting by F. Goodall, MA (1822–1904). A popular subject of dissolving views for the magic lantern (*Barnes Collection*)

the sky above the prostrate figure. 'Slowly the vision appears in the sky' is how the catalogue synopsis describes it. Such superimposed 'visions' had appeared in films as early as 1898, in G.A. Smith's *The Corsican Brothers* for example, but hitherto these visions had appeared suddenly. Paul improved the effect by making the vision gradually appear and then just as gradually disappear. How Paul obtained this effect is revealed by Talbot:

> Where gradual disappearances and appearances were desired, instead of using a rectilinear diaphragm stop in the lens as is now usual, Paul occasionally resorted to the chemical dissolution of the emulsion and image from the film—an intricate and delicate mani- pulation entailing considerable time and care, because if the dissolution process were carried too far or undertaken by unskilled hands, the film was spoiled and much labour fruitlessly expended.
>
> Sometimes the desired result was brought about by means of two special detachable stops, which were placed in the lens. Each of these stops had a V-shaped opening of iden- tical dimensions, and were set at right-angles to one another. As they were gradually drawn apart the aperture formed by the intersection of the V-openings through which the light passed to the film was enlarged, while on the other hand, as they moved towards one another, the aperture was decreased, until at last the film scarcely recorded any impression of the subject photographed. The gradual synchronous movement of these two V-shaped stops was somewhat difficult. Today their place is taken by the rectilinear stop in the lens, whereby the same effect can be produced much more easily.[17]

We cannot be sure which of these two methods Paul employed in *His Mother's Portrait*, as no copy of the film survives. But whichever method was used, this is the first recorded use of the fade-in and fade-out technique. Other trick films produced by Paul during the year included *Diving For Treasure*, *Kruger's Dream of Empire*, *The Hindoo Jugglers*, *Britain's Welcome to Her Sons* and *The Yellow Peril*. All made use of effects that had already been used by other film–makers, such as stop-motion substitution, dissolves and superimpositions on a black ground.

The Boer War was the theme of three of Paul's trick films, while *The Yellow Peril* referred to the Boxer Rebellion. *Diving for Treasure* consisted of three shots, one of which was an underwater scene photographed through an aquarium tank with live fish swimming about (Plate 7). A similar effect had already been used by Georges Méliès in *Visite Sous-Marine du Maine* (1898), but Paul's film was probably the first use of the effect in an English film. *The Hindoo Jugglers* depicted the instant growth of a mango tree from a seed, and the well-known Indian basket trick (Plate 8). Both had been performed at the Egyptian Hall as early as 1865 by the magician Colonel Stodare (Alfred Inglis)[18] and have been performed countless times since by other conjurors. Paul's film may have been performed in the traditional manner by a professional magician (Walter Booth perhaps?) and merely recorded on film, but it was more likely produced by trick photography using the stop-camera technique.

In *A Railway Collision* (Plate 9) Paul made use of models and a specially constructed layout on which to stage a railway collision between two trains. This was probably the first use of models in an English film. According to Talbot, 'many people marvelled at Paul's good fortune in being on the scene to photograph such a disaster. They were convinced that it was genuine. 'As a matter of fact, the scene of the accident was a field, in which scenery was erected with considerable care and a

Plate 7 *Diving for Treasure* (R.W. Paul, 1900). The underwater scene was photographed through an aquarium tank with live fish swimming about (*Barnes Collection*)

Plate 8 *The Hindoo Jugglers* (R.W. Paul, 1900). A re-creation of the well-known stage illusion of the Indian basket trick (*Barnes Collection*)

Plate 9   *A Railway Collision* (R.W. Paul, 1900). Probably the first use of models in an English film (*Barnes Collection*)

long length of model railway track was laid down, while the trains were good toy models.'[19] It is difficult to believe how audiences could possibly have been deceived, so unconvincing does the model work appear to the modern viewer. Yet apparently such was the case, for Paul informs us that the effect on the screen was regarded as very thrilling and the film had a large sale. Furthermore, he was informed that a great number of pirated copies of the film appeared in America.[20]

So few of Paul's films have survived from this period that we are forced to rely on the published descriptions (reproduced in Appendix 1) to get some idea of their content and flavour. Many of them are longer than Paul's previous films, some even reaching a length of 120 feet. The plots are also a little more developed and often require more than the customary single shot to tell their story. Films containing two, three and even five shots are to be found. Nearly all the films, both fiction films and topicals, reflect in some way the war in South Africa. The trick films have obviously been influenced by Georges Méliès, although not in style. The nearest to a Méliès production is *The Yellow Peril*, which is full of transformations and imps. In some respects it must have been one of Paul's most advanced films, and it is a pity that no copy survives.

Paul also produced films of a more realistic type such as *Plucked from the Burning* (Plate 10), which seems to anticipate James Williamson's *Fire!* of 1901. *His Mother's Portrait* is a rather more melodramatic example of the realist style, as is *The Hair-Breadth Escape of Jack Shephard* (Plate 11). Paul also appears to be the first to have tackled a classical subject, and his *Last Days of Pompeii* (Plate 12) is surely the

Plate 10 *Plucked from the Burning* (R.W. Paul, 1900). Mother and child are saved by the fireman amid clouds of smoke, just as the ceiling comes crashing down (*Barnes Collection*)

Plate 11 *The Hair-Breadth Escape of Jack Shephard* (R.W. Paul, 1900). A dramatic reconstruction in two scenes of an incident in the life of the notorious criminal (*Barnes Collection*)

Plate 12   *The Last Days of Pompeii* (R.W. Paul, 1900). This first attempt at a classical subject is replete with destructible set with falling columns and erupting volcano (*Barnes Collection*)

Plate 13   *A Naughty Story* (R.W. Paul, 1900). A study in facial expression, a subject which calls for a medium close-up (*Barnes Collection*)

precursor of all spectacle films. It even contains a destructible set, with falling columns and an erupting volcano. A few comedy films form part of his repertoire. Examples include *Punished*, *The Drenched Lover*, *A Wet Day at the Seaside*, *A Morning at Bow-Street* and *A Naughty Story* (Plate 13). This last is a study in facial expression. All are single-shot films which rely on visual anecdotes.

We cannot now be sure who the directors of these films were. Walter Booth may have been responsible for some and R.W. Paul for others; some films may have been co-directed. Unlike the films of Georges Méliès, they do not bear the unmistakable individual style of the artist. If anything, they have the hallmark of Paul himself, a rather methodical down-to-earth character with the precise and innovative flair of the scientist, who was certainly not averse to team work. Paul chose his team well. Some of its members, such as G.H. Cricks and J.H. Martin, went on to achieve success in their own right. Another Paul employee was Frank S. Mottershaw. After serving with Paul from 1900 to 1902, he returned north to his old firm, the Sheffield Photo Co., where he set about reorganizing the film department. Among the films he subsequently directed for the company was *A Daring Daylight Robbery* (1903), which was to become a key film in the early history of the cinema.[21]

As the staff at the Muswell Hill studio were fully occupied, the taking of topical films was entrusted to Jack Smith and his assistants.[22] A number of important home events were filmed, many of which concerned the comings and goings of the Boer War heroes. More tranquil pursuits, such as the Oxford and Cambridge University Boat Race, the Derby and the Cowes Regatta, were also covered. One of the big events of the year was Queen Victoria's visit to Dublin, and Paul's camera recorded the great review by the Queen in Phoenix Park in a film which ran to 120 ft. Royalty was always deemed a fit subject for the cinematograph, and in June the Prince and Princess of Wales were filmed at Chelsea Hospital interviewing soldiers' wives. As the royal couple approached the camera, 'most effective portraits' resulted, and the Princess was reported to have asked for a copy of the film, which was due to be shown at the Alhambra Theatre.[23] As Paul relates, 'So soon as a topical film had been taken all likely purchasers were informed by telegram or post, and the dark room staff, under J.H. Martin, worked hard to turn out prints, often continuously throughout the night.'[24]

One of Paul's biggest undertakings in the non-fiction class was a two hour documentary depicting life in every branch of the army, called *Army Life, or How Soldiers are Made*. According to advertisements the film was shot by Paul himself, with the permission of Sir Evelyn Wood, Adjutant-General, and with the assistance of the officers commanding the various depots.[25] To begin with, the whole film was offered to exhibitors on a sharing basis, and only later was it available for sale, in shorter lengths, on the open market. Proprietors and lessees of suitable halls throughout the kingdom were invited to forward terms and vacant dates.[26] It was Paul's intention to recruit experienced staff to accompany the film on provincial tours, and to this effect the following appeal appeared in the press:

> Operators who have been previously engaged by me, and others who are thoroughly com-
> petent and used to the working of the New Century Animatograph [sic], are requested to
> forward their addresses stating if and when they are disengaged. In connection with the
> above projected tours, vacancies will occur for a few competent and reliable men, as
> lecturers, managers, and working staff . . .[27]

To launch the film, a special press and private view was arranged at the Alhambra Theatre, Leicester Square, for Tuesday afternoon, the 18 September, at four p.m. A report of the performance in *The Era* the following Saturday, sets the scene:

> The Alhambra was crowded on Tuesday afternoon to assist at a private view of an original series of animated photographs, taken by Mr R W. Paul, M.I.E.E., inventor of the Animatographe, of the life of the soldier, from the recruiting stage until he becomes a smart linesman, cavalryman, or gunner. The pit was a mass of red coats—the old Chelsea pensioners, who had very considerately been invited by Mr Dundas Slater [manager of the Alhambra]; and in the upper parts of the house the boys of the Duke of York's School were seated. The audience in the stalls largely consisted of officers of various branches of the army, and a number of military drill instructors were also present by invitation . . . Each series of films is explained by excellent letter press thrown upon the screen, so that the pictures have a distinct educational value. They are besides very attractive, and no one who takes an interest in our Imperial land forces—and what Briton does not?—should miss the admirable series of representations of military life which have been so industriously and cleverly caught by the camera.[28]

The reference to the letter press thrown on the screen was to the series of slides shown with the film. Paul's new Animatographe could function equally well as a slide or film projector. The slides were available to exhibitors at one shilling and sixpence each, and were described in Paul's catalogue as 'essential where a lecturer is not employed'. The catalogue adds: 'The announcements are in clear letter-press, and give a quantity of useful and interesting information.' Also available were picture slides (taken from Paul's own negatives) which helped 'to illustrate in a vivid manner the humour and pathos of a soldier's life, and the characteristics of the various regiments in the British Army'. The price of each picture slide was the same as for the explanatory slides, but could be supplied with the titles clearly printed at the foot of the picture at an additional charge of one shilling.[29]

From the Alhambra, the *Army Life* pictures were transferred to the Royal Agricultural Hall, Islington, where they formed the first part of a lively entertainment of patriotic songs and music, to which *The Era* devoted a lengthy column:

> Mr R.W. Paul's series of animatograph [sic] pictures depicting the life of a soldier, originally seen at the Alhambra Theatre, are now exhibited nightly at the Agricultural Hall, a short season opening on Monday last [8 October]. From these pictures one obtains a thorough insight into the methods employed in converting the raw recruit into a smart soldier. Information concerning such an important branch of our national defence, and conveyed in so interesting a form, cannot but be of supreme interest at the present time, when a General Election has been contested on the South African War question. As to the excellence of the pictures shown by Mr Paul at the Agricultural Hall there can be no difference of opinion. The films are remarkably clear, the vividness of the military scenes depicted being a distinctive feature of the exhibition.[30]

As a supplement to the film, Paul published a special twenty four-page souvenir brochure, priced at sixpence and including numerous frame illustrations (Plate 14).[31]

On 14 April, Paul advertised a series of lantern slides depicting 'all the most interesting phases of the war, being actual photographs by officers at the front'.

Plate 14 *Army Life; or How Soldiers are Made*. Front cover of brochure issued in conjunction with R. W. Paul's feature documentary (*Cinémathèque Française*)

Prospective customers were urged to write at once for a new price list. The slides, it was stated, had been successfully exhibited for several weeks at the Alhambra.[32] Paul had previously prepared a magnificent photographic lantern slide showing his Animatographe camera on the battlefield ready for action, together with a Boer Cape cart used for its transport. This slide was presented free to any exhibitor who applied for it.[33] Enlargements of war pictures suitable for exhibition at the doors were also to be had at a nominal price.[34]

At the outbreak of war in South Africa, Paul had sent out two cameras to cover the conflict. As he notes in his reminiscences, 'one of them was lent to Colonel Beevor, RAMC, of the Scots Guard, one of the first regiments to leave. He was able to get about a dozen good films, including one of the surrender of Cronje to Lord Roberts'. (Plate 15)[35] The film showed General Cronje in a cart after his defeat at Paardeberg, and according to the catalogue entry, was the only film taken of the subject. Another successful film was *The Entry of Scots Guards into Bloemfontein* (Plate 16). Other films shot by Colonel Beevor included *Lord Roberts Crossing the Vaal River*; *Manhandling a Naval Gun by Blue-Jackets;* and *Royal Engineers with Balloon near Pretoria* (Plate 17). This latter was singled out for special mention by *The Era* in a review of Paul's New Century Animatographe at the Alhambra on 28 July. The programme included 'some most interesting war films', one of which, reports the paper, 'shows in a deep ravine on the road to Johannesburg, the balloon section of the Royal Engineers with their waggons coming towards the spectator. The balloon itself, which is hitched to the waggon, gives a fine effect as it

Plate 15   *Cronje's Surrender to Lord Roberts* (R.W. Paul, 27 February 1900). Photographed by Colonel Walter Beevor, RAMC. Frame illustration from a contemporary print in the National Film and TV Archive (*British Film Institute*)

Plate 16 *Entry of Scots' Guards into Bloemfontein* (R.W. Paul, 13 March 1900). Photographed by Colonel Walter Beevor, RAMC. Frame illustration from a contemporary print in the New Zealand Film Unit Archive (*Clive Sowry*)

Plate 17 The Royal Engineers' Balloon (R.W. Paul, 1900). Filmed on the road from Johannesburg to Pretoria by Colonel Walter Beevor, Paul's representative in South Africa (*Barnes Collection*)

approaches, until it almost fills the picture. This is a very novel subject' . . . [36] Paul's second camera was in charge of Sidney Melsom, who (with Paul's two brothers) was in the City Imperial Volunteers (CIV). But, as Paul later admitted, Beevor's films were the more successful.[37]

Information is sparse regarding the technical details of the ciné cameras produced by Paul at this period. One account states that the *movement* was the same as that used in the New Century Animatographe projector and that the outfit included 'five 200 ft spool boxes and accessories—all in a satchel no bigger than a whole plate outfit'.[38] Two photographs of cameras produced by Paul, both published at about this time, are not very helpful in enlarging our knowledge. The photograph of the camera mounted on its track outside the studio at Muswell Hill (first reproduced in *The Optician*, 5 October 1900, p. 74) is devoid of detail, but the one pictured with the Cape cart in South Africa published in one of Paul's catalogues (see my vol. 4, p. 22) shows a similar camera, but with a spoked crank wheel visible on one side.[39] These photographs show the cameras to be of the compact box-type. Mounted on their tripods, they could be quite easily manipulated by one man.

Paul had been one of the first to stage dramatic scenes purporting to show incidents in the war, and several of these reconstructions or 'faked' war films were produced the previous year. Throughout 1900, however, only one such film seems to have been made. Instead, an allegorical approach to the subject was preferred, expressed in patriotic tableaux replete with transformations and trick effects. The sole exception to this non-realistic approach was *Briton versus Boer*, described as 'two-minutes of white-heat excitement'. The 100 foot-long film depicted 'a magnificent display of swordsmanship' between the two protagonists, which ended, of course, in the Boer's defeat. According to the catalogue, the fight was staged by Lewin Fitzhamon, who was also one of the participants. Fitzhamon was to become a noted film director for Cecil M. Hepworth. Denis Gifford lists him as the director of Paul's *His Mother's Portrait*. He is yet another example of a former Paul employee making good, indicating what a formidable team Paul had at his Muswell Hill studio.[40]

Of the literature published by Paul during the year, very little survives. In April, a list of 'new genuine war films' was issued, which was briefly mentioned in *The Amateur Photographer*,[41] but this is now lost, as is also a list of 'The Hundred Best Films' mentioned in the same journal in December. Many of the films listed 'being what are called "trick subjects", for the production of which Mr. Paul has a special studio, one side of which can be completely opened'.[42] This is a clear reference to the studio at Muswell Hill. Both the British Film Institute and the Cinémathèque Française have a prospectus for *Army Life, or How Soldiers are Made*. Fortunately, many of Paul's films for 1900 are described in catalogues of later years, which have survived. A search of national and regional newspapers is likely to provide information not to be found elsewhere in the literature of the period, but this is a task I have not yet been able to undertake.

In 1900, cinematography was first used to animate drawings whereby a series of sequential diagrams were photographed one after the other to give the illusion of motion. The man responsible for this revolutionary first step in the history of the animated film was Professor Silvanus Thompson, and the man chosen to accomplish the task was R.W. Paul.

Wishing to demonstrate the electrical phenomenon in which lines of force 'snap

across' from tooth to tooth in an alternator, Professor Thompson, in association
with Dennis Coales, prepared a series of drawings of the magnetic lines stage by
stage. Paul, himself a notable electrical engineer, was asked to photograph the
diagrams one after the other on cinematograph film. The resultant film was
presented by Thompson, in a lecture entitled 'Faraday und die Englische Schule der
Elektriker', on 9 January 1901, at the Urania Theatre, Berlin. In October 1911,
Robert Paul—to whom the film belonged—showed it to Edison, at West Orange,
New Jersey, and presented it to him with the original negative.[43] The method by
which this animated film was made was revealed in a lecture given by Thompson on
24 November 1904 at the Institution of Electrical Engineers, Savoy Place, London:

> I am going to show you this by means of coarse diagrams put on the screen by an
> animatograph [sic]. I ought to tender my thanks to Mr Paul for having so kindly brought
> his instrument here in order to show the films. Those films were made by myself and Mr
> Dennis Coales, now of the University College, Nottingham. We got a number of cards,
> each about foolscap size. These cards had two holes punched in the corners of them, so
> that they could be put upon two pegs to register exactly. We drew diagram after diagram of
> the magnetic lines, stage by stage. Mr Paul photographed the diagrams one after the other
> on animatograph [sic] films, that they might be put through the lantern, exactly as though
> they had been taken by a camera from the moving magnetic apparatus.[44]

Modern animators will recognize here the fundamental principals of the animated
film cartoon.

This was not Paul's only involvement with scientific cinematography. He was
associated with Professor Wood's series of films recording sound waves, three of
which were offered for sale at five shillings each from Paul's establishment at 44
Hatton Garden. He also assisted Professor C. Vernon Boys by filming a dynamite
explosion showing the shadow of the sound wave, the resultant film selling at ten
shillings.[45]

Electrical work always remained dear to Paul's heart, and he never abandoned this
side of his business. He considered himself first and foremost an electrical engineer,
and when films became more of an industry than a one-man enterprise, he felt he
would rather quit than become embroiled in the cut-throat competition that came
with the rise of the international giants such as Pathé, Gaumont and Vitagraph. He
therefore had no compunction in winding up the film side of the business to devote
himself entirely to the electrical trade. Paul was only a little over forty years old
when he left the film industry for good in 1910.

The Northern Photographic Works Limited (Birt Acres)

By the beginning of 1900, the Northern Photographic Works, of which Birt Acres
was the head, underwent a marked change in policy. The supplying of cinematograph film stock to the trade was no longer its priority. Instead, the company
switched to film production, making some twenty films during the year, in marked
contrast to the single title recorded for 1899 and the five titles for 1898. The average
length of each film was now eighty feet, whereas previously it had seldom, if ever,
exceeded seventy-five. This clearly indicates that a new camera was in use, and this

probably accounts for the increase in output. In none of the advertisements issued by the firm in the pages of *The Era* during 1900 was there mention of the availability of film stock or processing facilities, as was formerly the case. This was because Birt Acres was in the throes of moving yet again, this time to 'extensive works' at Whetstone, a couple of miles or so away, where it was his intention to manufacture cinematographic film 'warranted not to separate from the celluloid'.[46] It was a brave move, especially now that L. Gaumont et Cie. had recently entered the field,[47] thus supplementing the considerable output of firms such as Lumière, Blair and Eastman, which were already firmly established in this country.

The films Acres produced at this time were mainly news items, but there were a couple of comedies, each 100 feet in length, and a remarkable 'interest' film shot from a moving crane. With the camera pointing downwards from the skip of a colossal steam crane, the Acres camera was raised 200 feet into the air over a busy London thoroughfare and then lowered about 100 feet. 'The view when projected on the sheet gives a most extraordinary effect, as people walking in the street gradually diminish in size until they appear to be no bigger than ants, whilst at the close of the film the traffic appears to increase in magnitude with a rapidity which is positively startling'.[48]

Another film which received high praise was a staged war scene called *Briton v. Boer*, in which the British are seen driving the Boers from the trenches at the point of the bayonet. Other films relating to the Boer War showed troop embarkations, and an exclusive film of Sir George White, the hero of Ladysmith, arriving at Portsmouth on 24 April. Another news film was of the comedian Dan Leno at the Music Hall Sports.

Birt Acres' inventive spell seems finally to have deserted him, and there is no mention in the photographic press for the year of any new developments in this sphere. In fact, after 1900, Acres' film career gradually declined. According to an article by M. Tummel, Birt Acres was born of English parents on 23 July 1854 in the state of Virginia in the United States. Made an orphan early in life, he finally settled in England, living first in Ilfracombe, North Devon.[49] By November 1889 he had moved to London, with an address at 131 Richmond Road, Hackney.[50] His next move was to High Barnet, where in March 1895 he was living at Clovelly Cottage, the scene of England's first successful Kinetoscope film. He was still at this address on 27 February 1896,[51] but some time before April 1897 he moved to Wrotham Cottage, Hadley (Plate 18).[52] Here he is reputed to have first achieved screen projection, presumably using Kinetoscope films. He later established his Northern Photographic Works, which in June 1897, were situated at 45 Salisbury Road, Barnet (Plate 19), relocating in November to Nesbitt's Alley, High Street, Barnet. His next move was in 1900, when the business was transferred to Athenaeum Road, Whetstone, about two miles from his previous address. His final move was to Rawreth Lane, Rayleigh, Essex (Plate 20).[53] His death occurred on 27 December 1918. What are we to make of these constant changes of address? I think the inference is that he found it difficult to compete in the market place and that his business never achieved the stability needed to keep pace with that of his rivals. It is no surprise, therefore, that he was finally declared bankrupt in 1909.[54]

There is still some mystery surrounding Birt Acres' origins, and there is some suspicion that he had German ancestry and that the family name was originally Akers. Peter Jewell, who has been researching the inventor's stay in Ilfracombe,

Plate 18   Wrotham Cottage, Barnet, the residence and workshop of Birt Acres 1896–1897. The captions on this and the following two photographs were probably added by his son, Sidney, for exhibition purposes (*Mrs Sidney Birt Acres*)

Plate 19   The Film Coating Machine, used by Birt Acres in 1896 at his workshop in Salisbury Road, Barnet (*Mrs Sidney Birt Acres*)

Plate 20   The Film Splitting Machine, used by Birt Acres at his workshop in Rawreth Lane, Rayleigh, Sussex, in 1918 (*Mrs Sidney Birt Acres*)

Devon, where it is reputed he stayed on first arriving in England from America, has come up with some interesting revelations. His residence in that town was the Royal Clarence Hotel and the local paper, *The Ilfracombe Chronicle*, lists him there at various periods during 1884 and 1885.[55] On two occasions (26 April and 18 October 1884) 'recent arrivals' to the town include 'Mr and Mrs Akers' staying at the Royal Clarence Hotel. There are regular reappearances of Akers/Acres at Easter, Whitsun, and in October and in November, but he was possibly a semi-permanent resident of the Royal Clarence during those two years. The Clarence advertised itself as 'Agent to the Anglo-Bavarian Brewery Company' and this German connection may have played some part in drawing Acres there in the first place.

At the outbreak of World War I, the Foreign Office suspected Acres of being an alien, no doubt owing to his American birth, but according to the film historian Richard Brown, Acres was able to prove to the authorities that his deceased parents were indeed English. This would seem to dismiss any theory that his ancestry was German. So far, no one has been able to turn up his birth certificate.

Birt Acres has recently been the subject of a German book by Hauke Lange-Fuchs (Kiel, 1987) which draws heavily on my own work. There is an illustration on p. 63 of this book, which is wrongly supposed to be Birt Acres with assistant Edward Cash in Germany. In fact, it depicts the two men in the main street of Totnes, Devon.[56]

Cecil M. Hepworth

In 1900, there was no one more versed in the theory and practice of cinematography than Cecil M. Hepworth, and although still a young man in his twenties at the turn of the century, he may well be regarded as the scholar of the trade. In his autobiography, *Came the Dawn*, Hepworth described his early life as involving 'photography—limelight—lantern shows—lectures'.[57] It was inevitable, therefore, that when the time came, cinematography would also be included among these pursuits.

His connection with films began in 1896, when he assisted Birt Acres at a Royal film performance at Marlborough House, but it was not until the summer of 1899 that he commenced film production on his own account. There was nothing very remarkable about these first films of Hepworth's except their photographic quality, which is not too surprising considering he was already an expert photographer. The subjects first chosen followed the usual pattern: simple, short actualities, topicals and comic incidents. Aware of the increasing length of the films being produced by the Warwick Trading Company, with which he was closely connected, Hepworth was 'determined to construct a camera big enough to take a thousand feet of film at a time'. As he explained:

> What eventually emerged was a long, narrow, black box, rather like a coffin standing on end. It had three compartments. The centre one contained a 'Bioscope' mechanism, modified to do duty as a camera instead of a projector, and the top one held a thousand feet of film on a spool, while the bottom compartment held a similar spool on which the film was automatically rewound as it came out of the camera.[58]

Plate 21   Cecil M. Hepworth in Algiers preparing to film the solar eclipse on 28 May, 1900 (*Hepworth Collection*)

This camera was used to take the series of views photographed from the front of a railway engine passing through the Devon countryside. This had an overall length of 600 feet, although it was also made available in shorter lengths of fifty, seventy five, 100, and 200 feet. This mammoth *phantom ride* had been taken in the summer of 1899, but except for one or two 125 foot-long films, Hepworth's productions in 1900 seldom exceeded fifty feet in length. As his memoirs imply, his large capacity camera was obviously made for the sole purpose of filming the locomotive scenes.[59]

Hepworth was a very practical man, capable of making all kinds of innovations applicable to his trade. A case in point is the technical expertise he revealed in filming the eclipse of the sun on the 28th May 1900, from a vantage point in North Africa (Plate 21). This is how Hepworth describes the event:

I went out to Algiers on the steam-yacht *Argonaut* with apparatus which I had carefully constructed at home before leaving. This was a very strong oaken stand to hold the camera at ground level, a fourteen-inch focus, large-aperture lens, a motor to drive the camera steadily at slow speed and a storage battery to work the motor. On the auspicious morning the astronomical party drove out to a spot near Algiers where the duration of the eclipse would be at its longest, and there on a large concrete platform we all set up our respective gear.

I so set my camera that in the time at my disposal the diminishing image of the sun would enter the top right corner of my picture and leave again in about fifteen minutes at the bottom left. The lens was stopped down to its very smallest and had, in addition, a deep red glass screen covering its hood. Although there was only a little crescent of the sun showing when operations began it would have been fatally over-exposed without these precautions.

Then when the instant of totality arrived I whipped off the red screen and at the same time opened the lens aperture to the full extent, reversing the operations directly totality was over and the sun's rim began to re-appear. By good luck, everything happened according to plan and I secured an excellent picture of the beautiful corona with enough of the before-and-after to give it point'.[60]

The trip also presented Hepworth with the opportunity to take street scenes in Algiers and Tangier, as well as some pleasant views of life aboard the *Argonaut* during the voyage. Other notable events of the year covered by Hepworth were Queen Victoria's visit to Dublin, the Paris Exhibition, and the arrival of HMS *Powerful* with the returning heroes of Ladysmith. A series of films of life in the British Army and Royal Navy were also produced, photographed by a new member of the Hepworth staff, H.V. Lawley. Lawley bought himself into the firm as a partner, injecting much needed capital.[61] Of the fiction films produced during the year, perhaps the most memorable were *Explosion of a Motor Car* (Plate 22) and *How it Feels to be Run Over* (Plate 23). Copies of both films have survived, and have received detailed study by film historians.[62] In the first film, 'a motor car containing four passengers drives towards the camera. It stops suddenly and explodes. The wreckage and passengers are thrown into the air. A policeman rushes to the spot and scans the sky with a telescope. The bodies start falling to the ground and the policeman collects the parts and enters his observations in a notebook'. The film is noteworthy for its use of off-screen space (body fragments fall from above). The driver of the car was Hepworth himself and the passengers were H.M. Lawley and his brother.[63]

In the second film, a cart moves along a narrow country road forward and past the camera. It is followed by an automobile travelling at high speed. Seeing the buggy, the driver of the automobile tries in vain to avoid a collision. The screen then suddenly goes dark and a series of interrogation and exclamation marks appear, followed alternately by the words 'Mother will be pleased'.

Hepworth was a keen motorist who was not averse to including his vehicles in a film whenever the occasion arose. '*The Explosion of a Motor-car* (cat no. 130) was one which attracted a great deal of attention at the time', wrote Hepworth,' for it was typical of the attitude towards "horseless carriages" in those days, and had for an alleged "comic", quite a germ of genuine humour in it'.[64] He added that the sales of the film were the biggest they had had up till then.

Two lost films may even be of more significance than the motoring films. *The Excentric Dancer* (cat no. 137) for instance, used slow-motion cinematography, probably the first calculated use of the effect in the history of the cinema. 'I remember', recalls Hepworth, 'we had to hand-turn the camera at a tremendous speed to get the effect, which was exceedingly comic until continued use dimmed its infinite variety'.[65] The other film, *Leap-frog as Seen by the Frog*, in which the audience is placed in the position of one of the 'frogs',[66] is an amusing example of the use of the subjective camera. Although there is no catalogue entry for this film, the effect is obviously achieved by getting the participants to leap-frog over the camera.

To increase the variety of subjects, producers realised that some sort of studio was needed so that subjects which required an indoor setting could be made. In his

Plate 22 *Explosion of a Motor Car* (Cecil M. Hepworth, 1900). This film proved to be Hepworth's biggest success up to that date (*British Film Institute*)

Plate 23 *How it Feels to be Run Over* (Cecil M. Hepworth, 1900). Hepworth was the first British film-maker to use the automobile as the subject for a comic film. This, and the above, featured his own dog-cart style 'horseless carriage' (*British Film Institute*)

autobiography, Hepworth described the first primitive studio which he employed for the purpose:

> Soon we began to feel the necessity of indoor sets, for the ideas for outdoor comics began to wear thin. So we set up a sort of stage in our little back garden. It measured fifteen feet by eight and had a few upright posts against which scenery flats could be propped. It faced due south so as to give us the longest possible spell of sunlight.[67]

Hepworth made a sketch of this studio from memory, reproduced here (Plate 24). Compared with Paul's studio at this time, Hepworth's appears very elementary indeed. The first film to be made on this little open-air stage was, according to Hepworth, *The Egg-Laying Man* (cat no. 132), which shows a big close-up of a man's head (Hepworth's own) from whose mouth issue a succession of eggs.[68] In 1896, Paul had made a film of the same title with David Devant.

We do not have a complete list of Hepworth films for 1900; a supplementary list mentioned in *The Photogram* for March 1900[69] is now lost, as is a catalogue published at the beginning of October of the same year. *The Amateur Photographer* informs us that the latter 'includes a large variety of well chosen subjects ranging from the serious and instructive to the refined and comic'.[70] By this time, Gaumont et Cie., of 25 Cecil Court, Charing Cross Road, were Hepworth's London agents,[71] although some films were also handled by J. Wrench & Son and the Warwick

Plate 24   Hepworth's First Studio consisting of a simple open-air stage on which painted flats were propped against the wooden uprights. From a sketch by Cecil M. Hepworth (*Hepworth Collection*)

Trading Company.[72] This led some to suppose that Hepworth & Co. were under the control of the Warwick Trading Company, but this was strongly denied in a letter sent to leading photographic and trade journals:[73]

The Manufacture of Cinematograph Films.

To the Editor of THE PHOTOGRAPHIC NEWS.

SIR,—Our attention has been called to an article in the *British Journal of Commerce*, in which it is erroneously stated that our film factory at Walton-on-Thames is under the control of the Warwick Trading Company. This mistake has obviously arisen from the fact that we do a very large proportion of the film work of that company, while they handle the bulk of the output of our own series of 'Hepwix' films. We are fully sensible of the honour done us by the coupling of our name with that of a firm the quality of whose work is well known to be second to none, but we feel it to be only due to ourselves, and in justice to the trade generally, to contradict the impression conveyed—doubtless inadvertently—and to state that we are not connected in any way whatever with this or any other firm.

We should also like to point out that the Patent Developing Machine—which is also credited to the same company—and by virtue of which alone it is possible to develop and print from negatives 1,500 ft. long in one piece, is in reality part of the equipment of our Walton factory, and we are sole possessors of the entire patent rights.

We are equally certain that the Warwick Trading Company would be the last to wish to convey an erroneous impression, and the first to desire to see it corrected if by any accident it should gain currency.

Apologising for thus trespassing upon your space, and thanking you for the courtesy which permits us to do so, we are, dear Sir, yours, &c. HEPWORTH & CO.
Hurst Grove, Walton-on-Thames,
January 23rd, 1900.

In line with other producers at the time, Hepworth travelled to Ireland to cover the Queen's visit to Dublin on 4 April. His coverage of the event is reported to have totalled 325 feet of film, but if the Dublin films listed in subsequent catalogues are anything to go by, it is unlikely that individual negatives exceeded 125 feet in length. Hepworth regarded the event as of some importance, and as the *British Journal of Photography* reported:

This entire series of cinematograph pictures has a length of 325 feet—that is, nearly seven times the usual length of such films. It is noteworthy that, on the evening of the same day upon which the negatives were taken, they were travelling to London. Early on Thursday morning they were developed at the factory at Walton-on-Thames, and on the same evening, at eight o'clock, they were exhibited to a delighted and enthusiastic audience at the London Hippodrome. When we consider the great length of this film, comprising no fewer than 5200 pictures, and remember that the negative had to be developed, fixed, and dried, and that positives from it had to go through the same operations, we must consider this a very creditable photographic feat. Positive copies of this unique film were sent the same evening by post to Dublin and other chief cities, so that the loyal inhabitants of Britain were able to follow the movements of their Queen in the Emerald Isle very shortly after the chief ceremonial connected with her visit there had closed.[74]

Described as 'a cinematographic feat', this report elicited an immediate response from the British Mutoscope & Biograph Company:

A CINEMATOGRAPHIC FEAT.

To the EDITORS.

GENTLEMEN, Knowing your desire for accuracy in noting any photographic achieve-ment, I beg to point out the fact that the feat you give publicity to has been beaten some time ago by the British Mutoscope and Biograph Company, Limited, and a record estab-lished which will be very difficult to break.

   I will not trouble you by citing innumerable parallel cases with the above, as they are an every-day occurrence with the above Company, but, as an instance of marvellous dispatch and organisation, the following, I think you will agree, makes the record: At the Crystal Palace, in May last, at the opening of the Article Club by HRH the Duke of Connaught, the arrival of the Duke and Duchess, just before one o'clock, was photographed on a film of considerable length, the negative developed, dried, and a positive printed, developed, dried, and prepared for exhibition, and shown upon the screen at the Crystal Palace (Biograph Pavilion), at three o'clock the *same afternoon.*

   The developing, printing, &c., was all done in an improvised dark room, fitted up expressly for this picture, where the great facilities the Company have in their extraordinary dark rooms at Windmill-street were missing. I may also instance, as an equally great feat (showing what perfect organisation can do), the Grand National Race of last year, when the finish of the race at Liverpool, late in the afternoon, was brought to London and shown at the Palace Theatre the same evening, all the developing, printing, &c., being done at Windmill-street. Every week at the Palace Theatre events taking place in the afternoon are shown the same evening, and, during the last few months, war pictures have been shown with marvellous quickness after the event, that to give you any details would occupy too much of your valuable space. Hoping you will insert this, as your leaderette might create a false impression, except to those familiar with the Biograph at the Palace Theatre. I am, yours, &c., W.P. DANDO.
18 & 19 *Great Windmill-street, London, April* 13, 1900.[75]

According to information kindly supplied by Graeme Cruickshank, the present curator of the Palace Theatre archives, the signee of the letter, Walter Pfeffer Dando (1852–1944), received some fame as a theatrical engineer, and was at one time stage manager of the Royal English Opera House (now the Palace Theatre). In April 1896, he apparently resigned his position at the Palace in order to open a Phantom Theatre where he intended to show a cinematograph with coloured pictures and a phonograph working together.[76] This project evidently never transpired and instead he ended up working for the Mutoscope & Biograph Company, but in what capacity we do not know. No doubt his knowledge of stage effects and his inventive turn of mind was thought to be a welcome asset to the company.

   Filmmaking was not the only function of the Hepworth Company; developing and printing for the trade was also undertaken (Plate 25). At the Photographic & Allied Trades Exhibition held at the Portman Rooms (27 April-5 May), Hepworth lectured and exhibited the cinematograph.[77] In July he issued a booklet, *The Making of an Animated Photograph*, describing the whole process from raw film to finished print. It also included illustrations of some of the rooms in the factory at Hurst

It is Easy (Comparatively Speaking)

To TAKE Animated Photographs, but it is a very different matter to DEVELOP and PRINT them. Send your exposed Negatives to

HEPWORTH & CO., Cinematographers,

Telegrams: Hepworth, Walton-on-Thames.
Telephone No. 16.   WALTON-ON-THAMES.

Makers of the Celebrated "HEPWIX" FILMS, of which there is now a very large variety.

Send for Catalogue, and, if convenient, call and inspect Stock at

22 CECIL COURT, CHARING CROSS, LONDON, W.C.

N.B.—The **"HEPWORTH" ARC LAMPS** are the Best on the Market.

Plate 25   Advertisement announcing Cecil M. Hepworth's developing and printing services, November, 1900. (*Photograms of the Year 1900*, p. xlix)

Grove, where the various operations were carried out.[78] A second edition of his book *Animated Photography: the ABC of the Cinematograph* (first published in 1897) also appeared, revised and brought up to date by Hector Maclean.[79] A new preface and two additional chapters on 'Alternate Projection With Two Lenses' and 'Notes on Cinematography in 1900' were added. Of particular interest is the illustration on p. 121, showing three frames from a film photographed by Maclean with the Birtac, which reveals that there were only two perforations per frame at one side. The advertisement pages differ from those in the first edition.

2 The South Coast Filmmakers— Smith, Williamson, and West

G.A. SMITH

More than half of Smith's film output for 1900 consisted of what came to be referred to by early filmmakers as 'facials' (Plate 26). These simple films depicted comic characters engaged in situations which were conducive to the wildest forms of facial expression. The actors were filmed in close-up or medium close-up so that every movement of the face could be clearly seen by the audience.

Smith's first film of this type was made in 1897 and bore the simple title, *Comic Faces*. It showed a man enjoying a glass of beer and an old woman taking snuff. This has been called the first movie close-up. It was certainly not the first 'screen' close-up, for similar comic faces were already familiar in magic lantern shows. One of the most popular was *The Grimacer*. An example in the Barnes Collection is truly remarkable in the variety of expressions the painted face is made to undergo by the simple manipulation of a pivoted glass slide (Plate 27).

Plate 26 *A Quick Shave and Brush-up* (G.A. Smith, 1900). The actor (Tom Green) is photographed in medium close-up so that his facial expressions are clearly seen. Frame enlargement (*British Film Institute*)

Plate 27 *The Grimacer*. Articulated magic lantern slide, by Carpenter & Westley, London, circa 1850. By the simple manipulation of a pivoted glass slide, the face assumes a variety of comic expressions. Films of comic faces in close-up, known as *facials*, were first introduced by G.A. Smith (*Barnes Collection*; Photos: Denis Crompton)

Like so many other innovations in film technique (the dissolve, for instance), the idea of the *facial* was clearly derived from magic lantern slides, but Smith was the first to transfer the idea to film. In doing so he created a popular genre that was soon to be taken up by other filmmakers. Paul, for instance, in 1900 contributed to the genre with *A Naughty Story*. Smith's examples were particularly successful because he employed competent professional actors to register the emotional responses evoked by the situations. So successful did the genre become that Smith embarked upon a series of *facials* based on the characters of the 'Two Old Sports'. The original film of this title was made in 1899, and the second and third in the series appeared the following year as *Two Old Sports' Political Discussion*, and *Two Old Sports' Game of 'Nap'*. The 'political discussion' as the catalogue noted, needs no description of the action. 'It is simply an exchange of opinion regarding a *Daily Mail* and *Globe* article, the expressions of the faces telling the tale.' The parts were played by two prominent comedians, Messrs Hunter and Green, who also appeared in the sequel.[1] Descriptions of other films in the genre can be found in the Appendix.

Smith also used the close-up as a magnified image. In *Grandma's Reading-Glass*:

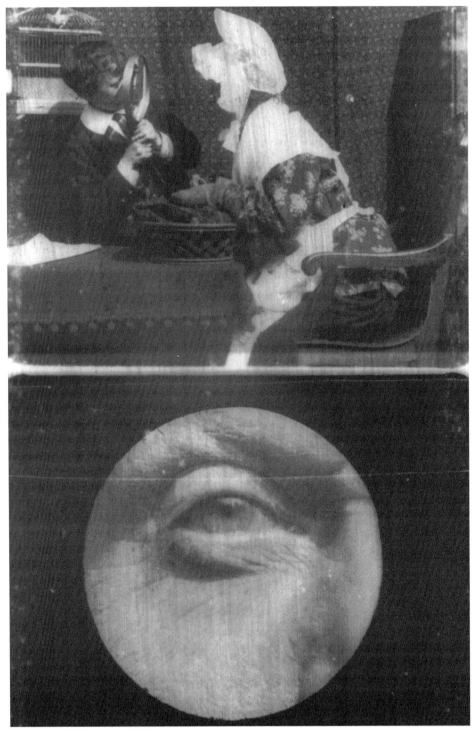

Plate 28   *Grandma's Reading Glass* (G.A. Smith, 1900). The objects looked at are photographed in close-up through a circular matte to simulate images seen through a magnifying glass. Frame enlargements (*British Film Institute*)

Grandma is seen at work at her sewing-table, while her little grandson is playfully handling her reading-glass, focusing same on various objects, viz., a newspaper, his watch, the canary, grandma's eye, and the kitten, which objects are shown in abnormal size on the screen when projected. The conception is to produce on the screen the various objects as they appeared to Willy while looking through the glass in their enormously enlarged form. The big print of the newspaper, the visible working of the mechanism of the watch, the fluttering of the canary in the cage, the blinking of grandma's eye, and the inquisitive look of the kitten, is most amusing to behold. The novelty of the subject is bound to please every audience.[2]

Smith photographed the objects looked at through a circular matte to give the impression that they were being viewed through the actual magnifying glass (Plate 28). The first object to come under the inspection of the reading glass is a newspaper, which the camera scans in a slow *panning* shot. If we freeze the picture at the appropriate spot, one can read an advertisement for Bovril: 'an appetising sandwich for Henley'. The Royal Henley Regatta took place in July, which is probably when the film was made.

Smith employed a similar effect in *As Seen Through the Telescope*, made at about the same time. Here the Professor with his telescope uses it to obtain a better view of a young man tying the lace of a lady's shoe (shown in close-up through a circular matte as in the former film). What is doubly interesting about these two films is that each scene is divided up into a number of shots, the close-up insert in each case acting as a 'point of view shot' (POV), showing what the person in the scene is looking at. In both films Smith used the close-up as a magnified image, not to give a closer view of the object, but to provide an enlargement of it.

The actual location of Smith's *As Seen Through the Telescope* is the entrance to St Ann's Well and Garden, Furze Hill, Hove (Plate 29). The man with the telescope stands in the street outside the porch of the gate-house. The upright posts of the gate-house are clearly visible in the film, as is the vending machine which stands against the wall (Plate 30). The spot where the girl stops with her bicycle is just beyond the lamp-post shown in the right-hand side of the picture postcard, reproduced in our illustration.[3]

This use of the close-up as magnified image goes back to the phantasmagoria, when the projected image was seen to increase in size as the lantern was moved closer towards the screen. The sensation of the image increasing in size rather than getting closer to the audience is cleverly demonstrated in Méliès' *L'Homme à la tête en caoutchouc/The Man with the Rubber Head* (1902). The professor's head, normal size, is seen on the laboratory table. The assistant connects it to a rubber tube attached to a pair of bellows and proceeds to inflate it. The head (Méliès' own) then appears to grow in size until it finally bursts. The head was of course, photographed independently of the main scene, with the camera stationary, but the object arranged on a travelling carriage which was moved slowly up a ramp towards the camera. When the shot was superimposed on the rest of the scene, the effect was of the head expanding.[4]

In the early days of cinema, there was some confusion over how the close-up should be 'read'. Was it an enlargement of the image, as in the reading-glass and telescope films, or simply a form of animated portrait like the simple *facial*? Or was it something else besides? The idea of using the close-up as detail, for taking a closer

Plate 29   The Entrance to St Ann's Well, Furze Hill, Hove. This provided the location for Smith's film *As Seen Through the Telescope* (*Barnes Collection*)

Plate 30   *As Seen Through the Telescope* (G.A. Smith, 1900). The scene is located at the entrance to St Ann's Well. Note the vending machine against the wall, also visible in the postcard view above. Frame enlargement (British Film Institute)

look at a particular aspect of a scene, did not occur to Smith, or to anyone else, until the following year when he made *The Little Doctor*. In this film, Smith inserts a close-up so that the audience may better see what is taking place in the general view that preceded it. But even here he is not quite sure how to describe the effect, as is apparent from the catalogue description:

> Children playing at 'doctors' with the kitten in a cradle as patient. When the medicine is administered a magnified view of the kitten's head is shown, the manner in which the little animal receives its dose (of milk) from a spoon, being most amusing. Length 100 feet.[5]

The interpolated close-up in this film is not a closer shot along the axis of the camera, as Barry Salt would lead us to believe in his book *Film Style*, but is in fact a different set-up altogether.[6] No attempt has been made to match the position of the kitten across the two shots, as Salt implies. It is quite plain to see that the person holding the kitten in long shot is a different person to the one holding it in close-up. This is most obvious from the different apparel worn by each sitter. The little girl in the first shot wears a white pinafore which is nowhere visible in the close-up. The person in close-up also appears to be older. However, this does not distract from the intention of the director, to show us more clearly what is going on in the scene.

Another aspect of film technique explored by Smith in 1900 was the use of the subjective camera. *Snapshotting an Audience* shows a photographer's preparations

Plate 31   *A Photograph Taken From Our Area Window* (G.A. Smith, 1901). Legs and feet only are seen, as if the spectator were looking up through a basement window. Frame enlargement from a 17.5 mm Biokam reduction print (*G.A.F. Ramsden*)

Plate 32   *The House That Jack Built* (G.A. Smith, 1900). This simple trick film relies for its effect on reverse motion, signalled in the film by a title. This is possibly the first use of an inter-title in an English film. Frame enlargement (British Film Institute)

for taking a group photograph of an imaginary audience which in reality is us, the spectators of the film. He tells various imaginary persons amongst us, to look this way or that, to look pleasant, and so forth. He is, of course, directing his instructions towards the camera, as if it were a member of the audience.

The following year, Smith used the same idea to even better effect in *A Photograph Taken From Our Area Window*. In this film the point of view is from the basement window, looking out at the feet and legs of passers-by on the pavement. The catalogue description is succinct: 'What do we see? Nothing but feet and legs, but oh! what a variety.' The original film was 100 feet in length and is now lost, but a short extract of about 25 ft is preserved in a 17.5 mm version prepared for use in the Biokam (Plate 31).

In *Let Me Dream Again*, Smith took an equally imaginative approach to the handling of a dream sequence transition. This opens with a scene of a loving couple enjoying themselves at a masquerade ball. The scene then goes out of focus and comes into focus again on the next scene which shows the man waking up in bed to find himself next to his unattractive wife. Smith affects the transition from dream to reality by the simple expedient of using a focus-pull.[7]

In *The House that Jack Built* (Plate 32), a little girl builds a house of toy bricks, which her young brother then proceeds to demolish. By reversing the film the boy is made to appear to restore the house to its former state. This simple trick using reverse motion had been used as early as 1897,[8] but Smith introduced an innovation by signalling the effect with a title which reads 'reversed'. This is possibly the first use of an inter-title in a British film. Smith may also have been the first to use a main title on a film, for instance in *Santa Claus*, made in 1898.[9]

Except for a very brief pan at the beginning of *Grandma's Reading Glass*, Smith does not seem to have used this effect at all in any of the other films that he made in 1900, though he had a tripod fitted with a panoramic head as early as the summer of 1899. A correspondent of *The Brighton Herald*, who interviewed Smith at St Ann's Well in that year, mentions 'a camera specially adapted for taking panoramic views'. The correspondent explained:

> Most of us, probably, have seen the pictures where long stretches of a river bank, the Grand Canal at Venice,[10] or a harbour quay, glides slowly before us. Mr Smith has a method whereby he can stand still and take such views, by merely turning the camera slowly round on its tripod.[11]

Smith had already successfully put the new tripod to the test with a panning shot of Brighton seafront. He 'chose a bright sunny day in August when the town was filled', notes the correspondent of *The Herald*, who then went on to describe the film:

> A splendid picture resulted, including a big sweep of the front, from west to east, coming down to the Lower Esplanade, crossing the beach, and winding up at the head of the West Pier. There are four-in-hands, carriages, donkey boys, bathing machines, and steamers, and the usual holiday crowd. But most prominent of all, slowly wending its ponderous way, appears the giant of whom we see so much,—the steam-roller. 'Charming characteristic of Brighton, isn't it', remarked Mr Smith, 'the height of the season and a steam-roller'.[12]

The film appears in the WTC catalogues as no. 3053—BRIGHTON. 'A panoramic view of the Queen of Watering Places, taking in the upper and lower esplanades and beach, and finally conducting the observer up to the head of the Pier'.

The number of technical innovations which Smith introduced into his films from 1897 to 1903 is truly remarkable. He can be credited with the first close-up, the superimposed inset, the practice of dividing a scene up into a number of shots, the point of view shot, the focus-pull, the panning shot, and even special lighting effects such as those used in the film *After Dark, or the Policeman and his Lantern* (1903). Smith also pioneered the use of titles. In some respects he was the equal of Méliès as far as technical matters were concerned, but it would be foolish to equate his artistry with the French master, for Méliès was an artist of considerable talent, whereas Smith was little more than a clever innovator.

If we look into Smith's cash book for the year 1900, we find that laboratory work occupied a great deal of his work load. He was also heavily involved in Biokam affairs and a darkroom was equipped specifically for this purpose. The bulk of his film stock was now bought directly from WTC, which had acquired an interest in the Blair film factory at Foot's Cray. Smith's accounts show that he paid on average of about £430 per month to WTC for film. His only paid assistants remained T.G. Brocksopp and Dora Shaw. Sundry equipment continued to be supplied by Alfred Darling, and chemicals by Fuerst Brothers. L.E. Smith supplied material for Biokams, title slides, and so forth. On 3 August, Smith received from John Benett-Stanford the sum of £5 as commission on the sale of his war films. *The Brighton Herald* had described these war films earlier in the year:

> Living Photographs from the Seat of War. It is interesting to know that Brighton has played a prominent part in the production of some unique living photographs from the seat of war in South Africa. The photographs, which have been exhibited at the latter part of this week in some of the London Halls, were taken by Mr Benett-Stanford, of Brighton, with apparatus with which he was equipped by G. Albert Smith, of Brighton, at whose factory at St Ann's Well, in Furze-hill, the prize films were developed, immediately on their receipt in carefully sealed boxes from Southampton. The events portrayed, which are exciting the keenest interest, are:
>
> Lancers under the Earl of Airlie fording the Modder River on their return from the Enslin engagement, December 8th, 1899.
>
> The Hospital Corps attending the wounded on the battlefield after the Modder River engagement.
>
> Troop train carrying the Seaforth Highlanders over the Modder River, crossing on a temporary bridge, erected in place of the one blown up by the Boers. Both ends of the train are guarded by an armoured car and engine.
>
> The ('Fighting Fifth') Northumberland Fusiliers making trenches at Orange River, and the passing of an armoured train'.[13]

The film business does not seem to have been a very lucrative one for Smith: his receipts from January 1897 to the end of December 1900 amounted to only £8278.4s.3d. Perhaps that is why he finally threw in his lot with Charles Urban. At about the same time as Urban left the Warwick Trading Company to form his own 'Trading Company', Smith handed over the lease of St Ann's Well to A.H. Tee, a pioneer film exhibitor (Plate 33). Henceforth the Urban catalogues listed Smith's 'film works and theatre studio' at Southwick, where he had re-established himself under Urban's auspices.[14]

Telephone: Nat. No. 08927.

A. H. TEE

Now booking engagements for
exhibitions of the Best

Animated

.. Pictures

High-Class Entertainments,

Moral, Amusing, Instructive.

*None but selected Pictures
exhibited.*

No connection with other exhibitors.

Full particulars gratis.

ONLY ADDRESS:

St. Ann's Well Garden's, Hove

Agents: Messrs. LYON & HALL,
Brighton and Hove.

Plate 33   Advertisement for A.H. Tee's Animated Pictures. From a printed programme for The Dome, Brighton, 27 October 1904. Tee succeeded Smith as lessee of St Ann's Well in 1904 (*Barnes Collection*)

But in 1900, Smith still had three more productive years at St Ann's Well, during which time he was to make some of his most memorable films. There is a photograph of him at this period, seated at his desk in his office at Furze Hill (Plate 34), which was first published in the Warwick catalogue of September 1900, where he is described as 'Mr G.A. Smith, Manager of the Brighton Film Works of the Warwick Trading Co., Limited'.[15] Also appearing in the same catalogue is an illustration of Smith's simple out-door studio (Plate 35) with the caption: 'The lawn and gardens at the Brighton Film Works—arranging a "Set" '.[16]

A statement in *The Photogram* for February 1900 states that WTC 'have concluded arrangements whereby they command the output for the next few years of the firm of G. Albert Smith the well-known kinetographer of Brighton'.[17]

Charles Urban, the Warwick Trading Company's domineering manager, seemed intent on taking over Smith and his tranquil establishment at St Ann's Well. A new building was erected in the Gardens with a sign proclaiming 'Warwick Trading Co., Ltd. Brighton Works'.[18] A section of the new building was illustrated in the September catalogue, which showed three members of the female staff standing at the main entrance (Plate 36). Urban must have thought very highly of Smith, for he retained his services after his departure from WTC in 1904, to the Charles Urban Trading Company.

Like so many early filmmakers, Smith had come to cinematography via the magic lantern. His name first came into prominence in the Brighton area, with his 'Dioramic Lecture Entertainments' at the Brighton Aquarium, on the seafront. This

Plate 34   G.A. Smith in his office at Furze Hill, Hove. Photograph first published in September 1900 (*Science Museum, London*)

Plate 35   G.A. Smith arranging a film set in the gardens of St Ann's Well, Hove. Photo first published in September 1900 (*Science Museum, London*)

Plate 36   The Warwick Trading Company's Brighton Works at St Ann's Well, September 1900 (*Science Museum, London*)

Plate 37   Brighton Aquarium, in the theatre of which G.A. Smith gave a series of magic lantern lectures, which he later augmented with films (*Barnes Collection*)

Plate 38   Interior of the Brighton Aquarium showing stage and auditorium where Smith lectured with lantern and cinematograph (*Barnes Collection*)

place of entertainment included a theatre where dramatic or operatic entertainments were given, along with instrumental concerts by the Aquarium Band. In addition to the theatre, the Aquarium, as its name implied, also housed marine specimens (displayed in the usual tanks) as well as diving birds, seals and sea lions (Plates 37 and 38).[19]

On several occasions Smith presented a series of three dioramic lectures at the Aquarium theatre, given on alternate days throughout the week, including afternoon and evening performances. The first lecture was called *The Glories of the Heavens, or a Tour Through Space*. This was 'a grand Astronomical Entertainment, with brilliant dissolving views and beautiful mechanical and dioramic effects'. The second lecture was *Twenty Thousand Leagues Under the Sea*, 'a romantic and startling trip with Jules Verne, introducing numerous electrical effects and dioramic changes. Charming to young people. Pleasing and entertaining to all'. The third was a patriotic entertainment called *Our Glorious Empire*, 'a pictorial and dioramic tour through John Bull's Dominions, our Colonies, Possessions and Defences in all quarters of the Globe, with charming optical changes and effects.'[20] During a re-engagement for the week commencing 29 March 1897, the entertainment was concluded with a display of 'Animated Photographs', which included local subjects, some no doubt taken by Smith himself (Plate 39).[21]

Tom Green was a frequent performer at the Aquarium. In a Christmas pantomime of *Cinderella* in 1896, for example, he played the part of Baron Hardup, and the performance concluded with a grand comic harlequinade and shadow pantomime 'invented and arranged by Mr Tom Green' (Plate 40).[22] It was probably at the Aquarium that Smith and Green first met, and who better to cast in the Smith photoplays than this local comedian?

Plate 39 Brighton Aquarium programme for the week commencing 29 March 1897, featuring Smith's popular 'Dioramic Lecture Entertainments', augmented with a display of 'Animated Photographs' (*Brighton Reference Library*)

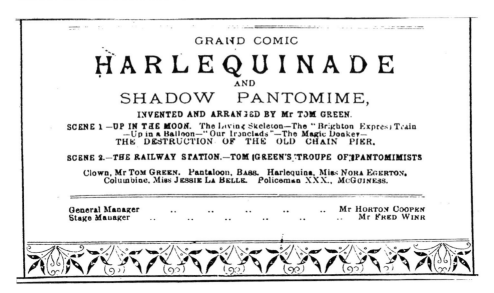

GRAND COMIC

HARLEQUINADE

AND

SHADOW   PANTOMIME,

INVENTED AND ARRANGED BY Mr TOM GREEN.

SCENE 1 —UP IN THE MOON. The Living Skeleton—The " Brighton Express Train
—Up in a Balloon—" Our Ironclads "—The Magic Donkey—
THE DESTRUCTION OF THE OLD CHAIN PIER.

SCENE 2.—THE RAILWAY STATION.—TOM GREEN'S TROUPE OF PANTOMIMISTS

Clown, Mr TOM GREEN. Pantaloon, BASS. Harlequina, Miss NORA EGERTON.
Columbine. Miss JESSIE LA BELLE. Policeman XXX., McGUINESS.

General Manager   ..   ..   Mr HORTON COOPER
Stage Manager   ..   .. Mr FRED WINR

Plate 40   Notice of a comic harlequinade and shadow pantomime devised by Tom Green for the Christmas pantomime *Cinderella*, presented at the Brighton Aquarium, 1895–96 (*Brighton Reference Library*)

James A. Williamson

Williamson had already made at least 122 films by the time he tackled his first major work, *Attack on a China Mission*. Previously he had been noted for his 'one-minute comedies', which were simple one-shot comic incidents with no attempt at continuous narrative. He had also filmed a number of actualities, but these too were encompassed within a single shot and were restricted in length to the film capacity of the camera.

Attack on a China Mission—Blue Jackets to the Rescue (41–44) was his first attempt at a serious dramatic reconstruction of a contemporary theme, in this case, the Boxer Rebellion.[23] He was following the precedent set by Georges Méliès with his film of the Dreyfus affair, and the numerous reconstructions of incidents in the Boer War which the Méliès film had triggered off. However, the Williamson film broke new ground in narrative technique. This is one of the key films in the history of the cinema and has the most fully developed narrative of any film made in England up to that time. With a cast of over two dozen, including what appears to be a contingent of professional sailors, the story is staged in four shots and runs to an unprecedented length, for an English fiction film, of 230 feet. The plot more or less speaks for itself and can just about be understood without the help of a commentator. The official catalogue description of the film can be found in the Appendix, but here I wish to analyse the construction of the film in a little more detail:

Shot 1. First we are shown the outside of the mission compound, with the Boxers forcing an entry. We know it is a Chinese Mission that is being attacked because the words are clearly painted on the front gates.

Shot 1

Shot 2

Shot 3

Shot 4

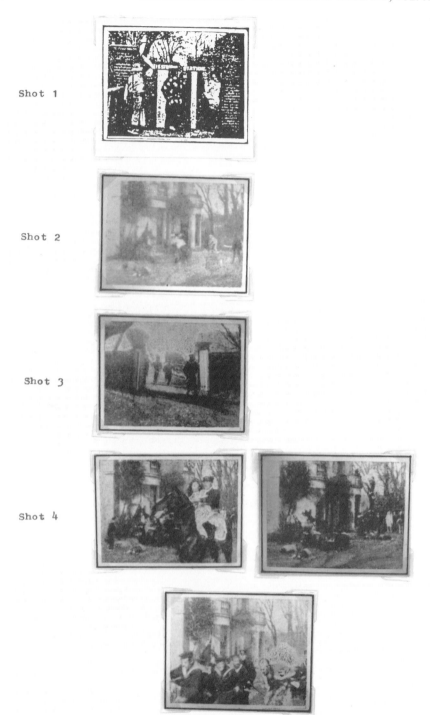

Plate 41 *Attack on a China Mission* (Williamson, 1900). A dramatic reconstruction of an incident in the Boxer Rebellion, comprising four shots. Six frame illustrations from the catalogue of the Charles Urban Trading Co., 1903–1904. pp. 113–114, film no. 4126 (*Science Museum, London*)

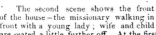

4123 ATTACK ON A CHINA MISSION.—BLUEJACKETS TO THE RESCUE

The scene opens with the outer gate of the premises; a Chinaman with flourishing sword approaches and tries the gate. Finding it fastened, he calls the others who come rushing up; one leaps over the gate, and the combined attack results in forcing it open; nine Boxers in Chinese costumes of varied character now swarm in, stopping occasionally to fire in the direction of the house.

The second scene shows the front of the house—the missionary walking in front with a young lady; wife and child are seated a little further off. At the first alarm, the missionary drops his book and sends the young lady into the house to fetch rifle and pistols; he then rushes to his wife and child, and sees them safely into the house; takes cover behind some bushes, discharges his revolver at the Boxers advancing in different directions, kills one, then picks up rifle and discharges it at another; his ammunition exhausted, he comes to close quarters with another Boxer armed with a sword, and, after an exciting fight, is overcome, and left presumably killed. Meanwhile, others of the attacking party have closed round the young lady and followed her, retreating into the house.

Missionary's wife now appears waving handkerchief on the balcony; the scene changes and shows party of bluejackets advancing from the distance, leaping over a fence, coming through the gate, kneeling and firing in fours, and running forward to the rescue, under command of a mounted officer.

The fourth scene is a continuation of the second. The Boxers are dragging the young lady out of the house, which they have set on fire, at the moment the bluejackets appear; a struggle takes place with the officer rides up Boxers; mounted young lady out of and carries off the the melée.

The missionary's wife now rushes out of the house pointing to the balcony, where she has left her child; a bluejacket has secured it, but his passage down the stairs being blocked, three sailors mount on each other's shoulders and land the child safely in the mother's arms.

The struggle with the Boxers continues, but they are finally overcome and taken prisoners.

This sensational subject is full of interest and excitement from start to finish, and is everywhere received with great applause.

Length 230 feet.

Plate 42 *Attack on a China Mission* (Williamson, 1900). Text and illustrations published in Urban's catalogue of 1903–1904, pp. 113–114 (*Science Museum, London*)

114

quarters with another Boxer armed with a sword, and, after an exciting fight, is overcome, and left presumably killed. Meanwhile, others of the attacking party have closed round the young lady and followed her, retreating into the house.

Missionary's wife now appears waving handkerchief on the balcony; the scene changes and shows party of bluejackets advancing from the distance, leaping over a fence, coming through the gate, kneeling and firing in fours, and running forward to the rescue, under command of a mounted officer.

The fourth scene is a continuation of the second. The Boxers are dragging the young lady out of the house, which they have set on fire, at the moment the blue-jackets appear; a struggle takes place with the Boxers; mounted officer rides up and carries off the young lady out of the melée. The mission- ary's wife now rushes out of the house pointing to the balcony, where she has left her child; a bluejacket has secured it, but his passage down the stairs being blocked, three sailors mount on each other's shoulders and land the child safely in the mother's arms.

The struggle with the Boxers continues, but they are finally overcome and taken prisoners.

This sensational subject is full of interest and excitement from start to finish, and is everywhere received with great applause.

Length 230 feet.

Plate 43 *Attack on a China Mission* (Williamson, 1900). Page from Urban's catalogue of 1903–1904 (*Science Museum, London*)

Plate 44   *Attack on a China Mission* (Williamson, 1900). Frame enlargement from a contemporary print in the National Film Archive (*British Film Institute*)

Shot 2. The scene then changes to the front of the house with the missionary and his household becoming alarmed at the intrusion and taking the necessary steps for their defence. After a short skirmish in which the missionary is left for dead, the wife, who has taken refuge in the house, appears on the balcony waving a handkerchief.

Shot 3. Evidently the signal has alerted a party of sailors who race to the rescue. A reverse angle to shot one, from inside the compound, shows the bluejackets in the distance climbing over a fence and advancing through the open gates, firing as they approach.

Shot 4. This is a continuation of shot two, showing the front of the house where the rest of the action takes place.

Williamson, who was himself a chemist, seems to have devised special cartridges to give off the maximum amount of smoke when the guns are discharged so as to enhance the dramatic effect of the fighting. The action is staged in depth and with a fair degree of realism. The characters taking part in the film have been identified as Florence Williamson (girl), Mr Lepard (missionary) and Mr James (officer).[24] The location was a derelict property in Hove which was soon to be demolished known as

Plate 45   Postcard from J. A. Williamson sent during a trip to Ireland where he had probably gone to film the Queen's visit to Dublin. The text reads:

Belfast. April 9

Dear Janet,
    I was away on the Mourne Mountains yesterday and did not get your wages till late. Mr Maclean's proofs were therefore not returned till this morning 80 ft Neg. film sent same post. Hand to Stevens [?] for developing & printing. Tell him to take very *small* piece from inside and for trial. Cannot say yet whether I shall be returning to-night or tomorrow night. Will telegraph
Yours faithfully
J. Williamson.

The original postcard is in a Williamson album in the possession of the British Film Institute

Plate 46   Advertisement for James A. Williamson's Cinematograph Film Works, 55 Western Road, Hove, offering developing and printing services to the trade (*The Optician*, 6 April 1900, p. 80)

Plate 47   Hove town hall, venue for Williamson's popular saturday night entertainments, where *Attack on a China Mission* received its debut on 17 November 1900. *Top:* Interior—the stage where the film was shown (*Barnes Collection*)

Ivy Lodge.[25] Williamson's film should not be confused with another film based on a similar subject, called *Attack on a Mission Station*. This latter film was issued by J. Wrench & Son and recorded the incident in a single take 87 feet long. A synopsis of this film, too, can be found in the Appendix. Its simple treatment goes to show what a tremendous stride Williamson had taken by breaking up his story into a number of separate shots.

No doubt the making of *Attack on a China Mission* occupied much of Williamson's time during part of 1900, and prevented him from producing his usual number of fiction films. In fact, there is only one other title for the whole of the year, *The Jovial Monks*, a simple *facial* comedy made in two parts which involves a couple of monks and a bottle of wine.[26] Williamson did, however, manage to film a few topical subjects, one of which took him to Ireland to film Queen Victoria's visit to Dublin (Plate 45). This trip resulted in two films of the event, one 75 feet long and the other 150 feet. He also went to London to cover the City Imperial Volunteers procession. The rest of the year's films were of subjects taken closer to home, but even these were few in number.

Filmmaking was not, however, Williamson's only occupation. He still carried on his pharmaceutical business in Western Road, where he developed and printed his own films as well as those for the trade (Plate 46).[27] He was also something of an impresario, and in the winter months he presented a series of Saturday night shows at the Hove Town Hall under the banner of 'Williamson's Popular Entertainments' (Plate 47).[28] These shows included concert items, vocalists and comedians, as well as the cinematograph. The films were always accompanied on the piano by a local pianist, usually a Mr Norman Richards.[29] It was at just such an evening's entertainment at the Town Hall, Hove, that Williamson's *Attack on a China Mission* received its première on 17 November 1900. It delighted the audience to such an extent that they wanted to see it again, but, as the local paper reported, 'those in authority were alas! inexorable'. The accompanist on this occasion was Mr E.H. Killick, 'who showed much tact in his selection of airs with which he enlivened the kinematograph display'.[30] Extracts from the local paper capture something of the flavour of these Victorian evenings:

> Those who visited the Hove Town Hall on Saturday evening last could not possibly have been disappointed or dissatisfied with the bill of fare placed before them. The hall was well filled with an appreciative audience, and a free and easy air prevailed throughout the evening.
>
> The entertainment opened with a piano selection by Mr Norman Richards, A.R.C.O., and was followed by the Aeolian Glee Singers . . .
>
> The Kinematograph then followed, Mr Norman Richards enlivening the proceedings with appropriate music.
>
> In the second part, Miss Edith Welling and Mr A. Galloway opened with a duet.[31]

The review closed with a list of the twenty or so films shown. The majority were taken by Williamson himself, but there were a few Boer War subjects obtained from another source. On 8 December, the same paper reviewed the third entertainment of the season:

> Another of Williamson's attractive Saturday 'pops' was given at the Town Hall last Saturday evening, when an excellent programme was presented in a perfectly satisfactory

way. The room was very fairly filled with a rather larger audience than that of the week before. Several quartettes were sung by the Cecilians in a refined and artistic way, that won the people's warmest approval. The Cecilians consist of Miss F. Donovan (soprano), Miss Maud Foreshew (contralto), Mr H.E. Hedgcock (tenor), and Mr W.A. Lauder (baritone). Among other things, they gave 'The Miller's Wooing', 'The Little Church', 'Joy and Sorrow', and 'Annie Laurie'. Miss Foreshew and Mr Lauder sang 'Keys of Heaven', a pretty old English ditty, with silly words, in such a taking way that they were encored in a most determined manner. They returned and sang, 'Oh! that we two were maying'. Miss Foreshew's rich contralto was heard to excellent advantage in 'Love the Pedlar', and Mr Hedgcock's 'Lorna' was a delightful contribution. Two songs were pleasingly given by Miss Donovan. The humorist of the evening was Mr C.T. West, whose funny songs, cleverly accompanied by himself, were enormously popular, so that he had to give more than he was booked for. Extremely interesting kinematograph pictures were shown. These included a splendid series, taken by Mrs Aubrey le Blond, illustrative of winter sports in the Engadine. There was skating at St. Moritz, figure skating by Mr Vail, tobogganing on different runs at St. Moritz, bob-sleigh, racing, hockey on the ice, sleighing, and snow-balling.

The fourth entertainment of the season will be given to-night, with a new programme'.[32]

It is interesting to note Williamson's sponsorship of Aubrey le Blond (Mrs Main), England's first woman filmmaker. Her *Winter Sports in the Engadine*, consisting of ten short films, were considered by Williamson interesting enough to be included in his future catalogues. This was not the first time he had shown her work, for he had included two of her films in a previous Saturday night's entertainment at the Hove Town Hall.[33] At present, little is known about this lady, but her career surely deserves to be rescued from oblivion.

Williamson's career as a filmmaker, like Paul's, had come to an end by 1910, but unlike Paul, he did not desert the film industry, instead conducting a profitable business as a manufacturer of cinematographic equipment. As a filmmaker, he will be principally remembered for *Attack on a China Mission* (1900); *The Big Swallow* (1901); *Stop Thief* (1901); *Fire!* (1901); *The Soldier's Return* (1902); *Wait Till Jack Comes Home* (1903); *An Interesting Story* (1904); and *Our New Errand Boy* (1905).[34]

G. West & Sons ('Our Navy')

Whereas West's film performances are quite well documented, there is very little information available about the actual films made by the firm.[35] Here and there one finds a reference to a particular title, but even this does not provide a definite clue as to the film's identity. Many of the films shown were made by other producers, such as the ones taken in South Africa, where West had no cameras operating. Likewise, not all those taken on the home front can be attributed to West, since films from other sources were invariably used. The kind of show that West was now presenting under the title of 'Our Navy' called for scenes of the present conflict, and if the Boer War had not been represented, then audiences would surely have found the programmes wanting. After all, was not the very nature of the programme a call to patriotism? Such a sentiment is clearly expressed in the following review written for the *Hove Echo*:

Plate 48   Brighton sea front at the turn of the century, showing Hove and West Pier in the distance (*Barnes Collection*)

'Our Navy', which is still at the West Pier (Plate 48), is one of the most interesting, educative, and inspiring entertainments imaginable. At the present time interest is centred in our fighting forces, and not the least interesting portion of those forces is the little band of blue-jackets who have done such brilliant work in conjunction with our troops in South Africa. Messrs West and Son have obtained a remarkably complete and clear set of animated pictures illustrating the drills, the life, and the fighting abilities of English sailors, and the collection is brought up-to-date by pictures of Khaki-clothed troops embarking for South Africa, and of the sailors and naval guns actually at the front. These pictures cannot but work upon the patriotic feelings of most people, and if anyone is suffering from depression concerning events in South Africa, we would advise them to pay the West Pier a visit in order to gratify their patriotic pride in our great naval strength, and to have their spirits raised by a sight of our mirthful, hardy, and energetic sailors. Messrs West's pictures show Jack exactly as he is, always at work, yet never done with play, and after enjoying this pictorial entertainment no one can deny or wonder at the words of the song, 'they all love Jack'. Among the most wonderful pictures shown are those of the *Turbinia*, steaming at immense speed; of the Queen's review of the Household troops before their departure for the seat of war; of the embarkation of the West Surrey Regiment; and of various yacht-races. The musical accompaniments are good, and the verbal descriptions of the pictures are delivered by a fine elocutionist.[36]

Naturally, West's home base of Southsea, close to Portsmouth with its naval con-nections, provided another ideal venue for the new season's programme, and consequnetly 'Our Navy' was consequently booked for a three-week run at the

Victoria Hall.[37] The opening night of 26 March was given in aid of the Mayor of Portsmouth's Fund for sailors and marines engaged in the war. The gross proceeds of the performance, amounting to £30.6s.8d., was handed over to the Mayor during one of the intervals. The evening's performance was an unqualified success, and next day the *Portsmouth Evening News* printed the following account:

> On Monday evening, at the Victoria Hall, Southsea, Messrs West and Son, the well-known local photographers, commenced an exhibition of their photographic views depicting life in the British Navy. The pictures shown were simply splendid. Not only were they examples of the art of animated photography at its best, but the whole made up a complete history [of] a sailor's life, from the time when he first joins until he is shaped into the most highly trained fighting man that the world has ever seen. Also nearly every class of vessel in the Navy was shown upon the screen in the course of the evening. Besides 'Our Navy' proper, which has been exhibited with great success all over England, some splendid general war pictures were on view. All our leaders in South Africa were shown, and the bluejackets who saved Ladysmith were to be seen, tugging their 4.7's through the ruts in the roads *en route* to the threatened town. Then a troop of French's cavalry scouts was pourtrayed [sic], skirmishing in lively fashion against retiring Boers. The audience which attended by far the best entertainment of its kind to be seen in England, was very large, and included a number of Naval officers.[38]

Performances took place every evening at 8 p.m., with matinées Wednesdays and Saturdays at 3 p.m.[39] After a successful run of three weeks, the performances at the Victoria Hall came to a close on 6 April.[40] But with one week still to go, the *Portsmouth Evening News* wrote:

> 'Our Navy', Messrs West's splendid patriotic entertainment, now being produced nightly at the Victoria Hall, Southsea, entered, on Monday, on the third and last week of its stay at Portsmouth. This unique photographic display has drawn crowded audiences during the past fortnight, nor is its popularity surprising, for the entertainment shows almost every imaginable phase in Naval life, from a dance and 'jollification' on deck to the march of the Naval Brigade to Ladysmith, and every description of Naval craft, from the *Victory* to the *Powerful*. Last night a picture of special interest was introduced at the finish of the entertainment—the entry of Her Majesty into Dublin. It is worth recording that 'Our Navy', has produced no less than £300 for the sufferers from the war, for Messrs. West have generously given to various local war funds the proceeds of a large number of entertainments held in different towns'.[41]

After several weeks, 'Our Navy' again visited its home town of Southsea for a short season at the Victoria Hall from 20 August to 22 September.[42] The programme was arranged in three parts:

> Part I. Bluejacket's career from his entry on board a training ship.
> Part II. On board H.M.S. Jupiter during the recent manoeuvres, by permission of the Lords of the Admiralty.
> Part III. Various scenes in naval life, including 'Jack' at play.[43]

Each scene was graphically and clearly described by H. Wright Scadden, whilst a band played appropriate music. Among the films singled out for mention in the local press, were: 'some splendid yacht racing scenes', 'the two turbine boats *Turbinia* and *Viper*', 'collection of war pictures, which include the Naval Brigade with their guns and the welcome extended by Portsmouth to the gallant men of the *Powerful*'.[44] Other films shown during the season included Southsea Regatta, showing the start of the 'All Comers Race' and 'Walking the Greasy Pole', both filmed by West on Friday, 24 August.[45] A local gymkhana was also filmed.[46]

In addition to the show running at Southsea, West had three other touring companies on the road. On 3 September, 'Our Navy' opened simultaneously at Leicester, Hull and Herne Bay. Furthermore, two other companies were about to be established, and a colonial company was to be despatched to Canada, South Africa, Australia and New Zealand.[47] The Australian tour was under the management of Captain Edwards, R.N., who was accompanied by G.H. Snazelle.[48] 'Our Navy' was becoming a national institution, taking its place alongside Poole's Myrioramas and Hamilton's Excursions as Britain's best known touring entertainments. During 1900, 'Our Navy' visited the Curzon Hall, Birmingham (October–November);[49] Free Trade Hall, Manchester (October–November);[50] Wisbech (November);[51] Guildhall, Cambridge (November);[52] Drill Hall, Peterborough (November);[53] and the Temperance Hall, Bolton,[54] as well as other venues for which there are no records.

West's show place, however, was the old Polytechnic, Regent Street, London, which was shortly to become semi-permanent home for 'Our Navy' (Plate 49). One review described its appeal:

> We must not forget our sailors in the rush of sympathy with our soldiers. The boys in blue are at the front fighting just as well, just as calmly, as they do always. In peace Jack is trained to be a thoroughly capable fellow, to use his hands and his brains. If you want to see how this is done, you may see everything at the Polytechnic, in Regent Street, where, at three and eight daily, Messrs West and Son's excellent lantern and cinematographic representation of life in our Navy is being shown to crowded audiences. The exhibition has been running since October [1899], and the interest shows no sign of slackening. For youngsters no entertainment could be better.[55]

As the season at the Polytechnic drew to a close, the *British Journal of Photography* advised its readers who had not yet witnessed the exhibition to do so forthwith:

> The Exposition of 'Life in the Royal Navy' concludes its stay at the Polytechnic, London, on July 7 next. The crowded audiences that have visited it each day for the past nine months, and the keen interest and enthusiasm that has been shown during the presentation of this series of animated pictures, warrant one in strongly advising those who have not as yet been able to witness it to take advantage of the remaining two days of its stay at the Polytechnic. I understand that Messrs. West intend to open again in London, during the forthcoming winter, with some new scenes of naval life of still greater interest, and that they are arranging to send this Exhibition to Australia and our other colonies.[56]

It is necessary to add that West's film production existed solely for the purpose of supplying films for the 'Our Navy' entertainments. The films were never intended to be sold on the open market; this is the main reason why seeminly none of them have survived. West's intentions are clearly stated in this advertisement in *The Era*:

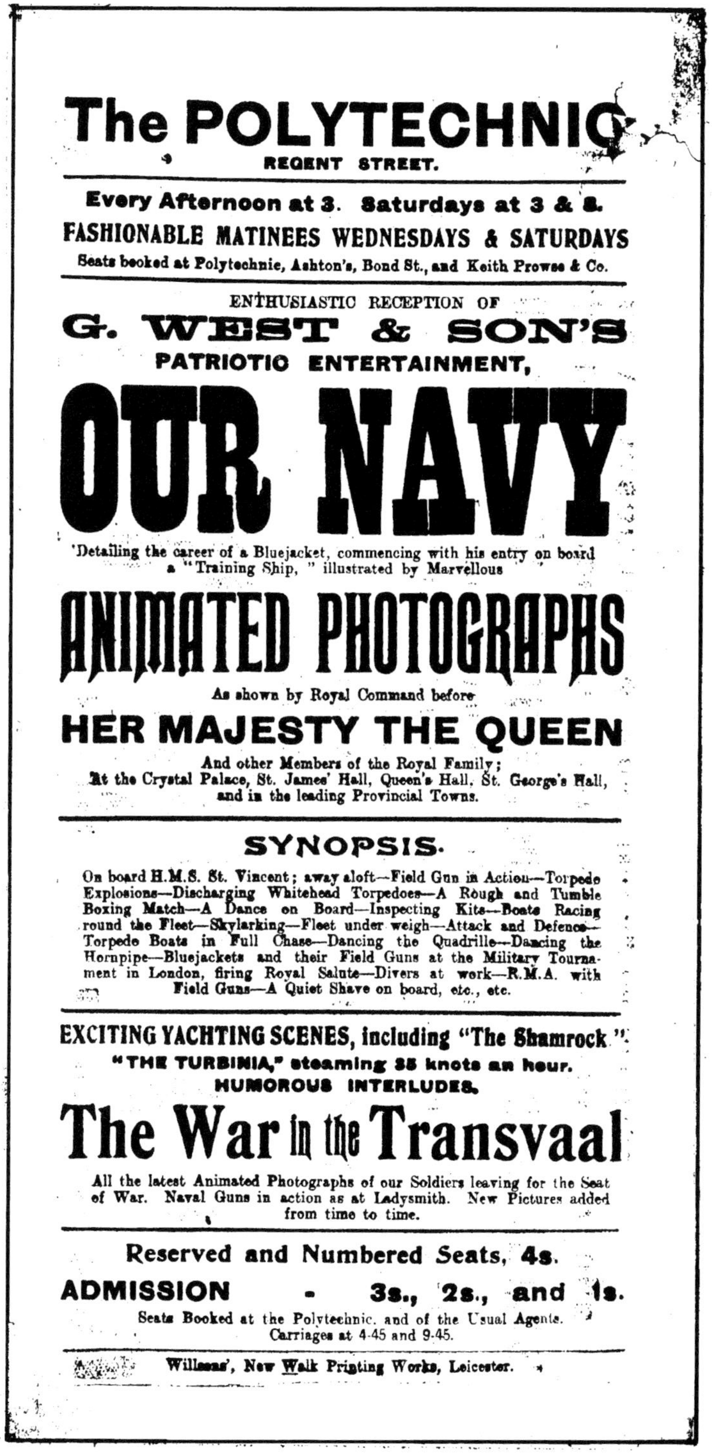

The POLYTECHNIC

REGENT STREET.

Every Afternoon at 3. Saturdays at 3 & 8.

FASHIONABLE MATINEES WEDNESDAYS & SATURDAYS

Seats booked at Polytechnic, Ashton's, Bond St., and Keith Prowse & Co.

ENTHUSIASTIC RECEPTION OF

G. WEST & SON'S

PATRIOTIC ENTERTAINMENT,

OUR NAVY

Detailing the career of a Bluejacket, commencing with his entry on board
a "Training Ship, " illustrated by Marvellous

ANIMATED PHOTOGRAPHS

As shown by Royal Command before

HER MAJESTY THE QUEEN

And other Members of the Royal Family;
At the Crystal Palace, St. James' Hall, Queen's Hall, St. George's Hall,
and in the leading Provincial Towns.

SYNOPSIS.

On board H.M.S. St. Vincent; away aloft—Field Gun in Action—Torpedo
Explosions—Discharging Whitehead Torpedoes—A Rough and Tumble
Boxing Match—A Dance on Board—Inspecting Kits—Boats Racing
round the Fleet—Skylarking—Fleet under weigh—Attack and Defence—
Torpedo Boats in Full Chase—Dancing the Quadrille—Dancing the
Hornpipe—Bluejackets and their Field Guns at the Military Tourna-
ment in London, firing Royal Salute—Divers at work—R.M.A. with
Field Guns—A Quiet Shave on board, etc., etc.

EXCITING YACHTING SCENES, including "The Shamrock".

"THE TURBINIA," steaming 35 knots an hour.

HUMOROUS INTERLUDES.

The War in the Transvaal

All the latest Animated Photographs of our Soldiers leaving for the Seat
of War. Naval Guns in action as at Ladysmith. New Pictures added
from time to time.

Reserved and Numbered Seats, 4s.

ADMISSION - 3s., 2s., and 1s.

Seats Booked at the Polytechnic, and of the Usual Agents.
Carriages at 4-45 and 9-45.

Willsons', New Walk Printing Works, Leicester.

Plate 49   Handbill announcing G. West's 'Our Navy' at the Polytechnic, Regent Street, London, which was to become the permanent home for this entertainment (*Theatre Museum, Covent Garden*)

'OUR NAVY'

G. WEST and SON beg to Announce that their Marvellous Naval and Yachting Animated Photographs are not for Sale, and are only used, and can only be seen at their 'Exposition of Life in our navy'

The following are a few of the subjects:

HOISTING BOATS

CLEAR LOWER DECKS

GUNNERY DRILL

TORPEDO EXPLOSION

THE SHIP'S BARBER

ROPE YARN SUNDAY

COALING SHIP

CLEANING SHIP

ANCHORS WEIGHED

SHIPS IN A HEAVY SEA

DANCING THE HORNPIPE

BARBETTE GUNS IN ACTION

MANNING THE CUTTER

HEAVING THE LEAD

YACHTS RACING IN ROUGH SEA

TURBINIA AT FULL SPEED

&c., &c., &c.

G. WEST and SON Photograph their own Pictures, and have a répertoire of over Seventy different Scenes of Naval Life, which are now being shown at the

POLYTECHNIC, REGENT-STREET

Every Afternoon at 3.0

G. WEST and SON are Open for Bookings of part or whole of this Interesting, Instructing, and Amusing Entertainment, including complete Staff, Lecturer, Operator, Music, &c.

Morning Post, Nov. 10th, 1899.—Is as good as a course of Naval Instruction.

Westminster Gazette, Oct. 21st.—We have certainly seen nothing to equal this entertainment.

All Communications to be made to

'OUR NAVY' BUREAU,

THE ANCHORAGE

SOUTHSEA

N.B. 'Our Navy' is the registered title of this entertainment.[57]

The exhibition side of West's activities is quite well documented, but reports of the filmmaking side of the business are sadly lacking. A brief glimpse of this aspect of West's work appeared in the *British Journal of Photography* at the end of August:

> We are pleased to hear that Messrs West, of Southsea, are adding fresh pictures to 'Our Navy', and are keeping it well up to date. By permission of the Lords of the Admiralty, one of the firm has spent the last three weeks on H.M.S. *Jupiter*, and has secured some excellent cinematograph series of the naval manoeuvres, such as evolutions of the fleet, ships in a heavy sea, heaving the lead, officers playing cricket on the quarter-deck, and sailors running along the boat boom to man the cutter, with one of them falling overboard and his mates to the rescue.[58]

3 American and French Connections

Although the Mutoscope & Biograph Company (M&B) and the Warwick Trading Company (WTC) both originated in the United States, they nevertheless thoroughly adapted themselves to the British market. This is not so surprising when one recalls that at M&B, the leading light was William Kennedy-Laurie Dickson, who had Scottish and English origins, while the guiding hand at WTC was Charles Urban, a rabid Anglophile who was to end his days in Brighton, the cradle of English cinematography.

Both companies established a secure footing in Britain very early on and WTC in particular was soon to dominate the British market in apparatus and films. As yet, American produced films had no appreciable effect on British cinema. It was the French who mattered most, and their influence was felt in both America and England. L. Gaumont et Cie was the first of the major French companies to establish a base in Great Britain, where its affairs were managed by the Englishman A.C. Bromhead. In this survey for 1900, I will consider the two Anglo-American companies first and then pass on to the French.

The Mutoscope & Biograph Syndicate Ltd (Biograph)

The Mutoscope & Biograph Syndicate Ltd remained outside the mainstream of British film production in that all its product was made solely for the company's own use. The Biograph films themselves could not be used by outsiders because of their unique size and format. The wide gauge film adopted by M&B was both taken and exhibited by the company's own apparatus, which remained under the control of its staff. Thus it was only in the field of exhibition that it could pose any threat to others.

The company had a semi-permanent home at the Palace Theatre of Varieties, Cambridge Circus, London (Plate 50), where its daily presentation of films was exhibited under the name of the American Biograph, as part of the general music hall programme. It retained its privileged position here until the beginning of 1903 when the large format film was gradually phased out in favour of the regular 35 mm gauge.

The manager of the Palace Theatre during the Biograph's engagement, was the flamboyant Charles Morton (Plate 51), who died not long after the Biograph's departure on 18 October 1904 at the ripe old age of 85. He seems to have had a special relationship with the Biograph people and even appeared in a Biograph film. 'Here we see Mr Morton advance, bow to the audience, and retire before a background where the English and American flags are tastefully united.'[1]

The American Biograph was not exclusive to the Palace Theatre, but played in various theatres throughout the kingdom. According to one report, there were five Biographs in operation in Great Britain, and 8,000 Mutoscopes.[2] Wherever they were shown, the highlights of the 1900 Biograph programmes were the war films being sent back from South Africa by W.K.-L. Dickson (Plate 52).

London   Palace Theatre, Cambridge Circus.

5207 B.

Plate 50   *Above:* Palace Theatre of Varieties, Cambridge Circus, London, where Casler's American Biograph remained a regular feature on the programmes for a number of years.
Below: Premises of the British Mutoscope & Biograph Co., 18 & 19 Great Windmill St., London. The building was erected in 1897 and the exterior is still more or less intact. When the company was wound up, the contents of the building were sold by public auction on 19 September 1905. Included in the sale were Mutoscopes, Kinoras and Biograph apparatus (*Barnes Collection*)

Plate 51   Charles Morton (1819–1904). Manager of the Palace Theatre, home of the American Biograph. He also appeared in a Biograph film (*Barnes Collection*)

Dickson was perhaps the most remarkable of all the early pioneers of cinematography. He was born in Brittany, France, of an English father and a Scottish mother, and spent much of his early youth in Scotland. In about 1879 Dickson and his mother went to America and for four years settled in Richmond, Virginia, where they had relations. In 1883 he went to New York and got a job with Edison. There he did important work in various departments including the laying of electric cables under the streets of New York and Brooklyn, and assisting Edison's ore-milling work. He is, of course, best remembered for his work at the Edison laboratories, where he was responsible for the first practical method of cinematography. His invention of the Kinetograph and Kinetoscope marks the true birth of modern cinema.

After leaving Edison's employ on the 2nd April 1895, he assisted the Lathams in their cinematographic work and went on to become a founding member of the Mutoscope & Biograph Company, where he was largely responsible for designing the Mutagraph (camera) and Biograph (projector). Dickson was twice married, first to a lady of Virginia, and then to a Scotswoman. According to the passenger list of the ship on which he sailed to South Africa, Dickson gave his nationality as 'Scotch'. He finally settled in Twickenham, Middlesex, where he died on 28 September 1935.[3]

Dickson had arrived in South Africa on 30 October, 1899, and by the end of December had already recorded many historic scenes with the cumbrous Mutagraph camera (Plate 53).[4] After taking part in the Battle of Colenso, he pushed on with

Plate 52   Photographers arriving in South Africa to cover the Boer War. The Mutagraph camera is seen in the centre with Dickson, in top hat, standing at right. (*War Pictures*, vol. 1, no. 1, 10 February 1900, p. 31)

Lord Robert's Naval Brigade to the relief of Ladysmith and eventually reached Pretoria on 4 June. At times he was in the thick of battle and suffered appalling hardships. Sometimes short of food, he also had to endure intense heat by day and bitter cold by night. As the South African historian Thelma Gutsche wrote:

> Moving constantly over rough and steeply inclined ground, Dickson and his assistants had great difficulty in getting their cart in position. They ran extraordinary risks and endured great hardships for the sake of their films. Constantly exposed to heavy fire to which it offered a clear target, the Biograph camera succeeded in taking excellent films not only of the actual hostilities but also of the crude life of the camps. Officers wrote home describing its activities and the Naval Brigade itself came almost to take pride in its curious companion.[5]

One story attributed to Dickson in *The Era* concerned a cavalry charge near Spion Kop. 'The sortie was suddenly ordered and there was only time to half-hitch the horses to the Biograph waggon and gallop after the troops. The Biograph held one Kopje, while Lord Dundonald's men got round another, and the action began. The machine recorded it all, and the fight is one of the Palace's best pictures.'[6] Such stories probably gave rise to the following paragraph in *The Optician*, which appeared under the heading 'Photography and Modern Warfare':

> The heavy guns were trained.
> 'Why the delay?' thundered the general.

Plate 53   W.K .-L. Dickson with Mutagraph camera in South Africa (*War Pictures*, vol. 1, no. 6, 17 March 1900, p. 164)

'The moving-picture operators have signalled that their machine is out of order', elucidated the Colonel.[7]

If nothing else, it certainly shows the growing importance accorded to cinema-tographers in war time.

The lack of action shots of actual battle was a criticism sometimes raised by the press, but some of Dickson's material came very close to supplying this need, as a correspondent in the *British Journal of Photography* pointed out:

So far, photographers at the theatre of hostilities in South Africa have not succeeded in securing negatives of fighting at close quarters, although every other phase of the war, including long-distance firing, appears to have been shown in the illustrated papers. We note, however, at a London place of amusement, The Palace Theatre, a series of animated photographs is being shown which take us very near to the representation of the actualities of carnage by means of photography. These include views of the bridging of the Tugela; Mounted Colonials returning from reconnaissance; the bombardment of Colenso; and the seizure of a Kopje near Spion Kop. Hand-to-hand encounters have yet to be photo-graphed, it would seem, although some of the stay-at-home artists have given us, in the illustrated papers, some vivid and striking pictures of such subjects.[8]

During the trek to Pretoria, Dickson suffered several misfortunes. During an unguarded moment, his Cape cart was looted by troopers. 'As soon as I yelled', Dickson wrote in his diary, 'they retreated in the gloom, carrying with them everything we had in the shape of food, cups, dishes, cooking utensils, and all our film and plates'.[9] Luckily, the Mutagraph camera was untouched, but the other losses necessitated a return trip to Durban, an estimated journey of some 625 miles. A far more serious calamity occurred when his assistants Cox and Seward came down with enteric fever. They became so ill that Dickson was forced to take the two men to Durban Sanatorium. In their absence Dickson had to make do with an incompetent sailor as his assistant. Eventually Dickson himself succumbed to the fever, but fortunately in a much milder form.

In spite of his difficulties, Dickson entered Ladysmith on 1 March, being one of the first civilians to do so. Here he was able to secure several historic scenes for the Biograph, including the beleaguered Gordon Highlanders *en route* from the camp to welcome the entrance of the relief column, headed by General Buller and Staff. Buller's entry was filmed from the back of the Cape cart. 'The cart had to displace the soldiers, the back reaching out into the street as we had no tripod; this we found impossible to drag over the mountain, and so had left it behind',[10] recorded Dickson in his diary.

Dickson was forced to remain seven days in Ladysmith. 'Terrifically hot, the town is rendered almost unendurable with the stenches', he wrote. It was here that Dickson contracted enteric fever, but fortunately the disease postponed its development until he had reached Durban. From there he had planned to go on to Cape Town to pick up a new camera, but his illness obliged him temporarily 'to retire from public life', as he stoically put it.[11] The diary does not make clear whether or not the new camera was waiting for him when finally he got to Cape Town.

The camera he was expecting was probably the 35 mm version of the Mutagraph which, although still using an unperforated film, was much smaller and thus more portable than the one he had been using. Referring to one military engagement in his diary, he observed, 'had we had a light camera these movements could have been secured and many others of an invaluable nature, but the enormous bulk of our apparatus which had to be dragged about in a Cape cart with two horses, prevented our getting to the spot'.[12]

From Cape Town he took the train to Bloemfontein, leaving his assistant behind to follow with the Cape cart and horses. All arrived in time for Dickson to film the Annexation Ceremony at Bloemfontein on 28 May (Plate 55b). The next day the party continued its difficult journey to Pretoria, eventually reaching there on 4 June, just in time to film Lord Roberts and his Staff on the outskirts of the town, and the eventual raising of the flag in front of the crowd assembled in the town square. 'Thus was the principal aim of our enterprise accomplished, and the heart of the Biographer was at rest',[13] noted Dickson triumphantly. But was Dickson's famous film *Raising the Flag at Pretoria* (54f) really all it professed to be? According to Thelma Gutsche, 'it appears that Dickson arrived too late for the actual ceremony which was filmed by Edgar Hyman for the Warwick Trading Company, and resorted to 'staging' the scene. When both his and Hyman's films of the hoisting of the Union Jack at Pretoria were shown in South Africa, it was noticed that the 'Biograph' showed a much larger flag than the 'Bioscope'. Letters were published in the Press . . .'[14] Dickson's own account of the event is as follows: Had the raising of the flag been done in the middle of the Square, then the surrounding crowd as well as the flag could have been photographed; but as it was raised several hundred feet high on the peak of the Rathouse, the unfurling of the flag alone is shown on the Biograph'.[15]

Dickson also informs us that the shot was taken 'from a fine position in the window'. Perhaps the experienced Dickson realised at once that the original flag was far too small to be seen clearly in a shot taken on the Square, and for dramatic purposes hoisted a larger flag expressly for the Biograph after the true ceremony had taken place.

In due course, Dickson's historic footage would be received back in London, where it was immediately developed and printed and promptly added to the programmes of the Palace Theatre of Varieties, sharing the bill with the other distinguished music hall turns, but invariably singled out for special mention in the press. Here are some typical reviews selected from *The Era*:

The American Biograph keeps up its high reputation for vivifying daily events, and the war pictures are, of course, immensely popular. The Review of Gordon Highlanders by Lord Wolseley, the same Scottish regiment on board the transport. The Landing of General Buller at Cape Town, the New South Wales Lancers, and the Armoured Train leaving Durban for the front are pictures that prove intensely interesting, and are watched with unconcealed admiration. (6 January 1900)[16]

The Biograph will enter on Monday, March 19th, upon its fourth year, during which period it has been exhibited over 1,000 times at the Palace Theatre, and its popularity, far from waning, is ever on the increase, the present realistic war pictures having added another popular item to the usual excellent programme. (10 March, 1900)[17]

The American Biograph, which Mr Charles Morton [Manager of the Palace] has made a pictorial companion to the newspaper, on Monday commenced its fourth year at the Palace. To mark the occasion, the management presented the audience with souvenirs consisting of a book of illustrations of incidents of the Transvaal War, many of which had already been seen through the medium of the biograph. To the war pictures there are frequent additions, and two of the views of the entry of General Buller's relieving force into Ladysmith will be exhibited. (24 March, 1900)[18]

Three new Biograph pictures, representing scenes in the relief of Ladysmith, were shown at the Palace Theatre on Thursday evening [19 April], when they were most enthusiastically received. (21 April, 1900)[19]

The Palace has justly won a reputation for the excellence of the pictures shown by the American Biograph, and this week some of the illustrations of the South African War have been replaced by new and interesting views. Amongst these may be mentioned Lord Roberts at his headquarters receiving a despatch from the front, and another notable picture is the meeting of the Commander-in-Chief and General Baden-Powell at Pretoria. Patriotic feeling is stirred by the sight of the British flag being unfurled at Bloemfontein, and hoisted at Pretoria on June 5th, a third film showing the arrival of a courier with despatches for Lord Roberts from Heilbron. A cheer greets the men of the Naval Brigade as they are seen dragging 4.7 guns into Ladysmith. (28 July, 1900)[20]

(a) *Battle of Spion Kop: Ambulance Corps Crossing the Tugela River* (25 January 1900)

(b) *An Armoured Train Leaving Durban for Escourt* (17 November 1899)

Plate 54 (a-l)   Biograph films of the Boer War. Photographed by W.K.-L. Dickson. From contemporary bromide prints taken from the original negatives. Prepared by the Kodak Research Laboratories, Rochester, N.Y. (*South African National Film Archive*)

(c) *Naval Guns Firing at Colenso* (13–14 December 1899)

(d) *Lord Roberts and Staff on the Outskirts of Pretoria* (4 June 1900)

(e) *Transferring Wounded From Red Cross Wagons to the Train at Colenso* (26 February 1900)

(f) *Raising the Flag at Bloemfontein* (27 May 1900)

(g) *Boer Prisoners at Bloemfontein* (27 May 1900)

(h) *Boer Prisoners at Bloemfontein* (27 May 1900)

(i) *Repairing the Broken Bridge at Frere* (29 November 1899)

(j) *An Armoured Train Leaving Durban for Escourt* (17 November 1899)

(k) *Naval Guns Firing at Colenso* (13–14 December 1899)

(l) *Rifle Hill Signal Station Near Frere Camp* (7 December 1899)

The souvenir booklet presented to patrons to mark the third anniversary of the Biograph at the Palace Theatre on 19 March 1900, mentioned above, was a nicely produced quarto publication called *The War by Biograph*. It contained extracts from Dickson's diary, together with frame illustrations from Biograph films and still photographs taken during his South African assignment. Dickson was later to publish a fuller account of his experiences under the title *The Biograph in Battle* (1901), but the souvenir publication provides a foretaste of his experiences up until the beginning of January 1900.[21] Dickson's diary entries in the souvenir book differ somewhat from those subsequently published in *The Biograph in Battle*. Some of the illustrations also differ, and are reproduced much better than those in the later publication. Furthermore, the frame illustrations are indicated by an asterisk so that there can be no confusion between scenes from actual films and still photographs.

With the fall of Pretoria and talks of peace, there was a decided lull in the fighting which led some to believe that the conflict was as good as over. On 17 June, Dickson wrote, 'we have sold our horses and Cape cart, saddles, tent and general camping outfit, and are now waiting the end of the campaign'.[22] Although the war was to drag on for another twenty-two months, on 18 July Dickson sailed for England aboard the *Carisbrook Castle*; for him the war was already over.

As well as his inventive skills, Dickson was a capable musician and singer, often performing in drawing room concerts. He was also a good linguist and spoke French, German and Italian. He was thus the ideal person to represent the Biograph company in Europe, and he sailed for England in this capacity on 12 May, 1897.

For Biograph, Dickson took many sensational subjects such as Pope Leo XIII;[23] Queen Margharita of Italy; The Coronation of the Queen of Holland; President Faure of France; and the majoirty of the British Royal Family; not to mention some outstanding sporting events. However, his most difficult assignment was undoubtedly the coverage of the Boer War, where he showed amazing courage and fortitude.

The photographic quality of the Biograph films is remarkably good and it is absolutely appalling that so little of this historical material has survived, and this more by accident than design. When the late Dr Thelma Gutsche was researching her splendid book on the history of the cinema in South Africa, the only Dickson relics she was able to locate in the whole of the United States were twelve bromide prints taken from Dickson's original negatives of the Boer War (Plate 54). The following paragraph from a document, now in the South African National Film Archives, reveals the outcome of her search:

At the request of Miss T. Gutsche who was engaged on research into the history and present position of the cinema in South Africa, Mr Glenn E. Matthews of the Kodak Research Laboratories, Kodak Park, Rochester, New York, instituted a search for the films taken by the Biograph expedition led by W.K.-L. Dickson in the front line during the Boer War during 1899–1900. It was subsequently discovered that all the stock of the original Biograph company was intentionally destroyed by fire in 1909 and that nothing remained of the films. Further search revealed the existence of a dozen Bromide stills reproduced from the original films. Mr Matthews had duplicate negatives made of these stills and presented the set of negatives to Miss Gutsche in trust for the South African Council of Educational and Social Research with the compliments of the Kodak Research Laboratories, Rochester, New York. One set of photographs reproduced from these negatives has been presented to the Africana Museum, Johannesburg'.[24]

The material sent to South Africa by Kodak, designated the 'Kodak Presentation', comprised the following items:

1. Letters
2. Original Bromide Prints from Dickson's Original Negatives—Prints made 1900 to 1902:
2.1 Rifle Hill Signal Corps
2.2 Lord Roberts and Staff
2.3 Raising the Flag at Pretoria
3. Copies made from original bromide prints made from Dickson's negatives—exact size of negative
3.1 Raising the Flag at Pretoria
3.2 Battle of Spion Kop—Ambulance train crossing the Tugela River
3.3 Armoured train
3.4 Boer prisoners
3.5 Rifle Hill Signal Station
3.6 Lord Roberts and his Staff
3.7 Unidentified—field guns
3.8 Armoured train
3.9 Unidentified—field guns
3.10 Boer prisoners
3.11 Wounded unloaded from ambulance
3.12 Bridge destroyed by Boers
4. Article illustrated with 6x4 prints of 2 and 3 above
[This entry has been crossed through]
5. Twelve negatives on two sheets—Duplicate negatives obtained from copying paper prints made from original Dickson Boer War film.
Enlargements of these negatives same as prints under 3.[25]

According to an unidentified press report, a cache of Biograph films was discovered in Holland in the 1940s.[26] At first I thought that this may have been the origin of the Schultze Collection, now in the British National Film and Television Archive (NFTVA) (Plate 55). Dr Rolf S. Schultze was curator of the Kodak Museum at Wealdstone, Harrow, Middlesex (1953–1968), but it is not known how he came by the Biograph films. At his death, his widow presented the collection to the NFTVA. The collection consisted of exactly 100 separate reels of 70 mm film in fifty cans, and was received by the archives at Aston Clinton in November 1969. At the time of writing, the task of transferring the material to 35 mm film stock and the identification and cataloguing of the films is still proceeding. Some of the reels contain footage shot by Dickson in South Africa.

Information about the cache of Biograph films discovered in Holland has recently been sent to me by Geoffrey N. Donaldson of Rotterdam.[27] It appears that the Biograph films were found in the attic of the office of the newspaper *Haagsche Courant* in The Hague, back in 1948. The films subsequently disappeared until they were rediscovered in 1991 in the vaults of the Nederlands Filmmuseum, where they must have lain forgotten. Frame illustrations from the British productions have recently been sent by the Netherlands Film Museum to the cataloguing department of the British Film Institute, where they can be inspected. Among the films are a number of Boer War subjects.[28]

(a) *Boys of HMS Terrible Getting their Guns into Position* (12 December 1899)

(b) *Annexation Ceremony at Bloemfontein* (28 May 1900)

Plate 55   Biograph films of the Boer War, photographed by Dickson. Frame illustrations from contemporary prints in the Schultze Collection at the National Film & TV Archive (*British Film Institute*)

Although Dickson's pictures of the Boer War dominated the Biograph programmes, there were plenty of other subjects taken by the company's cinematographers in various parts of the world. *The Era* reported the selection shown at The Palace Theatre, London, in July:

> There are several pictures illustrative of the German naval manoeuvres at Kiel, the first being boat B 89 under full steam discharging torpedoes. Next we see the battleship *Kaiser Wilhelm II*, leaving Kiel Harbour, and another war vessel, the *Odin*, with her guns in action. While black smoke issues from her funnel, the smoke from her guns is white, and soon the ship is completely hidden from view, the general effect being remarkably striking. Another naval picture that arouses considerable interest shows H. M. torpedo-boat destroyer *Viper* steaming at the extraordinary fast rate of thirty-six knots an hour. Very clear and distinct is the film showing HRH Prince Edward of York at drill in the grounds of Marlborough House, attended by his younger brother and sister, Prince Albert and Princess Victoria. Other pictures in which Royalty figures include the Prince and Princess of Wales and the Duke of York and Princess Victoria witnessing the cattle parade at the York Agricultural Show; the Prince of Wales at the opening of the London Central Railway, and welcoming his guests at Wolferton. Every loyal subject of Her Majesty must be specially interested in the picture representing the Queen in Phoenix-park, Dublin, receiving a large bouquet from a little girl. Other films represent Italian cavalry officers forcing their horses down a precipitous incline, garden fêtes at Sheen House Club, the recent international sports, the razing of a tall chimney at Bolton, and a panoramic view of the Paris Exhibition as seen from the moving platform.[29]

Although variety in subject matter made for a more balanced programme, it seems to have been the policy of the Biograph to act primarily as a presenter of news, and in this respect it anticipated the news reel companies of later years. The following review from *The Era*, for example, reads very like a summary of an early *Pathé Journal*:

> The Palace Theatre was fortunate enough on Monday night [27 October] in being able to show on the Biograph the only animated pictures permitted to be taken on board the *Aurania* on her arrival in Southampton Water. The pictures are exceptionally fine, showing a group of officers including Colonel Mackinson, Colonel Cholmondeley, the Earl of Albermarle, and other distinguished soldiers; also a view of a number of Privates crossing one of the bridges, and, in addition, a view of the *Aurania* coming to her anchorage, the reception of Colonel Mackinson by Colonel Stackpole, the landing of the C.I.V. at Southampton Docks, and views of their march through London. As may be expected, these examples of the theatre's enterprise were received by the enormous audience— amongst whom were Lord Wolseley and Lord Pirbright—with the greatest enthusiasm.[30]

Victorian music hall audiences were very demonstrative and their behaviour sometimes continued to be expressed during the screening of the cinematograph pictures. Popular heroes were invariably cheered as soon as they appeared on the screen and the 'enemy' hissed and jeered. Sometimes the reactions of the audience could be decidedly unpleasant, as witness this comment from an irate correspondent in the pages of *The Outlook*:

At a certain Theatre of Varieties in the Charing Cross Road one may see the Biograph in action, and one of the pictures shown by it is of Boer prisoners taking exercise. A door opens, there issue forth some six or eight Boers, young and old, sullen, dejected, but defiant; the orchestra plays our National Anthem, and the prisoners are seen to touch their hats in a perfunctory fashion; and they are greeted with a tremendous storm of yells, hoots, jeers, hisses, &c., from the smug counter-jumpers, the office boys, the yahoos, and the brainless bar-crawlers who form the vast majority of the audience.

In the first place, was it fair or sportsmanlike, was it even decent of the Biograph Company to photograph these poor devils for the amusement of a music-hall crowd? In the second, apart from the utter childishness of yelling and hooting at a photograph of anybody or anything, when the photograph happens to be one of your enemies in captivity, is it not absolutely despicable?

It used not to be the custom of our people to jeer an enemy who fought bravely in a cause that to him was sacred, even though he was 'ignorant', 'dirty', 'cunning', &c. I am not a pro-Boer. I am a jingo filibustering Imperialist of the most rabid description; but those hoots and howls made me feel sorry I was an Englishman (and that is a very dreadful sensation indeed). The only crumb of comfort was vouchsafed by the conduct of a fine young Tommy of the Buffs, who expressed his disgust at the whole proceeding in no uncertain fashion.[31]

By Command of HRH the Prince of Wales, soon to become King Edward VII, an exhibition of the Biograph was given on 29 June at Sandringham, the royal residence in Norfolk. The programme consisted of twenty-four items and included some of the Boer War subjects taken by Dickson. This was not the first time that the Biograph had been so honoured. Three years previously, the Prince had commanded the Biograph to appear at St James' Palace. It is some measure of the Biograph's prestige that it should have received the future king's favour on two occasions and to be summoned to two such stately venues.[32]

Turning our attention once again to the Mutoscope side of the business (Plate 56), an interesting first-hand account of the manner in which the Mutoscope reels were prepared has been brought to my attention by Dr Nicholas Hiley of Cambridge. The article in question was written by Jack Wiggins (Plate 57), who, at the turn of the century, was a laboratory assistant for the British Mutoscope & Biograph company. Here is part of his account of the procedures involved:

[The] pictures were printed on one strip of bromide paper from 210ft to 250ft in length, 70 mm wide. The machine used for printing these pictures was almost human—when anything went wrong with the negative the machine would stop automatically until the experienced operator put the trouble right. No ripping up of negatives or doing damage of any kind. The movement of the machine was intermittent and during the period of exposure punched a hole top and bottom of the picture for registration in cutting and mounting and to ensure steadiness.

These strips of printed bromide paper were developed on iron drums 6ft long and 4ft in diameter which were lowered into a shallow tank and the process continued till complete. Then transferred to a wooden frame 6ft high and placed in the drying room with continual changing of hot air by means of fans.

When dry the strips were wound in a roll and consecutively numbered on the back of each print. A foot press was used for cutting the strip into separate pictures, each with a

Plate 56 W.K.-L. Dickson with E.B. Koopman (seated) the Director of the British Mutoscope & Biograph Co. Ltd. Note the framed picture of Loïe Fuller on the wall (*Cinéemathèque Française*)

Plate 57 Jack Wiggins, laboratory assistant at the British Mutoscope & Biograph Company (*Barnes Collection*)

notch on either side. They were then ready for mounting. The apparatus used for this purpose was two steel flanges, mounted on a wooden stand. The pictures were placed singly in the 'Rig' with a plain card between each picture. These interposing cards were used for giving a spring to the pictures when passing the 'Tripper', a small gadget similar to the human thumb. Each reel was mounted in two sections and while still in the 'Rig' was glued on the inside with a special white glue and strengthened with a piece of fabric known as 'Leno'. When dry the two halves were placed between metal flanges and screwed together, forming a complete reel. They were then 'steamed' by a special machine and forced into a metal band of slightly smaller diameter. This gave the pictures the curve which made them flat when passing the 'Tripper'.

The reel is now ready for placing in the machine for exhibition. You screw the machines all in a row—you choose your subject—you put a penny in the slot and turn the handle. No regulation speed. Turn as you like. Linger or stop until the reel is finished'.[33]

The Warwick Trading Company

By the turn of the century, Charles Urban had succeeded in making the Warwick Trading Company the leading film company in Britain and the headquarters for a considerable overseas trade (Plate 58). Noted primarily for its wide range of non-fiction films, of which the latest news items were a speciality, WTC also traded in cinematographic equipment. Its Bioscope cameras and projectors were world renowned, the name Bioscope ultimately becoming a generic term to denote a cinematograph show of any kind. As well as cameras and projectors, the firm also issued numerous accessories for cinematographic work. Urban was not much interested in producing fiction films, but he realized their popularity and accordingly secured the rights to the films of two of the world's most inventive and successful film-makers, Georges Méliès and G.A. Smith.

With the outbreak of the Boer War, Urban was determined to obtain the fullest possible coverage of the campaign and consequently enlisted the services of three remarkable men. One was the South African impresario, Edgar M. Hyman, with whom Urban already had dealings as an exhibitor of Warwick films. Being domiciled in South Africa, Hyman was perfectly placed to commence filming as soon as hostilities began and so it is not surprising that the first films to arrive in England from the seat of war were taken by him. Another of Urban's cameramen in South Africa was a Brighton aristocrat by the name of John Benett-Stanford, who had already distinguished himself as a war cinematographer in the Sudan, where he was the only person to take a film at the Battle of Omdurman. Moreover, he already had connections with South Africa in a private capacity, so was no stranger to that country. His films were the first by an Englishman to arrive in England, being received shortly after those of Hyman's. The third cameraman was Joseph Rosenthal (Plate 59), an obvious choice as he was already an experienced cinematographer with WTC in England. He left England on 1 December 1899 aboard the *Avondale Castle*, so he was rather late on the scene. Benett-Stanford had left England on 7 October 1899 on the steamer *Mexican*, and Dickson's departure took place a week later. Paul's cameraman Walter Beevor sailed on 21 October.[34]

According to one source, Rosenthal was born in London in 1866,[35] but the passenger list of the ship on which he sailed to South Africa lists him as a foreigner.

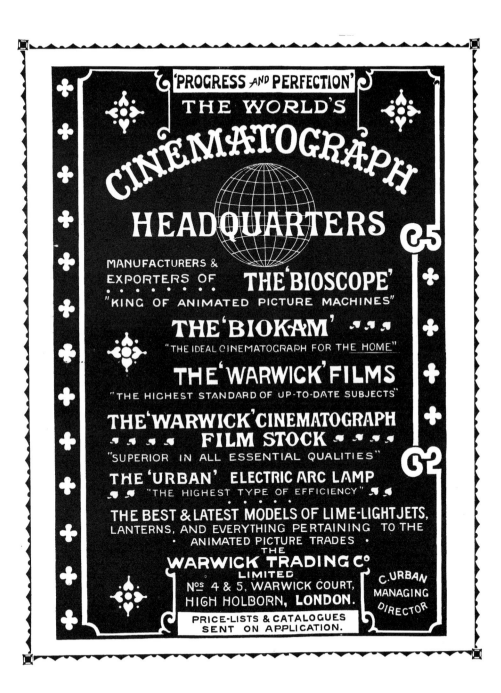

Plate 58   Advertisement for the Warwick Trading Company. From *The Optician* (6 April 1900) p. 97

(a)

(b)

Plate 59   Boer War (a) Joseph Rosenthal with pony and Bioscope cameras. (b) The Bioscope cart crossing the Orange River (British Film Institute)

It could be that he was the son of Jewish emigrants who had not applied for British nationality. By profession, Rosenthal was a pharmaceutical chemist, with a decided penchant for the scientific side of photography. For some years he worked as a dispenser at St George's Hospital London. He joined the Warwick Trading Company in 1897, and soon afterwards was appointed head of staff.[36]

Rosenthal was much more fortunate than Dickson, for he was equipped with cameras which were easily manageable by a single person, whereas Dickson was burdened with the cumbrous Mutagraph. The two Bioscope cameras Rosenthal took with him were said to have film capacities of 165 feet and 650 feet respectively,[37] although the finished films taken by him in South Africa never exceeded 150 feet in length. This extra reserve of film must have freed him from the anxiety of having to reload at a critical moment or under difficult conditions. Once shooting had begun he could be sure of a reasonable supply of negative in his camera whatever the circumstances (Plate 60).[38]

From the outset, WTC's three war cinematographers were assigned to specific areas of operation. John Benett-Stanford was assigned to the Orange Free State, Edgar M. Hyman to the Cape Colony and Joseph Rosenthal to the Natal.[39] As the war progressed, however, these boundaries were no longer adhered to. Rosenthal became attached to General French's Column, Stanford to Lord Methuen's, whereas Hyman was left to cover Cape Town and its vicinity.[40] Even these arrangements were not permanent. At one time Rosenthal was with General Clements' forces while Hyman moved as far north as Pretoria, where he managed to film the victorious

Plate 60   Boer War. Joseph Rosenthal filming field ambulance and transport wagons crossing the Vaal River Drift, entering the Transvaal. From a photograph first published in WTC catalogue, September 1900, p. 124 (*Barnes Collection*)

A THUMBNAIL CINEMATOGRAPH. YOU CAN MAKE IT YOURSELF.

From a cinematograph photo by the Warwick Trading Co.]
LORD ROBERTS AT CAPETOWN.   (See page 296.)

Plate 61   A thumbnail cinematograph, depicting Lord Roberts at Capetown, 10 January 1900 (WTC no. 5540, Frame illustrations published in *War Pictures*, vol. 1, no. 10 (14 April 1900), p. 309. Instructions on page 296 indicate how the pictures may be cut-out and assembled as a flip-book)

Plate 62   Boer War. War correspondents with their carts and apparatus awaiting Lord Roberts' entry into Kroonstad, 12 May 1900 (*Barnes Collection*)

troops entering the town (WTC no. 5725). Of particular interest to us today, were the film still to exist, is a shot of Rosenthal himself crossing a pontoon bridge on the Orange River. Hyman's film shows him walking towards the camera carrying his own Bioscope camera and tripod (WTC no. 5652). Other historically opulent films photographed by Hyman showed Lord Roberts' arrival and reception at Cape Town on 10 January (WTC no. 5540) (Plate 61); the entry of the general and his troops into Pretoria on 5 June (WTC nos. 5724–5725); and the ceremonies connected with the annexation of the Boer Republics on 25 October (WTC no. 5885). Hyman can also be definitely credited with nos. 5541, 5550 and 5652, but the remainder of his work has yet to be identified with certainty.

Rosenthal's more important films included: *A Skirmish With the Boers Near Kimberley* (WTC no. 5545), which comprised three scenes and was 150 feet long; *The*

Surrender of Kroonstad to Lord Roberts on 12 May (WTC no. 5678) (Plate 62); *War Balloon and Transport Crossing the Vaal River* (WTC no. 5733); *The Essex Regiment Going into Action* (WTC no. 5721), reported to be one of the few scenes of actual battle; *Guns in Action at Pretoria* (WTC nos. 5722 and 5723); and *Lord Roberts Hoisting the Union Jack at Pretoria* on 5 June (WTC no. 5726). Rosenthal is also credited in the WTC catalogues with nos. 5546, 5549, 5653 and 5654.

For some reason no films are credited by WTC to John Benett-Stanford, although he is still listed as one of their cameramen. In fact no films are credited to Benett-Stanford after the Modder River Engagement, which took place towards the end of 1899. Perhaps, as Stephen Bottomore suggests,[41] Benett-Stanford was wounded in the conflict and had to retire. However, when the last consignment of Stanford's films were received by WTC towards the end of January 1900, they were given an exclusive run at the Olympia. The programme was reviewed in the *Daily Mail* on 22 January under the heading 'Triumph of the War Bioscope. Arrival of Films from the Seat of Operations'. It declared:

> Many of the best films have been taken by Mr Bennett [sic] Stanford, who is a millionaire with a strong love of adventure who has chosen to see the war as the head of the bioscope war staff.
>
> The pictures are interesting and novel. One can see the armoured train rushing rapidly by, with the muzzles of guns projecting from its sides. The train consists of only two carriages. One of the most vivid and striking pictures of the series, and also one of the most successful bioscope films ever taken, shows the Lancers under the Earl of Airlie fording the Modder River on their return from the Enslin engagement. Another extremely fine film depicts the hospital corps on the battlefield after the Modder River fight picking up the dead and wounded. The rapidity of the movement is remarkable, and the celerity with which a wounded man is picked up and driven away in the ambulance is a great compliment to the skill and energy of the Ambulance Corps.[42]

All negative shot in South Africa had to be sent back to England for processing, except for small test pieces developed in the field. Some of this negative never reached its destination, because it was either destroyed by enemy action or lost in transit. Other consignments were delayed for weeks before being delivered. The Warwick Trading Company were particularly hard hit in this respect, and this notice appeared in several issues of *The Era*:

> Owing to the activity of the Boers around Johannesburg after the British army occupied the town, and the difficulty in getting the convoy carrying the mails through to Cape Town, much delay was occasioned in receiving the negatives showing the Johannesburg incidents, so these latter have only just arrived, being four weeks overdue.
>
> Advices have also reached us that one of the consignments of 5,000ft sensitised film we forwarded to the front for use by our war staff of photographers was captured by De Wet, the Boer Commander, at Roodewal, and destroyed; the boxes were opened, and the film strewn all over the veldt. This loss, together with several consignments of exposing [sic] negatives which have gone astray in the mails, as well as those lost by the sinking of the SS *Mexican* off the Cape, deprived us of the opportunity of placing on the market many more of the intensely interesting subjects, and adding them to the already extensive list of war films.[43]

Some negatives were also destroyed by the stupidity of censors. One such case was reported by a correspondent in the *Daily Mail*:

> The strips of film, which measure 100ft. in length, and sometimes considerably more, are afterwards packed in light-proof round tins, which remind one of nothing so much as an ordinary two-ounce tobacco-box. A dozen or two of these tins are then carefully packed in a larger tin, also light-proof, and the whole is sent by post to the factory in England, where the films are developed.
>
> A representative of the 'Daily Mail' was shown one of these tins which has a curious history. It bears upon its side the words, written in violet-coloured pencil, 'Opened under martial law', and beneath, the signature, in initials, of the censor at Capetown.
>
> It seems that this box, which contained some interesting and unique films, was opened by the censor, and many feet of film were spoiled by being exposed to the light. 'Martial Law' is thus responsible for the loss to the British public of some exceedingly interesting pictures.[44]

In June, Rosenthal was recalled from South Africa. The Boxer Rebellion had broken out and all eyes were now turned towards China. The Boer War no longer held the centre of attention and WTC needed a crack cameraman to cover the Chinese situation. Rosenthal left England for Shanghai in the second week of August.[45] According to a statement in *The Era* he was to join Warwick's other photographer, Mr Seymour, who had left India for China on 22 June.[46]

Joseph Rosenthal's place in South Africa was taken by Sidney Goldman,[47] a newspaper reporter, who does not appear to have had any previous experience of film work, but no doubt received instruction from Rosenthal before he left. Goldman proceeded to join Lord Roberts' army at the front. He must have proved quite a capable cinematographer, for he is credited with the historic film showing the hoisting of the Royal Standard in front of the Government Buildings at Pretoria during the formal annexation ceremony by Lord Roberts on 25 October 1900.[48]

During 1900 someone at Warwick came to appreciate the panning shot, no doubt remembering G.A. Smith's effective use of the device in his panoramic view of Brighton (WTC no. 3053) taken in August 1899.[49] Formerly, the term panoramic view had denoted a shot taken from a moving vehicle, such as a boat, train or tramcar. The first example of this kind was a shot taken from a moving gondola on the Grand Canal, Venice, by Lumière's roving cameraman Alexandre Promio in 1896. There have been countless examples ever since, one of the most notable of the earlier examples being Biograph's phantom ride taken from the front of a railway locomotive travelling at high speed. The use of an actual panning shot, however, with the camera itself turning on a revolving tripod-head, did not come into general use until 1900, when the effect was termed a 'circular panoramic view'.[50] A shot of this kind is clearly indicated in the catalogue description of *The University Boat Race* (WTC no. 5637), where it states that, 'the camera is gradually turned so as to include the crowds lining the river,' and, again 'the camera is again slowly revolved gradually, following the crew up the river with an ever-changing panorama as a background'. Should there be any doubt that these are indeed true panning shots, the next example provides irrefutable evidence. It occurs in the description of the film depicting Conway Tubular Bridge (WTC no. 5805): 'the panoramic turn table of the camera was again brought into play, disclosing a view of the fields and hills in the background'. Indeed, the *Conway* series of films (WTC nos. 5803–5808) provides excellent examples of *panning*.

When Joseph Rosenthal set out on his journey to China to cover the Boxer Rebellion, he took with him WTC's new panoramic tripod-head. Evidently he had been impressed with the films using this new panning technique, which he had probably seen at Warwick Court on his return to London from South Africa. The only moving shots he had been able to take of the Boer War were from moving vehicles. Some of the Boer War films were quite stunning in this respect. For instance, a couple of films shot from projecting platforms mounted on a transport and an armoured train were quite spectacular. (WTC nos. 5632–5633). But these were *travelling* shots, not panning shots. The first batch of Chinese subjects received from Rosenthal showed a number of 'circular panoramic views' in which the camera actually revolved on its tripod. These were true panning shots, and were used to good effect by Rosenthal in presenting these exotic views of the Far East.

Rosenthal's Chinese films were advertised by Warwick at the beginning of November,[51] and included scenes taken in Shanghai, Port Arthur,[52] Taku, and Tientsin (WTC nos. 5886–5897). Actual scenes of the Boxer Rebellion were sadly lacking. But so much interest in China had been stirred up by the uprising that audiences seemed content just to view everyday scenes of this distant land. It was left to the filmmakers in Britain to provide the dramatic content of the Rebellion with their fictional reconstructions, such as Williamson's *Attack on a China Mission*.

After his assignment in China, Rosenthal undertook many more foreign missions, first for WTC and then for the Charles Urban Trading Company. He went to the Philippines and put in four months there with the American army. His next move was to Australia where he went with the Prince and Princess of Wales when they sailed on the *Ophir*. After a trip to Canada, he went to Port Arthur, 1904, when it was beseiged by the third Japanese Army under General Nogi during the Russo-Japanese War. His next trip was through the jungles of Borneo. A trip through India with the Prince of Wales followed, and then another journey through Burma and Central China. From China Rosenthal came back to England and settled down in Croydon where in 1907 he established the Rosie Film Company.[53]

We may well marvel at the Lumière cameramen who travelled the world to obtain pictures for the Cinématographe, but not one of them is quite the equal of Joseph Rosenthal, whose quest for pictures took him to so many distant lands and danger spots of the world. His name surely deserves to rank alongside those of Herbert Ponting and Alec Hurley, to name but two of those intrepid cameramen who sought to bring real-life adventure to the screen.

Another roving cameraman employed by WTC in 1900 was F.B. Stewart, about whom little is known. He was responsible for a series of films taken in India. At the beginning of December, Warwick announced that 'a splendid consignment of negatives of Indian Life and Customs' had just been received from their photographer now travelling through India.[54] These were issued as nos. 5898–5916 in the Warwick catalogues, a total of nineteen short films averaging from 50 feet to 65 feet each, except for one which was 150 feet. This latter film depicted the Race for the Governor's Cup at Bombay, and consisted of four views (WTC no. 5916).

If the Boer War and Boxer Rebellion dominated the thoughts of film producers during the year, there were plenty of other subjects offered by WTC which must have caught the interest of the public. The usual functions of Royalty were filmed, as were the main sporting events of the day. The Paris Exposition, naturally, merited coverage and resulted in a splendid panorama 625 feet long taken from a moving vehicle (WTC nos. 5668–5670). Some of the leading music hall artistes of the day appeared in two films taken at their Annual Outing (WTC nos. 5679 and 5680), and the Music Hall Sports were also filmed (WTC nos. 5687–5700). Of particular interest to film historians was the appearance at the Crystal Palace of the Kansas City Fire Department (WTC no. 5810) under its Chief, George C. Hale, who was later to achieve fame as the originator of *Hale's Tours*. Mention should also be made of the series of films showing the Austrian strongman Eugene Sandow, known as the Modern Hercules (WTC nos. 5623–5628), who had also performed for W.K.-L. Dickson in the Edison Black Maria Studio in 1894.

One other point of interest concerns a short film called *The Diver* (WTC no. 5865), which shows a diver descending into the water several times from a small boat. The catalogue entry suggests this should be joined to no. 4147, which is the Méliès film *Visite sous-marin du Maine* (*Divers at Work on the Wreck of the Maine*), Star catalogue no. 147.

Apart from the intrinsic interest of many of the Warwick films, some showed a decided advance in narrative technique well ahead of anything being attempted in the fiction film at that time. The material for *Badger Digging* (WTC no. 5744) seems to have been shot and assembled in a manner reminiscent of later documentary films, and the film was extended to 200 feet. Although it no longer exists, much of its style and content can still be gathered from the catalogue description which reads almost like a shot by shot breakdown:

> Showing incidents connected with the badger hunt, as follows: The meet. The arrival of the pack. Climbing the hills. Locating the badger, and putting the terriers into the hole. Digging for the badger. The badger escapes. The hunters, with terriers, chase, and return with the badger bagged. Killing and skinning the badger. Holding up the carcass and skin, giving the former to the terriers. Distribution of trophies of the hunt, consisting of head and the pads.

There are other examples in the Warwick catalogues which show the same advanced technique achieved by the makers of non-fiction films, and one begins to wonder whether the language of film was being more skilfully developed in this class of film than in the rather stagy theatrical productions emanating from the makers of fiction films.

The film stock used by WTC production was supplied by the European Blair Camera Company (Blair) whose factory was situated at Foot's Cray in Kent (Plate 63). WTC and Blair had a close working relationship which allowed the factory to be referred to in a catalogue of 1900 as 'Warwick's Cinematograph Film Works'.[55] Blair also supplied the 17.5 mm film stock for the Biokam, and the film cans for holding the 25 foot strips are embossed with the WTC trade mark on the lid and the initials E.B.C.C. on the bottom, under which are the words 'Film Makers Foots Cray'.[56] When Urban left WTC to form his own company, the connection established with Blair was carried over, and the Charles Urban Trading Company's catalogue of 1903–4, devotes a number of pages to the film works at Foot's Cray illustrated with photographs.[57] The manager of the Blair Film Works at this time was John Haddow.

Plate 63   Blair Film Works, Foot's Cray, Kent, 1900, suppliers of film stock for WTC, including 17.5 mm film for the Biokam (Science Museum, London)

Plate 64   The Warwick Bioscope 35 mm Projector (Model E). Note the enlarged film spools in this 1900 version (*Barnes Collection*)

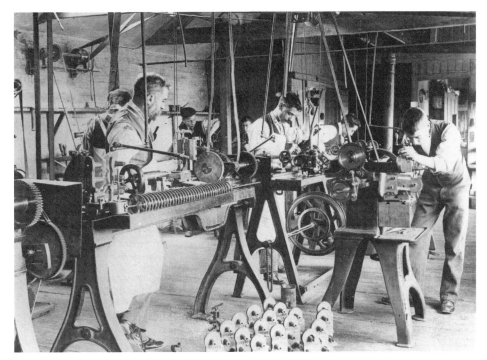

(a)

(b)

Plate 65   Assembling Warwick Bioscope Projectors at Prestwich's Lansdowne Works at Tottenham
(*Science Museum, London*)

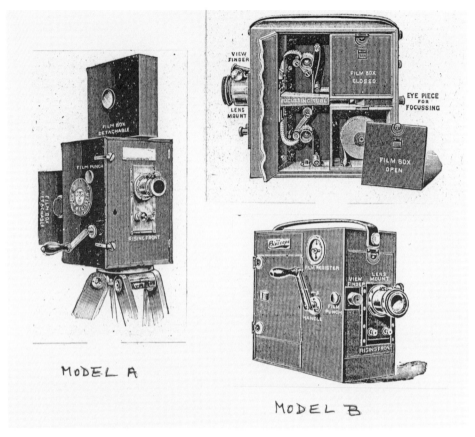

MODEL A

MODEL B

Plate 66   The Warwick Bioscope cameras (Models A and B) as used in South Africa by Joseph Rosenthal (*Barnes Collection*)

We will conclude this survey of the Warwick Trading Company with a review of some of the equipment issued by the firm during 1900. WTC referred to the new Model E Bioscope Projector (Plate 64) as 'The King of Cinematographs', and the influential journal *The Optician* called it 'a handsome cinematograph'. It was constructed entirely of metal and 'the continuous feed and eccentric movement are so designed as to admit of no jumping of the film when passed through the machine'.[58] New features included an enlarged lantern or lamphouse, some minor improvements to the shutter which was now mounted on a sliding shaft, and a greatly improved film-trap or gate incorporating an automatic pneumatic safety light cut-off.[59] The Bioscope Projector was the brainchild of Charles Urban, who had first promoted a machine of this name in the United States before coming to England. According to Terry Ramsaye, its manufacturer had been a former acquaintance of Urban's named Walter Isaacs.[60] The English version, was made by the Prestwich Manufacturing Company of London (Plate 65).

The Bioscope Camera Model B (Plate 66) was establishing a record equal to that of the Bioscope Projector. It had stood the test of operating in the South African campaign, and was about to gather laurels in China.[61] It was a compact apparatus with a claw mechanism and interior film boxes with a capacity of 150 feet. The lens

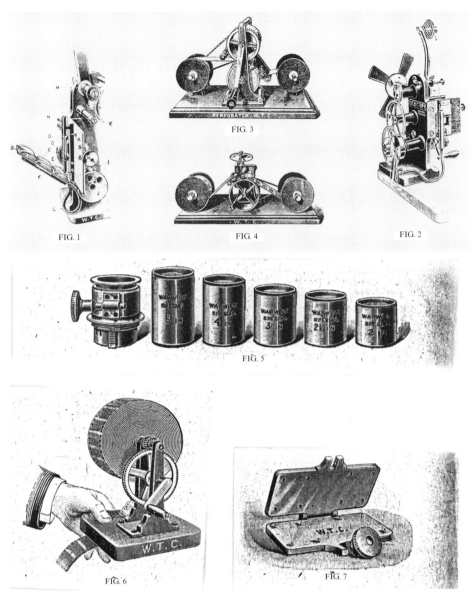

Plate 67   Warwick cinematographic accessories (1900). (1) Improved film-gate for Bioscope projectors; fine steel springs replace the former velvet pressure pads (2) Pneumatic automatic light cut-off (3) Rotary film perforator (4) Film measuring machine (5) Rack and pinion lens tube and lenses (6) Film winder (7) Film splicer (*Barnes Collection*)

was a Dallmeyer stigmatic of 3 inch focus.[62] The Bioscope Camera Model A (Plate 66) was of somewhat heavier construction, employing exterior film boxes for longer films up to 500 feet. This, too, was used in South Africa by Joseph Rosenthal and proved very successful. A number of accessories for cinematographic work, including film splicers, perforators, film measurers, winders, and lenses were also issued by the firm, (Plate 67). Charles Urban made sure that Warwick apparatus received full coverage in the photographic press, and he was prepared to take part personally in any promotional campaigns that ensured increased sales for WTC products. On 14 March we find him taking part in an entertainment given in aid of soldiers and their children, held at a large public hall in Croydon under the auspices of the Croydon Camera Club. As the *British Journal of Photography* noted:

> The chief hit of the evening was, however, the bioscope, which was worked by Mr. Charles Urban himself. It ran for half an hour, and provoked an amount of enthusiasm which rivalled the plaudits that greeted Baden-Powell and "Bob" earlier in the evening. To particularise the films shown is not possible. Those who contemplate arranging for a bioscope at any similar lantern show can see what it is like by visiting the London Hippodrome, where it is used every night.[63]

L. Gaumont et Cie

The Gaumont Chrono-Projector (Plate 68) made a greater impact on the British market than the Gaumont films. The Chrono had received the only prize in its class at the Paris Exposition of 1900,[64] and had formerly won prizes at Monaco.[65] The merits of the machine were detailed in the *Amateur Photographer*:

Plate 68   The Gaumont Chrono 35 mm Projector (1900). Made by L. Gaumont et Cie., Paris (*Barnes Collection*)

GAUMONT'S 'PROFESSIONAL' CHRONO-PROJECTOR

The cinematograph apparatus emanating from Messrs. Gaumont and Cie., of 25, Cecil Court, Charing Cross Road, has already earned for itself the high repute it deserves, and there is now introduced an additional machine called the 'Professional Chrono'. The object aimed at in this strong and powerful machine is *complete elimination of flicker*, and to obtain this result the *cam* has been designed to give the maximum movement in the shortest time, and a small mica shutter is employed. The simultaneous movement of lens and film-trap ensures exact framing of the picture, a milled-head screw instantly controlling any inaccuracy. All parts are strongly made of well- finished metal, the *spools* (carrying about 700 feet) being protected by metal sheaths, *sprockets*, and *clamps* are hollowed in the centre to prevent any part of the film but the edge being subjected to friction. The *film-trap* is on the same principle; both sides are moveable, and can be instantly replaced, while only the edges of the film are touched. The action is transmitted to the sprockets and take-up by steel chains, while the whole mechanism works with the precision and smoothness of a high-grade bicycle, answering the least movement of the handle with ease and regularity. It is made to work by hand or motor at will.

The price of the Professional Chrono, with handle, 4 in. projection lens and mount, two double spools, one single spool (in tin box), and extra gate springs to carry 650 feet of film, is £25. Or, with extra large spools, to carry 1,000 feet of film, £27 10s. The Chrono can be inspected and seen at work at 25, Cecil Court, London, W.C.[66]

The company's French produced films were not as yet a threat to British producers. In fact, Gaumont in Britain were distributing the Hepwix and Lumière films, as well as their own.[67] However, before the year ended, five films were deemed interesting enough to British audiences to be given prominence in advertisements on this side of the channel.[68] They were: *Marie Goes to Bed*; *Venus and Adonis*; *The Four Seasons Ballet*; *How Children are Born*; and *Descent From Mont Blanc*. The English advertisements quote the original Gaumont catalogue numbers against each film, so it is a simple matter to ascertain their original French titles. Four of these films are by the remarkable French woman director, Alice Guy (Plate 69), and warrant a full description of their subject matter, taken from advertisements in *The Era*:[69]

359. MARIE GOES TO BED/COUCHER D'UNE PARISENNE 120ft. 40 m.
'A beautiful Parisian lady disrobes at her bedside. Her thoughts meanwhile are apparently concerned about her "best boy", as she mimics the way he strokes his moustache, and in other amusing ways plainly shows she has him in mind. Having undressed, put on and arranged a very charming night-robe, she jumps into bed. There is nothing in the least offensive about this exceedingly well-arranged and artistic picture'.

361–5. VENUS AND ADONIS/SÉRIE VÉNUS ET ADONIS 300ft. 100 m.
Ballet de M. G. de Dubor, Musique de M. Mestres. Danse par Mlles Boos et Meunier de L'Opera.
1. Badinage. 20 m.
2. Valse lente, 20 m.
3. Danse du voile. 20 m.
4. Mort d'Adonis. 20 m.
5. Le sang d'Adonis donnant naissance à la rose rouge. 20 m.
'Charming Ballet, arranged by Mons. G. Dubor, set to music by M. Mestres, Danced by

Plate 69   Alice Guy (1873–1968) pioneer French director in charge of production at Gaumont from 1897 to 1907. Her films were available in Britain through Gaumont's London office (*Barnes Collection*)

Mdlles Boos and Meunier of the French Opera. There are five scenes to this popular Ballet, comprising the Meeting of Venus and Adonis, illustrating the story and showing the death of Adonis and his blood giving birth to the Red Rose. It is a remarkably fine work of art'.

367–70. THE FOUR SEASONS BALLET/SÉRIE DANSE DES SAISONS. 240ft. 80 m.
1. Le printemps: danse des roses. 20 m.
2. L'été: danse de la moisson. 20 m.
3. L'automne: danse des vendanges.
4. L'hiver: danse de la neige. 20 m.
'Springtime, the Dance of Roses; Summer, Golden Grain Dance; Autumn, Vines and Grapes; Winter, Snow. Admirable from all points of view and extremely popular'.

379. HOW CHILDREN ARE BORN/LA FÉE AUX CHOUX, OU LA NAISSANCE DES ENFANTS. 60ft. 20 m.
Une fée dépose les bébés vivants qu'elle retire de choux. Trés gros succès. Interprète: Yvonne Mugnier-Sérand.
'A bountiful Fairy is producing Living Babies, which she finds growing in a garden on huge Cabbages. An immense success'.

Alice Guy remembers this as her first film made in 1896, but as Francis Lacassin has pointed out in his 'Filmographie d'Alice Guy',[70] this is clearly a memory lapse. Among the five films advertised in *The Era*, the only one not directed by Alice Guy is:

Plate 70 Leon Gaumont (1864–1946) founder of L. Gaumont et Cie., Paris, manufacturers of cinematographic equipment and films. Gaumont films first began to hit the English market in 1900, with the films of Alice Guy (*Barnes Collection*)

390–4. DESCENT FROM MONT BLANC. 120ft
'Magnificent Mountain Scene, showing long chains of climbers, all roped together, descending a most difficult pass, over ice and snow, crossing a glacier and icebridge, Unsurpassably picturesque'.

The price of these French productions was one shilling per foot, but the two ballet pictures could be supplied coloured at twenty-five shillings per scene extra.[71]

In December, Gaumont (Plate 70) advertised two more films which were considered of special interest to British audiences, as they concerned the Boer War and the arrival in France of the President of the Transvaal. One was *Kruger at Marseilles* (180 feet) and the other, *Kruger in Paris* (60 feet). They were described as 'authentic pictures taken by own operators', and priced at £9 and £3, respectively.[72] As the year came to a close, Gaumont claimed to have 'three thousand first-class film subjects to choose from'.[73] In charge of Gaumont's London office at 25 Cecil Court (Flicker Alley) was A.C. Bromhead, whose biography I have briefly sketched in volume four.[74] Gaumont had not yet commenced filmmaking in England, so the business here was chiefly concerned with the sale of Gaumont's French products. The London office did however provide the chief outlet for the films made by Cecil M. Hepworth, which were sold under the Hepwix label,[75] and in due course Gaumont was also to handle the films of several other English filmmakers such as William Haggar, Clarendon, Williamson, Mitchell & Kenyon.

Gaumont was not the only French firm trading in Britain, of course, although it was becoming one of the most important. Clement & Gilmer (140 Faubourg St Martin, Paris) continued to advertise their Vitagraph machines in this country. There were two models, No. 1 was priced at 18 and No. 2 at £30.[76] Both have already been described and illustrated in a previous volume of this history.[77]

A. Lumière et fils was another firm catering to the English market at this time. Their products were handled by several English agents such as Fuerst Brothers and the Warwick Trading Company. French films were readily available on the British market, including not only those made by the leading producers such as Gaumont, Lumière and Méliès, but the films of the lesser known French filmmakers. There were several English dealers specializing in French films, among whom we may number Philipp Wolff, Rosenberg and Warwick.

4 Manufacturers and Dealers

By the turn of the century, the technology of cinematography had advanced sufficiently to allow filmmakers a greater choice of subject matter and a greater freedom in the manner in which it was treated. Films were no longer restricted, as formerly, to the short lengths of about 40 to 75 feet, which was then the maximum capacity of most makes of camera and projector. Cameras holding as much as 500 feet of film were now common, and projectors could accommodate reels of 1,000 feet or more. Many cameras were being fitted with exterior view finders which, together with the introduction of the panoramic tripod-head, permitted cameramen to follow the action without the characters disappearing unwittingly out of frame. Equally importantly, the camera could enlarge its field of view by turning on its axis or even tilting upwards or downwards.

Cinematographic equipment was now evolving from its first primitive state and taking the form that was not to be seriously challenged until the introduction of the Pathé studio camera, and more particularly, the Bell & Howell in about 1912. Rectangular box-type cameras developed in England by manufacturers such as Darling, Warwick, Prestwich; Williamson and Moy were commonly used the world over during the first decade of the twentieth century. In 1900, Warwick, Prestwich, and Paul were the chief suppliers of movie apparatus, although there were also a few less important manufacturers around at this time. What follows is an account of those manufacturers and dealers who were active during this closing period of the Victorian era. Some of these firms dealt in films as well as in apparatus and some were even engaged in film production, whereas others confined themselves solely to the sale of films. The names are arranged in alphabetical order, omitting those which have already been described in chapters 1, 2 and 3.

R.R. Beard

Beard was the manufacturer of the cinematograph projector which bears his name, but the machine does not seem to have survived the end of the century. None the less, he continued to be known as a manufacturer of lantern appliances and in 1900 was forced to install additional machinery to deal with increasing demands for his services.[1] The year under discussion is chiefly memorable for improvements made to his popular projection arc lamp.[2]

F. Brown

Frederick Brown was a manufacturer of lantern appliances and was chiefly noted for his limelight jets. At one time his name was associated with the Rosenberg Cinematograph. He had started business in a very small way some ten years previously by making jets in a garden shed at 13 Assulston Street, Euston Road. He then sought larger premises at No. 11 of the same street. He subsequently moved to 13 Gate Street, off Holborn, where he was still to be found in 1900.[3]

Plate 71   Blackheath village at the turn of the century, showing the shop of W. Butcher & Son situated at extreme right of picture (*Barnes Collection*)

W. Butcher & Son

William Butcher (1840–1903) was a pharmacist by profession but his interests turned increasingly towards photography. Around 1896, he opened a small factory in Blackheath producing cheap still cameras and accessories chiefly aimed at the amateur market. He also dealt in magic lanterns and slides and eventually included cinematographs and films among his stock-in-trade. By 1897 he was producing and exhibiting his own films intended mainly for local consumption. Butcher & Son were notable suppliers of all kinds of lantern and cinematographic apparatus (Plate 71). They acted as agents for various manufacturers and were among the first to import toy cinematographs from Germany. Two such examples are illustrated in the previous volume of this history.[4] In 1900, Butcher introduced a home cinematograph which, although a little more substantially built, still carried the film in a loop. Its construction, however, allowed it to be used with a regular lantern body thus making it capable of giving a larger, clearer and more steady image (Plate 72a). Butcher also handled Wray's 'Perfection' cinematograph, which sold at £6.6.0. and the popular Matagraph projectors.[5] Films also formed part of the firm's trade: they acted as wholesale agents for the films of J. Williamson, for instance.[6]

The Improved Model 'Primus' Matagraph projector, which Butcher advertised in 1900, was not of their own manufacture either, but was the product of Levi, Jones & Co, formerly well known manufacturers of optical lanterns, microscopes and electrical goods, which they made on their premises in Farringdon Road, until their move to Old Street in 1898.[7] Several different models of the Matagraph are known, some of which are illustrated in a previous volume of this series. Like earlier models, the new 1900 version was also a combined cinematograph and slide projector (Plate

(a)

(b)

Plate 72 Two popular 35 mm film projectors retailed by W. Butcher & Son, Blackheath, London, in 1900. (a) Home Cinematograph, with Maltese-cross movement, for use with 35 mm film loops (b) The 'Primus' Matagraph (Improved Model), a combined 35 mm film and slide projector manufactured by Levi, Jones & Co (*Barnes Collection*)

72b). It was supplied with two spools for 400 feet of film, safety shutter, slide carrier, lantern attachment, $4^{1}/_{2}$ inch condensers, and high power mixed jet. It was priced at £22.10s.[8]

As Butcher's business grew he was forced to acquire more space, and in April 1902 leased a building on the corner of St Bride Street and Stonecutter Street in the City of London, which he named 'Camera House'. The pressure of business undermined his health, and on 20 December 1903, he took his own life by jumping from an upstairs window. However, the business was to survive until the present day.

Fuerst Brothers

This firm is best remembered as the agents for the Cinématographe-Lumière and for films. They were also producers of their own films but only in a small way, filming topicals or news films. During January a film of the departure of Lord Roberts on the *Dunottar Castle* was advertised.[9] Other films advertised during the same month included, *Arrival of the Lord Mayor, in state, on board the S.S. 'Briton'*; and *Embarkation of the City of London Volunteers on board the Union Liner 'Briton'*; both of which were filmed at Southampton on 13 January.[10]

Harrison & Co

With the intense interest in China which had been aroused by the Boxer Rebellion, Harrison & Co. were fortunate in acquiring a number of films taken in that country by a British member of Parliament, E.F.G. Hatch, who made a cinematographic record of a world cruise he had been on.[11] Amongst the material he brought back were about a dozen good films shot in various parts of China just prior to the uprising. These scenes alone were enough to ensure the sale of the rest of his material, which included scenes taken in Korea, Japan and the Rocky Mountains of Canada.[12] In all there were about fifty films, each averaging about 75 feet in length. In addition to the films, there were several hundred lantern slides of places he had visited, providing a golden opportunity for lecturers who availed themselves of the material.[13] The Chinese scenes were shown at several London halls, including the Empire and the Hippodrome.[14]

Harrison & Co. seem to have acquired their films from several sources, but it seems doubtful that they produced any films of their own. A pantomime film of the fairy-tale *Hop o' My Thumb*, composed of twenty tableaux and 350 feet in length, would seem to be a French production.[15] It was apparently available from other dealers, and is also listed by the Micrograph Company.[16] Other films issued by Harrison included an extensive series on the Paris Exhibition; one on the late King of Italy; and a comedy called *A Gallant Rescue*, which relied on reverse motion for its humour.[17] A dramatic incident in the Boxer Rebellion is depicted in *Boxers Sacking a Missionary Station*, which is more than likely the Wrench film *Attack on a Mission Station*.[18]

Haydon & Urry Limited

There is very little information to hand about the Islington firm of Haydon & Urry.

Four small advertisements in *The Era* during January and February announce the 'latest war films', but only two titles are given, both depicting troops leaving for the Transvaal, 'taken by special permission'.[19] Customers were requested to 'send for latest list of films', but no such list is known to have survived. At the beginning of March, a series of five 'war pictures for Erascopes, Kalloscopes, &c.', were advertised, but these were still pictures presented as lantern slides and priced at ten shillings per dozen.[20]

It would seem that cinematography no longer played an important part in the activities of the firm, and all its attention was now directed towards its light engineering products, such as penny-in-the-slot machines. Whether or not the firm's Eragraph projector was still in production is not known, but more than likely it was found to be too outdated to warrant further modification. However, there was a reorganization of the firm at the beginning of the year, when a public prospectus was issued announcing a new limited liability company under the name Automatic Machines Ltd. Among the property which the new company was to acquire were the patent rights in the Eragraph, together with the existing stock of Eragraph films and the plant for their manufacture. The company's address was to remain at 353 Upper Street, Islington.[21]

After the death of Queen Victoria in January 1901, Haydon & Urry reissued two films of the Queen taken the previuos year. One showed her last appearance in public, leaving Netley Hospital on 11 November 1899, after visiting the wounded soldiers returned from South Africa. The other film showed the Queen in her state carriage during a royal procession, but the actual occasion is not identified. 'These two subjects', stated the advertisement, 'have been acknowledged by the trade to be two of the finest pictures ever taken of Her Majesty the Queen.'[22]

W. C. Hughes

Hughes, of Kingsland Road, London, were specialists in optical projection and offered a wide range of goods for lanternists and cinematographists. Their 'single' and 'duplex' street cinematographs, or Photo-Rotoscope Peepshows, were among their most popular products, and were consistently advertised throughout the year.[23] Very little change had taken place in the design of the two models since their initial appearance in 1898, but a slight modification had been made to the screened sightholes, which made for clearer viewing for the twenty to forty spectators which the respective models were capable of accommodating.[24] Little or no improvements seem to have been made to the Photo-Rotoscope projectors used in the peepshows, and they continued to be sold as a separate commodity for as little as seven guineas.[25] Outside their use as projectors for peepshow movies, their limited capabilities restricted their use to the home or to very small exhibitions, although it was specifically stated in advertisements that the Photo-Rotoscope was not a toy.[26]

For theatrical exhibition, Hughes offered a choice of two machines, the Moto-Photoscope Double-Action Reversing Cinematograph and the Motor-Pictoroscope with its special piston action intermittent movement, which was patented by Hughes in 1898.[27] The former machine was fitted with two cam striking movements so that the film could be projected either in the usual way or reversed, the change being made simply by turning the handle in the opposite direction. It also had large spools capable of holding about 700 feet of film.[28]

In addition to these 35 mm machines, Hughes placed on the market a sub-standard gauge apparatus for amateurs called 'La Petite', a combined camera and projector which is described and illustrated in Chapter 6. Hughes' La Petite Projector, designed for projection only, made its appearance at about the same time. This too is described and illustrated in Chapter 6.

Micrograph Co. Ltd

The Micrograph Company, which had been situated in Fleet Street in 1899, moved to 7 Great Queen Street, Lincoln's Inn. The cinematograph, bearing the same name as the company's, was still being advertised, but unless it had been transformed, was now only suitable for the small exhibitor.[29] It was priced at £10, but second-hand apparatus and films were also to be had. Among the new films which the company advertised for Christmas was a special pantomime feature called *Hop o' My Thumb*, which was 350 feet long.[30] This was a foreign importation, most likely French, and was composed of twenty tableaux, including:

Hop o' My Thumb's Home
Bound for the Forest
The Ogre's Castle
His Wife Hides the Children
The Ogre's Home-coming
The Escape
The Pursuit
The Ogre Falls Asleep
Children Steal his Seven-League Boots
The King's Palace
Dances and Revels, and numerous other scenes.

The same film was also offered by Harrison & Co.,[31] q.v.

Newman & Guardia Ltd

The camera and projector made by this company underwent little or no change during the year.[32] Both instruments were driven by an eccentric released spring-claw. An advertisement in Hepworth's *Animated Photography* shows the projector on its stand ready for operation (Plate 73).[33]

Prestwich Manufacturing Co.

The Prestwich Manufacturing Company, of 744 High Road, Tottenham, still held its position as one of the most important and reliable manufacturers of cinemato-graphic equipment, with a worldwide reputation. Most of their products of the previous year still remained on the market[34] and have already been dealt with in previous volumes, but during 1900 an improvement was made to their Reversing

Plate 73   Newman & Guardia advertisement in Cecil M. Hepworth's *Animated Photography* (London, 2nd ed. 1900) p. i

Cinematograph Projector (Plate 74) by the addition of a new picture racking device.[35] This was described in the *Magic Lantern Journal*:

In the new cinematograph projector lately introduced . . . there is a very ingenious method of ensuring that the pictures shall appear in the correct relation to the mask. Some instruments are so arranged that the mask is made to move upwards or downwards, but this occasions a dodging about on the screen, whereas with the method adopted in the instrument in question, the mask or aperture remains stationary and the film itself is shifted. At the lower part of the illustration a small crank handle will be seen, this controls the position of the sprocket wheels with relation to the mask, which is thus enabled to be stationary. In this manner the exact framing of the pictures can be assured quickly and without trouble, even whilst the machine is running'.[36]

Prestwich also marketed a simple and effective safety device to prevent the buckling or igniting of films when the projector stopped. This new automatic light cut-off consisted of a shutter actuated by a small air-pump, which, being connected with one of the quick-moving parts of the projector, kept the shutter raised as long as the machine was working. When the latter stopped, the air supply failed and the shutter dropped, cutting off the light from the lamphouse (Plate 75). The price of this safety device was £2.10s.[37] The Prestwich Camera and Printer Model 4 remained on the market unaltered since its introduction the previous year.[38]

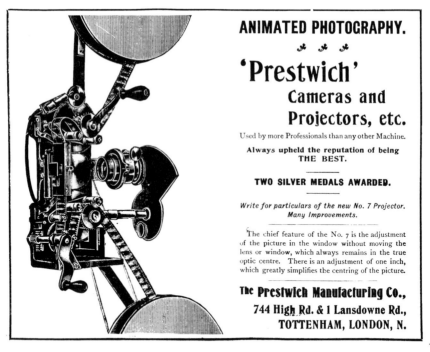

Plate 74   Prestwich No. 7 reversing cinematograph projector, 1900. Made by the Prestwich Mfg. Co., Lansdowne Road, Tottenham, London (*Barnes Collection*)

Plate 75   Prestwich automatic light cut-off, 1900. (*Barnes Collection*)

Riley Brothers

There is little to report on this firm for the year. A series of lantern slides on the Boer War were issued, along with 'a good number of cinematograph films'.[39]

A. Rosenberg & Co.

A. Rosenberg is chiefly known as the manufacturer of the cinematograph that bears

A. ROSENBERG & CO.,

PATENTEES AND MANUFACTURERS OF SCIENTIFIC AND OPTICAL INSTRUMENTS.	❊ CINEMATOGRAPH FILMS ❊ CAMERAS AND PROJECTORS. DEVELOPING OUTFITS . . . PRINTING MACHINES . . . PERFORATORS, &c. . . .
Apparatus for WIRELESS TELEGRAPHY, RONTGEN X-RAYS, TESTA AND HERTZ EXPERIMENTS, &C.	PERFORATING, PRINTING, AND DEVELOPING FOR THE TRADE. The Famous "CARBUTT" BLANK FILM. Rapid, for Negative Work, Quality Guaranteed. Slow, for Positive Work ,, ·5 in thickness, 3d per foot Large stock always on hand. Used by all the leading film manufacturers
Telegraphic Address— "PURGAMENT," LONDON.	Liberal Discount to the Trade.

Sole Agents in Europe and the British Colonies for **JOHN CARBUTT, Philadelphia.**

A. ROSENBERG & CO.,
12 & 17, SOUTHAMPTON ROW, HOLBORN, LONDON, W.C.

Plate 76   Advertisement published by A. Rosenberg & Co., in *The Optician*, 6 April 1900, p. 71

his name, although when it first appeared in 1896, it bore the name Kineoptograph. The machine appears to have served its purpose admirably for two or three years, but by 1900 it was obviously outmoded and consequently disappeared from the market. However, the firm continued to deal in apparatus and films (Plate 76). By the beginning of the year, Rosenberg was boasting the 'largest and most comprehensive list yet issued of unique subjects, including some from the seat of war'.[40] One film in particular, which appeared in June, was remarkable by any standards. It was called *Aladdin and the Wonderful Lamp*, and ran to about 750 feet. 'It was a complete show in itself', which the advertisement did not fail to point out. Unfortunately, there is no clue as to its origin. The film was described as 'the triumph of animated photography, consisting of a series of forty-five scenes. The most wonderful set of pictures ever taken, showing processions, quick changes, illusions, beautiful scenery, and tricks specially invented for these scenes, gorgeous dresses, with good acting. No exhibitor is up to date without a set of these most wonderful pictures'.[41] Although the production follows the pattern of Georges Méliès, it is not to be found among his *oeuvres*. It must surely be French, since no other country at that time had the capacity to mount such a lavish spectacle. Yet it seems too early to be Pathé, which would later specialize in films of this sort. Neither does the style quite suit Gaumont, the only other company capable of producing such a film. For the time being the mystery remains unsolved. Could it be yet another key film lost to posterity?[42]

Rosenberg also offered views of the Paris Exhibition, and undertook to photograph special views for customers which, it claimed, would be ready the same day if desired. In addition it advertised 'operators with camera sent to any part of the world on the shortest notice'.[43]

Watson & Son

Makers of the Motograph, 'one of the most compact on the market'. This was still available, but had undergone no changes and so does not warrant any further description.[44]

Philipp Wolff

Philipp Wolff offered a wide choice of films from various sources. He was quick to exploit the Chinese crisis and issued a series of views of China, which had been taken before the troubles began.[45] The Boxer Rebellion created a sudden interest in all things Chinese, and every available film depicting China was used as a stop gap until cameramen could be sent out there to cover the actual situation. The photo-grapher of Wolff's Chinese films is not named, but could have been the MP, E.F.G. Hatch, who supplied Harrison's.

Other sensational subjects offered by Wolff during the year, were *Panorama from a Steam Crane*, '100ft in the air' (surely Birt Acres' film),[46] and *Aladdin and the Wonderful Lamp*, described on p. 107).[47] Wolff also offered a large number of new and up-to-date films,[48] and, in line with other dealers, lantern slides to supplement the war films.[49] It is noticeable that Wolff's advertisements are less frequent and occupy less space in the pages of *The Era* compared with former years, which would seem to indicate that the business was in decline. And, indeed, within the next few years the company would be wound up.

Cecil Wray

This firm underwent a complete transformation. A new company was to be formed under the name of the Automatic Cinograph Company Limited, with a capital of £5,000 in 1 shares. An agreement was entered into with Cecil Wray and Arthur W. Thornton to acquire any patents, rights and so forth, connected with the cinematograph trade.[50]

John Wrench & Son

Noted primarily as manufacturers of high quality lantern and cinematograph equipment, this firm also produced its own films, although not on a very grand scale. It also acted as an agent for other filmmakers and professed to be able to supply films from any source.[51]

With the situation in China receiving most of the headlines, Boer War subjects were taking second place to the Boxer Rebellion. This uprising in Northern China caused the deaths of hundreds of people. It was essentially an anti-Western movement and the Boxers (so called because of their fondness for boxing and callisthenics) set out to destroy everything they considered foreign. They slaughtered Christian-Chinese, missionaries, and anyone they thought supported Western ideas. The Rebellion was finally put down by the intervention of foreign troops.

In line with other producers, Wrench issued a series of films about the Rebellion which purported to show the barbarities of which these Boxers were capable.[52] Among this class of film were: *Attack on a Mission Station*; *Attempted Capture of an English Nurse and Children*; *Assassination of a British Sentry*; and *The Clever Correspondent*. A full synopsis of each film can be found in the Appendix.

Attack on a Mission Station sounds remarkably like the now famous Williamson film *Attack on a China Mission*. The Wrench film preceded Williamson's by about three months. However, I do not think there was any deliberate copying, but rather that both filmmakers happened to draw on an identical source for their respective scenarios, possibly an account of a similar incident reported in the daily press. In any case, the Wrench film merely consisted of a continuous action recorded in one shot, whereas Williamson's made use of a more complex narrative technique by splitting the action into a number of separate shots. Besides, the Wrench film was only 87 feet long whereas Williamson's was 230 feet.

Wrench's series of 'faked war films' (as producers were wont to call them) may not have contained any innovations in film technique, but the intention behind them is explicit in the following statement which appeared in *The Era* when the films were released:

Important Notice

We intend issuing from time to time a number of these so-called 'Faked War Films', like the above, as we find from our experience that they are infinitely more exciting and interesting to an audience than the so-called 'Genuine War Films', as the latter will never be anything more than scenes of soldiers or sailors parading &c., before the camera in time of peace. It would be more appropriate to call them 'Genuine Peace Films', for it is a sure thing that the times were never more peaceful than when the films were taken. It is absolutely impossible to take a film of a genuine battle scene or any film of fighting, as, apart from the danger, modern warfare is carried on with the armies or navies miles apart, and therefore the subject does not lend itself to cinematography.[53]

As naive as some of these 'fakes' may have been, there is no doubt they provided filmmakers with the impetus to experiment with the dramatization of reality that was finally to lead to more complex forms of film narration such as we begin to witness, for example, in the films of Williamson and see more fully developed in *A Daring Daylight Robbery* of 1903.

With a company such as Wrench, which dealt in films from so many different sources, it is often impossible to be sure which films were actually made by the firm itself. Denis Gifford, in his *British Film Catalogue*, identifies the producers of the Boxer films, emanating from Wrench, as Mitchell & Kenyon.[54] He may well be right, but I have found no contemporary evidence to support him in this matter. However, we do know that a series of films depicting the 'Procession of the City Imperial Volunteers', also listed by Wrench, were in fact made by Hepworth. So I am inclined to side with Gifford regarding the attribution of the Boxer films. To keep the record straight I have listed them in the filmography under both names, with the necessary proviso. However, some war films from South Africa can be accredited to Wrench, if we are to believe the following statement in *The Optician* for 18 May:

Films from the Front.

We are informed that several new war films have been received from Mr A. Underwood, one of Messrs John Wrench and Son's war staff now with Lord Roberts, of which the three following are of special interest: Sir Alfred Milner arriving at the Presidency at Bloemfontein; change of guard outside the Presidency; and the wounded being carried on stretchers out of the hospital into the ambulance waggon, the scene changing to the driving off of the waggon.[55]

The same source also lists eight other films which Messrs Wrench are said to be 'publishing'. The majority seem to be 'fake war films', with such titles as *Winning the Victoria Cross*; *The White Flag Treachery*; *The Nurse's Brother*; *Shelling the Red Cross*; *The Dispatch Bearer*. The rest appear to be genuine news films. There is *The Volunteer Parade*, probably a parade of the City Imperial Volunteers; *Discharging Wounded Soldiers at Netley Hospital*, and two further films which may have been sent back from South Africa by Underwood, *Washing Boer Prisoners*; and *The Military Train*.

The Despatch Bearer, mentioned above, is another of Wrench's 'faked war films' to survive. The NFTVA catalogue entry for this film reads:

A 'faked' newsfilm representing an incident in the Boer War. A party of riflemen are attacked by the Boers and left for dead; one of the enemy removes a despatch from one of the fallen men; another of the fallen Britishers struggles to his feet, shoots the Boer and proceeds on his way with the despatch. (72ft).[56]

The National Film & Television Archive also holds three more 'faked war films, which have not been identified. Each has been given a descriptive title in lieu of the original, which is unknown. The NFTVA catalogue entries for the three films are as follows:

(BEHEADING A CHINESE BOXER). A 'faked' newsfilm representing the execution of a Chinese Boxer. A group of armed 'Chinese' soldiery are seen at the foot of a hillside; the victim is led into the centre of the group and decapitated; the head is stuck on a pole, around which the group circle, brandishing their weapons. The whole scene is photographed from a distance. (33ft).[57]

(BOER ATTACK ON A RED CROSS OUTPOST). A 'faked' newsfilm representing an incident in the Boer War. A nurse is seen receiving wounded British soldiers at a Red Cross tent; a Boer emerges from behind the tent and beats a hasty retreat after throwing a bomb in front of the tent; the wounded are brought out of the tent and amongst the casualties is the nurse. (69ft).[58]

(RESCUE OF A WOUNDED GUNNER). A 'faked' newsfilm representing an incident in the Boer War. Four gunners are seen under fire; one falls wounded as the others advance; a cavalryman rides up, drags the wounded man on to his horse and rides off in the direction from whence he came. (58ft).[59]

Film trading was only a small part of Wrench's business. First and foremost they were manufacturers of equipment and claimed to 'have manufactured and sold more

April 6, 1900.   ¦THE OPTICIAN AND PHOTOGRAPHIC TRADES REVIEW.   127

JOHN WRENCH & SON (*WHOLSALE ONLY*).

THE CELEBRATED

"WRENCH"

CINEMATOGRAPH.

No. 100 D.

Price Complete, **£50**

The Celebrated

"WRENCH"

Cinematograph.

No. 100 B.

Price Complete, **£36.**

For full particulars of above send for Illustrated Catalogue which will be sent (with schedule of discounts) post free on application.

50, GRAY'S INN ROAD, LONDON, W.C., ENGLAND.

Plate 77   Advertisement for Wrench cinematographs. From *The Optician*, 6 April 1900, p. 127

cinematographs than anyone else in the world'.[60] By February, a new projector had just been completed and was ready for sale. It was called 'The Grand' (Model 100 D) and could be seen working each week day from 10.00 a.m. to 6.00 p.m., by appointment at their premises, 50 Gray's Inn Road.[61] It was priced at £50, but the previous year's model, the 100 B machine, was still on the market, selling at £36 (Plate 77).[62]

As the advertisements proclaimed:

> Two special features in the Wrench cinematograph are that the films can be used thousands of times without damaging them, and that the machine will effectively and properly exhibit without the slightest hitch any film, no matter how torn or damaged it may be, provided there are perforations left on one side of the film.[63]

Towards the end of the year, an improvement in 'The Grand' was announced. It was now fitted, without extra charge, with an automatic shutter, which, it was claimed:

> Absolutely prevents the firing of films. The instant the cinematograph handle is turned the shutter rises, and immediately the handle is at rest the shutter falls. The mechanism of this new automatic shutter is very simple, works with perfect smoothness, and will not get out of order. It is made entirely of metal, and is a perfect mechanical device.

At the end of this 'important notice' the following words were added:

> 'THE GRAND'
> is, without doubt
> *THE* CINEMATOGRAPH OF THE AGE[64]

In May, a new cinematograph camera was announced.[65] It was provided with two film boxes to hold 100 feet of film. The optical system comprised a Voigtlander Collinear lens of $2\frac{1}{8}$ inch focus, with iris diaphragm. Each turn of the handle brought down six inches of film, exposing eight frames, thus a double turn of the crank per second exposed one foot. The price of the camera complete was £20; and extra metal spools loaded with 100 feet of negative, ready for insertion into the spool boxes of the camera, cost 27s.6d. each.

5 Exhibitors

For an overall picture of film exhibition in Britain at the turn of the century, one would need to search practically every provincial newspaper in the country. No one is ever likely to undertake such a formidable task, but a growing body of local historians has begun the task of researching the history of the cinemas in their own localities. Inevitably, this has uncovered material relating to early film shows that took place before regular cinemas were established. The exhibition pattern that emerges from this research seems to confirm Colonel A.C. Bromhead's argument, detailed in my previous volume, that exhibitors tend to fall into three distinct categories—the music hall exhibitor; the town hall showman; and the fairground travelling showman.[1] It would appear that all three types of exhibitor were to survive throughout the first decade of the twentieth century, until the screen found a permanent home.

These local cinema histories are now too numerous to be considered here, but film historians will do well to bear them in mind. In this chapter, I shall not attempt a comprehensive survey of British film exhibitors, but will confine myself to a selection of the better known names.

Gibbons' Bio-Tableaux

Walter Gibbons had now become the foremost exhibitor in England. This was a rapid rise to fame and fortune considering that he only became known to the public towards the end of 1898. Originally billed as the 'Anglo-American Bio-Tableaux', he now traded under the name of 'Gibbons' Bio-Tableaux'. From the start, Gibbons seems to have had a working relationship with Charles Urban.[2] It was Urban's Bioscope projector that provided the model for his own machine, hence the Bio part of his trade name. However, he had completely transformed the machine since then, and was able to proclaim that the 'New Bio-Tableaux' was his own invention, of which he was also the patentee. This was the machine now used for all his bookings, and was first introduced on 6 September 1900. A notice to managers and proprietors, published in *The Era* on 15 September, stated that, 'an order for twenty of these machines has been placed with a large firm, and these will replace all those in present use in the provinces as quickly as possible'.[3] It was this machine that was used twice daily at the London Hippodrome, the theatre in Cranbourne Street, Leicester Square,[4] which provided Gibbons with his chief venue, and where all his most important films were first shown to the public (Plate 78).

The Bio-Tableaux at the Hippodrome was in the capable hands of Matt Raymond, the former electrician/operator for the Cinématographe-Lumière under Félicien Trewey (Plate 79). In 1900 Matt Raymond left Walter Gibbons' employment to set up on his own account as an independent exhibitor, informing the managers of the various music halls that it was he who was responsible for bringing the Bio-Tableaux show at the Hippodrome to the 'standard of excellence it has attained'. This naturally displeased his former employer, who forced him to retract the

Plate 78   The London Hippodrome, the music hall where Gibbons' Bio-Tableaux became a regular item on the programme (*Barnes Collection*)

Plate 79   Matt Raymond, electrician/operator for Gibbons' Bio-Tableaux at the London Hippodrome, seen here adjusting the glass globe condenser in the lantern of the Cinématographe-Lumière, circa 1897 (*Barnes Collection*)

statement in the form of a full-page announcement printed in *The Era* under the heading 'London Hippodrome/Gibbons' Bio-Tableaux/An Apology'.[5]

Gibbons' Bio-Tableaux had its offices at 60 Chandos Street, The Strand. The premises were reputed to have seventeen rooms, 'all devoted to Animated Photography, where everything is accomplished'. Gibbons wrote in one of his advertisements, 'This magnificent place is one of the sights of London, and I invite everyone interested in this wonderful business to pay me a visit.'[6] Here were offered for sale a wide range of films, emanating from various sources, including Smith and Williamson. The fiction films he offered during November included: *A Funny Story* (Smith); *The Burning of a Missionary and the Dispersing of the Infamous Monsters by the Allied Troops*; *Attack on a Mission Station: Saved by Bluejackets* (Williamson); *The War in China: Boxers Decapitating a Prisoner*; *Living Statues*; and *The Fisherman's Luck*.[7] Second-hand films, lamps and machines, were also offered for sale.[8]

In November, Gibbons introduced the Phono Bio-Tableaux, which was advertised as 'the most wonderful invention of the age. No longer a silent picture'.[9] As the *Photographic News* reported:

> It is well worth seeing and hearing even if not absolutely perfect, and as the first attempt of the kind in London it is decidedly encouraging. Three special turns of the combination [phonograph and cinematograph] are given, two of a quartette who come on to the stage kinematographically and sing phonographically, and the other the arrival of a train, the latter being by far the more realistic of the two. As a beginning, the author, Mr. Gibbons, of the Bio-Tableaux is to be congratulated, and we wish him more success in future attempts.[10]

Another series of sound films was shortly presented, featuring the famous music hall artiste Vesta Tilley in *The Midnight Sun*; *Algy* and *Louisiana Loo*. Gibbons expressed his gratitude to the actress in an advertisement which read: 'Many thanks to Miss Vesta Tilley for the trouble she took in enabling me to take the pictures and records.'[11] Here is proof that Gibbons was also a filmmaker. The Phono films were fairly successful, being shown twice daily at the London Hippodrome. There were, of course, other attempts by various inventors to synchronize moving pictures with recorded sound, the best known contemporary example being the Gaumont Phono-Cinema-Theatre.

Before the year ended, Gibbons updated his Bio projector, and introduced it as the Royal Randvoll, a great feature of which was that 'the film only comes in contact with six teeth of both sprocket wheels, thus ensuring the easy running of any different gauge perforation'.[12] The price of the machine was £45. There was also an arc lamp and rheostat to go with it priced at £6.10s and £4.10s, respectively.[13]

H. Spencer Clarke

H. Spencer Clarke has some claim to fame as the exhibitor of the film shows sponsored by Messrs Lever and Nestlé during a nationwide advertising campaign undertaken in 1897–1898. Equipped with Lumière apparatus, he was responsible for a great number of performances throughout Great Britain, and at one time employed as his assistant the future British film producer Cecil M. Hepworth.

Clarke was also a capable cinematographer in his own right, and some of the films he shot were included in the shows.

Clarke's exploits during this period have already been recorded in previous volumes of this history, but new information has come to light concerning his association with William Hasketh Lever, the first Lord Leverhulme and founder of Port Sunlight where the famous brand of soap was manufactured.[14] Lord Leverhulme was one of the first industrialists to realize the value of the cinemato-graph as an advertising medium, and in association with the Nestlé milk company, recruited Clarke to undertake the task of promoting their products by means of popular film shows at greatly reduced prices.

A Swiss man by the name of Lavanchy-Clarke is also known to have been associated with Lumière and to have reached an agreement to exploit the Cinématographe in Switzerland for a year, with a preference right for Lever & Nestlé in England. Whether or not he is the same person as our Spencer Clarke, or a relative, has not been determined.[15]

By 1900, Spencer Clarke had already severed his connections with Lever and Nestlé and also with Lumière, and although he continued to function as an exhibitor, his performances were now billed under the name of 'Clarke's Royal Bioscope', which seems to suggest that he was operating the Warwick machine. In January 1900, he is reported at the Empire Theatre of Varieties at Deal, showing a series of war films,[16] and a poster of 31 December of the same year announces a two week engagement at the Alhambra Theatre of Varieties at Sandgate, Kent.[17] Among the films advertised were: *Hoisting the Union Jack at Pretoria*; *Review of Troops at Pretoria before Lord Roberts*; *Naval Guns and Ammunition Crossing the Vet River*; *Landing the Famous 4.7 Gun at Port Elizabeth*.

Maskelyne & Cooke

The Egyptian Hall, which was reputed to be the oldest house of entertainment in London (Plate 80), still continued a policy of mixing magic with 'animated photo-graphs' as the films were still referred to. Surprisingly, the subjects chosen for display were not trick and phantasy films, but topical scenes of the Boer War. For the moment, war subjects were thought more popular than any other, no matter what the venue or mode of entertainment. The weekly illustrated journal *Black and White* reviewed the latest programme on 21 April 1900:

> Nevil Maskelyne has quite a new series of Animated Photographs, which represent in the most vivid way the stirring scenes of the present war and the chief actors therein. The whole course of events which followed Lord Roberts's arrival at the Cape is brought in a wonderfully realistic way before the audience in the scene which shows the assured and quiet confidence of his lordship as he gets into the carriage awaiting him on his arrival.[18]

The same programme was reviewed in *The Era*, but with some interesting details of the accompaniments:

> It is quite a droll bit of comedy that Mr Devant silhouettes on a large screen, and the pictures are keenly appreciated. Not more so than the animated photographs introduced

(a)

(b)

Plate 80   The Egyptian Hall, Piccadilly. (a) As it appeared in 1902 (b) The stage. Maskelyne's Mechanical
Orchestra can just be glimpsed at the right of the stage (*Barnes Collection*)

by Mr Nevil Maskelyne, who makes appropriate observations, which are often witty and never too long. The views, which include general subjects, besides scenes from the war in South Africa, are accompanied by Mr Maskelyne's mechanical orchestra, which is controlled by that expert organist and pianist Mr F. Cramer. From this resumé it will be seen that all the conditions of a popular entertainment are fulfilled in the latest Egyptian Hall programme.[19]

On the 28th May there was to be an eclipse of the sun. Cecil M. Hepworth had gone off to Algiers to record the phenomenon. J.N. Maskelyne likewise was intent on filming the event and chose a spot in North Carolina for the purpose. Following in the footsteps of his ancestor Nevil Maskelyn, the Royal astronomer to King George III—'J.N.' took a keen interest in the subject and was already a Fellow of the Royal Astronomical Society when he set off for America. Evidently, his film of the solar eclipse turned out satisfactorily for it was featured in the programmes at the Egyptian Hall (Plate 81) and was duly commented on in *The Era*:

> The finest and most exclusive series of Animated Photographs ever exhibited, including all the latest subjects from the seat of war; also an animated photograph of the recent Solar Eclipse, of much scientific interest, being the first occasion that animated photography has been successfully employed in astronomical research, taken in North Carolina by Mr Nevil Maskelyne, F.R.A.S.[20]

It is not strictly true that this was the first successful employment of cinematography in the field of astronomical research. Maskelyne had himself attempted to film a solar eclipse from a position in Buxar, India in 1898, but the negative had been stolen before it could be developed. Another expedition had, however, filmed that eclipse from Viziadurg, and there is no reason to doubt that the outcome was successful, if not for regular showing, then at least for scientific purposes.

David Devant was a regular performer at the Egyptian Hall, and when in 1904 the company moved to its new home at St George's Hall, Regent Street, he became a full partner in the firm. Meanwhile, whenever he was not performing at the hall in Piccadilly, he was prepared to undertake private engagements of 'prestidigitation' 'mental phenomena' 'hand shadows' 'illusions' and, of course, 'animated photographs'.

The Royal Viograph Co. Limited

An interesting programme of films was presented on 22 May 1900, by The Royal Viograph, at a special evening for the Municipality and Press of Bordeaux, France.[21] The second part of the programme was devoted entirely to 'episodes de la guerre du Transvaal', taken by the operators of the Warwick Trading Company, and made available for the occasion by Charles Urban. No information has come to light regarding this cinematograph, but a machine with a similar sounding name but spelt 'Vieograph' was exhibited at the International Universal Exhibition of 1898 at Earl's Court, London.

Among the French films included in the performance at Bordeaux that night were *Cendrillon* by Georges Méliès, and *Histoire d'un crime*.[22] This latter has received

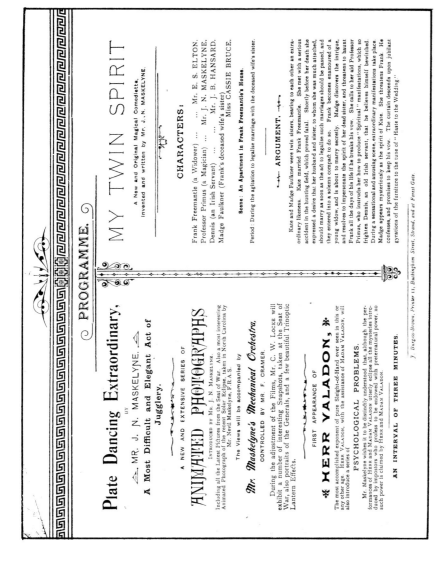

Plate 81 Egyptian Hall programme announcing a new and extensive series of Animated Photographs, including the film of the solar eclipse taken in North Carolina by Nevil Maskelyne. Note also Maskelyne's Mechanical Orchestra which accompanied the films (*Barnes Collection*)

some notoriety for its use of flashbacks showing the criminal's past life, which are depicted on a small open stage seen through an aperture in the back wall of the prison cell. Evidently Pathé, the producers of the film, were not yet aware of the 'balloon' method of showing dreams and visions by double exposure, pioneered by G.A. Smith in 1898. The fact that *Histoire d'un crime* was shown as early as May 1900 will require film historians to revise their dating of this film, which hitherto was thought to have been made in 1901.

A. D. Thomas, and Some Others

Little was heard at this time of the flamboyant exhibitor A.D. Thomas, whose previous film performances were regularly reported by the theatrical press. Perhaps his fortunes had taken a down turn. A performance of his was recorded at the Brighton Alhambra on 19 February, where his cinematograph show was billed as the Edison-Thomas Royal Vitascope, in a programme of Boer War films.[23]

Other exhibitors besides Thomas linked their names with the great Edison. A programme at the Alhambra Theatre of Varieties at Attercliffe, on 29 October, included Edison-Rodgers' Electrograph,[24] and a Northern exhibitor of 4 Newby Terrace, Stockton-on-Tees, who advertised under the name of Edison-George.[25]

Messrs Inman, Holt and Woolfenden, cinematographers and photographers of 80 Dale Street, Milnrow, Rochdale, Lancashire, were exhibitors of WTC's latest Bioscope projector. Warwick films and those of Hepworth made up their programmes, together with films of local interest which they shot themselves. They were prepared to undertake shows in 'the largest or smallest hall in the United Kingdom'.[26]

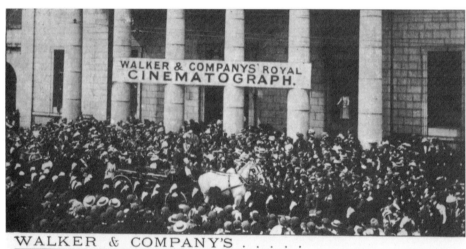

Plate 82   Walker & Company's Royal Cinematograph advertised on the exterior of an unidentified town hall (*Barnes Collection*)

Plate 83   Schoolchildren attending a Bioscope show at the turn of the century (*Barnes Collection*)

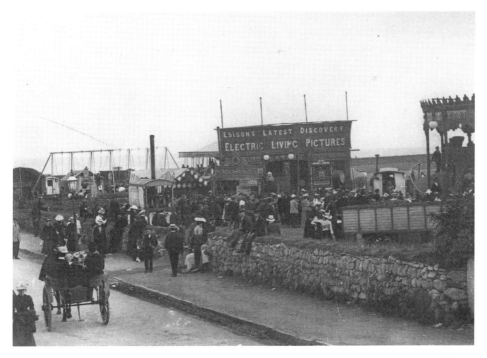

Plate 84   Fairground Bioscope show at Tranmore, near Waterford, Ireland, circa 1900, exhibiting 'Edison's Latest Discovery—Electric Living Pictures' (*Barnes Collection*)

Plate 85   The Great American Bioscope. An early travelling show, with a castle-style front. Among the films advertised on the billboard are *The Last Cartridge*; and *Defence of the Colours*, two Lumiére films of 1897 (650. Le défense du drapeau; 745. Les dernières cartouches). The photograph was probably taken at Altrincham Fair in April 1900. From a lantern slide in the collection of Trafford Leisure Services (*Douglas Rendell*)

A London-based exhibitor of 43 Bellamy Street, Balham, named Saye, specialized in showing films of the Boer War and aptly named his cinematograph the Wargraph.[27] A Scottish itinerant showman, by the name of R. Silvester, placed an advertisement in *The Era* in order to dispose of a copy of the Fitzsimmons-Jeffries fight, in eleven rounds, which he had originally acquired from E.H. Bostock of the Zoo, Glasgow. The reason he gave for selling was that he intended to go the same route with new pictures. His address is given as 19 Chisholm Street, Glasgow.[28]

On 5 October, C. Goodwin Norton was exhibiting at Alnwick Castle,[29] where he showed an assortment of twenty films some of which he had produced himself. The second part of the programme consisted of fifteen films relating to the war in South

Plate 86   The Picture House, Hill Street, Lydney, the proprietor of which was the pioneer film exhibitor Albany Ward, whose name appears on the theatre marquee (*Barnes Collection*)

Plate 87   Open-air theatre, Westcliff-on-Sea, Southend, circa 1911. Owned by the pioneer film exhibitor, Jasper Redfern (*Barnes Collection*)

Africa. The performance concluded in fitting manner, with *H. M. The Queen*; *Garden Party at Buckingham Palace*; and lastly, *Good Night*, the latter showing the front of Norton's shop at closing time, with the window shutters being put in place and on which were displayed the words 'Good Night'. Norton's career has already been dealt with in Volume 4 of this series.

The Scottish exhibitors Walker & Co., of Aberdeen gave a notable performance of Boer War films, in October, to a distinguished audience of Royals and aristocracy at Abergeldie Castle, the home of the Earl and Countess of Clanwilliam.[30] Although based in Scotland, Walker & Company exhibited extensively throughout the United Kingdom at various venues, including the Royal Polytechnic, Queen's Hall and Royal Court Theatre in London (Plate 82).

During the summer months, seaside piers continued to attract film exhibitors. The Northern showmen, Tweedale & Hargreaves, for example, enjoyed a successful season at the Central Pier, Morecambe with their Bio-Motograph.[31] Until the outbreak of the First World War, Bioscope shows continued to be well represented in the fairgrounds. (Plates 83–85) A novel form of travelling cinema was proposed by Chadwick's Patent Advertising Company Limited, of Manchester. At the tail end of a large van a screen was erected so that by means of a cinematograph projector placed at the other end, advertising films could be projected on the screen as the van was hauled about the streets.[32]

Some pioneer exhibitors ended up owning or running cinema theatres. Albany Ward, for example, acquired the first permanent cinema in Weymouth, and a picture postcard reveals that he was also connected with the Picture House in Hill Street, Lydney, where the marquee displays the words 'Albany Ward's Pictures!' (Plate 86). Arthur Cheetham became a cinema proprietor, Walter Gibbons became the owner of the Holborn Empire of Varieties, and Jasper Redfern ran an open-air seaside theatre at Westcliff-on-Sea, near Southend (Plate 87).

6   Home Movies

It is some measure of the importance with which the trade accorded amateur cinematography, that Henry V. Hopwood (author of *Living Pictures*) deemed it appropriate to write an article on the subject for *The Optician*, called 'Cinematography for All'.[1] In it he describes the Birtac, Biokam, La Petite, the Pocket Chrono, Mirographe, Kammatograph and the Kinora. However, Hopwood's article does not deal with home cinematographs using the 35 mm gauge, nor does it include those of the toy variety, some of which find a place in this chapter.[2]

The idea of sub-standard gauge cinematography originated with Birt Acres, whose 17.5 mm Birtac first appeared in 1898, closely followed by the 17.5mm Biokam manufactured by Alfred Darling of Brighton and marketed by both Warwick and Wrench. Both machines have already been dealt with in previous volumes of this history.

By May 1900, W.C. Hughes was advertising the 'La Petite' Living Picture Camera and Projector (Plate 88).[3] Like the Biokam, this used 17.5 mm film, but perforated down the centre of the frame lines; the Birtac used film perforated along one side. The mechanism of 'La Petite' was geared so that two turns of the handle per second was sufficient in the way of speed.[4] Like the Biokam, it too employed a claw mechanism for the intermittent motion. A developing frame was also supplied with the outfit and the same apparatus could be used as a printer as well as camera and projector (Plate 89). In addition to 'La Petite' camera/projector, Hughes issued a little machine for projection only, which they named 'La Petite Projector' (Plate 90). This took a small gauge film $^5/_8$ in $\times$ $^1/_2$ in. With limelight it would throw a picture from 5 feet to 7 feet. It was described as 'a little gem machine for amateurs', and cost £3.15s.0d.[5]

Two French machines using sub-standard gauge film also appeared on the market. One called the Chrono de Poche, or Pocket Chrono, and the other the Mirographe. The Pocket Chrono (Plate 91), as its name implies, was manufactured by L. Gaumont et Cie, of Paris, and used a 15mm film with perforations at the centre. The intermittent movement was supplied by the well known Demeny beater or 'dog'. The apparatus is described and illustrated in *La Nature* for 22 September 1900,[6] and it is from this source that our own illustrations are taken.

The Mirographe (Plate 92) made by Reulos & Goudeau (Reulos was once in partnership with Georges Méliès) had some novel and interesting features.[7] It used a 22 mm film notched at intervals down one side. The intermittent movement was applied to the film by an eccentric snail cam which interacted with the notches on the film and drew down a length of film equal to one frame at each revolution of the cam wheel. Both these French machines also operated as cameras and projectors. It is not known whether either machine was widely used in England.

The instruments discussed so far in this chapter were all designed to take a small gauge film. The Kammatograph (Plates 93 and 94) took no film at all—'a filmless cinematograph' as it was designated in the literature of the time.[8] Instead of film, the pictures were recorded on a glass disc 12 inches in diameter.[9] The tiny photographs, 550 in number, were arranged spirally on the circular plate. A second model took larger pictures, 300 in number, but in both cases the principles remained the same.

(a)

(b)

(c)

(d)

Plate 88   W.C. Hughes' 'La Petite' Living Picture Camera and Projector, 1900. A sub-standard gauge cinematograph for amateurs (*Barnes Collection*)

"La Petite"
Living Picture Camera
and
Projector,

Also acts as a Snap-shot Camera.

A LIVING PICTURE CAMERA, PRINTER & PROJECTOR IN ONE.

Price £6 6 0

reduced to

£5 10 0

A SUPERB PIECE OF
MECHANISM.

PRICES.

	£	s.	d.
The "La Petite" with one Magazine and 2in. Lens with Waterhouse stops ... Price £6 6, reduced to	5	10	0
Extra Magazines	0	5	0
Russian Iron Lantern with cowl, tray, and brass front	1	10	0
4in. Menisen's Condensor in brass mount	0	8	0
First-class Front Lens with rack and pinion	1	5	0
Safety Blow-through Jet	0	12	6
Special Folding Tripod	0	5	0
Developing Frame	0	2	6
12in. by 10in. Xylonite Developing Dish	0	4	0
6ft. by 5ft. Lantern Screen and Portable Frame ...	1	5	0
Dark-room Lamp	0	3	6
Alum Trough, glass or metal	0	9	0
Film Cement	0	1	0
Developing Customers' own Negative	0	4	0
Printing and Developing (including cost of Film) ...	0	10	0

W. C. HUGHES,

Specialist in Optical Projection.   Established over 30 Years.

Brewster House, 82, Mortimer Rd., Kingsland, N.

Plate 89   Publicity sheet issued by W.C. Hughes for 'La Petite' sub-standard gauge cinematograph (*CinéMathèque Française*)

Plate 90   Hughes' 'La Petite' Projector, for small films $^5/_8$ inch×$5^1/_2$ inch. Made by W.C. Hughes, London, 1900 (*Cinémathèque Française*)

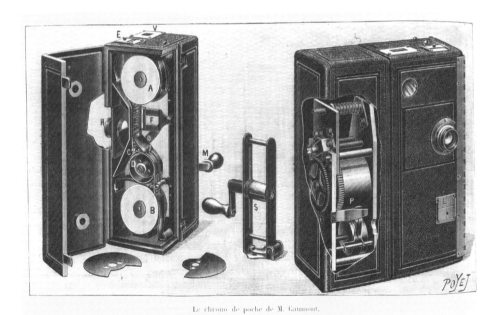

Le chrono de poche de M. Gaumont.

Plate 91   Chrono de Poche, or Pocket Chrono. Sub-standard gauge cinematograph made by L. Gaumont et Cie., Paris, 1900 (*La Nature*)

Fig. 1. — Le Mirographe.
Mécanisme d'entraînement et d'obturation.

Fig. 2. — Le Mirographe.
Disposé pour prendre une photographie.

Plate 92   Le Mirographe. Sub-standard gauge cinematograph made by Reulos & Goudeau, Paris, 1900
(*La Nature*)

Plate 93   Advertisement for the Kammatograph. Invented and patented by L. Kamm in 1898. It used a 12-inch diameter glass plate, with the pictures arranged in a spiral (*Barnes Collection*)

Plate 94   The Kammatograph. Interior view (*Barnes Collection*)

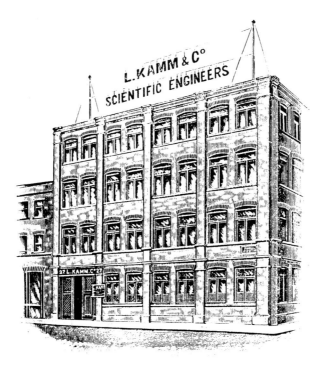

Plate 95   Factory of L. Kamm & Co, 27 Powell Street, London, manufacturers of the Kammatograph
(*Fox Talbot Museum, Lacock*)

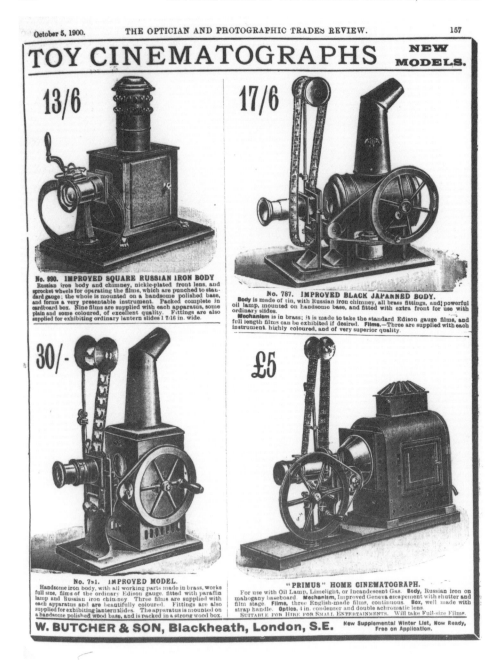

Plate 96   German Toy Cinematographs. Distributed in England by W. Butcher & Son, of Blackheath. Advertisement in *The Optician*, 5 October 1900, p. 157

Each apparatus served as a camera and projector combined and was the invention of Leonard Ulrich Kamm, an electrical engineer of 1 Gresley Road, Hornsey Rise, London. The Kammatograph was patented in 1898 (Pat. No. 6515) but was not available on the market until 1900.[10] The makers were L. Kamm & Co., Scientific

Engineers and Manufacturers. The company had a large factory at 27 Powell Street, Croswell Road, London, E.C. (Plate 95), and was later to manufacture the successful 35mm Kamm Film Projectors which were widely used in cinemas throughout Great Britain.[11]

By the end of the century amateur cinematographers already had a choice of six different instruments with which to photograph and project their own movies. In addition to this sub-standard gauge apparatus, there were a number of 35 mm film projectors such as Watson's Motograph and Hughes' Photo-Rotoscope, which although aimed at the professional, were suitable for home use.

For the juvenile trade, the German toymakers began the manufacture of tin-plate magic lantern-cinematographs, which were distributed in England by dealers such as W. Butcher & Son of Blackheath (Plate 96).[12] These toy lanterns projected small glass lantern slides as well as film loops. The pictures on the loops were not photographic images, but sequential chromolitho designs, often traced from live-action films of the period.[13] They can thus be regarded as progenitors of the animated film cartoons.

The Photogram mentions a 'parlour kinetograph' called the Omniscope, in which the pictures are 'enlarged not by projection but by inspection through a magnifying lens'. The address of the company selling it was 15 Abchurch Lane, London, E.C.[14]

It might be as well to include here that class of book-form apparatus in which a series of sequential pictures are flicked over like the leaves in a book, with either the thumb or some mechanical contrivance. The simplest form of such apparatus is the common flick book which has its origins in the days before motion photography when drawings were used instead of photographs. J.B. Linnett patented such an idea using drawn pictures in 1868, which he named the Kineograph (Plate 97).[15] In 1896, the same principle was applied to cinematographic images and was sometimes referred to as the pocket kinetoscope. The pictures in these simple flick books were taken from contemporary films, and those examples that survive today have a particular interest and value, as they often preserve the only visual record we have left of

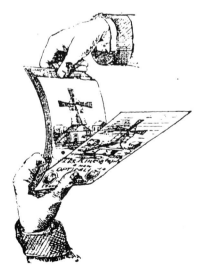

Plate 97   Kineograph. Patented by J.B. Linnett in 1868 (Pat. No. 925). A series of sequential drawings are flicked over one after the other to give an illusion of motion (*Living Pictures*, 1899, p. 35)

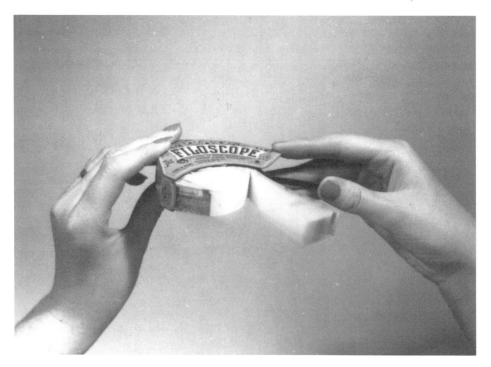

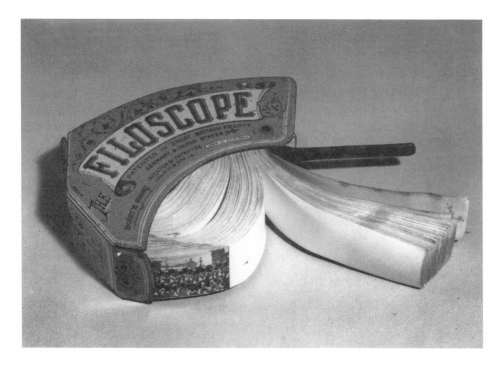

Plate 98   The Filoscope. Patented by H.W. Short in 1898 (Pat. No. 23,158). Later reissued by the British
Mutoscope & Biograph Company. The subject shown is Paul's film *The Gordon Highlanders*, taken in
1896 (Science Museum, London)

4   THE " NOAH'S ARK " MAGICAL DEPOT,

No. 5042.—**Latest Novelty.**—Most wonderful effect ever seen. Perfectly natural movements, exactly the same as life. A proper description of the marvellous effect of the " Filoscope " cannot be written owing to the space it would take to give an adequate description of its wonderful, amusing, and pleasing effect. This article has been selling in thousands, and for the winter season the demand will be greater than the supply. Below will be seen the list of different " Filoscopes." The views and effects are precisely the same and are taken from those shown in the Animated Pictures or Cinematograph.

Price **6d.**   *Post free* **8d.** *each.*

1. The Prince's Derby.
2. Chirgwin, the White-Eyed Kaffir.
3. Prince & Princess of Wales.
4. David Devant.
5. Soldier's Embrace.
6. Spanish Dance.
7. Train entering Station.
8. Skirt Dance, Sisters Hengler
9. Gordon Highlanders.
10. The Long Drink.
11. The Troopship.
12. Here we are again.

No. 6034. **The Surprise Pack of Cards.**—A pretty little card case is laying about on your table, say on a card table. Of course some one immediately picks the case up and at once opens it to see what kind of cards it contains, but to his surprise he receives a great shock, as instead of a pack of cards he finds that something jumps out at him. Much fun may be had with the surprise pack of cards.

Price **2/3.**   *Post free* **2/6.**

Plate 99   Page from Hamely's toy catalogue circa 1900, listing twelve different subjects depicted in the Filoscope (*Douglas-Jewell Collection*), Bill Douglas Centre, Exeter

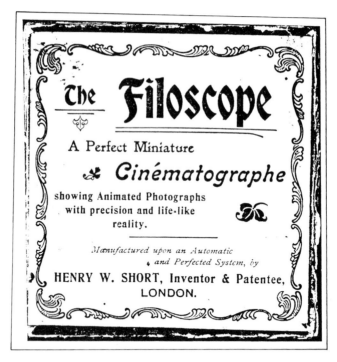

Plate 100   Printed label on the lid of a Filoscope box (*Lester Smith Collection*)

some lost film. The same holds true for the mechanical forms of flick book, such as the Filoscope and Kinora.

The Filoscope (Plate 98)[16] was patented in 1898 by H.W. Short, and according to a list published in a Hamley's toy catalogue of about 1900,[17] twelve different subjects were issued (Plate 99). Elsewhere, I have shown that these subjects were taken from films originally made by R.W. Paul.[18] Each Filoscope came in a little box with a printed label on the lid (Plate 100)[19] and inside was a sheet of instructions (Plate 101).[20] On one of the preliminary leaves attached to the Filoscope a few particulars were printed about the film. *The Soldier's Courtship*, for instance, states:

> The scene of which the present incident forms a portion was enacted upon the roof of the Alhambra Theatre, London for the purpose of exhibition in the Cinematographe [sic] and remained for some time one of the most popular subjects.
> The principals are Mr Fred Story and Miss Julie Seale, both familiar figures in the well-known gorgeous Alhambra Ballets.[21]

It seems that at some time the Mutoscope & Biograph Company acquired an interest in the Filoscope, as their name has been rubber-stamped on the backs of some examples.[22] It is not surprising that M&B should show an interest in this little toy, for Herman Casler, one of the founder, members of the firm, was co-patentee of the Kinora, another toy based on the same principle. He also held the patent on the Mutoscope. This latter was readily adaptable as a flick book, and Mutoscope pictures were issued in book form as the Bio-Gem, or Pocket Biograph. An example

THE FILOSCOPE.

Patented in Great Britain, France, Germany, Italy, Austria and the United States.

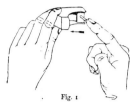

To use the FILOSCOPE to its best effect and maintain it in good working order, observe carefully the following instructions :—

FIRST—Holding the case in the left hand as shown in Fig. 1, push the book right out of the case backwards—that is—away from the observer—by means of the handle, taking care that all the leaves, including the frontispiece, pass right out clear at the back.

Fig. 1

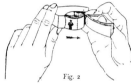

Fig. 2

THEN—Holding the Handle between the thumb and fore-finger of the right hand, and resting the tip of the second finger on the back of the book, Fig. 2, draw the handle steadily forward. The book will curve as it re-enters the case from behind, and sliding through, the leaves will be successfully released and will spring clear of the line of vision. The exposure of the whole book should occupy from 10 to 15 seconds according to the subject.

To repeat, continue to rotate the book in the same direction as for the previous exposure, until the handle passes back through the case to its original position. **Do not push the book back through the case and start afresh.**

When finished with reverse the direction and press the book **by means of the handle** (Fig. 3) back into the case, until the frontispiece is just enclosed, taking care that none of the leaves are protruding from the back. Squeeze the leaves together in such a manner that the book is left at rest evenly and compactly curved within the outline of the case.

Too great stress cannot be laid upon this latter condition, for it is to this curved form of the leaves whilst at rest that the FILOSCOPE owes its sharpness and "snap" in working, and which forms the most important claim in the Patents by which it is protected.

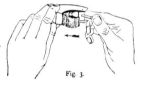

Fig. 3.

The action of the FILOSCOPE improves with age, and with ordinary care in following these directions, it will remain in good order for years. In examining individual leaves care should be taken not to force them too far apart or to disturb their normal curve.

New subjects of an amusing and topical nature will be published from time to time.

The Filoscope is a British invention, produced exclusively by British skill and labour.

HENRY W. SHORT,
Inventor and Patentee,
LONDON.

Plate 101   Instructions supplied with the Filoscope (*Lester Smith Collection*)

in the Barnes Collection bears the imprint of the 'Biograph Studio, 107 Regent St. W.' and depicts what seems to be a garden party for the actress Ellen Terry. In America, a series of flick books using Mutoscope pictures, reduced in size, were marketed by the Winthrop Press, 419 Lafayette Street, New York, under the name 'Winthrop Moving Picture Book'. Among the Biograph film subjects used in the series was no. 46 *The Elopement* of 1898. But other subjects seem of a later date. The

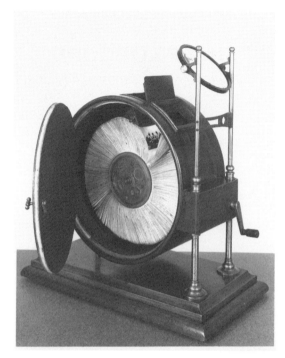

Plate 102   Casler's Parlour or Home Mutoscope, for use with standard reels (*Science Museum, London*)

Winthrop flick books were sold under license from the American Mutoscope & Biograph Company under patent number 838,610.[23]

Casler's regular Mutoscope was described and illustrated in a previous volume of this history, but no mention was then made of the model designed for home use.[24] An example of this portable form of the apparatus is preserved in the Science Museum, London (Plate 102). With it is a reel of pictures showing the children of the Duke and Duchess of York 'playing at soldiers', which was filmed in the garden of Marlborough House by W.K.-L. Dickson in 1900. An article on the filming of this event was published in *The Harmsworth Magazine* and includes an illustration which shows the Royal children looking into a similar apparatus (Plate 103).[25] The Harmsworth article was published in the issue for October, but there is an earlier reference to a portable Mutoscope in *The Amateur Photographer* for 27 April. Whether this refers to the model just mentioned, or to the Kinora, is impossible to say at this stage. The report simply states that:

> The Biograph Company has decided to form circulating agencies all over the country, by which films for a new patented mutoscope for private use will be exchanged day by day. These machines will only cost some £2 or £3 a year, and will bring to every household who desires to be in touch with a sort of pilgrim's progress, living representations of the stirring events of the moment.[26]

The Kinora (Plate 104) had also appeared on the market about this time, in France, with the names of Casler and Lumière as co-patentees.[27] The pictures were much smaller in size than those for the Mutoscope and the reels were clockwork driven

Plate 103 Royal children and the Mutoscope. Prince Edward, Prince Bertie and Princess Victoria, the children of the Duke of York, in the garden of Marlborough House viewing a home Mutoscope. (*The Harmsworth Magazine*, October 1900, p. 194). *Below*: A similar model now in the Victoria & Albert Museum

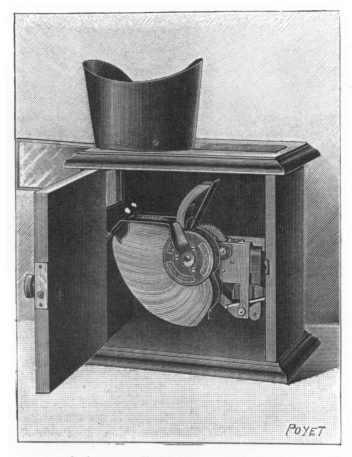

Le kinora. — Vue du mécanisme intérieur.

Plate 104   Le Kinora (Casler-Lumière Patent). This French model was first introduced in 1900. The reels were composed of prints taken from early Lumière films (*La Nature*)

instead of manually operated. The subjects were taken from existing films photographed with the Cinématographe-Lumière. The Kinora was advertised in 1900 by L. Gaumont et Cie, who presumably were responsible for its manufacture;[28] but sometime after the turn of the century, two different models of the apparatus appeared in Britain under the Kinora label, bearing the inscription: 'Kinora Patent Casler-Lumière British Mutoscope and Biograph Co., Ltd, London.' Model 1 (Plate 105) was a combined hand or table instrument, and Model 2 (Plate 106) a double viewer mounted on an ornate pedestal stand.[29] Both models were manually operated and the pictures were formed from existing Biograph films and Mutoscope reels, although much reduced in size. As the years passed, the Kinora enjoyed a considerable vogue and several different models were placed on the market, including a Kinora Camera for those wishing to take their own subjects. By this time however, the enterprise was being conducted under the trade name of Bond's Limited, of 138 New Bond Street, London.[30]

Plate 105   Advertisement issued by the British Mutoscope & Biograph Company, showing the Kinora
Model 1, first introduced in about 1904. From the theatre journal *The Play* (*Barnes Collection*)

Plate 106   The Kinora Model 2. The double lenses allowed two persons to view the pictures at one time. Introduced by the British Mutoscope & Biograph Company in about 1904. The reels were composed of prints from early M&B films (*Barnes Collection*)

Appendix 1

British Films of 1900

Abbreviations

BC	Barnes Collection
BKS	British Kinematograph Society
DF	David Francis
F	Fiction
M & B	Mutoscope & Biograph Co
M & M	Mander & Mitchenson Theatre Collection
NFTVA	National Film and Television Archive
N	News films
N-F	Non-fiction
OMLJ	*Optical Magic Lantern Journal*
PTA	Palace Theatre Archive
RB	Richard Brown
S	Science
SM	Science Museum, London
TM	Theatre Museum, Covent Garden
WTC	Warwick Trading Company

NB   A filmography has since been compiled by Barry Anthony using some of the above sources plus a Company catalogue at the Museum of Modern Art, New York which I have not consulted. Barry Anthony's list is due to appear in R Brown & B Anthony, *The History of the British Mutoscope and Biography Company* (Flicks Books) 1997

BRITISH MUTOSCOPE & BIOGRAPH CO. LTD. (Biograph)

All films 70 mm, unperforated.

This Biograph filmography has been compiled almost entirely from the list of films to be found in the printed programmes of the Palace Theatre, collections of which exist in the Palace Theatre Archive; The Theatre Museum, Covent Garden; the Mander & Mitchenson Theatre Collection; the Barnes Collection; and in various private collections. W.K.-L. Dickson's book *The Biograph in Battle* (London, 1901) has also proved a valuable source, as has also the souvenir booklet, *The War by Biograph*, published by the British Mutoscope and Biograph Co. Ltd (London, 1900), a copy of which has been kindly made available to me by Richard Brown. I have also been greatly aided by Graeme Cruickshank, archivist at the Palace Theatre.

1   ROYAL FUSILIERS STRIKING CAMP NEAR COLENSO (2 January) (N)

Ref: Dickson, *The Biograph in Battle* (London, 1901) p. 104 (1 frame illus.)

2   MARCH PAST OF SOUTH AFRICAN LIGHT HORSE INFANTRY HEADED BY LORD DUNDONALD (2 January) (N)

Ref: Dickson, pp. 104–5

3   LOCOMOTIVE AND CARS BEING ARMOURED IN A NEW WAY (2 January) (N)

Ref: Dickson, pp. 105–6 (1 frame illus.)

4   PANORAMA OF THE UPPER VALLEY OF THE TUGELA (17 January) (N)

Ref: Dickson, p. 124 (1 frame illus.)

5   RECEIVING A MESSAGE BY FLAG (18–24 January) (N)

Ref: Dickson, p. 127 (1 frame illus.)

6   BATTLE OF SPION KOP—AMBULANCE CORPS CROSSING THE TUGELA RIVER (25 January) (N)

'After the Battle of Spion Kop. Red Cross ambulance waggons and coolie stretcher-bearers bringing in the dead and wounded over pontoon bridge.'
Refs: Dickson, p. 130 (1 frame illus.)
   Sandringham programme, 29 June 1900 (SM URB 12/6–2)
   Copy in the NFTVA (Schultze Collection, nos. 12, 40b and 45c)

7   AFTER THE BATTLE—CORTEGES OF STRETCHER BEARERS (25 January) (N)

Ref: Dickson, p. 132 (1 frame illus.)

8   SEIZING A KOPJE NEAR SPION KOP BY LORD DUNDONALD'S TROOPERS (January) (N)

Ref: Palace Theatre programme 6 August 1900. (BC)

9   NAVAL GUNS IN ACTION (6 February) (N)

Ref: Dickson, p. 143 (1 frame illus.)

10   LORD MAYOR AND CITY OFFICIALS ON S.S. 'BRITON' (February) (N)

Ref: Palace Theatre programme, 19 February 1900 (TM)

11   CITY OF LONDON IMPERIAL VOLUNTEERS ON S.S. 'BRITON' (February) (N)

Ref: Palace Theatre programme, 19 February 1900 (TM)

12   IMPERIAL YEOMANRY (PAGET'S HORSE) REVIEWED BY HRH PRINCE OF WALES AT CHELSEA BARRACKS (February) (N)

Ref: Palace Theatre programme, 19 February 1900 (TM)

13   H.M.S. TORPEDO BOAT DESTROYER 'ALBATROSS' (February) (N)

'Steaming at 32 knots an hour on the measured mile off Maplin Bank, Sheerness.'

Refs: Palace Theatre programme, 19 February 1900 (TM)

Sandringham programme, 29 June 1900 (SM)

14   TRANSFERRING WOUNDED FROM RED CROSS WAGGONS TO THE TRAIN AT COLENSO (26 February) (N)

Ref: Dickson, p. 157

15   RELIEF COLUMN, HEADED BY GENERAL BULLER, ENTERING LADYSMITH (3 March) (N)

Ref: Dickson, pp. 170–73 (1 frame illus.)

16   GORDON HIGHLANDERS IN LADYSMITH (3 March) (N)

Ref: Dickson, pp. 170–3 (1 frame illus.)

    Copy in NFTVA

17   BUGLER DUNN AT NETLEY BARRACKS (March) (N)

Ref: Palace Theatre programme, 8 March 1900 (PTA)

18   H.M. THE QUEEN LEAVING WINDSOR CASTLE (March) (N)

Ref: Palace Theatre programme, 19 March 1900 (TM)

19   H.M. THE QUEEN LEAVING BUCKINGHAM PALACE (March) (N)

Ref: Palace Theatre programme, 19 March 1900 (TM)

20   H.M. THE QUEEN REVIEWING THE GUARDS AT BUCKINGHAM PALACE GARDENS (March) (N)

Ref: Palace Theatre programme, 19 March 1900 (TM)

21   NAVAL BRIGADE DRAGGING 4.7 GUNS INTO LADYSMITH (March ?) (N)

Ref: The Era, 28 July 1900, p. 17a

Palace Theatre programme, 6 August 1900 (BC)

Copy in NFTVA

22   THE OXFORD & CAMBRIDGE UNIVERSITY BOAT RACE (31 March) (N)

Ref: Palace Theatre programme, 2 April 1900 (TM)

23   LORD LIEUTENANT OF IRELAND ENTERING PHOENIX PARK (4 April) (N)

Ref: Palace Theatre programme, 28 April 1900 (TM)

24   H.M. THE QUEEN ENTERING PHOENIX PARK (4 April) (N)

Ref: Palace Theatre programme, 28 April 1900 (TM)

25   PRESENTING BOUQUET TO H.M. THE QUEEN IN PHOENIX PARK, DUBLIN (4 April) (N)

'The Queen's visit to Ireland. Children's Review: Presentation of flowers to Her Majesty at Dublin.'

Refs: Sandringham programme, 29 June 1900 (SM)
        The Era, 28 July 1900, p. 17a
        Palace Theatre programme, 6 August 1900 (BC)

26   LANDING OF SIR GEORGE WHITE AT SOUTHAMPTON (April) (N)

Ref: Palace Theatre programme, 28 April 1900 (TM)

27   S.S. 'MINNEAPOLIS' ENTERING LONDON DOCKS (May) (N)

'Arrival off Tilbury Docks (Atlantic Transport Line)'

Ref: Palace Theatre programme, 8 May 1900 (TM)

28   SCENES ON THE HORSE GUARD'S PARADE (7 May) (N)

'Inspection of the Naval Brigade from H.M.S. *Powerful*, by H.R.H. the Prince of Wales and the Lords of the Admiralty.'

Ref: Sandringham programme, 29 June 1900 (SM)

29   LADYSMITH NAVAL BRIGADE AT WINDSOR (May) (N)

Ref: Palace Theatre programme, 8 May 1900 (TM)

30   H.M.S. TORPEDO BOAT DESTROYER 'VIPER' STEAMING 36 KNOTS AN HOUR (Parson's Turbine Company) (May) (N)

Ref: Palace Theatre programme, 15 May 1900. (M & M)
        The Era, 28 July 1900, p. 17a
        Palace Theatre programme, 6 August 1900 (BC)

31   DRAGGING A 6 INCH GUN BY TRACTION ENGINE (12 May) (N)

Ref: Dickson, p. 190.

32   GENERAL KELLY-KENNY AND STAFF REVIEWING TROOPS AT BLOEMFONTEIN (26 May) (N)

Ref: Dickson, p. 204 (1 frame illus.)

33   BOER PRISONERS AT BLOEMFONTEIN—EXERCISE OF WAR PRISONERS (27 May) (N)

Ref: Dickson, p. 207
        Palace Theatre programme, 3 July 1900 (BC)

34   ANNEXATION CEREMONY AT BLOEMFONTEIN (28 May) (N)

'Unfurling the flag—March Past of Howitzer Battery.'

Refs: Dickson, pp. 207–8 (1 frame illus.)
     Palace Theatre programme, 14 August 1900. (London Cinema Museum)
     Copy in the NFTVA

35   BLOEMFONTEIN—UNFURLING THE FLAG (28 May) (N)

'Our new territory, Orange River Colony. Reading the Proclamation of
Annexation and unfurling the Royal Standard in the Square, Bloemfontein.'

Refs: Sandringham programme, 29 June 1900 (SM)
     The Era, 28 July 1900, p. 17a
     Palace Theatre programme, 6 August 1900 (BC)

36   DERBY RACE (30 May) (N)

'HRH the Prince of Wales wins for the second time.'

Ref: Sandringham programme, 29 June 1900 (SM)

37   LORD ROBERTS AND STAFF ON THE OUTSKIRTS OF PRETORIA
(4 June) (N)

Refs: Dickson, p. 237 (1 frame illus.)

The Royal Magazine, vol. 6, 1901, p. 122 (1 frame illus.)

38   RAISING THE FLAG AT PRETORIA (5 June) (N)

'With the flag to Pretoria—The Union Jack being hoisted at Pretoria on the
arrival of Lord Roberts.'

Refs: Dickson, p. 237 (3 frame illus.)
     Palace Theatre programme, 6 August 1900 (BC)
     The Royal Magazine, vol. 16, 1901, p. 121 (1 frame illus.)

39   LORD ROBERTS AND STAFF—FIRST DAY IN PRETORIA AT
HEADQUARTERS (6 June) (N)

'British flag at Pretoria—Lord Roberts and Staff. A courier arrives with
despatches from Heilbron.'

Refs: Dickson, p. 238 (1 frame illus.)
     The Era, 28 July 1900, p. 17a
     Palace Theatre programme, 6 August 1900 (BC)
     The Royal Magazine, vol. 6, 1901, p. 128 (1 frame illus.)

40   PEACE COMMISSIONERS LEAVING PRETORIA BY STAGE-COACH (12
June) (N)

Ref: Dickson, p. 249 (1 frame illus.)

41   LORD ROBERTS AT HIS HEADQUARTERS IN PRETORIA (16 June) (N)

Refs: Dickson, p. 255
     Palace Theatre programme, 6 August 1900 (BC)

42   LORD ROBERTS RECEIVING MAJOR-GENERAL BADEN-POWELL AT PRETORIA (18 June) (N)

Refs: Dickson, p. 262.
     The Era, 28 July 1900, p. 17a
     Palace Theatre programme, 6 August 1900 (BC)

43   YORK AGRICULTURAL SHOW (21 June) (N)

'Their Royal Highnesses the Prince and Princess, Duke of York and Princess Victoria witnessing cattle parade. Champion Shire and Shetlands.'

Refs: Sandringham programme, 29 June 1900 (SM)
     The Era, 28 July 1900, p. 17a
     Palace Theatre programme, 6 August 1900 (BC)

44   HIS ROYAL HIGHNESS THE PRINCE OF WALES OPENING THE CENTRAL LONDON RAILWAY (27 June) (N)

'Arrival of H.R.H. the Prince of Wales at the opening ceremony of the new Central London Electric Railway.'
Refs: Sandringham programme, 29 June 1900 (SM)
     The Era, 28 July 1900, p. 17a
     Palace Theatre programme, 6 August 1900 (BC)

45   TROOPING THE COLOURS—MARCH PAST (June or July) (N)

Ref: Palace Theatre programme, 3 July 1900. (PTA)

46   SIR GEORGE WHITE ARRIVING AT THE NATIONAL BAZAAR (July) (N)

Ref: Palace Theatre programme, 3 July 1900 (PTA)

47   HIS ROYAL HIGHNESS THE PRINCE OF WALES AND GUESTS AT WOLFERTON (July) (N)

Refs: *The Era*, 28 July 1900, p. 17a
     Palace Theatre programme, 6 August 1900 (BC)

48   THE INTERNATIONAL SPORTS (July) (N)

100 Yards Race
120 Yards Hurdle Race
Final of the Quarter Mile
Refs: *The Era*, 28 July 1900, p. 17a
     Palace Theatre programme, 6 August 1900 (BC)

49   GARDEN FÊTES AT SHEEN HOUSE CLUB (July) (N)

Refs: *The Era*, 28 July 1900, p. 17a
     Palace Theatre programme, 6 August 1900 (BC)

50   THE RAZING OF A TALL CHIMNEY SHAFT AT BOLTON (July) (N)

Refs: *The Era*, 28 July 1900, p. 17a
      Palace Theatre programme, 6 August 1900 (BC)

51   THE THREE CHILDREN OF THE DUKE AND DUCHESS OF YORK AT PLAY (July) (N)

Taken in the garden of Marlborough House.
(a) H.R.H. Prince Edward of York (future king of England) playing soldiers.
(b) H.R.H. Prince Edward of York executing 'Manual of Arms' attended by Prince Albert of York and Princess of York.
(c) H.R.H. Prince Edward of York and his army at manoeuvres
Commander-in-Chief, Prince Edward, age 6
Second in Command, Prince Albert, age 4
Hon Colonel, Princess Victoria, age 2
Refs: *The Era*, 28 July 1900, p. 17a
      Palace Theatre programme, 6 August 1900 (BC)
      The Harmsworth Magazine, vol. 5, no. 27 (October 1900) pp. 194–200 (24 frame illus.)
      Copy in the Paul Killiam Archive (The film is included in the TV programme *Movie Museum*)

52   HIS ROYAL HIGHNESS THE PRINCE OF WALES'S HORSE PERSIMMON (August) (N)

Ref: Palace Theatre programme, 6 August 1900. (BC)

53   SWEET NELL OF OLD DRURY—MISS JULIA NEILSON (October) (F)

English Nell: Miss M. Tempest

Ref: Palace Theatre programme, 9 October 1900 (SM)

54   ROYAL DUBLIN SOCIETY'S HORSE SHOW (October) (N)

'The champion jump over stone wall, 5ft 6in high, won by Billy Costello, owner J. D. Lambert.'

Ref: Palace Theatre programme, 6 October 1900 (BC)

55   INSTITUTE OF JOURNALISTS—COMMITTEE AT WORK (October) (M)

Ref: Palace Theatre programme, 6 October 1900. (PTA & BC)

56   MOTOR CAR RACE IN REGENT'S PARK (October) (N)

Ref: Palace Theatre programme, 9 October 1900. (SM)

57   THE 'AURANIA' AT ANCHOR OFF NETLEY (24 October) (N)

Ref: Palace Theatre programme, 12 November 1900 (PTA & BC)

58   VIEW OF THE CITY IMPERIAL VOLUNTEERS ON BOARD (24 October) (N)

Ref: Palace Theatre programme, 12 November 1900. (PTA & BC)

59   COLONEL   MACKINNON,   LORD   ALBERMARLE,   COLONEL
      CHOLMENDEY ON BOARD THE 'AURANIA' (24 October) (N)

      Ref: Palace Theatre programme, 12 November 1900. (BC)

60   THE C.I.V.S DISEMBARKING AT SOUTHAMPTON (29 October) (N)

      Ref: Palace Theatre programme, 12 November 1900 (PTA & BC)

61   THE C.I.V.S PASSING THROUGH HYDE PARK (29 October((N)

      Ref: Palace Theatre programme, 12 November 1900 (PTA)

62   SCENE FROM 'FLORADORA'—"Tell me pretty maidens" (November) (F)

      Ref: Palace Theatre programme, 12 November 1900. (PTA)

63   GENERAL SIR REDVERS BULLER AT SOUTHAMPTON (10 November)
      (N)

      Refs: *Amateur Photographer*, vol. 22, no. 841 (16 November 1900) p. 381.
         Palace Theatre programme, 24 November 1900 (PTA)

64   LORD MAYOR'S PROCESSION (November) (N)

      Ref: Palace Theatre programme, 24 November 1900. (M & M)

65   GENERAL SIR REDVERS BULLER AT ALDERSHOT (November) (N)

      Ref: Palace Theatre programme, 28 November 1900. (BC)

WALTER GIBBONS

1   THE MIDNIGHT SUN (F) Synchronised

      Dir: Walter Gibbons
      L.p.: Vesta Tilley
      Musical number recorded and filmed for the Phono Bio-Tableaux.
      Ref: *The Era*, 26 December 1900, p. 27e

2   ALGY (F) Synchronised

      Dir: Walter Gibbons
      L.p.: Vesta Tilley
      Musical number recorded and filmed for the Phono Bio-Tableaux.
      Ref: *The Era*, 26 December 1900, p. 27e

3   LOUISIANA LOO (F) Synchronised

      Dir: Walter Gibbons
      Lyrics: Leslie Stuart
      L.p.: Vesta Tilley
      Musical number recorded and filmed for the Phono Bio-Tableaux.
      Ref: *The Era*, 26 December 1900, p. 27e

HARRISON & CO

The following films (catalogue nos. 1–55) were taken during a world tour undertaken by E.F.G. Hatch, MP.

1   STREET SCENE IN PEKIN (N-F) 125 ft

    'Showing the quaint conveyances and traffic of a purely native quarter, including a drove of camels; altogether a busy and animated scene likely to remain unique for a very long time, considering the isolation of Pekin.'

    Ref: *The Era*, 25 August 1900, p. 24b

3   PANORAMA TAKEN FROM THE BACK OF A TRAIN MOVING OUT OF LUFA STATION ON THE TIENTSIN TO PEKIN RAILWAY (N-F) 65 ft

    'As the train recedes, the platform is disclosed crowded with Chinese hawkers, flower vendors, &c., who leap on the line and offer their wares to the passengers in another train standing in the station.'

    Ref: *The Era*, 25 August 1900,p. 24b

4   CHINESE FACTORY HANDS (N-F) 65 ft

    Chinese factory hands arriving at a cotton mill, mostly being wheeled in barrows six to the load, and seated sideways—most amusing.'

    Ref: *The Era*, 25 August 1900,p. 24b

5   AN OLD CHINESE WOMAN SPINNING (N-F) 65 ft
    'A most charming picture, and realistic. One of the best pictures ever taken, and bound to be popular.'

    Ref: *The Era*, 25 August 1900,p. 24b

6   CRAFT ON THE CANTON RIVER (N-F) 125 ft

    'A most entertaining and beautiful scene on this celebrated river, on which a large portion of the population of Canton permanently have their home. This film is bound to be a most popular one, and no letterpress or ordinary photograph can possibly give an idea of life on a Chinese river as here shown.'

    Ref: *The Era*, 1 September 1900, p. 28b

7   CHINESE 'PUNCH AND JUDY' SHOW (N-F) 65 ft

    'The attention of the spectators is more directed to the cinematograph at work, to the advantage of the picture taken by it. A good and amusing study of Chinese facial expression.'

    Ref: *The Era*, 1 September 1900, p. 28b

8   8. A CHINESE LAUNDRY (N-F) 65 ft

    'The Celestials are famous washerfolk; they are here seen in their native glory. A good film.'

    Ref: *The Era*, 1 September 1900, p. 28b

9   NATIVE BOAT RACE IN SOUTH CHINA (N) 100 ft

'The rival crews, who row standing and with great energy, get a tremendous pace on their long boats, carrying about a hundred rowers. An exciting and novel scene, showing the race at start and finish.'

Ref: *The Era*, 1 September 1900, p. 28b

10   A CHINESE THEATRE (N-F) 125 ft

'The performers, among whom is the leading actor of China, display great agility in their acting; and numerous sword combats take place, whilst the curious groupings and action keep up the interest to the finish.'

Ref: *The Era*, 15 September 1900, p. 28c

11   PARADE AND EXERCISE OF SIKHS (N-F) 65 ft

'The first regiment of Sikhs which recently forced its way into Pekin is here shown. The men advance towards the camera and then double. An interesting subject at the present moment, and a good representation of the fine body of men who defend our Empire in the east.'

Ref: *The Era*, 15 September 1900, p. 28c

12   COALING A MAN-OF-WAR AT NAGASAKI (N-F) 65 ft

'Another subject of the day, illustrating the operation of coaling with baskets.'

Ref: *The Era*, 15 September 1900, p. 28c

13   SCENE IN COREA [sic] (N-F) 65 ft

'The market place at Chemulpo, one of the treaty ports of Corea. The only film taken of this little known country, and a purely native scene, showing costumes different from those of China or Japan.'

Ref: *The Era*, 15 September 1900, p. 28c

14   CHINESE AT MEAL (N-F) 50 ft

'A capital subject. Four or five grave Celestrials are seated round a table, whilst their host dispenses hospitality in hearty style.'

Ref: *The Era*, 29 September 1900, p. 27c

15   CHINESE IRONING (N-F) 65 ft

'A companion to the laundry scene, No. 8. The work is done in the open street by a portly Chinaman and his assistant. Persons bringing in the washing and passers-by give the scene the necessary animation. As we are about to be invaded by China laundrymen this film and No. 8 are of special interest at the moment, and show there is nothing slip-shod about the Chinaman in dealing with our linen. At the finish an English soldier passes and stops to view the proceedings.'

Ref: *The Era*, 29 September 1900, p. 27c

The Chinese subjects (nos. 1–15) were also listed in an advertisement in *The Optical Magic Lantern Journal* for October 1900 at one shilling per foot. Also advertised was a series of lantern slides of Chinese views (nos. 1–24). I wish to thank John Townsend for kindly bringing this advertisement to my attention.

16   CHINESE MILL-HANDS LEAVING WORK (N-F) 65 ft

'A companion to the very successful No. 4 of our series, the men being searched at the gates by the inspector.'

Ref: *The Era*, 29 September 1900, p. 27c

17   CHINESE RETURNING HOME FROM VANCOUVER (N-F) 50 ft

'The Chinaman, having made his "pile", is seen leaving the train arrived from San Francisco, and numbers make their way in their best clothes, with their baggage, across the line to the Pacific steamer lying alongside the quay.'

Ref: *The Era*, 29 September 1900, p. 27c

16[sic]   VOLUNTEER TURN-OUT AT SHANGHAI (N) 65 ft

'The band, preceded by two batteries, is followed by the regiment and spectators, Chinese and Europeans. This film is interesting from the news that the Volunteers have just been called out for the defence of Shanghai.'

Ref: *The Era*, 13 October 1900, p. 27e

18   VANCOUVER STATION (N-F)

'Passengers, including Chinese, making for the Canadian Pacific steamer for Japan, China, &c'.

Ref: *The Era*, 15 December 1900, p. 32b

19   PANORAMA OF HONG KONG HARBOUR (N-F) 50 ft

'The finest harbour in the world, also now being put into defence against the threatened rising in South China.'

Ref: *The Era*, 13 October 1900, p. 27e

20–30 (No titles available).

31   STATION YARD SCENE AT KIOTO (N-F) 65 ft

'Full of life, with Jinrickshaw hurrying away laden with fares.'

Ref: *The Era*, 15 December 1900, p. 32b

32   RAPIDS AND BOAR SCENE ON JAPANESE RIVER (N-F) 50 ft

'A good picture of seething water.'

Ref: *The Era*, 15 December 1900, p. 32b

34–35   GEISHA DANCERS (N-F) Each 50 ft

Ref: *The Era*, 15 December 1900, p. 32b

36   STREET TOP-SPINNER (N-F) 50 ft

          'A familiar sight in all Japanese towns.'

          Ref: *The Era*, 15 December 1900, p. 32b

37   COMBING RICE (N-F) 65 ft

          'A most artistic picture of a very curious operation and primitive method of
          shucking the grain.'

          Ref: *The Era*, 15 December 1900, p. 32b

SCENES IN A JAPANESE SCHOOL:

38   PROCESSION OF SCHOLARS INTO EXERCISE GROUND (N-F) 50 ft

          Ref: *The Era*, 15 December 1900, p. 32b

39   BOYS AT EXERCISE (N-F) 65 ft

          Ref: *The Era*, 15 December 1900, p. 32b

40   GIRLS PRACTISING EXTENSION MOTIONS (N-F) 65 ft

          'These three subjects (nos. 38, 39 and 40) appeal to the very large class who take
          delight in anything in which little children are concerned. The wistful faces of the
          little Japs are very comical by the earnestness with which they go through their
          exercises, and their lips move in time as they sing some measured song.'

          Ref: *The Era*, 15 December 1900, p. 32b

41   JAPANESE FUNERAL PROCESSION (N) 65 ft

          'Burly Shinto priests pass along in starched vestments, some carrying on trays
          offerings for the ancestors of the departed and others bearing huge paper maces
          and other curious paraphernalia, whilst the magnates are borne along in cumber-
          some conveyances. Interesting all through, and a good steady film.'

          Ref: *The Era*, 15 December 1900, p. 32b

ROCKY MOUNTAIN SERIES (N-F):

50   ENTERING HELL'S GAP AND TUNNEL SCENE. 65 ft

51   PANORAMA OF THE CANADIAN PACIFIC RAILWAY THROUGH THE
          ROCKIES, NEAR HOPE. 65 ft

52   DITTO, NEAR MISSION. 65 ft

53   PANORAMA ALONG THE SELKIRKS. 65 ft

54   RECEDING TRAIN IN THE ROCKIES. 65 ft

55   TRANS-CONTINENTAL EXPRESSES WITH 'TOUR ROUND THE WORLD' PASSENGERS BOUND FOR THE FAR EAST. 80 ft

Ref: *The Era*, 15 December 1900, p. 32b

BOXERS SACKING A MISSIONARY STATION (F) 87 ft (?)

This is almost certainly the same film issued by J. Wrench & Son as Attack on a Mission Station, q.v.

Refs: *The Era*, 11 August 1900, p. 27e

  The Era, 14 July 1900, p. 24e

LATE KING OF ITALY (N)

Ref: *The Era*, 11 August 1900, p. 27e

COAL-MINING SCENE (N-F)

Ref: *The Era*, 11 August 1900, p. 27e

HOP O' MY THUMB (F) 350 ft

'New pantomime film. The fairy tale of "Hop o' My Thumb", in twenty tableaux, with dissolving effects.'

Production: unknown (French ?)

For synopsis see the same film issued by the Micrograph Co. Ltd.

Refs: *The Era*, 22 September 1900, p. 27d

  The Era, 15 December 1900, p. 32b

A GALLANT RESCUE (September) (F) 100 ft

'A fisherman, in landing a gigantic fish, falls off a barge into the water. The dock-keeper, divesting himself of his coat and waistcoat, plunges after him. Presently the fisherman emerges the same way as he fell in, and is followed out of the water by his rescuer feet foremost. The dock-keeper puts on his numerous clothing and the fisherman warmly embraces his heroic preserver.

They depart arm-in-arm to refresh.

New reversing film (most laughable, absurd).

Note. This film is run straight through, and needs no rewinding to produce the reverse effect.'

Ref: *The Era*, 6 October 1900, p. 28c

THE PARIS EXHIBITION (N)

Ref: *The Era*, 11 August 1900, p. 27e

HAYDON & URRY LIMITED

GRENADIER GUARDS LEAVING FOR THE TRANSVAAL (January) (N)

Ref: *The Era*, 6 January 1900, p. 7a

20th BATTERY ROYAL HORSE ARTILLERY IN KHARKI LEAVING FOR THE TRANSVAAL (January) (N)

Ref: *The Era*, 6 January 1900, p. 7a

QUEEN VICTORIA LEAVING NETLEY HOSPITAL AFTER VISITING THE WOUNDED SOLDIERS RETURNED FROM SOUTH AFRICA (11 November) (N) 75 ft

Ref: *The Era*, 26 January 1901, p. 26c

QUEEN VICTORIA IN HER STATE CARRIAGE DURING A ROYAL PROCESSION   (Date uncertain) (N) 75 ft

Ref: *The Era*, 26 January 1901, p. 26c

CECIL M. HEPWORTH (HEPWIX FILMS)

Hepworth began film production in 1899 and each film was catalogued and numbered chronologically, starting with the numeral 1. He continued this practice for a number of years, so it is relatively easy to assign any one film to a particular year. Films with numbers in the range 1 to 77 were made in 1899; those in the range 78 to 227, in 1900; and so on.

The Hepworth films, or 'Hepwix' films as they were soon to be called, were sold through agents, firstly the Warwick Trading Company and then L. Gaumont & Co., and John Wrench & Son. WTC issued the Hepwix films with the serial numbers in the 2000 range, but the original Hepworth numbering was retained in the last numerals. For example WTC no. 2077 is equivalent to Hepworth no. 77. Gaumont, I believe, retained the numbers originally assigned to them by Hepworth, as Wrench may also have done. Hepworth published a catalogue in October 1900, which does not seem to have survived. However, a catalogue of 1903 in the British Film Institute, includes a number of films made in previous years. It is from this that most of the descriptions below are taken.

78   THAMES RIVER SCENERY—UNDER STAINES BRIDGE (Date uncertain) (N-F) 50 ft

'This photograph is a panoramic view of the scenery of the River in the neighbourhood of Staines. Several boat houses and boat-building sheds are passed, and the picture finishes as the steam launch from which it is taken glides past the Bridge Hotel, and under the old stone bridge.'

Ref: Hepworth catalogue 1903, p. 19.

79   THAMES RIVER SCENERY—MAGNA CHARTA ISLAND AND PANORAMA OF HOUSE BOATS (Date uncertain) (N-F) 100 ft

'The scenery here represented is higher up the River, and of a more pastoral character than the last. The beautifully wooded island opposite Runnymede, on which King John signed the Magna Charta, is shown throughout its length, and a very picturesque little cottage is said to have been built upon the site where the great charta was signed. The latter portion of the picture shows a long panorama of a great number of beautifully decorated house-boats of all designs and sizes.

Flags are fluttering from the roofs and numerous fishing parties are rapidly passed. The effect of the sunlight on the rippling water is very beautifully rendered, and the scene is one of much interest and animation.'

Ref: Hepworth catalogue 1903, p. 19
   Copy in the NFTVA (925)

80–84   (No titles available).

85   S.S. 'NEW YORK' LEAVING SOUTHAMPTON DOCKS (January) (N) 50 ft

'This magnificent vessel, one of the largest of the "Ocean Greyhounds", makes an imposing picture as she glides majestically by, overhauling and leaving behind the stout little tug which has pulled her out of the dock.'

Ref: Hepworth catalogue 1903, p. 20

86   C.I.V.S MARCHING ABOARD S.S. 'GARTH CASTLE' (13 January) (N) 75 ft

'An excellent photograph showing the first detachment of the City of London Imperial Volunteers (the Lord Mayor's Own) stepping aboard the ship which is to convey them to the seat of war. By kind permission, this photograph was taken from a commanding position on the deck of the vessel, just facing the gangway over which the Volunteers pass. The men pass so close that every face is an actual portrait, and every detail of their uniform is plainly visible.'

Ref: Hepworth catalogue 1903, p. 20

87–92   (No titles available).

93   ANIMATED CARTOON. 'WIPING SOMETHING OFF THE SLATE' (F) 75 ft

'At the opening of this picture clouds of smoke rolling away, reveal the figure of a "gentleman in kharki" near a huge slate, on which the word "Majuba" is written, and over which the Boer flag proudly waves. The British soldier tears down this emblem, trampling it underfoot, and goes aside for a moment to fetch some water in his helmet. Then, with the bedraggled, saturated flag, he wipes the offensive word from the slate. He has just finished this, when a shell bursting near, wounds him in the temple. Almost fainting, he yet manages to bind up the wound, pick up his rifle and to take up position at the "ready" in the well known pose of "The Absent-Minded Beggar". The wound, however, proves too much and he staggers and falls just as the Union Jack floats out behind him, forming a striking background to the picture.'

Ref: Hepworth catalogue 1903, p. 20

94   NEW 'TRICK' FILM. 'THE CONJUROR AND THE BOER.' (F) 75 ft

'This is a patriotic 'trick' film of a very interesting and highly popular nature. A conjuror enters and advancing to the footlights, requires a gentleman to come up from the audience, who proves to be a typical Boer. The conjuror then borrows a lady's handkerchief, which he rolls up in his hands for a moment and unfolding it, shows it to be changed into a Union Jack. The small flag then grows in the conjuror's hands until it is sufficient to entirely envelope the Boer, which last operation is performed much to the victim's disgust. A moment after, the big flag is removed, and the Boer is seen to have changed to a figure of Britannia, who rises from the seat, hangs up the flag on her trident and waves it backwards and forwards, so that it covers almost the entire stage. At the same moment, the conjuror transforms himself into a puff of smoke, which rapidly disperses, while the words "Rule Britannia" appear in large letters all along the bottom of the picture.'

Ref: Hepworth catalogue 1903, pp. 20–21

95   (No title available).

96   THE QUEEN'S VISIT TO DUBLIN, ROYAL PROCESSION ENTERING THE CITY GATES (4 April) (N) 125 ft

'This is one of the finest procession photographs ever made. The scene shows the gaily decorated streets lined with soldiers, and in the background is a realistic representation of the ancient city gate of Dublin. The gates are thrown open by the Beefeaters in attendance, and the Royal procession of several carriages and the Queen's body-guard, etc., pass through. As the last carriage showing Her Majesty, comes into the field of view, the crowds cheer enthusiastically and wave handkerchiefs and hats in great excitement.'

Refs: Hepworth catalogue 1903, p. 21
      The Era, 26 January 1901, p. 31c

97   (No title available).

98   RECEPTION OF THE MAYOR AND CORPORATION (N) (4 April) 75 ft

'The Queen's carriage is here seen drawn up in front of the space where the Lord Mayor and Corporation are waiting to present Her Majesty with the keys of the City. This ceremony is proceeded with amidst enthusiastic cheering on the part of the crowd all round, which, with the restless movements of the many horses and the continual fluttering of the bunting in the breeze, makes up a scene full of animation and life. At the conclusion of the ceremony the Queen's carriage drives off and is immediately followed by mounted soldiers who bring up the rear of the procession.'

Refs: The Era, 26 January 1900, p. 31c

99–100   (No titles available).

101   H.M.S. 'POWERFUL' ARRIVING IN PORTSMOUTH HARBOUR (24 April) (N) 50 ft

'This photograph was taken from the pier at Portsmouth, and has for a background Nelson's Flag Ship, the Victory, gaily decorated with bunting in honour of the home-coming of the modern war vessel. The Powerful is bringing home those heroes who fought so well and so successfully at Ladysmith, to whom indeed the credit for preventing the fall of that gallant garrison should be accorded. As the famous war ship passes slowly into the harbour an excellent panoramic view of the vessel is obtained.'

Refs: Hepworth catalogue 1903, p. 21
    Copy in the NFTVA (N.78)

102–103   (No titles available)

104   PANORAMA OF THE PARIS EXHIBITION (N) 50 ft

'This photograph was taken from a very swiftly moving steamboat travelling close by one bank of the river Seine, so that an excellent panoramic picture of the other bank is obtained. The photograph starts with the extreme end of the Exhibition frontage by the Place de la Concorde, and shows several of the buildings of the Rue des Nations. The stereoscopic effect of the buildings passed is very fine.'

Ref: Hepworth catalogue 1903, pp. 21–2
    Copy in the NFTVA (N.79)

105   PANORAMA OF THE PARIS EXHIBITION. No.2 (N) 50 ft

'This is a continuation of the previous picture, and shows several of the most picturesque pavilions in the Rue des Nations. At times the intervals between the buildings afford glimpses into the most distant portions of the Exhibition, and this photograph gives a good general idea of the appearance of this vast Fair.'

Ref: Hepworth catalogue 1903, p. 22

106   PANORAMA OF THE PARIS EXHIBITION. No. 3 (N) 100 ft

'The remainder of the entire river front of the Exhibition is beautifully portrayed in this photograph. The boat passes under several of the well-known bridges of the Seine, and many of the new temporary bridges erected for the purposes of the Exhibition. Buildings of all descriptions are seen; from the Eiffel Tower and the wonderful erection forming the Schneider exhibit, to the merest palace of amusement, and marvellous, stereoscopic relief is yielded by the buildings, at different distances, passing one another at varying rates. Crowds of sightseers are seen walking about, and the numerous steamboats on the river lend extra animation to the beautiful scene.'

Ref: Hepworth catalogue 1903, p. 22
    Copy in the NFTVA (D. 69177)

107   (No title available).

108   THE SOLAR ECLIPSE (28 May) (N) (S) 75 ft

'The only Cinematograph Representation of an Eclipse on the market. It shows first the constantly narrowing sun's crescent. Then totality is reached and the corona is seen in all its brilliancy and beauty, and finally the sun's disc reappears at the other side.'

Refs: Hepworth catalogue 1903, p. 22

Optical Magic Lantern Journal, vol. 11, no. 136 (September 1900), pp. 110–12; 119–20

Hepworth, *Came the Dawn* (London, 1951) pp. 48–49 & illustration

109–110   (No titles available).

111   STREET SCENE IN ALGIERS (May) (N-F) 50 ft

'A very characteristic view of one of the streets in the Arab quarter of this remarkable town. The natives are seen passing and repassing and conversing together quite naturally, in spite of their abhorrence of being photographed, for the camera was concealed in a specially selected building.'

Refs: Hepworth catalogue 1903, p. 22
Hepworth, *Came the Dawn*, p. 49

112   TANGIER—THE LANDING STAGE (May) (N-F) 50 ft

'A remarkable scene, showing a group of tourists mounting mules preparatory to a jaunt in this very Oriental town. The Moors and Arabs surround them on all sides, gesticulating wildly in their efforts to arrange terms to their own satisfaction, makeing [sic] up a scene of great confusion and liveliness.'

Refs: Hepworth catalogue 1903, p. 23
Hepworth, *Came the Dawn*, p. 49

113   TANGIER—THE MARKET PLACE (May) (N-F) 50 ft

'This is a very remarkable picture considering the great difficulties there are in photographing Moors and Arabs. The picture shows the Market Place, Tangier, on market day, one of the most curious Oriental scenes to be found anywhere.'

Refs: Hepworth catalogue 1903, p. 23
Hepworth, *Came the Dawn*, p. 49

114   PILLOW FIGHT ON THE S.Y. 'ARGONAUT' (May) (N-F) 50 ft

'For the purpose of this sport a spar is stretched across the deck, at a suitable height, and the combatants take their places, one at either end, sitting astraddle upon it. Each is provided with a pillow, with which he vigorously attacks his opponent, with the result that, as they are quite unsupported, one or other—or more often both—swing round head downwards before many blows have been struck. In this picture the fighters are speedily set up again by friendly hands, and they renew the onslaught with redoubled vigour every time they are upset.'

Refs: Hepworth catalogue 1903, p. 23
Hepworth, *Came the Dawn*, p. 49

115   COCK FIGHT ON THE S.Y. 'ARGONAUT' (May) (N-F) 75 ft

'A very interesting and exciting deck sport. A ring is chalked upon the deck, and around it the non-combatant passengers group themselves, eager to see the fun. The belligerents are "trussed" in the approved fashion, and, aided or hindered, as the case may be, by the rolling of the vessel, one speedily succeeds in rolling another out of the ring. A fresh pair immediately take the place of the last couple and the fighting is resumed. Again and again this happens, and the picture is full of excitement and animation, and is very comic and interesting.'

Refs: Hepworth catalogue 1903, p. 23

Hepworth, *Came the Dawn*, p. 49

'NOTE. The films, Nos. 108–115 inclusive, were taken during a Mediterranean cruise on the steam yacht "Argonaut", to view the Solar Eclipse at Algiers.'

116   EXPRESS TRAINS AT DAWLISH (N-F) 50 ft

'Visitors to this beautiful watering place will remember how the railway line runs along the sea-wall for a considerable distance. This photograph embraces a view of the portion of the sea-wall, with visitors walking about, and shows the passing of two express trains, one in either direction. The trains are travelling very rapidly, and there is a beautiful effect of clouds of steam issuing from the funnels of the engines. The picture forms an attractive variation to the usual run of train films.'

Refs: Hepworth catalogue 1903, pp. 23–4.

Amateur Photographer (12 October 1900), p. 295

117   EXPRESS TRAIN AND SLIP CARRIAGE (N-F) 50 ft

'In this photograph an important station on a main line is shown; a very rapid through train is seen coming towards the camera and dashing past, and as the dust raised by it clears away, the slip carriages are seen coming on behind. These carriages are pulled up in full view, and a large number of passengers dismount. A very interesting station scene.'

Ref: Hepworth catalogue 1903, p. 24

118–123   (No titles available).

124   BREAKING WAVES (N-F) 50 ft

'Of all the myriads of subjects which have come within the ken of the cinematographic lens, none is more beautifully shown than the breaking waves on the seashore. In this picture, which was taken on an exposed portion of the coast during a gale, wave after wave is seen rolling in towards the camera, and curling over and dashing itself into clouds of spray upon the shingle. In the distance the white-crested waves are roaring and tossing in their wild race for the shore, and ever and again a tuft is torn off by the gale and carried off in fine blinding spray.'

Refs: Hepworth catalogue 1903, p. 24.

  Amateur Photographer (12 October 1900), p. 295

125   DOVER PIER IN A STORM (N-F) 75 ft

'The Admiralty Pier at Dover has withstood the onslaught of many a furious sea, for it is in an exceedingly exposed portion of the coast. In this photograph the waves are seen dashing furiously against it, and slashing themselves into a frenzy as they career madly towards the beach, and on the beach they wreak their vengeance, dashing stones and seaweed into the air, while the fine blinding spray is torn away in filmy clouds. This is an exceedingly fine picture of breaking waves.'

Ref: Hepworth catalogue 1903, p. 24

126   ROUGH SEA (N-F) 100 ft

'This is another view, taken in a somewhat similar position, and shows a portion of the Admiralty Pier as seen during the onslaught of a very heavy sea. In this case the sunlight is reflected by the crest of every wave as it dashes on towards the spectator, and the gleam of the sunbeams on the dancing water lends additional beauty to the scene. At the foot of the pier are big masses of seaweed torn up and cast ashore by the fierce waves, and the effect of the white foamy water dashing upon these dark masses of weed, while the sunlight makes silver tracery on the walls of every wave, is very beautiful and fascinating.'

Ref: Hepworth catalogue 1903, pp. 24–5
    Copy in the NFTVA (D 69175).

127   (No title available).

128   THE PUNTER'S MISHAP (F) 75 ft

'This is a very comic photograph representing an accident which happened to a man who, though inexperienced, thought he would have no difficulty in punting. So confident was he that he asked a couple of ladies to go with him on a trial trip, and the picture opens as the boat starts along a wonderfully picturesque little backwater of the Upper Thames. The ladies have just settled down to comfortably enjoy their expedition, and the punter, proud in the assurance of his fancied skill, has just waved his hat and bowed to the audience when he becomes aware that the punt pole is firmly stuck in the mud. His endeavours to drag it out again, while the punt gradually drifts farther and farther away, are very amusing, and as he is obliged bit by bit to shift his position on the boat, and come farther every moment towards its edge as it glides from under his feet, it is easy to see what must ultimately happen. In the end a last despairing pull proves too much for the punter's equilibrium, and he falls heavily into the water, clinging tightly to the pole, while the punt and its frightened occupants drift rapidly away. The picture finishes with the struggles of the unfortunate young man as he flounders out of the mud towards the shore.'

Refs: Hepworth catalogue 1903, p. 25.
    Hepworth, *Came the Dawn*, p. 44
    The Era, 24 November 1900, p. 27(e)

129   THE GUNPOWDER PLOT (F) 50 ft

'Scene, a country garden. Enter an old man carrying a canvas chair, which he places to his satisfaction in a quiet corner and settles himself with a book for a comfortable afternoon. But the heat proves oppressive, the book drops from his fingers, and he falls asleep. A mischievous boy next enters, carrying in his hand a very formidable Chinese cracker; this he places surreptitiously under the chair, and after quietly lighting the fuse he runs away. There is a few moments pause and then a terrific explosion, and as the smoke clears away it is found that the chair and occupant have entirely disappeared. A few moments more and they begin to come down in bits, first an arm and leg, and then the bits of the chair and the remainder of the body fall through the air on the scene of the explosion.'

Ref: Hepworth catalogue 1903, p. 25
   The Era, 24 November 1900, p. 27e

130   EXPLOSION OF A MOTOR CAR (F) 100 ft

Driver: C.M. Hepworth
Passengers: HV Lawley and his brother
'This is a somewhat similar scene to the last, but of a much more elaborate description. The picture opens with a view of a quiet country road, with, in the distance coming rapidly forward, a motor car with four passengers. The car comes along at a high speed, and its occupants, recognising friends, wave and raise their hats, until, just as the carriage comes to the centre of the picture there is a sudden mishap, followed by a big explosion which entirely wrecks the motor car and blows the passengers high into the air. A policeman rushes to the spot, and seeing nothing but wreckage of machinery, searches in the sky with a telescope; he soon sees the bodies falling down, and only runs away in time to escape being hit. When all the pieces have fallen to the ground he comes up again and collects them in to classes—so many legs, so many arms, etc., and we lose sight of him as he enters the results in his official note-book. A bewildering trick film full of comic interest.'

Refs: *The Era*, 24 November 1900, p. 27e
   Hepworth catalogue 1903, pp. 25–26
   BKS Proceedings, pp. 10–11
   Copy in the NFTVA (F 181)
   (Plate 22)

131   (No title available).

132   THE EGG-LAYING MAN (F) 75 ft

'In this film the entire field of view is filled by the head and shoulders of a man, who, at the commencement of the picture is smoking a cigarette. After making a few comic grimaces which clearly reveal the fact that his mouth is empty, he seems to be in considerable difficulty with something swelling up in it, which, in a few moments, turns out to be an egg, and this he takes from between his lips immediately after, in full view of the audience. Another egg commences to protrude, and so on, until five eggs are lying on the table before him. Then, resuming his cigarette, he proceeds to break one of the eggs into a cup, but, in spite of the fact that it would seem to have been newly laid, the odour is so powerful as to overcome the man and bring the picture to an end.'

Refs: Hepworth catalogue 1903, p. 26
   The Era, 24 November 1900, p. 27e

133–135   (No titles available).

136   HOW IT FEELS TO BE RUN OVER (September) (F) 50 ft.

'The eccentric artist Wiertz has powerfully depicted the supposed feelings of a decapitated head, but it has remained for the cinematographer to show large audiences what it feels like to be run over. In this very sensational picture a pretty country road is seen, and in the distance a dog-cart travelling at a fair speed. The road is narrow, but the cart successfully passes, and as the dust which it raised clears away, a motor car is seen approaching very rapidly indeed. Perhaps it is the dust of the previous vehicle, or perhaps sheer carelessness on the part of the driver, but he does not see the obstruction in the road until it is too late to steer past it. The car comes forward at tremendous speed, and the occupants, realising the danger, get wildly excited in their efforts to clear the obstruction. The steersman makes one or two frantic swerves and is seen to apply the brake with all his might, but to no purpose, the car dashes full into the spectator, who sees "stars" as the picture comes to an end.'

Refs: *Amateur Photographer*, vol. 32, no. 836 (12 October 1900), p. 295
      The Era, 29 December 1900, p. 31c
      Hepworth catalogue 1903, p. 26
      Copy in the NFTVA (F 652)
      (Plate 23)

137   THE ECCENTRIC DANCER (F) 50 ft

'The interest of this picture, which is an extremely comic one, bears upon an entirely new trick in cinematography. The scene is of a room, through the door of which a clown enters in a very peculiar manner. He dances about and cuts screamingly funny capers, which are utterly bewildering in their peculiar novelty. This film is one which is bound to produce roars of laughter wherever shown.'

Refs: *The Era*, 29 December 1900, p. 31c
      Hepworth catalogue 1903, pp. 26–27

138   THE BATHERS (REVERSING FILM) (F) 100 ft

'The first half of this film is devoted to an ordinary representation of a couple of bathers who arrive at the river's brink and take off their clothes, throwing them down in reckless disorder. Underneath they wear bathing suits, and when they have arrived at this stage they each take a header into the water. Scarcely have they done so, however, when the action is reversed, and the men are seen to be leaving the water feet first. After performing a graceful curve in the air they land on their feet, dry, and their clothes are seen to be flying up into their hands, one by one, producing an effect which is weird and extremely comic.'

Refs: *The Era*, 29 December 1900, p. 31c
      Hepworth catalogue 1903, p. 27

1139–141   (No titles available).

142   GREASY POLE COMPETITION (N) 100 ft

'There can be no doubt that by far the most comic and laughable item on the programme of an up-river Regatta, is the competition in walking the greasy pole A scaffold pole is placed in a horizontal position, over deep water, smeared with grease, and the competitors have to walk from one end to the other to win the prize. Many of them fall off almost immediately, others get half-way before their feet slip and they are precipitated in all sorts of strange attitudes into the water below. There are dozens of attempts within the compass of this one film, which is very comic and laughable.'

Refs: *The Era*, 29 December 1900, p. 31c
   Hepworth catalogue 1903, p. 27

143   (No title available).

144   WALKING THE GREASY POLE (N) 75 ft

'This is a similar subject to the above, but taken from an entirely different point of view. The photograph is taken from the shore, looking out across the river, and the figures are seen very much larger, in their frantic struggles to walk the pole. Here again there are many gallant attempts to reach the coveted goal, but they all result in a ducking of a more or less grotesque character.'

Ref: Hepworth catalogue 1903, p. 27

145   WALKING THE GREASY POLE, FURTHER EFFORTS (N) 50 ft

'This is a similar picture to the last, to which it may with advantage be joined if a longer film is required. It shows the renewed efforts of the competitors to reach the flag at the further extremity of the pole, and their attempts to traverse this inconvenient bridge are as ludicrous as their gestures are extraordinary.'

Refs: *The Era*, 29 December 1900, p. 31c
Hepworth catalogue 1903, pp. 27–28

146   THE BEGGAR'S DECEIT (F) 50 ft

'In this photograph—which may be described as a translation of a famous French film—a cripple is seen laboriously propelling himself along the pavement on a little trolley, as he has lost the use of his legs. In the distance a policeman is walking slowly up the street. Numerous passers-by, taking pity on the beggar's apparent plight, show their sympathy in a substantial manner, and the cripple appears to be reaping a good harvest, when the policeman comes up with him. The constable suspecting something wrong, taps the man on the shoulder, and the man being seized with a sudden fright, springs up and takes to his heels right down the street with marvellous rapidity. The policeman hardly expecting such a result to his enquiries, starts off in pursuit, but is handicapped at the commence-ment by falling heavily over the beggar's deserted trolley. He is a corpulent man, but he gets to his feet again with considerable agility, and tears off down the street after the retreating figure of the fraudulent beggar.'

Ref: Hepworth catalogue 1903, p. 28

147   (No title available).

148   THE BURNING STABLE (F) 100 ft

'This is a very interesting and exciting representation of a burning stable, the rescue of the horses from the flames, and the salvage of carts, carriages, etc. In the opening, the smoke and the flames are seen to be appearing from the doors of the stables, and a number of men rush in to rescue the property. As they are running out the carts, other men come upon the scene and bring a number of buckets to a pump in the foreground, and carry them full to pour on the flames; while two firemen direct a stream of water from a hose upon the burning building. Lastly, the horses from the inner stables are led, unwillingly, through the smoke to the outer air—it being necessary in some cases to envelope their heads in a sack before they will pass the fire.'

Refs: *The Era*, 29 December 1900, p. 31c
   Hepworth catalogue 1903, p. 28

149–150   (No titles available).

151   THE TOPSY-TURVY VILLA (F) 75 ft

'A very remarkable cinematograph trick of an entirely novel character is here successfully carried out. In a well-furnished kitchen the cook is seen walking about, only she is walking on the ceiling instead of on the floor. A small boy, also moving in the strange manner, is cuffed by the cook for some offence, and swears revenge as he climbs out over the lintel of the door. Next a policeman enters in much the same way, and while flirting with the cook is seen by the small boy, who reports the irregularity to the mistress of the house. That lady, also walking on the ceiling, comes rapidly into the apartment, and chases the policeman and his sweetheart round the room. The effect produced by this strange trick of animated photography is very curious and remarkable.'

Ref: *The Era*, 29 December 1900, p. 31c

152   C.I.V.S KILLING TIME ON THEIR VOYAGE HOME (October) (N) 50 ft

'After their exciting and heroic adventures in the Transvaal, the C.I.V.s found the time hang heavily on their hands during their voyage from Cape Town to Southampton. This photograph, taken on the upper deck of the *Aurania*, shows the men engaged in playing quoits. An interesting and pleasing picture.'

Refs: Hepworth catalogue 1903, p. 28.
   The Era, 29 December 1900, p. 31c
   The Showman, December 1900, p. 3 (advert)

153   C.I.V.S PLAYING LEAP-FROG (October) (N) 50 ft

'The excitement of deck quoits palls after a while upon anybody, and in this photograph the C.I.V.s are seen engaged in the more boisterous pastime of leapfrog, and they appear to thoroughly enjoy the exercise.'

Refs: Hepworth catalogue 1903, p. 29
   The Showman, December 1900, p. 3
   The Era, 3 November 1900, p. 31a

154   (No title available).

155   C.I.V.S DISEMBARKING AT SOUTHAMPTON (29 October) (N) 75 ft

'London's brave citizen soldiers step for the first time upon their native soil after their perilous sojourn in the Transvaal. No sooner does the *Aurania*, which has brought these brave soldiers from Cape Town, draw up to the quay, then the gangways are placed across and the men run gladly ashore. In this photograph, although it was of necessity taken early in the morning, the men are splendidly defined, and the photograph is a really excellent one of a most interesting subject. The faces can be very clearly seen and easily recognised by those who are familiar with them.'

Refs: *The Era*, 3 November 1900, p. 31a
    The Showman, December 1900, p. 3

156   TRAIN LOAD OF C.I.V.S LEAVING SOUTHAMPTON FOR LONDON (29 October) (N) 50 ft

'On disembarking from the *Aurania* the City Volunteers immediately entrained for London. This photograph shows the train steaming along the quays at Southampton immediately after taking in its load of soldiers. The train is drawn by a gaudily decorated engine bearing the magic letters C.I.V., and as it steams past the men lean out of their windows and wave their hats and shout merrily to their acquaintances on the quay.'

Refs: Hepworth catalogue 1903, p. 29
    The Showman, December 1900, p. 3

'The following four films were taken from a special position in Hyde-park, commanding a view along the Edgware-road, and they show the procession coming forward from the extreme distance and turning round right in the foreground of the picture. The views are all most effective, and are at the same time very picturesque and beautiful representations of an unique ceremony.'

157   C.I.V. PROCESSION. THE BATTERY (29 October) (N) 75 ft

'This film shows the earlier portion of the procession, consisting of the C.I.V. Battery and the mounted infantry. First come the men belonging to the Battery, with their khaki-coloured gun carriages, &c. They are followed by the Bands of the London Rifle Brigade, the Victoria and St George's Rifles, the Inns of Court Rifles, and the Pipers and Buglers of the London Scottish. Following these, again, comes a portion of the C.I.V. Mounted Infantry. An exceedingly beautiful effect is obtained where the men wheel round a refuge in the roadway and come right past in the foreground of the picture.'

Refs: *The Era*, 3 November 1900, p. 31a
    The Showman, December 1900, p. 3

158   C.I.V. PROCESSION. CYCLISTS AND INFANTRY (29 October) (N) 100 ft

'In this photograph the procession in London is excellently reproduced. Follow-ing the massed bands of the Civil Service Rifles, the Queen's Westminsters, and the Artists, comes a little group of volunteers with their kharki-coloured cycles which have done such excellent service in the Transvaal. Immediately behind them march the first half of the C.I.V. Battalion, chatting, and laughing, and smoking, and seemingly quite indifferent to the tumultuous cheering of the huge crowds on either side of the roadway. In their midst proudly marched a trooper who carried the flag of the late United Dutch Republic, the flag which was captured by the C.I.V.s at Jacobsdaal.'

Refs: Hepworth catalogue 1903, p. 29
   The Showman, December 1900, p. 3 (advert)
   The Era, 3 November 1900, p. 31a

159   (No title available).

160   C.I.V. PROCESSION—SECOND HALF OF THE BATTALION (29 October) (N) 100 ft

'This photograph opens as the band of the 21st Middlesex is passing into the picture. Immediately behind follows the band of the 1st Middlesex, and then, marching steadily and splendidly together, come several hundreds of the brave City Imperial Volunteers. This photograph having been taken at an early portion of the route, the procession passes exactly as it was originally formed, for it had not yet felt the stress of the too eager crowds which a little later on transformed it into a struggling line of soldiers.'

Refs: *The Era*, 3 November 1900, p. 31a
   The Showman, December 1900, p. 3

161   (No title available).

162   C.I.V. PROCESSION—THE SICK AND WOUNDED (29 October) (N) 50 ft

'Last, but very far from least, in this memorable procession, came the invalids, marching steadily and bravely after their more fortunate brothers, and, indeed, only distinguishable from them by the fact that they carried no arms, and immediately after them came the char-a-bancs carrying those of the sick and wounded who were unable to march with the others. The rear of the procession is brought up by the Life Guards.
This last film is of intrinsic interest, and its great variety makes a very pleasing and effective film.'

Refs: *The Era*, 3 November 1900, p. 31a
   The Showman, December 1900, p. 3

163   EXPRESS TRAIN (N-F) 50 ft

In this photograph, which was taken at Dawlish, where the railway runs alongside the sea wall, a train is seen rushing towards the camera at express speed, the clouds of steam emitted by the engine as it passes adding considerably to the beauty of the effect. Some tourists who happen to be on the wall at the time add human interest to the picture, which is an exciting example of railroad photography.'

   Ref: Hepworth catalogue 1903, p. 29.

THE BRITISH ARMY:

164   SWORD v. SWORD (N-F) 50 ft

'A competition between two mounted Dragoon Guards, who slash at one another furiously with fencing sticks. The excellent control which the competitors exercise over their well trained steeds is admirably shown in the photograph, which is one full of interest and movement. The judges stand around, and stop the competition whenever a hit is scored, in order that the marks may be duly awarded.'

Ref: Hepworth catalogue 1903, p. 30

165   LEMON CUTTING COMPETITION (N-F) 50 ft

'The principal objects in the field of view are a couple of gallows-like arrangements, from whose projecting arms lemons are suspended by a wire. The competitors—who are beautifully mounted—gallop at lightning pace from the distance towards the camera, and as they pass each lemon they slash at it; cutting the first one with a forward stroke, and the second with a back-handed sweep with their swords. The lemons are then replaced, and another competitor enters the arena. The very rapid movements of the horses, the clouds of dust raised by their feet, and the skilfully contested competition, makes up a subject which is of high interest.'

Ref: Hepworth catalogue 1903, p. 30

166   (No title available).

167   TENT PEGGING COMPETITION (N-F) 50 ft

'The first three competitors in this contest do not succeed in capturing the tent peg with their lances as their horses carry them at break-neck speed along the course, although the third man knocks the peg out of position. It is immediately replaced by the attendant, and the remaining competitors all succeed in impaling the peg upon the end of their lances as they rush past.'

Ref: Hepworth catalogue 1903, p. 30

168   GALLOPING COMPETITION (N-F) 50 ft

'A team of six horses drawing a five-pounder gun, with its equipment mounted on a separate carriage, have to gallop round the field and pass between two posts, which are only just far enough apart to allow of the passage of the gun carriage. The horses perform their part under the leadership of a Commissioned Officer and three other drivers of the R.H.A., with such exactitude that the posts are never displaced, although the competitors traverse the field in rapid succession.'

Ref: Hepworth catalogue 1903, p. 30.

169–170 (No titles available).

171   FENCING—SWORD V. SWORD, DISMOUNTED (N-F) 50 ft

'This is an excellent bit of fencing between two men who are evidently masters of their craft. The blows are well delivered and as cleverly parried, and it is some time before one of the adversaries scores a hit. At that point the play is stopped for a few moments while the hit is recorded, and then it proceeds again with redoubled energy. An excellent subject full of life and movement.'

Ref: Hepworth catalogue 1903, p. 31

172   (No title available).

WAR: MILITARY REVIEW OF 30,000 MEN:

173   INFANTRY MARCHING (N-F) 50 ft

'Two contingents of Infantry march past the camera in long lines, each being preceded by its band. As the men march in orderly procession, 100 men or more abreast, a curious and beautiful effect is obtained as a glimpse between each line is caught. The men are seen marching splendidly together almost as far as the eye can reach.'

Ref: Hepworth catalogue 1903, p. 31

174   (No title available).

175   MARCH PAST OF MOUNTED DRAGOONS (N-F) 150 ft

'Mounted soldiers are never seen to better advantage than when cantering from the distance, in one large company, straight to the spectator. At the beginning of the picture the men are seen far away in the distance cantering easily forwards, and as they come nearer, one can easily distinguish regiment after regiment, and all are seen to be in splendid form. There are several companies of the Royal Horse Artillery, several more of the Dragoon Guards, and others again of the 7th Hussars; while in the rear, last but not least, are the Pontoon and Balloon Sections of the Royal Engineers. Each company has a field gun or two with it, and as the horses come past right up close to the camera a very excellent idea is obtained of the splendid physique and fine training of England's second line of defence. This is a really excellent film, and one which is highly interesting from its exciting nature and on account of its fascinating subject.'

Ref: Hepworth catalogue 1903, p. 31

176–177 (No titles available).

178   ROYAL   HORSE   ARTILLERY   AND   MOUNTED   DRAGOONS
         GALLOPING (N-F) 50 ft

'A very spirited picture of several picked companies from each regiment galloping over a plain. Each man bears his lance aloft with a pennant streaming from the point. Company after company passes in rapid style, each man accurately keeping his place in the line, and the picture is a very beautiful representation of a subject which is of interest to every loyal Englishman.'

Ref: Hepworth catalogue 1903, pp. 31–32

179   MARCH PAST OF THE LANCERS (N-F) 125 ft

'Company after company of mounted soldiers—Lancers, Dragoons, and others—march slowly past in company formation with intervals of 100 yards or so between each group. The men sit erect on their splendid steeds, all keeping their places in the line with absolute exactitude. Among the last company are the Royal Horse Artillery, with their kharki-coloured field guns. The steady, rhythmic movements of the horses, and the light glistening on their coats and the accoutrements of the men, make up a picture whose beauty will not readily be forgotten.'

Ref: Hepworth catalogue 1903, p. 32

180   (No title available).

THE BRITISH NAVY:

181   'CURTAIN' PICTURE—FURLING SAIL ON H.M.S. 'ST. VINCENT' (N-F) 50 ft

'In this unique photograph nothing is seen at the commencement except a huge white sail which occupies the entire view. The lower edge of this is gradually hoisted, discovering a whole group of bluejackets pulling the halyards, and a most attractive effect is produced as the sail gradually rises and discloses the sailors behind. This film would form a most excellent opening picture for any series descriptive of England's might, or the lives of her Naval Heroes.'

Ref: Hepworth catalogue 1903, p. 32

182   SAIL DRILL ON A TRAINING SHIP (N-F) 50 ft

'One of the most attractive portions of the life of the boys on the training ship *St. Vincent* is excellently portrayed in this film. The picture is taken from the cross-trees of the main mast, and shows a large group of boys in the rigging and on the yards of the mizzen. There are about 20 boys on the yard stowing the sail, while their comrades below hoist it into position. Other boys swarming up and down the rigging lend much animation to the interesting scene.'

Ref: Hepworth catalogue 1903, p. 32

183   (No title available).

184   PHYSICAL DRILL—VAULTING HORSE (N-F) 50 ft

'Showing a number of marines in gymnastic uniform vaulting over a "horse" placed in the foreground of the picture. The men run up from the distance, and each takes the horse in a different manner, some of them actually taking headers right over without touching it. This is one of the ways by which the "Handy Man" acquires such wonderful agility that he is equal to any emergency requiring active limbs and cool courage.'

Ref: Hepworth catalogue 1903, p. 33

185   JACK TAR PLAYS AT 'LEAP FROG.' (N-F) 75 ft

'It is probably not generally known to everybody that the familiar schoolboy exercise—leapfrog—finds a place in the curriculum of the British Navy. In this picture there are 20 'frogs', who form up in line and leap over one another towards the camera. Then there is a curious high step exercise, which appears to appeal to the bluejacket's love of fun, and this is followed by the better known arm exercises. The whole forms a very interesting and varied film.'

Ref: Hepworth catalogue 1903, p. 33

186   JACK ON THE PARALLEL BARS (N-F) 50 ft

'Various motions associated with the parallel bars are here shown with very good effect. A large number of men take part in the exercise, and each one makes some variation upon the mode of his predecessor. There is no lack of "swing" about the movements, as the men rapidly replace one another in the field of action.'

Ref: Hepworth catalogue 1903, p. 33

187   EXERCISE WITH THE 'BAR-BELLS' (N-F) 50 ft

'There is hardly a prettier or better performed exercise in the repertoire of the gunnery school of Whale Island than that which is depicted in this photograph. The bar-bells take the place of dumb-bells, one set only being provided to each man. The usual dumb-bell exercises are preceded with, finishing up with that quaint frog-like movement, which is so excellently portrayed in an animated photograph, and causes so much amusement not unmixed with admiration.'

Ref: Hepworth catalogue 1903, p. 33

188   ON THE HORIZONTAL BAR (N-F) 50 ft

'A squad of bluejackets at Whale Island disporting themselves upon a horizontal bar in a manner which would put many members of athletic associations to shame. The performers follow one another in very rapid succession, and each takes his part in a most exemplary manner. A row of guns in the background lends a characteristic touch to the scene.'

Ref: Hepworth catalogue 1903, pp. 33–34

189   PHYSICAL DRILL—INDIAN CLUBS (N-F) 50 ft

'This exercise is so well known that a description of it is hardly necessary. As the photograph was taken at Whale Island Training Station (known as H.M.S. *Excellent*) it need not be said that the exercise is well performed. The photograph is an exceedingly clear and brilliant one and should prove of considerable interest.'

Ref: Hepworth catalogue 1903, p. 34

190   THE USE OF 'ITALIAN SABRES' (N-F) 75 ft

'Those exercises in physical drill in which the sword plays a prominent part are always most interesting. In this case the various passes, thrusts, and parries are skilfully performed by the men taking part in the drill, and the photograph forms an interesting study of the "art of self-defence".'

Ref: Hepworth catalogue 1903, p. 34

191   SWORD V. SWORD (N-F) 50 ft

'The two participants in this contest are exceedingly well matched, and the picture forms an interesting representation of the manner in which fencing for points should be carried out. The single sticks are chalked at the commencement of the fray, and every time a "hit" is scored the chalk mark localises it exactly. Near the finish one of the men has his single stick struck out of his hand, and a stop is made for a moment while a new one is fetched.'

Ref: Hepworth catalogue 1903, p. 34

192   BAYONET EXERCISE (N-F) 50 ft

'This photograph represents a detachment of bluejackets performing in splendid style their bayonet exercise. Thrust, parry and lunge follow one another in rapid succession, and all the movements are performed with the utmost regularity and precision. On seeing this picture one begins to understand the Boers' well-known objection to facing "cold steel" especially when handled by our "Jacks" ashore. Eastney Barracks forms an appropriate and picturesque background to the lively scene.'

Ref: Hepworth catalogue 1903, p. 34

193   BLUEJACKETS SKIRMISHING (N-F) 75 ft

'The picture shows a number of bluejackets kneeling in a trench in a long straight line. They load their rifles and fire two rounds in succession. Then their leader rushes forward brandishing his bayonet, and takes up a position much nearer the camera. The men immediately follow and kneel in a line beside him, and fire two or three times straight towards us. Once again they change their position and fire another couple of rounds, and then rush rapidly in two directions across the field of view, and the picture comes to an end. One of the finest naval photographs ever taken.'

Ref: Hepworth catalogue 1903, p. 35
    The Era 10 November 1900, p. 30c

194   FIRING A MAXIM GUN (N-F) 50 ft

'At the commencement of this picture, two or three sailors run in with the tripod of a maxim gun, which is brought in immediately after by the remainder of the party. The gun is placed in position on the tripod and sighted, while those not actually engaged in the operations throw themselves prone upon the ground to watch the effect while sheltered from the enemy's fire. Then the gun is fired continuously for several seconds, giving a very good idea of the power of this remarkable weapon, for every one of the hundreds of little puffs of smoke means a leaden messenger started on its death-dealing journey.'

Ref: Hepworth catalogue 1903, p. 35
    The Era, 10 November 1900, p. 30c

195   FIRING A NINE-POUNDER GUN (N-F) 125 ft

'A most excellent example of the high efficiency which long training and severe discipline gives to our sailors. The precision and speed with which they handle the old muzzle-loading gun is most remarkable. The charge is placed in the muzzle, rammed home, the gun trimmed and fired in an incredibly short space of time. When the operation is repeated, the gun fired again, and, before many seconds have elapsed, the weapon is lifted from its carriage, which is then dragged out of the way, and, at the word of command, seemingly falls to pieces and is carried away in portions. Then it is brought back again, and in an equally rapid manner, the gun is once more mounted upon it and fired again. Then it is hitched to the ammunition waggon, and still smoking, is drawn rapidly away by a team of bluejackets at the "double".'

Ref: Hepworth catalogue 1903, p. 35

196   (No title available).

197   BLUEJACKETS FIRING A BREECH-LOADER (N-F) 100 ft

'Rapid as is their performance with the muzzle-loading weapon, it is naturally far out-stripped in speed when the bluejackets have the more modern breech-loader to deal with. The twelve-pounder gun is brought up into position from the distance by a team of bluejackets and fired. Then the still smoking cartridge case is thrown out and a second charge slipped into the breech in a few moments and the gun again fired. Then the gun carriage is supported, while men told off for the purpose take off the wheels, roll them away in the distance, bring a fresh pair and attach them to the gun. Then the gun is limbered up, attached to the ammunition waggon, and drawn rapidly away.'

Ref: Hepworth catalogue 1903, pp. 35–36

198   (No title available).

199   'HANDY-MEN' FIRING THE 4.7 (N-F) 75 ft

'This is a most excellent photograph showing the manipulation and firing of the famous 4.7 gun, painted kharki, and mounted on the special carriage designed by Capt. Percy Scott, exactly as used with such terrible effect in the Transvaal. The gun is seen firing two rounds almost immediately one after the other—such is the efficiency of this marvellous weapon—and then, before the smoke is half cleared away a team of sailors attach the ammunition waggon to the tail piece of the gun and run off with it.'

Ref: Hepworth catalogue 1903, p. 36

200   BLUEJACKETS MARCHING DOWN AN INCLINE (N-F) 125 ft

'An exceedingly fine photograph representing many hundreds of brave bluejackets marching down an inclined roadway right down towards the camera. Led by their band, the bronzed and handsome fellows march with splendid precisions and regularity, and when we remember the noble part played by our gallant bluejackets in many a hard-fought struggle lately, it is no wonder that eyes grow moist and throats sore with shouting when this picture is seen. Hundreds of men are represented, and as they pass quite close, and the photograph is an excellent one, it constitutes an admirable portrait of each man. This is a photograph which is certain to be popular wherever shown.'

Ref: Hepworth catalogue 1903, p. 36
    The Era, 10 November 1900, p. 30c

201   (No title available).

202   FIRING A 9-POUNDER GUN FROM A MOVING TORPEDO BOAT DESTROYER (N-F) 100 ft

'This photograph shows, in a marvellous and convincing manner, the kind of life which our sailors live on one of the speedy torpedo boat destroyers. Although the decks are crammed with engines of destruction, and the machinery for propelling the vessel takes up so much room that there is scarcely space to look about, the excellently disciplined bluejackets train their guns upon a distant target and fire with marvellous precision every time. In this film the gun is seen loaded and fired several times, and the effect of the rolling clouds of smoke and the sparkling moving water at the vessel's side are very realistic. The gun is a "Hotchkiss" 9-Pounder, and the photograph was taken on H.M.S. Torpedo Boat Destroyer *Daring*, travelling at 23 knots.'

Ref: Hepworth catalogue 1903, pp. 36–7
    The Era, 10 November 1900, p. 30c

203   (no title available).

204   'CURTAIN' PICTURE—UNFURLING SAIL (N-F) 50 ft

'This is the last photograph of the series, to which it forms a most appropriate termination. All having been made ready, the sail is dropped from the yard and hoisted into position by the bluejackets below. As the immense sheet drops it entirely obliterates the view, and this film would form a most effective finish to any series of Naval pictures.'

Ref: Hepworth catalogue 1903, p. 37

205   MUSICAL DRILL (N-F) 100 ft

'For the purpose of this photograph the usual musical drill performed at Eastney Barracks was somewhat modified in order that a representative collection of the various exercises should be comprised within the bounds of a film of reasonable length. In this photograph all the usual exercises are included, and none of them is continued sufficiently long to be at all tiring or monotonous. The photograph is an excellent one of a fine body of men performing their physical exercise in strict time to their band.'

Ref: Hepworth catalogue 1903, p. 37

206   (No title available).

207   COMPANY DRILL AND FIRING EXERCISES (N-F) 75 ft

'A squad of marines at Eastney Barracks perform several picturesque manoeuvres in a very admirable manner. In the opening of the picture the men are standing four deep, and there appears to be only quite a few. As they march towards the camera they open out in one straight line, and suddenly kneeling down, fire a volley. Then they break up into two detachments, and with the commanding officer between them, go through a number of firing exercises.'

Ref: Hepworth catalogue 1903, p. 37

208   COMPANY DRILL AT EASTNEY BARRACKS (N-F) 100 ft

'In this photograph a very large body of Royal Marine Artillery are seen performing their various evolutions under the watchful eye of their commanding officer. Commencing with "mark time", right away in the distance of the picture, the men, at the word of command, march steadily up to the foreground. Marching, wheeling, turning and counter-marching follow one another rapidly, and the whole scene is one of animation which reveals in a remarkable degree the wonderful precision which strict discipline has given to these men. The photograph is an exceedingly fine one, and the faces of the various men are clearly recognisable.'

Ref: Hepworth catalogue 1903, pp. 37–38

209   (No title available).

210   MARCH PAST OF A FIELD BATTERY (N-F) 75 ft

'This is a picturesque view, looking towards a roadway from which is seen approaching a battery of field guns. The battery consists of six 15-pounders, each complete, of course, with its gun carriage and squad of gunners. They march through the archway out into the broad sunlight and right towards the camera, passing close enough for the face of each man to be clearly seen. The perspective effect in this picture is very fine.'

Ref: Hepworth catalogue 1903, p. 38

211   RAISING A BIG GUN (N-F) 75 ft

'In this photograph are clearly shown the arrangements employed by the Royal Marine Artillery for lifting and placing big guns without the aid of complicated machinery. The simple machine by which the necessary leverage is gained is called a "gyn", and is in the form of a huge tripod. Lying prone upon the ground at the beginning of the picture, this tripod is very smartly erected, and "shoes" are placed under each leg to hold it firmly in position. Then the block and tackle with which it is fitted are attached to a 3-ton gun, and by means of a kind of horizontal capstan the little body of men rapidly succeed in lifting this immense weight from the ground.'

Ref: Hepworth catalogue 1903, p. 38

212   LOADING A BIG GUN (N-F) 50 ft

'The immense weapon which figures in this picture is an old muzzle-loading gun for coast defence, which is used now for practice. It is very interesting to watch the manner in which the huge projectile, weighing no less than 410 pounds, is slipped easily into the muzzle of the weapon after the charge of powder has been rammed home.'

Ref: Hepworth catalogue 1903, p. 38

213   MOUNTING AND DISMOUNTING A 3-TON GUN (N-F) 150 ft

'With this method of handling a very heavy weapon the men are not aided in their work even by block tackle or pulleys. The gun, which in the opening of the picture is lying prone on the ground, is stood in position by parbuckling up the sides of a common standing carriage, using a couple of huge beams for an inclined way, and other beams for levers to push the gun up into position. Then it is lowered bit by bit by knocking out the wedges which have held it up; and at the end of about 80 seconds it is ready placed for firing. Then, at the word of command, the gun is swung round sideways and dropped on the ground by the simple process of tipping over the carriage on which it rests. This film is full of life, and interest, as the men rush about in order to gain posts of advantage in moving this massive weapon.'

Ref: Hepworth catalogue 1903, pp. 38–39

214–215   (No titles available).

216   MANIPULATING A HUGE GUN (N-F) 75 ft

'In this fascinating photograph, the men succeed in lifting a 3-ton gun from the ground with the aid of block tackle only. When the gun has been raised about 4 feet from the ground, a common garrison carriage is wheeled underneath and the gun lowered into position upon it. The rapid movements of the men as they rush from side to side to make the necessary connections between the ropes and pulleys, lend considerable animation to a picture which is full of interest from beginning to end.'

Ref: Hepworth catalogue 1903, p. 39

217   A 25-POUNDER SIEGE GUN (N-F) 125 ft

'Although the royal muzzle-loading siege guns are now, of course, quite out of date, their manipulation forms excellent practice for the men, and incidentally makes most interesting watching. In this picture the gun is first seen in its travelling position on an iron carriage. The men of the Royal Marine Artillery attach block tackle to the gun and quickly haul it into firing position on the fore-part of the gun carriage. Then they load it and fire a round, and immediately replace the tackle and haul the gun back into its first position on the carriage ready for travelling. Lastly the huge weapon is hauled rapidly out of the picture.'

Ref: Hepworth catalogue 1903, p. 39

218   (No title available).

219   FIRING A FIELD GUN (N-F) 75 ft

'This is a beautiful picture representing the firing of a 15-pounder breech-loading gun. The view opens with an empty parade ground, and immediately from one of the arches in the distance a field gun is seen rapidly approaching, with its accompanying squad of gunners. The gun is brought right up into the foreground, with its muzzle pointing directly at the camera. It is loaded and fired, giving a very beautiful smoke effect, and as the cloud clears away the men are seen changing the wheels of the gun carriage. Then the gun is limbered up and drawn rapidly away once more.'

Ref: Hepworth catalogue 1903, p. 39

220   FIRING MODERN FIELD GUNS (N-F) 75 ft

'A very instructive photograph at the present time, when we hear so much about smokeless powder. There are six field guns drawn up into line and they fire in turn, one shot every ten seconds. The smoke from the gun is almost invisible, but the curious effect is obtained of a cloud of dust raised by the concussion of the air in front of the muzzle. When the gun is fired, it is seen to suddenly run backwards for several feet as the shot leaves its muzzle at marvellous velocity, and as it flies back a little cloud of dust rises rapidly from under the path of the projectile.'

Ref: Hepworth catalogue 1903, p. 40

221   DARTMOUTH FERRY BOAT (N-F) 50 ft

'A view taken from the pier at Dartmouth, looking across the mouth of the harbour, showing the ferry boat which conveys passengers from Kingswear, where the railway station is, to the ancient town at the mouth of the river. The steamer is seen coming towards the spectators from a considerable distance, and forms a pretty and interesting picture.'

Ref: Hepworth catalogue 1903, p. 40

222   RAZING A FACTORY CHIMNEY (N) 50 ft

'The manner in which a huge chimney is destroyed has never been more faithfully portrayed than in this picture. The factory chimney was 150 feet high, and the method of destroying it was very simple. The foundations were knocked away on one side bit by bit, blocks of wood being put in to take their place. Then a bonfire was lighted at the foot of the chimney, the wood burnt away and the chimney toppled over. As it does so a huge cloud of dust rises from the base and from a place half way up where the chimney breaks in half as it falls. The whole structure drops slowly to the ground and goes to pieces while immense clouds of dust rise to an even greater height than that attained so recently by the chimney itself.'

Ref: Hepworth catalogue 1903, p. 40

223   TROTTING MATCH (N) 100 ft

'A very picturesque corner of a racecourse, overshadowed by a huge chestnut tree, is here shown. The trotting race is a handicap, in which a very large number of contestants take part. These are seen coming from the distance, and passing quite close very rapidly, one after another faster and faster as the more heavily handi-capped drivers come round. At the end of the picture a close finish is seen in which the successful racer succeeds in overhauling and passing two of his most serious rivals.'

Ref: Hepworth catalogues 1903, p. 40

224   (No title available).

225   LAUNCH OF H.I.J.M.S. 'MIKASA' (18 November) (N) 50 ft

'The largest battleship in the world was launched from Messrs. Vickers, Sons & Maxim's slips at Barrow-in-Furness, last Thursday, 8th inst. We have secured the sole cinematograph rights for this event and obtained a most successful film. As the immense vessel glides away—imperceptibly at first, then faster and faster—a big paper balloon attached to her bows is burst open, and a number of pigeons and chrysanthemums and a quantity of confetti are liberated. Then the huge mass plunges into the water, starting immense foam-flecked waves on either side, and is quickly brought to rest by the many tons of mighty chains which she is forced to drag behind her. The launch took place during a storm of rain, but the film is, nevertheless, the finest representation of a launching which has yet been produced.'

Ref: *The Showman*, December 1900, p. 3 (advert)

226   GENERAL BULLER'S RETURN—ARRIVAL AT SOUTHAMPTON (9 November) (N) 50 ft

'An excellent photograph taken in the station yard, Southampton, through which pass in rapid succession the carriages containing General Sir Redvers Buller, Lady Buller, the Mayor and Town Clerk, and General Buller's staff. The crowds display the greatest enthusiasm as the General passes, and the picture is a remarkably fine one of a most interesting subject. It is only right to state, however, that General Buller's face is, unfortunately, hidden from view at the moment his carriage passes.'

Ref: *The Showman*, December 1900, p. 3 (advert)

227   GENERAL BULLER'S RETURN—RECEPTION AT ALDERSHOT (November) (N) 75 ft

'Showing the immense crowds assembled to welcome Sir Redvers on his return to his command at Aldershot. The General steps forward in full view, hat in hand, to deliver his speech in reply to that of the Chairman of the Aldershot Council. At the conclusion he gets into his carriage amid the wild cheering of the crowd, and the Aldershot Firemen remove the horses, and draw the carriage trium-phantly away.'

Ref: *The Showman*, December 1900, p. 3 (advert)

LEAP-FROG AS SEEN BY THE FROG (F) (September)

'In which the audience is placed in the position of one of the frogs.'

Ref: *Amateur Photographer*, vol. 32, no. 836 (12 October 1900)
There is no catalogue entry for this film.

THE NORTHERN PHOTOGRAPHIC WORKS LIMITED (Birt Acres)

BRITON v. BOER (January) (F) 80 ft

'Rifle Brigade driving the enemy from the trenches at the point of the bayonet.'

Refs: *The Era*, 20 January 1900, p. 27b; 3 February 1900, p. 27d

THE CITY IMPERIAL VOLUNTEERS (January) (N) 80 ft

'Showing the troop train steaming into the embarkation shed, and also the men going aboard S.S. *Briton*. This film is the best taken of the troops, the view of the men leaning out of the carriage windows and waving the national flag being exceptionally interesting.'

Ref: *The Era*, 20 January 1900, p. 27b

THE PRINCE OF WALES INSPECTING THE HONOURABLE ARTIL-
LERY COMPANY'S NEW GUNS (January) (N) 80 ft

Ref: *The Era*, 3 February 1900, p. 27d

CITY IMPERIAL VOLUNTEERS EMBARKING ON S.S. 'PEMBROKE
CASTLE' (January) (N) 80 ft

Ref: *The Era*, 3 February 1900, p. 27d

IMPERIAL YEOMANRY SHIPPING THEIR HORSES ON THE 'GOTH',
(January) (N) 80 ft

Ref: *The Era*, 3 February 1900, p. 27d

THE MEN WITH THE LONG KNIVES (Date uncertain) (N) 80 ft

'Thrilling cavalry charge by the 12th Lancers.'

Ref: *The Era*, 3 February 1900, p. 27d

THE SHIPWRECK (February) (N) 80 ft

'This is an exceptionally fine marine picture, showing a vessel on the rocks being battered to pieces by mountainous waves. The view of the heavy seas striking against the unfortunate ship, and in some cases completely covering her with spray, is intensely thrilling. If you want a picture of a raging sea, buy this film.'

Ref: *The Era*, 24 February 1900, p. 27e

OXFORD AND CAMBRIDGE BOAT RACE, 1900 (31 March) (N) 80 ft

Ref: *The Era*, 31 March 1900, p. 27e

THE GREAT STEEPLECHASE, 1900 / STEEPLECHASING AT
SANDOWN PARK (March) (N) 80 ft

'This film shows the horses clearing the water jump, and as the animals are taken close up the pictures will show them life size. The film concludes with a nasty fall, showing one of the horses falling, and his jockey, being flung heavily to the ground, is seriously hurt.'

Refs: *The Era*, 17 March 1900, p. 27e; 31 March 1900, p. 27e

PICKING UP THE MAILS AT SIXTY MILES AN HOUR (March) (N-F) 80 ft

Ref: *The Era*, 31 March 1900, p. 27e

WATER POLO MATCH (Date uncertain) (N) 80 ft

Ref: *The Era*, 31 March 1900, p. 27e

THE QUEEN'S ENTRY INTO DUBLIN (4 April) (N) 80 ft

Ref: *The Era*, 7 April 1900, p. 27e

H.R.H. THE DUKE OF CAMBRIDGE BIDDING FAREWELL TO HIS YEOMANRY (April) (N) 80 ft

Ref: *The Era*, 21 April 1900

ARRIVAL OF SIR GEORGE WHITE AT PORTSMOUTH (24 April) (N) 50 ft

'This film shows the "Hero of Ladysmith" getting into the carriage which was waiting for him at Fratton Station, and acknowledging the cheers of the crowd which was awaiting his arrival.
From the beginning to the end of the film Sir George White is the central figure, and, owing to the camera being close to the carriage, the portrait will be more than life size on the sheet.'
'An uninterrupted view.'
'This is the only view taken of his arrival.'

Ref: *The Era*, 28 April 1900, p. 27d

ARRIVAL OF SIR GEORGE WHITE AT PORTSMOUTH TO DINE WITH THE NAVAL BRIGADE (24 April) (N) 50 ft

Ref: *The Era*, 28 April 1900, p27d

THE GUNS OF THE NAVAL BRIGADE BEING ENTRAINED FOR THE ROYAL MILITARY TOURNAMENT (May) (N) 100 ft

'This gives a beautiful view of the Naval Brigade placing their big gun on an open railway truck, and finally getting on to the metals and pushing it out of the field of the camera.'

Ref: *The Era*, 26 May 1900, p. 28b

NAVAL BRIGADE MARCHING THROUGH WINDSOR (May) (N) 80 ft

Ref: *The Era*, 5 May 1900, p. 27

JAPANESE BATTLESHIP 'ASCHI' ASHORE OFF SOUTHEND BEACH (May) (N) 60 ft

Ref: *The Era*, 5 May 1900, p. 27

MILITARY MEDICAL TRAIN ARRIVING AT NETLEY HOSPITAL (May) (N) 80 ft

Ref: *The Era*, 5 May 1900, p. 27

A TERRIBLE ROW IN THE FARMYARD (May) (N-F) 100 ft

'This shows an old-fashioned farmyard and its occupants. The tranquillity of the scene is, however, completely shattered by a "difference of opinion" between several game cocks, who make things very lively to the end of the film.'

Ref: *The Era*, 26 May 1900, p. 28b

PANORAMA TAKEN IN A STEAM CRANE (June) (N-F) 50 ft

'A new and entirely novel film.'
'This view was taken under very singular circumstances, our operator being seated in the skip used for hoisting building materials, with his camera pointing downwards. It was then raised 200 ft into the air, over a busy London thorough-fare, and finally dropped for about 100 ft, the camera going the whole of the time. This view when projected on the sheet gives a most extraordinary effect, as people walking in the street gradually diminish in size until they appear to be no bigger than ants, whilst at the close of the film the traffic appears to increase in magnitude with a rapidity which is positively startling.'
'Has a wonderful balloon effect.'

Ref: *The Era*, 14 July 1900, p. 24c

DAN LENO'S CRICKET MATCH (10 July) (N) 100 ft

'This film shows the celebrated "comique" at the wickets, also riding about the cricket-ground on a bicycle. He is literally supported by nearly all the music hall "stars", who are in the most grotesque costumes, and the whole film is full of the most ludicrous and comical incidents that ever transpired on a cricket ground. Through the courtesy of Mr. Dan Leno, who on one occasion came and played in front of the camera, we were able to secure a most excellent view of himself and his fellow artists, and the facial expression of these gentlemen is a study.'
'Causes roars of laughter.'
'Absolutely unique.'

Ref: *The Era*, 22 September 1900, p. 27d

IT'S NO USE CRYING OVER SPILT MILK (September) (F) 100 ft

'The subject of this film shows a lady cyclist "coasting" down a steep hill, when she suddenly runs into a country yokel carrying two pails of milk, with disastrous consequences. Whilst the yokel is extracting himself from the debris, and trying to restore the fair sufferer to consciousness, he is again "floored" by the maiden aunt, who is riding some twenty-five yards behind. A passing carriage picks up the fragments, and a painful incident is closed.'

Ref: *The Era*, 6 October 1900, p. 28c

FARMER GILES AND HIS PORTRAIT; OR, AN AWFUL EXPOSURE (September) (F) 100 ft

'This film shows the farmer and his wife entering a photographic studio for the purpose of having their likeness taken. The positions and poses they assume are comical to a degree, and drive the photographer to despair. Eventually he succeeds in exposing a plate, but finds on returning to the studio that, yielding to curiosity, the country couple have managed to completely ruin his apparatus. Mutual recriminations follow, and the studio and its occupants are entirely wrecked at the finish.'

'Irresistibly comic and absolutely steady.'
Ref: *The Era*, 13 October 1900, p. 27e

R.W. PAUL

We have no catalogue of Paul's for the year 1900 and so the following list has been compiled from other sources, principally advertisements placed by Paul in *The Era*. Once a title has been established for that particular year, it is a simple matter to supply a description of the film from entries in Paul's later catalogues that have survived.

   Where known, each title is preceded by the code word. Unlike other film producers, Paul did not number his films but used instead a short title or code word for identification purposes. Here the numeral given against each film is my own.

1   VOLUNTEERS: IMPERIAL CITY VOLUNTEERS (January) (N) 50 ft & 100 ft

         'A fine portrait of each of the 1,000 men selected for the Transvaal as they leave Wellington Barracks. As each man looks round at the camera a clearly recognisable view is obtained.'

         Ref: *The Era*, 13 January 1900, p. 27

2   THE LORD MAYOR AT SOUTHAMPTON (January) (N) Issued 22 January

         Ref: *The Era*, 13 January 1900, p. 27

3   CITIZENS: EMBARKATION OF THE CITY IMPERIAL VOLUNTEERS FOR SOUTH AFRICA (13 January) (N) 50 ft

         'A close view of the men as they go up the gangway after their exciting struggle through London crowds. Concluding with the Lord Mayor and suite going on board to bid farewell to them.'

         Ref: Paul catalogue November 1901

4   KOPJE. DRAGGING UP THE GUNS (22 January) (N) 80 ft & 100 ft

         'This film shows the difficulties contended with by our soldiers and sailors in transporting the big naval guns which were used with such effect. They are seen working together pulling a big naval gun up a "ramp".' This part of the picture is preceded by an ammunition wagon.'

         Refs: Era, 24 February 1900, p. 27
            Paul catalogue November 1901

5   TRANSPORT: TRANSPORTING PROVISIONS TO THE FRONT (22 January) (N) 50 ft

'This is a most successful picture, illustrating the method of transporting provisions and ammunition at the front. The wagons are seen going through a ravine, which forms a very beautiful and striking background to the picture. It is full of the movement of teams of mules and oxen, and Kaffir drivers with their long whips.'

Refs: *The Era*, 24 February 1900, p. 27
      Paul catalogue November 1901

6   CRONJE: CRONJE'S SURRENDER TO LORD ROBERTS (27 February) (N) 60 ft

Photographed by Col. Walter Beevor, RAMC

'This historical film, which is the only one of the subject taken, shows Cronje in a cart after his defeat at Paardeberg, followed by an escort of C.I.V. As the cart passes the camera, Cronje is seen to look out in astonishment at it. The picture is most successful, considering the circumstances under which it was taken in the early morning.'

Refs: *The Era*, 31 March 1900, p. 18; 14 April 1900, p. 24
      British Journal of Photography, 6 April 1900, p. 221
      Paul catalogue, November 1901
      (Plate 15)
      Copy in NFTVA

6a   BOER SHELL-PROOF PITS (February) (N)

'A view of the Boer shell-proof pits in their camp, showing the camp exactly as it was left by Cronje's army on its surrender.'

Refs: *British Journal of Photography*, 6 April 1900, p. 221
      Not listed in Paul's catalogue for 1901

7   BERKS: THE BERKSHIRE YEOMANRY (28 February) (N) 60 ft & 50 ft

'Review of Berkshire Volunteers at Windsor Castle by the Queen.'
'A clear and interesting scene, showing the review of the Berkshire Yeomanry, at Windsor Castle, February 28th, 1900, by Her late Majesty the Queen, before leaving for South Africa.'

Refs: *The Era*, 3 March 1900, p. 27
      Paul catalogue November 1901

8   QUEEN'S VISIT TO LONDON (9 March) (N) 40 ft & 60 ft

Ref: *The Era*, 10 March 1900, p. 27

9   THE BRUTAL BURGLAR (March) (F)

Ref: *The Era*, 10 March 1900, p. 27

10   COLLISION: A RAILWAY COLLISION (March) (F) 40 ft

'A railway collision between two trains, purchased by Mr. Paul for the purpose. The most thrilling film ever witnessed.'

'Few have seen, or can even imagine, the scene revealed in this film. A railway track is seen, along which comes a slow train, which over-runs the signal. While the driver backs his train, and before he can reach a position of safety, an express dashes out of the tunnel and smashes into the goods train, which is thrown down an embankment.'

Refs: *The Era*, 10 March 1900, p. 27; 31 March 1900, p. 28
    Paul catalogue November 1901 (One frame illus.)
    Frederick A. Talbot, *Moving Pictures* (London, 1912), p. 205
    Copy in NFTVA (F 63339)
    (Plate 9)

11   DIVERS: DIVING FOR TREASURE (March) (F) 120 ft

'Divers at work above and below surface.'

'Divers at work. Dressing, going down, at work below water and coming up into the boat, the pumps are manned by bluejackets, and the whole scene one of breathless interest.'

'This wonderful film is a triumph in realism. The naval divers are seen going down from a boat, in which the bluejackets are manning the pumps. The scene changes to below water, where the divers, surrounded by live fishes, resuce the treasure and send it up to the surface. They come up and dress in the boat.'

Refs: *The Era*, 10 March 1900, p. 27; 31 March 1900, p. 28
    Paul catalogue November 1901 (One frame illus.)
    (Plate 7)

12   BATTLE OF POPLAR GROVE (7 March) (N)

'Artillery, Cavalry and Mounted Infantry going into action at Poplar Grove.'

Ref: *The Era*, 14 April 1900, p. 24

13   BLOEMFONTEIN: ENTRY OF THE SCOTS' GUARDS INTO BLOEMFONTEIN (13 March) (N) 120 ft & 80 ft

'This magnificent picture shows the Pipers, as they marched into the Market Place, and nearly every detail of the men's battle-stained uniforms is seen. This picture was taken after a forced march, and the men, although weary, are marching sturdily to the strains of the bag-pipes.'

Refs: *The Era*, 14 April 1900, p. 24
    Paul catalogue November 1901
    Copies in the Archive of the New Zealand National Film Unit and NFTVA
    (Plate. 16)

14   SAVED: PLUCKED FROM THE BURNING (March) (F) 100 ft

'A house on fire, showing the gallant rescue of a woman and child from the burning room by a fireman.'

'Interior of a house on fire.'

'A very realistic and thrilling picture of the interior of a house on fire; a mother and child are awakened by the smoke, and the distracted parent picks up the baby and rushes to the door, only to be beaten back by the flames. A fireman, climbing up to the window, carries away the child, but the mother faints and falls. The fireman returns and is unable to get the woman through the window, but hastily chopping out the sash he carries her out just as, amid clouds of smoke, the ceiling falls.'

Refs: *The Era*, 10 March 1900, p. 27; 31 March 1900, p. 27
   Paul catalogue November 1901 (One frame illus.)
   (Plate 10)

15   SHEPHARD: THE HAIR-BREADTH ESCAPE OF JACK SHEPHARD (March) (F) 100 ft (In two scenes)

'Jack Shepherd's [sic] escape over the roofs in which the police are thrown 30 ft into the street.'
'Jack Sheppard [sic] and his hairbreadth escape over the roofs, the police being thrown into the street, 30 ft below.'
'Jack is, when the scene opens, making love to the innkeeper's daughter, but an alarm is given by the boniface, who has caught sight of the watchman coming. The girl shows a way of escape, and the scene changes to the roofs; the pair throw a plank across the street, and carefully make their way across. When the watchman and his assistant attempt to follow, Jack, lifting one end of the plank, throws them one after the other, 30 feet into the street below.'

Refs: *The Era*, 10 March 1900, p. 27; 31 March 1900, p. 28
   Paul catalogue November 1901 (One frame illus.)
   (Plate 11)

16   A MORNING AT BOW-STREET (March) (F)

'A morning at Bow-Street, a screamingly funny film, showing four lively cases in the dock.'

Ref: *The Era*, 31 March 1900, p. 28

17   PHOENIX: GREAT REVIEW BY THE QUEEN IN PHOENIX PARK (4 April) (N) 120 ft

'Her late Majesty Queen Victoria reviewing troops in Phoenix Park, Dublin. This magnificent film includes all the most effective parts of a historical and striking pageant. It commences with the march past of the soldier lads of the Hibernian School, the two Companies of Marines with Maxims, the 21st Lancers and three Companies of Bluejackets from the Fleet in Dublin Bay. One of these Companies is seen breaking into a charge with their guns. The film concludes with the finest view of H.M. the Queen ever obtained. Preceded by the Life Guards and Out riders, her carriage is seen driving down the lines close to the camera. As Her Majesty was sitting at the side of the carriage next to the camera, and looking directly towards it, a splendid view was obtained. The picture closes with the Life Guards following the carriage. As only the best and most interesting parts of this long negative have been selected to form the 120 feet length, the result on the screen is very fine, and the entire film is full of movement, sharp and brilliant.'

Refs: *The Era*, 28 April 1900, p. 28
   Paul catalogue November 1901

18   MAJESTY: GREAT REVIEW BY THE QUEEN IN PHOENIX PARK
        (4 April) (N) 40 ft

        'The last portion, showing only the passing of the late Queen with her escort,
        may be had separately.'

        Ref: Paul catalogue November 1901

19   SIR GEORGE WHITE'S ARRIVAL (14 April) (N) 20 ft

        'A short but splendid film, showing clear portraits of the Hero, also Lady White
        and the Mayor of Southampton.'

        Ref: *The Era*, 21 April 1900, p. 28

20   BRIGADE: LANDING OF THE NAVAL BRIGADE (11 April) (N) 40 ft

        'The *Powerful* Naval Brigade leaving their ship for the reception in the Town Hall
        by the Mayor of Portsmouth. Taken by courtesy of the Admiral Superintendent.'
        'Taken at Portsmouth by special permission. This film gives a close view of the
        sailors descending the gangway from H.M.S. *Powerful*.'

        Refs: *The Era*, 28 April 1900, p. 28
              Paul catalogue November 1901

21   *POWERFUL*: RETURN OF THE NAVAL BRIGADE WHICH SAVED
        LADYSMITH (11 April) (N) 40 ft

        'H.M.S. *Powerful* is first seen steaming into Portsmouth Harbour, to the
        accompaniment of waving hats and handkerchiefs which fringe the picture. This
        film, apart from its special interest, is an unsurpassed view of one of our finest
        battle-ships, and will always remain a popular subject.'

        Refs: *The Era*, 14 April 1900, p. 24
              Paul catalogue November 1901

22   QUEEN AT WOOLWICH (April) (N)

        Ref: *The Era*, 14 April 1900, p. 24

23   OXFORD AND CAMBRIDGE BOAT RACE (31 March) (N)

        Ref: *The Era*, 14 April 1900, p. 24

24   FOOTBALL MATCH (April) (N)

        Ref: *The Era*, 14 April 1900, p. 24

25   THE NAVAL BRIGADE IN LONDON (7 May) (N)

        Ref: *The Era*, 19 May 1900, p. 27

26   KRUGER: KRUGER'S DREAM OF EMPIRE (May) (F) 65 ft

        'When the scene opens the stage is occupied by a bust of Oom Paul, and a large
        frame on which is boldly written, "On Majuba Day England was defeated", Oom
        Paul enters and observes this with evident delight. He sits down in an arm-chair
        and dozes.

The legend in the frame changes to a striking cartoon entitled "Kruger the Conqueror", in which Kruger himself is seen with one foot on a recumbent figure of Lord Roberts, and a rifle in one hand and a bible in the other. To the real Kruger in his chair enters Mr. Joseph Chamberlain with the British Crown on a silken cushion. He kneels and presents this to Kruger, but, as Kruger stretches forth his hands to grasp it, it vanishes in a puff of smoke.

Kruger is rudely awakened from his illusion, and while he gazes on the cartoon it suddenly changes to the words, "On Majuba Day Cronje surrendered." In his rage he rushes to seize Chamberlain, but the latter suddenly disappears, and at the same time the bust of Kruger changes to a bust of Queen Victoria, which Kruger endeavours to overthrow. While doing so four men in Khaki enter and seize him, placing him on a pedestal. They drape him with the Union Jack. Two of the men step forward and fire on Kruger. As the shot is fired Kruger vanishes, and his place is taken by a stately figure of Britannia, around which the soldiers group, forming a most effective tableau.

This film is exceptionally clear and brilliant and strongly recommended as a final picture in a series of war subjects.'

Refs: *The Era*, 19 May 1900, p. 27; 15 September 1900, p. 28
Optical Magic Lantern Journal, vol. 11, no. 133, (June 1900), p. 70
Paul catalogue November 1901

27   GRENADIERS: QUEEN'S BIRTHDAY CELEBRATION (23 May) (N) 120 ft
4 shots

'This extremely fine and clear film was obtained from a special position, giving a fine spectacular effect. It commences with the inspection of the Guards by the Prince of Wales, Duke of York, Prince Christian, Lord Wolseley, and principal staff officers and foreign attaches. 20 ft. This is followed by the ceremony of escorting the colour down the ranks, the standard being surmounted by a wreath of laurel. 20 ft. Then comes the march past of the Grenadier Guards (40 ft.), and a splendid picture of the Royal Artillery, firing a salute. This part shows clearly the loading and firing of the guns, and includes a fine smoke effect. 40 ft. Total length of film, strongly recommended, 120 ft.; 40 ft. lengths also supplied.'

Refs: *The Era*, 26 May 1900, p. 28; 2 June 1900, p. 28

28   CARNIVAL: WAR CARNIVAL (May) (N) 120 ft

'This film shows the finest example of the elaborate carnivals organised in aid of the War Fund, and illustrates the best part of a procession three and a quarter miles long, formed of elaborately decked cars, &c., organised by the principal houses of amusement in London. Each car represents a patriotic tableau, and as they pass through the lines of cheering spectators the effective nature of the display is vividly represented. Total length, 120 ft; 40 ft. or 80 ft. also supplied.'

Ref: *The Era*, 26 May 1900, p. 28

29   FACES: A NAUGHTY STORY—A STUDY IN FACIAL EXPRESSION (May) (F) 60 ft

'A Naughty Story. A very fine new comic film on original lines. Just the thing for holiday audiences. Strongly recommended.'

'A Study in Facial Expression. An elderly gentleman is reading a paper, when he comes across a naughty story; his wife seated alongside him wants to know what he is laughing at, and her struggle of emotions of assumed vexation and real amusement are most laughable.'

Refs: *The Era*, 2 June 1900, p. 28
  Paul catalogue November 1901 (One frame illus.)
  (Plate 13)

30   DIAMOND: THE 1900 DERBY (30 May) (N) 40 ft.

'A very successful film of this popular race.'

Ref: *The Era*, 2 June 1900, p. 28

31   PRINCESS: THE PRINCE AND PRINCESS OF WALES INTERVIEWING SOLDIERS' WIVES AT CHELSEA HOSPITAL (June) (N) 40 ft

'This film gives the best animated portrait of the Princess of Wales yet obtained. It was taken at a meeting of the Soldiers' Families' Association, and the Prince and Princess of Wales are seen walking down the lines of soldiers' wives until they approach the camera, giving a clear full length portrait.'

Refs: *The Era*, 30 June 1900, p. 28; 21 July 1900, p. 16; 28 July 1900, p. 24

32   KHEDIVE: KHEDIVE AT GUILDHALL (28 June) (N) 50 ft

'A fine animated portrait of the Khedive as he steps into his carriage, bids adieu to the Mayor, and drives away, followed by a picture of the Duke of York entering his carriage and leaving the Guildhall.'

Ref: *The Era*, 7 July 1900, p. 24e

33   STRUGGLE: BRITON VERSUS BOER / SWORDS (June) (F) 100 ft

'Realistic hand-to-hand fight between a Boer Field Cornet and a Colonial Officer. Two minutes' white-heat excitement. The sensational film of the day, containing a magnificent display of swordsmanship by Mr. Lewis Fitzhamon (inventor of the fight) and Mr. Henry G. Shore. After a desperate hand-to-hand encounter the Colonial Officer is disarmed by his enemy, but recovers his sword, and after an intensely exciting struggle succeeds, by a marvellous feat of swordsmanship, in slaying the Boer. The scene takes place on the open Veldt, and is bound to cause a sensation wherever exhibited.'

Refs: *The Era*, 7 July 1900, p. 24; 28 July 1900, p. 24

34   SCOUTING THE KOPJES (June) (N)

'It would be difficult to find a finer film than *Scouting the Kopjes*. An antelope is disturbed by the rushing of the scouts' horses, which come upon the screen in full gallop, and so realistic does the scene appear, that the occupants of the stalls involuntarily shrink from what looks like an irresistible onrush of horsemen.'

Ref: *The Era*, 21 July 1900, p. 16

35   PONTOON: CROSSING THE VAAL (June) (N) 55 ft

Photographed by Col Walter Beevor, RAMC

'This magnificent film shows Lord Roberts and a body of Guards crossing the Vaal River on a swing pontoon ferry. The ferry is shown in the distance as the picture opens, and, as it is hauled across the river, passes close to the camera, the men themselves being distinctly seen. They then land from the ferry down a wooden plank. This film is extremely brilliant and clear, and is strongly recommended.'

Refs: *The Era*, 28 July 1900, p. 24
    Paul catalogue November 1901

36   BALLOON: THE ROYAL ENGINEER'S BALLOON (June) (N) 60 ft

Photographed by Col. Walter Beevor, RAMC

'In a deep ravine on the road from Johannesburg to Pretoria, is seen the balloon section of the Royal Engineers with their wagons, coming towards the spectator. The balloon itself, which is hitched to the wagon, gives a fine effect, as it approaches the spectator until it almost fills the picture. This is entirely a novel subject in war films, and being sharp and clear is sure to be well received.'

Refs: *The Era*, 28 July 1900, pp. 16 and 24
    Paul catalogue November 1901 (One frame illus.)
    (Plate 17)

37   NAVAL GUN CROSSING THE VAAL RIVER (June) (N) 50 ft

Ref: *The Era*, 4 August 1900, p. 24

38   MULE TRANSPORT IN A RAVINE NEAR PRETORIA (June) (N) 50 ft

Ref: *The Era*, 4 August 1900, p. 24

39   ARTILLERY: ARTILLERY CROSSING A RIVER (June) (N) 58 ft

'A good scene on the Vaal River, showing naval guns and wagons being drawn over the rocky bed of the river by struggling teams of oxen. It includes two different aspects of a busy and lively scene.'

Ref: Paul catalogue November 1901

40   PORTRAIT: HIS MOTHER'S PORTRAIT; OR, THE SOLDIER'S VISION OF HOME (July) (F) 100 ft. (Two scenes+vision)

'Novelty this week. An extremely interesting and beautiful film . . . Introducing an entirely new effect in animated photography. This film will be found a great addition to any series of war or other pictures.

The scene opens with a City Volunteer taking leave of his mother. As he points to the clock and rises to say good bye, he sees on the wall a metal case containing his mother's portrait, for which he asks her. He puts it in his tunic and goes out to the front. He is next seen staggering alone on the Veldt. Wounded and exhausted he crawls to a rock, and while he lies insensible, in the sky gradually appears, at first with clouded outlines, but afterwards distinct, a vision of his mother at home praying for her son. In answer come a doctor and nurse, but they find no wound. They discover the bullet, stopped by the metal photograph case, and bringing him to, he is helped off by them.'

'The Transvaal War has caused loneliness and sorrow in many a home, and in this film a dramatic little incident connected with it is taken for illustration. A C.I.V. is tenderly parting with his aged mother in her little cottage, and as a parting gift, she presses upon him a portrait of herself in a small gilt frame. Kissing it, he places it within his breast-pocket, and tears himself away to turn to duty for Queen and Country. The scene now changes to the open Veldt, with the tents of the British in the far distance. Wounded and alone, the soldier of our first scene staggers towards them to gain the help of his friends, but sinks exhausted on the ground. Lying there in a fainting condition, he dreams of his mother and home, and slowly the vision appears in the sky of the room in which he last saw her. He sees her reading his last letter, and then she sinks to her knees in an agony of apprehension for the safety of her boy, praying for his return. The vision fades and as if in answer to her prayer, a Red Cross nurse and army surgeon appear upon the scene. Reviving the wounded man with a draft from her bottle, as the doctor examines him, the sister quickly brings him round. The surgeon discovers the mother's picture in the man's pocket, and draws the nurse's attention to the fact that his life has been saved by his mother's portrait.'

Refs: *The Era*, 21 July 1900, p. 24; 28 July 1900, p. 24; 15 September 1900, p. 28
Paul catalogue November 1901 (One frame illus.)
(Plate 5)

41   JUGGLERS: THE HINDOO JUGGLERS (July) (F) 70 ft

'The scene represents a street in India, which [sic] an Indian juggler is showing his tricks to an audience of tourists. He first plants a mango seed, which he covers with a cloth, and immediately a full-grown plant appears; next, taking an empty basket, he places his assistant in it, shuts down the lid, and pierces it through and through with a long sword. The basket is then raised and shown to be empty. He recovers it, and produces the boy alive and whole.'

'Many have read of, but few have seen, the much-vaunted feats of the Hindoo Fakirs. In this film the spectator is transported to the centre of a square in India, where he sees a group of European tourists enjoying the performance of the two Eastern magicians, while one beats the tom-tom the other places a mango seed in a small quantity of loose earth, and covers it with an empty cloth. Slowly the cloth is forced upward by some power beneath, and on reaching its full height is snatched away by the conjurer. A mango plant, some 18 in. high, is disclosed, which a Hindoo boy carries away. The two jugglers now take a large basket, and having shown it empty, place the boy within, closing the lid. To the great horror of the spectators one of the conjurers now takes a sword and stabs through and through the wicker work in every direction. Marvellous, however, to relate, though the basket is surrounded by watchers, and is raised some feet above the ground, on the lid being raised it is found perfectly empty. Taking the cloth, the juggler throws it over the basket, when the form of the boy is seen to develop beneath. The cloth is thrown off, and the apparently murdered youngster jumps down alive and well.'

Refs: *The Era*, 28 July 1900, p. 24
Paul catalogue November 1901 (1 frame illus.)
(Plate 8)

42   POMPEII: THE LAST DAYS OF POMPEII (July) (F) 80 ft & 65 ft

'This scene is taken from "The Last Days of Pompeii". It represents the interior of a Greek House, in which Ione is seated with Lydia, the blind girl. Her lover, Glaucus, enters, and presents a Greek dancer, who executes some graceful movements. While the dance is in progress, Vesuvius is seen in eruption; the slaves rush forward in alarm, and Lydia leads out her companions; the entire house is then shaken to its foundations; the volcano throws out lava, which rushes over the house, of which the pillars and walls fall in, making a complete wreck.'

Refs: *The Era*, 28 July 1900, pp. 16 and 24
       Paul catalogue November 1901 (1 frame illus.)
       (Plate 12)

43   PUNISHED (July) (F) 40 ft

'A new comic film, representing the interior of a music hall agent's office. A serio-comic enters, and his voice is tried for an engagement; he is interrupted by a clerk bringing in a parcel, which proves to contain the portrait of a lady. While the agent is examining this gleefully his wife appears on the scene, and tearing up the portrait, jumps on it, and thrashes her husband.'

Refs: *The Era*, 28 July 1900, pp. 16 and 24

44   GUN (July) (N-F) 80 ft

'A striking picture of the naval gun drill by bluejackets at Chatham. The gun is run up, loaded, and fired, and then limbered up and retired with a smartness which only well-trained blue-jackets can show.'

Ref: *The Era*, 18 July 1900, p. 24

SPECIAL PICTURES OF COWES REGATTA:

45   COWES: PANORAMA OF COWES FRONT (July) (N) 80 ft

'A beautiful panorama of the principal features of the sea front at Cowes, full of animation, and including a number of boats in motion in the foreground. The clearness of detail and interest are wonderful, and this picture forms a suitable introduction to those below.'

46   ROADS: YACHTS IN COWES ROADS (July) (N) 80 ft

'The harbour is shown in the panoramic style during the height of the regatta season, being crowded with yachts and craft of all descriptions, in motion and at anchor. Suitable to follow the above.'

47   RACING: THE RACE FOR THE ROYAL YACHT SQUADRON CUP (July) (N) 40 ft

'Yachts under weigh in the race for the R.Y.S. Cup. A very animated and interesting scene.'

48   ASHORE: H.M. THE KING'S YACHT 'BRITANNIA' (July) (N) 60 ft

'View of the *Britannia* as she comes to her moorings. The Prince makes ready to go ashore with his guests; his steam barge comes alongside; they step on board, and the barge steams away.'

49   YACHTS: RACING AT COWES (July) (N) 80 ft

'A lively film, containing views of a number of yachts of different types sailing rapidly past the camera.'

50   METEOR (July) (N) 40 ft

'The *Meteor*, belonging to H.M. the German Emperor, at the moment of winning the cup, racing towards the camera at full speed.'

51   STRIKING (July) (N) 40 ft

'A fine picture of H.R.H'.s yacht *Britannia* striking and stowing mainsail; taken from a launch which follows her closely to show the people on deck, including the Prince.'

52   ALBERT (July) (N) 50 ft

'Panorama of the Queen's yacht, *Victoria and Albert*, at Cowes. A beautifully clear film, full of detail and interest, and a good finish to the above series.'

This splendid series gives a striking and complete view of the principal yacht racing events. The pictures are extremely fine and of splendid definition.'

Refs: *The Era*, 4 August 1900, p. 24
      Paul catalogue November 1901 (2 frame illus.)

53   DRENCHED: THE DRENCHED LOVER (September) (F) 70 ft

'An old countrywoman is seen washing outside her cottage, assisted by her daughter, whose attention is called off by a young man. The mother calls her daughter and cannot find her, she having gone off with the lover. The father is called to help in the search, but meantime the girl runs into the house and appears at the first floor window. Her lover, climbing upon the washtub to escape, is detected by the old people, who belabour him with a broom handle, and he drops into the suds. His discomfiture is completed by the old lady, who picks up the tub and empties the contents over him as he is running away towards the camera. The finish is extremely striking and funny, and cannot fail to cause laughter.'

Refs: *The Era*, 15 September 1900, p. 28
      Paul catalogue November 1901 (1 frame illus.)

54   HOME: BRITAIN'S WELCOME TO HER SONS (September) (F) 100 ft (5 shots)

'A large curtain covers the front of the stage, on which is inscribed the above title. Britannia steps forward, and taking the side of the curtain draws it back, disclosing the exterior of a rustic cottage, in front of which a one-armed pensioner sits reading. Looking up, he sees the manly form of his son returning from the war, and joyously greets him, while Britannia holds out to the soldier lad a Victoria Cross. As she performs this gracious action, the scene slowly dissolves to an enlarged representation of the cross, in the centre of which is depicted the heroic deed by which he won it. This fades again to the home of an officer. His wife is discovered reading a letter from her husband, while her little girl plays with her toys. The door quietly opens and the husband unobserved watches the scene. Suddenly the child sees him, flies to his arms to be kissed, while the wife clings to her returned wanderer. This happy reunion melts into a large laurel leaf of fame, and in its centre is represented the soldier leading his men to an attack. The final transformation shows Britannia in front of a large group of national flags, by the open sea, supported by her sailors. The officer and his wife enter from one side, and the private and his father from the other. The two soldiers clasp hands, and Britannia lays her hand upon the two, ratifying the bond of fellowship and the levelling of class in the common cause of king and country.'

Refs: *The Era*, 15 September 1900, p. 28
 Paul catalogue November 1901

55   A WET DAY AT THE SEASIDE (September) (F) 50 ft

'This will be an extremely popular subject for children's parties. The scene is the interior of a seaside lodging, and a number of children are amusing themselves by pretending they are on the sands. On the bed, a fisherman, aged three, is at work, catching mackerel from a bath, and hauling them out in great glee, while a photographer, aged five, having rigged up a camera, is inducing a young lady to have her portrait taken. Meantime another party is at work on a bathing machine, disrobing and plunging into the water. The game is impeded by the entrance of a small nigger [sic], whose lively playing on a fire shovel causes all the children to dance round him. The film is extremely natural and entertaining.'

Ref: *The Era*, 15 September 1900, p. 28

56   THE YELLOW PERIL (September) (F) 100 ft (Multi-shot)

'In front of a Chinese temple a European conjuror walks forward, opens his black bag and lays it upon the ground. Extending his hands in the air, he proceeds to catch samples of one kind of yellow peril—i.e. gold. Each time he extends his hands a large bag full of the precious metal is seen to appear in each, each bag being labelled with the coin mark of one of the Allied Forces. As he puts the last catch down in his portmanteau the head of a Chinaman rise from it, while the conjuror retires, horror-struck, away. The Boxer emerges from the bag and chases the European from the scene, proceeding to appropriate the gold to himself. Seated on a stand in the centre of the stage, he commences to devour the yellow metal by the handful till the re-entrance of the magician, who transforms him into a tremendous head. This is a most extraordinary effect, a living head resting on a stand, nearly as large as the full-sized man. The conjuror crosses to his bag, gathering up the gold, while the head watches him blowing fire and smoke from its mouth in anger at the appropriation of the money. As the head blows the smoke towards him the wizard picks up a sword, and with one cut severs it from forehead to chin. As the head falls apart imps of anarchy, riot, and disorder emerge from it, but while they caper about representatives of the Allied Powers enter, and are about to attack them, when they magically change to China's floral emblem, the sunflower. Russia at once goes to cut this gigantic plant from its stem, but it resists his efforts, and to the joy of the Powers, Peace, waving her olive branch, emerges from the centre. The Powers lay their flags at her feet, and shaking hands, congratulate one another on the happy termination of events.'

Ref: *The Era*, 15 September 1900, p. 28

57   ARMY LIFE, OR HOW SOLDIERS ARE MADE (September) (N-F) 2530 ft

Photographed by R.W. Paul with the permission of Sir Evelyn Wood. Premiere: 18 Sept. at Alhambra Theatre.

Part I—General Outline of a Soldier's Life.

JOINING THE ARMY

'The recruit applies, and preliminary tests are made—Examination by the Medical Officer—Taking the Oath of Allegiance before a Magistrate—Recruits marching off to the Regimental Depot.'

TRAINING AT THE REGIMENTAL DEPOT

'The first day's squad drill, turning and saluting by numbers—Extension Motions—Manual exercises with rifle and bayonet—A fatigue party at work—Twelve o'clock: opening of the canteen—An afternoon game at cards.'

CAMP LIFE AT ALDERSHOT

'Cavalry and infantry firing at the ranges—A bathing party and soldiers diving—Cooking dinners at the camp kitchen—Dinner in camp—Afternoon amusements.'

ARMY GYMNASTICS AT THE CENTRAL GYMNASIUM, ALDERSHOT

'Physical drill and kneeling and bending practice—Pyramid building—Vaulting horses.'

THE COMMISSIONAIRE CORPS

'Church parade.'

Part II—Training in the various Branches of the Service.

TRAINING OF CAVALRY AT CANTERBURY

'Recruit's first ride—Mounting and dismounting practice—Sword exercise and pursuing practice—Lance extension and lance drill—Bareback riding—A charge of lancers—Musical ride by the 2nd Life Guards.'

ROYAL ARMY MEDICAL CORPS

'Detachment searching for wounded—First aid—Dressing station.'

ROYAL HORSE ARTILLERY AT WOOLWICH

'Gun drill—Watering horses—Hooking in and reversing at the trot—Battery galloping into column of route—Field gun going into action and firing.'

ARMY SERVICE CORPS
'Dismounting a wagon—Aldershot backeries—Butchers at the supply depot.'

GARRISON ARTILLERY
'Old style: Firing 9-in R.M.L. guns—6-in disappearing gun—Battery of Q.F. guns in action, and view of sea target.'

INFANTRY

'Mounted infantry—Digging trenches—Maxim gun drill—Cyclists going into action and retiring.'

ROYAL ENGINEERS
'Escalading and capturing a fort—Building a pontoon bridge—Defending a redoubt—Constructing a trestle bridge—Exploding a land mine—Royal Engineer Divers at work—Connecting, dropping and exploding 100-lb submarine mine.'

Refs: *The Era*, 15 September 1900, p. 21; 22 September 1900, pp. 18 and 28; 13 October 1900, p. 19
    Paul catalogue November 1901 (37 frame illus.)

58   MARCH: RETURN OF THE CITY IMPERIAL VOLUNTEERS (29 October) (N) 120 ft

'This is the most complete view taken of the historic entry of the City Imperials into London, and gives with great clearness the various sections of the procession, including band, infantry, cyclists, the captured flags, and the invalids in brakes.'

Refs: *The Era*, 27 October 1900, p. 28
    Paul catalogue November 1901

59   WELCOME: RETURN OF THE NAVAL BRIGADE (7 May) (N) 120 ft

'The visit to London of the Naval Brigade which saved Ladysmith. An extremely good view of the whole Brigade is shown as they march out from Victoria Station headed by a band, and pass towards the camera. The guns, dragged by the men in the rear, form a striking and interesting finish.'

Ref: Paul catalogue November 1901

60   NEWHAVEN: TO THE PARIS EXHIBITION BY THE NEWHAVEN-DIEPPE ROUTE (Date uncertain) (N-F) 100 ft

'An excellent series of three scenes, including the arrival of the boat train at Newhaven, the bustle of the station, the passengers going on board the steamer, and a very picturesque scene at the mouth of the harbour with the vessel leaving.'

Ref: Paul catalogue November 1901

G. A. SMITH

Smith's film work was now more closely linked with the Warwick Trading Company and his films were no longer given special numbers in the WTC catalogues. Previously, they had been allocated numbers in the 3000 range, but now they were numbered in accord with the other titles in the Warwick lists. This of course makes identification a little more difficult, but most of Smith's titles can be recovered with the help of other sources. The synopses are also to be found among the other WTC films described in the catalogues.

A general catalogue of Warwick films was published in September 1900, and a Supplement at the beginning of December. Copies of both these publications are in the Museum of Modern Art, New York. Later catalogues, listing some of the films for 1900, are to be found in the Science Museum Library, South Kensington. An undated catalogue (of April 1901), lists a number of Smith's films of various years and although the films are not identified by name, many reappear under the 'G.A.S.' heading in another catalogue in the Science Museum Library, which dates from 1903/4, issued by the Charles Urban Trading Co. Ltd (referred to below as 'URB catalogue'). When Urban left WTC in 1903 to form his own company, he retained control of the G.A.S. films which he now issued under Smith's name and with new catalogue numbers.

At the end of 1903, Smith relinquished the leasehold of St Ann's Well and moved his works, laboratory and studio to Southwick, a suburb of Brighton westward along the coast from Hove. Shortly thereafter regular film production ceased and he was mainly concerned with experimental work for Charles Urban, which culminated in the first successful colour process for cinematography known as Kinemacolor.

1   GRANDMA THREADING HER NEEDLE (F) (September) 50 ft

'Portrays the difficulty of threading a needle, causing much annoyance to the old lady seated at the table with her work basket before her, as she repeatedly jobs the thread towards the eye, but misses it, until finally she succeeds, as the triumpant (sic) expression on her countenance indicates. A cat, seated behind her, washing its paws, adds much interest to this industrious scene.'

Refs: *The Era*, 15 September 1900, p. 27e, no. 5779
      WTC catalogue (September 1900), p. 156, no. 5779
      URB catalogue (1903–4), p. 104, no. 3501

2   SCANDAL OVER THE TEACUPS (F) (August) 75 ft

L P: Eva Bayley
'Two gossiping spinsters exchanging confidences and talking scandal while par-taking of a cup of tea. They are evidently much shocked to learn of "John Smithers kissing Mary Green", &c. A study of facial expression. A subject which will meet with the success of Two Old Sports. Will make a big hit wherever shown.'

Refs: Smith's cash book, entry for 15 August 1900
      The Era, 15 September 1900, p. 27e
      WTC catalogue (September 1900), p. 156, no. 5780
      URB catalogue (1903–4), p. 156, no. 5780

3   TWO OLD SPORTS' POLITICAL DISCUSSION / THE POLITICAL DISCUSSION (F) (September) 50 ft

'After numerous enquiries regarding the possibility of placing on the market further humorous subjects similar to the original Two Old Sports and Legacy films, we have finally induced the two prominent Actors and Comedians, Messrs. Hunter and Green, to arrange for a series of equally interesting pictures which will be known as the Old Sports Series, of which No. 5781 is the second. A description of the action in this subject is not necessary. It is simply an exchange of opinion regarding a *Daily Mail* and *Globe* article, the expressions of the faces telling the tale.'

Refs: *The Era*, 15 September 1900, p. 27e
   WTC catalogue (September 1900), p. 156, no. 5781

4   TWO OLD SPORTS' GAME OF 'NAP' / A GAME OF NAP (F) (September) 50 ft

'This, the third of the "Old Sports Series" will appeal to all as one of the best humorous films published. A quiet social game for good stakes, each holds a splendid hand and bets accordingly; the game is played and ended. The Nap hand loses on the last trick, being won by the deuce of trumps. The surprise, triumph and disgust depicted in the faces of the players is a treat to witness. Every exhibitor will want this film.'

Refs: *The Era*, 22 September 1900, p. 27e, no. 5782
   WTC catalogue (September 1900), p. 156, no. 5782
   URB catalogue (1903–4), p. 104, no. 3504

5   TWO OLD SPORTS' GAME OF 'NAP'—No. 2 / GAME OF CARDS (F) (September) 125 ft

'A continuation of the preceding subject (although the former is complete in itself). The vagaries of this game will lend itself to such variety of facial expressions on the part of the players, that we prepared a longer film in which two hands are dealt, played and discussed. Splendid.'

Refs: *The Era*, 22 September 1900, p. 27e, no. 5782
   WTC catalogue (September 1900), p. 156, no. 5783
   URB catalogue (1903–4), p. 156, no. 3505

6   SNAPSHOTTING AN AUDIENCE (F) (September)

'A photographer is attempting to pose the audience (before whom this picture is shown) for the purpose of taking a "shot" at them, but is constantly correcting someone in the audience to "look this way or that", or "look pleasant", &c. After everything is arranged to his satisfaction, he takes the photograph, thanks the audience, and then departs with his camera. A novel subject, in which the audience takes a direct interest.'

Refs: *The Era*, 22 September 1900, p. 27e, no. 5777
   WTC catalogue (September 1900), p. 155, no. 5777

7   LET ME DREAM AGAIN (F) 75 ft

'A scene at a masquerade ball showing a couple having a tête-à-tête helped on by several bottles. He proves an ardent lover and progresses nicely when the scene gradually changes, dissolving to a view of a bedroom with an old fat couple peacefully sleeping, when the man suddenly starts up in bed (evidently awakening from his dream of which the preceding scene is the subject) and getting a view of

the stout Amazon to whom he is linked and with whom he quarrels, reclines on
his pillow to again dream of his youthful days and its follies.'

Refs: WTC catalogue (April 1901), p. 161, no. 5730
    URB catalogue (1903–4), p. 104, no. 3500
    WTC catalogue (September 1900), p. 149, no. 5730

8   A QUICK SHAVE AND BRUSH-UP (F) 50 ft

'Nothing is more conductive to a smooth shave than a good lather, but our friend
who is attending to his tonsorial duties evidently is plying a razor with none too
keen an edge, to judge by his grimaces. A cut and a twitch now and then, with a
wash up, lotion, powder and a hair brush, he gazes admiringly at his reflection in
the mirror and concludes that he has not made such a bad job of it after all. A
good subject.'

Refs: WTC catalogue (April 1901), p. 161, no. 5729
    URB catalogue (1903–4), p. 107, no. 3526
    (Plate 26)

9   THE DULL RAZOR (F) (September) 50 ft

'The individual herein depicted is seen lathering and shaving himself, to judge by
his grimaces, evidently with a dull razor. His back being to the camera, the face
and "scraping" manoeuvres are plainly seen by reflection in the mirror. As most
men have had a similar experience, this subject is bound to create much mirth
among an audience.'

Refs: *The Era*, 22 September 1900, p. 27e, no. 5778
    WTC catalogue (April 1901), p. 155, no. 5778
    URB catalogue (1903–4), p. 107, no. 3527

10   GRANDMA'S READING GLASS (F) (October) 100 ft

'This, the first of a series of most unique pictures, was conceived and invented by
us. Grandma is seen at work at her sewing-table, while her little grandson is playfully handling her reading-glass, focusing same on various objects, viz., a newspaper, his watch, the canary, grandma's eye, and the kitten, which objects are
shown in abnormal size on the screen when projected. The conception is to
produce on the screen the various objects as they appeared to Willy while looking
through the glass in their enormously enlarged form. The big print of the
newspaper, the visible working of the mechanism of the watch, the fluttering of
the canary in the cage, the blinking of grandma's eye, and the inquisitive look of
the kitten, is most amusing to behold. The novelty of the subject is bound to
please every audience.'

Refs: *The Era*, 20 October 1900, p. 30e, no. 5784
    WTC catalogue Supplement no. 1 (Nov/Dec 1900), p. 164, no. 5784
    URB catalogue (1903–4), p. 106, no. 3517
    (Plate 28)

11   AS SEEN THROUGH THE TELESCOPE (F) (October) 75 ft

'The professor with his telescope while resting by the wayside, notes a young
couple walking down the hill, when the young lady calls her gallant's attention to

her untied shoe-lace. She is seen placing her dainty foot on the pedal of his cycle, and kneeling down he proceeds to tie the lace. The professor, to obtain a better view of the incident, levels his telescope at the point of proceedings, and the picture on the screen changes to an enlarged view of the lady's foot and the busy hands which lingeringly perform the pleasant duty, as they appeared to the professor through his glass. While chuckling over the sight, the professor is sent sprawling in the road by the young man, who resents his inquisitiveness.'

Refs: *The Era*, 20 October 1900, p. 30e, no. 5785
    WTC catalogue Supplement no. 1 (Nov/Dec 1900), p. 164, no. 5785
    URB catalogue (1903–4), p. 106, no. 3518
    (Plate 30)

12   THE OLD MAID'S VALENTINE (F) (August) 50 ft

Old maid: Eva Bayley

'The old maid is seated at work, but continually leaves off to glance at the calendar which indicates February 14th, Valentine's Day. The maid entering gives her a large envelope which she coquettishly handles, showing she thinks there is still hope for a sweetheart. Her expression is speedily changed on seeing the contents, viz., a long picture of a baby, "Just like Mama". This she throw aside in disgust, and resumes her work with dignified air. All hope is gone! The old maid's cat seated on the table washing itself lends further interest to the picture.'

Refs: Smith's cash book, entry for 22 August 1900
    The Era, 20 October 1900, p. 30e, no. 5786
    WTC catalogue Supplement no. 1 (Nov/Dec 1900), p. 164, no. 5786
    URB catalogue (1903–4), p. 106, no. 3519

13   A BAD CIGAR (F) 50 ft

'This shows a portrait of a gentleman at his ease perusing a newspaper. He has evidently dined well, and to complete his enjoyment, helps himself to a cigar. After clipping the end and lighting it, he proceeds to smoke it, but to judge from his facial expressions it does not draw well, nor is the taste to his liking; he examines it, and finds a short hair which protrudes from the cigar. This he withdraws, and makes another attempt, but still finding it not to his taste flings it away in disgust. We have all had similar experiences. Decidedly humorous.'

Refs: *The Era*, 20 October 1900, p. 30e, no. 5787
    WTC catalogue Supplement no. 1(Nov/Dec 1900), p. 164, no. 5787
    URB catalogue (1903–4), p. 105, no. 3514

14   THE HOUSE THAT JACK BUILT (Reversing) (F) (October) 50 ft

'The picture opens showing an elaborately built house of toy bricks, which the builder, a little girl, has just completed and stands to admire. Her little brothers drawn to the scene by her exclamations, proceeds to poke his fingers mis-chievously among the bricks, toppling the house over in sections, much to her discomfiture. The second section of this picture shows the action reversed, producing a most startling and impossible effect assumed by the bricks in restoring themselves to their proper positions in the house which is thus mysteriously rebuilt without hands, finally appearing entirely complete as it did at the beginning of the picture.'

Refs: *The Era*, 20 October 1900, p. 30e, no. 5788
WTC catalogue Supplement no. 1 (Nov/Dec 1900), p. 164, no. 5788
 Plate 32)

15   THE JOLLY OLD FELLOWS / GOOD STORIES (Month uncertain) (F) 100 ft

'The course of conversation can readily be imagined from the countenances and expressions of the two old boys. Must be seen to be appreciated. Decidedly humorous.'

Refs: *The Era*, 17 November 1900, p. 30b, no. 5872
 WTC catalogue Supplement no. 1 (Nov/Dec 1900), p. 175, no. 5872
 URB catalogue (1903–4), p. 104, no. 3506

16   THE UNFORTUNATE EGG MERCHANT (Month uncertain) (F) 75 ft

'A scene on the edge of a wood showing a couple emerging from among the trees walking towards the camera. They discover a piece of board which they support on two stumps of trees, thus forming a rude bench upon which they seat themselves. Unperceived by them a farmer with a basket of eggs approaches, and evidently feeling tired, finds a resting place on the edge of the plank. The couple noting the farmer, and preferring seclusion, rise, and as the plank is relieved of their weight, it tips, upsetting the farmer, who angrily remonstrates with the couple for their lack of forethought. The young man pays him out by pelting him with his own eggs.'

Refs: WTC catalogue Supplement no. 1 (Nov/Dec 1900), p. 171, no. 5844
 URB catalogue (1903–4), p. 109, no. 3543

17   THE YOKELS DINNER—Reversing / THE YOKELS LUNCHEON—Reversing (Month uncertain) (F) 75 ft

'Two farmers are seen at their dinner, stuffing spoonfuls of pudding into their mouths, accompanied by all manner of grimaces and dumb talk (their mouths being too full to speak). At this stage the film is printed, showing reverse action. Instead of them shovelling food into their mouths they apparently put the spoons up to their lips and drag there from heaps of pudding, which they deposit on their plates. This looks more appetising than it sounds. Very funny.'

Refs: WTC catalogue Supplement no. 1 (Nov/Dec 1900), p. 172, no. 5855
 URB catalogue (1903–4), p. 110, no. 3549

18   THE VILLAGE CHOIR (?)

19   WHERE DID YOU GET IT (?)

WARWICK TRADING COMPANY

This list of WTC films is compiled from two sources: the Company's own catalogues and the advertisement columns of *The Era*. The latter gives detailed descriptions of the latest productions, although a number of the less newsworthy films are sometimes omitted. Even so, it is this source which receives priority in this present list, for not only are the descriptions for the most part identical to those subsequently adopted by the official catalogues, but it provides more precise dates for certain films. Copies of *The Era* may be consulted at the Westminster Public Reference Library, Leicester Square, and at the British Library's Newspaper Library at Colindale, North London.

The second source used comprises the WTC catalogues, of which there were two published during 1900; a general catalogue appearing in September and a supplement in November or December, this latter designated *Supplement No 1*. Copies of both these publications will be found in the Museum of Modern Art, New York. Another catalogue was issued in April 1901, which includes most of the films already described in the previous publications. A copy of this catalogue is to be found in the Charles Urban Collection at the Science Museum Library, London (URB 10 Box One). Owing to the convenient location for European readers, it is this catalogue which has been drawn upon for this list, rather than those at MOMA. However, where a particular film is omitted in the catalogue at the Science Museum, recourse has had to be made to those at MOMA.

Where no footage is indicated, the length of the film is usually less than 75 feet. Short descriptions of some of the Boer War films are also to be found in *The British Journal of Photography* (22 June 1900) p. 398, but this source has not been used in compiling the present filmography.

5526   THE AUSTRALIAN MOUNTED RIFLE VOLUNTEERS / THE AUSTRA-
            LIAN MOUNTED RIFLES MARCHING THROUGH CAPE TOWN—
            (23 December 1899) (N) 100 ft

            'A finer lot of troopers, in their picturesque uniforms and mounted on their
            splendid horses, can hardly be imagined than these, seen marching through
            Adderley Street, Cape Town, on their way to the front. This regiment has already
            distinguished itself in many a battle and skirmish with the Boers.'

            Refs: *The Era*, 10 February 1900, p. 27c
               WTC catalogue (September 1900), p. 125. See also WTC 5529 below.
               Copy in NFTVA

5527   THE LORD MAYOR OF LONDON AND FRIENDS BOARDING THE
            UNION LINER S.S. 'BRITON' AT SOUTHAMPTON / THE LORD MAYOR
            OF LONDON'S FAREWELL TO THE C.I.V. (13 January) (N)

            'Previous to their departure for South Africa, the Lord Mayor of London
            delivered a farewell address to the City Imperial Volunteers at Southampton.
            This picture depicts him and other officials boarding the S.S. *Briton*, January
            13th, 1900. Splendid photograph.'

            Refs: *The Era*, 10 February 1900, p. 27c
               WTC catalogue (September 1900), p. 125

5528   EMBARKATION OF THE 'C.I.V'. ON THE UNION LINER S.S. 'BRITON'
            AT SOUTHAMPTON / THE C.I.V. EMBARKING AT SOUTHAMPTON (13
            January) (N)

            'An excellent picture, showing the first detachment of the City of London
            Imperial Volunteers (The Lord Mayor's Own) stepping aboard the S.S. *Briton*. By
            kind permission of the Union-Castle Steamship Co. (Messrs. Donald Currie and
            Co., Agents).'

Refs: *The Era*, 10 February 1900, p. 27c
    WTC catalogue (September 1900), p. 125

5529   THE NEW SOUTH WALES LANCERS MARCHING THROUGH ADDERLEY STREET, CAPE TOWN / THE ARRIVAL OF NEW SOUTH WALES LANCERS IN CAPE TOWN (23 December, 1899) (N)

'These troopers arrived at Cape Town, December 23rd, 1899, and are here shown marching down Adderley Street. They are a fine body of soldiers, and the crowds of spectators cheering, the fluttering of numerous flags and bunting placed in their honour, add much to the picturesqueness of this film.'

Refs: *The Era*, 10 February 1900, p. 27c
    WTC catalogue (September 1900), p. 125

5530   A BRITISH 40-POUNDER BATTERY IN ACTION (N) 100 ft

'This subject shows a battery of five naval guns firing their full charge with fine smoke effects. As each gun is fired, the recoil sends the carriage back about six feet, when it is moved into its former position, the breeches opened, another shell introduced, and again fired. As there are five squads at work, the action and interest in the film is considerable.'

Refs: *The Era*, 10 February 1900, p. 27c
    WTC catalogue (September 1900), pp. 125–26

5531   TROOPS DANCING A JIG ON BOARD THE GOVERNMENT TRANS-PORT 'ARUNDEL CASTLE' ON THE WAY TO SOUTH AFRICA / PASTIMES OF 'TOMMY' ON BOARD A TRANSPORT (N) 75 ft

'Four of the "boys" are here seen dancing a jig to the tune of a concertina played by another, while surrounding them are their comrades, stamping and clapping their hands in time to the music. Others are seen amusing themselves in divers ways, performing gymnastic feats over the beams and ropes of the ship. Splendid definition, full of interest.'

Refs: *The Era*, 10 February 1900, p. 27c
    WTC catalogue (September 1900), p. 126

5532   TROOPS' PHYSICAL DRILL ON BOARD THE 'AVONDALE [sic] CASTLE' DURING THE TRIP TO SOUTH AFRICA / TROOPERS PHYSICAL DRILL ON BOARD A TRANSPORT (N) 100 ft

'The exercises themselves are most interesting to watch, but the endeavours of a fat soldier in the front ranks create considerable amusement by always being behind the others in his movements, constantly looking back to watch how the others do it, but never-the-less making wrong moves himself. Excellent definition, sharp and clear.'

Refs: *The Era*, 10 February 1900, p. 27c
    WTC catalogue (September 1900), p. 126

5533   A JIG ABOARD SHIP (N)

'Similar to No. 5531, but of shorter length. The precision with which the four troopers dance will surely procure them an engagement at a London Music Hall should they all return from the front and desire same. Bound to please any audience.'

Ref: WTC catalogue (September 1900), p. 126

5534   TROOPS EXERCISING ON BOARD A TRANSPORT (N)

'This photo was taken from the Captain's bridge, and depicts the troops taking their morning exercise of walking, drilling and running up and down the decks of the ship.'

Refs: *The Era*, 10 February 1900, p. 27c
    WTC catalogue (September 1900), p. 126

NOTE. Nos. 5531 to 5534 were photographed on the Government Transport SS. *Arundel Castle*, by kind permission of the Admiralty and the Union-Castle Steam ship Co. (Donald Currie & Co., Agents).

5535   HRH THE PRINCE OF WALES ARRIVING AND INSPECTING THE IMPERIAL YEOMANRY AT ALBANY BARRACKS / ARRIVAL OF HRH THE PRINCE OF WALES AT ALBANY BARRACKS (26 January) (N)

'The Prince, accompanied by various officers, is seen passing down the first rank of soldiers, inspecting and praising their appearance.'

Refs: *The Era*, 10 February 1900, p. 27c
    WTC catalogue (September 1900), p. 126

5536   HRH THE PRINCE OF WALES INSPECTING THE IMPERIAL YEOMANRY (26 January) (N)

'Another film of the inspection, but taken from a different point of view, giving a splendid portrait of the Prince and officers as they thread their way between the ranks of the I.Y., January 26th, 1900. This is perhaps the best film of the two, if only one section is desired.'

Ref: WTC catalogue (September 1900), p. 126

5537   THE PRINCE OF WALES ADDRESSING THE IMPERIAL YEOMANRY AT ALBANY BARRACKS / THE IMPERIAL YEOMANRY GIVING THREE CHEERS FOR HRH THE PRINCE ON [sic] WALES (26 January) (N)

'After the inspection, the Prince is seen delivering a farewell address to the troops, who respond by waving their hats and giving three hearty cheers for His Royal Highness.'

Refs: *The Era*, 10 February 1900, p. 27c
    WTC catalogue (September 1900), p. 126

5538   THE PRINCE OF WALES SHAKING HANDS WITH OFFICERS OF THE IMPERIAL YEOMANRY, ALSO SHOWING HIS DEPARTURE / THE PRINCE OF WALES GREETING THE OFFICERS OF THE IMPERIAL YEOMANRY BEFORE HIS DEPARTURE (26 January) (N)

'Before departing, the Prince shakes each of the officers by the hand, among them being Sergeant Patrick Campbell (who was recently killed in battle at the front). HRH the Prince then steps into his carriage and drives towards and by the camera. Nos. 5536 to 5538, make a splendid series.'

Refs: *The Era*, 10 February 1900, p. 27c
   WTC catalogue (September 1900), p. 126

5539   (No title available).

5540   LORD ROBERTS'S ARRIVAL AND RECEPTION AT CAPE TOWN (10 January) (N) 125 ft

Photographed by Edgar M. Hyman
'The view shows the *Dunottar Castle*, lying at the Docks at Cape Town. Troops acting as escort arrive at the wharf. Lord Roberts is seen coming down the gang plank from the ship, when he is enthusiastically received. He proceeds to inspect the troops, and finally steps into a carriage in company with other prominent officers. Lots of action, splendid portraits, and fine photographic quality. (Photographed by Mr Edgar M. Hyman, of our War Staff.)'

Ref: *The Era*, 3 March 1900, p. 27c

5541   SOUTH AFRICAN WAR SUPPLIES, TRANSPORTED BY MEANS OF THE M'KENZIE TRACTION ENGINES (N) 75 ft

Photographed by Edgar M. Hyman
'The heavy war stores, guns, and ammunition are thus transported from the ship to the railway, also across the country. These powerful engines draw from ten to fifteen heavily laden trucks. The view is full of life and action, and quite novel and picturesque. (Photographed by Mr Hyman.)'

Ref: *The Era*, 3 March 1900, p. 27c

5542   HORSES OF THE IMPERIAL YEOMANRY SHIPPING ON BOARD THE UNION LINER (TRANSPORT) 'GARTH' (N) 75 ft

'Showing many obstinate animals forcibly driven and pushed into the "boarding boxes" by means of which they are transported on board the ship.'

Ref: *The Era*, 3 March 1900, p. 27c

5543   LANDING OF THE SICK AND WOUNDED FROM THE S.S. 'SUMATRA' AT CAPE TOWN, EN ROUTE FOR WYNBERG HOSPITAL (N) 75 ft

'A pathetic scene as the stretcher bearers carry forth many of our men who were wounded at the front.'

Ref: *The Era*, 3 March 1900, p. 27c

5544   THE DISAPPEARING GUNS IN ACTION (N) 75 ft

'Showing these latest devices of Harbour Defence in service. The heavy guns are raised by hydraulic power, loaded with shell, aimed and fired, the gun automatically disappearing behind the casement of the fort by the recoil. Novel, lots of action, and fine smoke effects.'

Ref: *The Era*, 3 March 1900, 27c

5545   A SKIRMISH WITH THE BOERS NEAR KIMBERLEY BY A TROOP OF CAVALRY SCOUTS ATTACHED TO GENERAL FRENCH'S COLUMN (N) 150 ft

Photographed by Joseph Rosenthal
'One of the liveliest scenes yet photographed in three views—1. The Scouts in pursuit of the Boers. II. Bringing the Maxims into action. III. A charge and general fusillade. These scenes portray one of the many brushes with the Boers by a contingent of General French's Army during his march to relieve Kimberley. Several kopjes in background. Photographed by Mr. J. Rosenthal, of our war staff.'

Ref: *The Era*, 3 March 1900, p. 27c
   Copy in NFTVA

5546   WAR SUPPLIES AND PROVISIONS ARRIVING AT A BOER LAAGER BY A TRAIN OF OX TEAMS (N) 50 ft

Photographed by Joseph Rosenthal
'The slow but sure method of replenishing war material and food. Boer camp forming background. One of a very few pictures secured on the Boer side. Photographed by Mr. J. Rosenthal.'

Ref: *The Era*, 3 March 1900, p. 27c

5547   DRIVING THE OSTRICHES (N-F) 50 ft

'A scene on the Ostrich Farm of Mr N. Smit, Impanzi, Natal, showing the driving of hundreds of these huge birds by Zulus and farm hands. Fine definition, lots of action, and most novel scene.'

Ref: *The Era*, 3 March 1900, p. 27c

5548   SCENE ON MR N. SMIT'S OSTRICH FARM, IMPANZI, NATAL, SOUTH AFRICA (N-F) 100 ft

'Hundreds of Ostriches being fed by keeper. The driving and round up of these birds by Zulus lends most spirited action to this unique and interesting picture.'

Ref: *The Era*, 3 March 1900, p. 27c
   Copy in NFTVA 983

5549   A BOER SUPPLY CROSSING THE VELDT (N) 100 ft

Photographed by Joseph Rosenthal
'Hundreds of oxen drawing heavily laden waggons, trekking over the veldt. Many Zulus and drivers wielding 20-foot whips over their teams. A novel and most interesting scene. (Photographed by Mr J. Rosenthal, of our War Staff.)'

Ref: *The Era*, 3 March 1900, p. 27c

5550   THE ROYAL HORSE ARTILLERY ON THE MARCH TO THE FRONT (N)
            100 ft

            Photographed by Edgar M. Hyman
            'A splendid scene, with Table Mountain in the background, showing the Artillery
            Company winding its way along the roads leading from Cape Town, appearing
            from the distance like some huge serpent. (Photographed by Mr. Edgar M.
            Hyman, of our War Staff).'

            Ref: *The Era*, 3 March 1900, p. 27c

5551   CARRYING THE WOUNDED ON BOARD THE HOSPITAL SHIP AT
            DURBAN, S.A. (N) 75 ft

            'A continuous line of sick and wounded being transported by stretcher-bearers up
            the gangway to the ship.'

            Ref: *The Era*, 3 March 1900, p. 27c

5552   WINTER SPORTS IN SCOTLAND (N-F) 125 ft

            'Scene on the ice of a frozen lake near Edinburgh, showing scores of adepts at
            Curling engaged in this sport. A close view of one of the "sets" is depicted, giving
            the many who are not familiar with this pastime a good opportunity to gain a
            few pointers. The last section of the film shows hundreds of skaters gliding over
            the ice. A boy in kilts enjoys the sport hugely, irrespective of the cold. Full of
            action.'

            Ref: WTC catalogue (April 1901), p. 139
            Copy in Science Museum, London (URB 10 Box 2)

5553   (No title available).

5554   THE HANGING BRIDGE OF ROUEN (N-F)

            'An unique method of transporting passengers and vehicles across the River
            Seine at Rouen. The series of cables which span the river and support the hanging
            "car" are stretched between two high towers situated on either side of the water,
            the car gliding in mid-air over the same.'

            Ref: WTC catalogue (April 1901), p. 139

5555   THE DUKE OF CAMBRIDGE BIDDING FAREWELL TO HIS OWN
            IMPERIAL YEOMANRY (N) 50 ft

            'On the day of their departure to South Africa, from Southampton. Fine
            portraits.'

            Ref: *The Era*, 3 March 1900, p. 27c

5556   THE QUEEN'S LANCERS DISEMBARKING THEIR HORSES FOR THE
            FRONT AT PORT ELIZABETH, S.A. (N) 50 ft

            'A spirited and picturesque scene.'

            Ref: *The Era*, 3 March 1900, p. 27c

5557   LANDING THE 4.7 NAVAL GUNS AT PORT ELIZABETH, S.A. (N) 75 ft
(Two shots)

'These guns which are used at Ladysmith and elsewhere at the front will throw a
45-lb shell of Lyddite eight miles. Showing the loading from the ship to the R.R.
trucks.'

Ref: *The Era*, 3 March 1900, p. 27c

Nos. 5558 to 5617 allocated to films made by G. A. Smith during the years 1897
to 1899

For description of each film, consult the reference

Ref: WTC catalogue (September 1900), pp. 128–34

5618   LANDING OF THE NAVAL BRIGADE AT PORT ELIZABETH, S.A. (N)
50 ft

'The "Handy Man" climbing from the small boat on to the dock. A beautiful
picture full of action.'

Ref: *The Era*, 3 March 1900, p. 27c

5619   THE MARCH OF THE NAVAL BRIGADE TO THE STATION AT PORT
ELIZABETH, S.A. (N) 50 ft

'Their movement indicates their eagerness to reach the front.'

Ref: *The Era*, 3 March 1900, p. 27c

5620   THE NAVAL BRIGADE MARCHING THROUGH MAIN-STREET, PORT
ELIZABETH, S.A. (N) 50 ft

'A splendid view of main street of this bustling S.A. Port, showing our marines
marching to the front.'

Ref: *The Era*, 3 March 1900, p. 27c

5621   THE DERBYSHIRE REGIMENT (SHERWOOD FORESTERS) MARCH-
ING FROM THE JETTY, PORT ELIZABETH, S.A. (N) 100 ft

'This famous regiment is here seen to good advantage, leaving the docks for the
front. Fine definition, clear, and lots of action.'

Ref: *The Era*, 3 March 1900, p. 27c

5622   WRECK IN A GALE (N) 75 ft

'Showing a sailing vessel wrecked off the Jersey coast with tremendous sea
breaking over her. The grandest film of a storm in the Channel ever produced.'

Ref: *The Era*, 3 March 1900, p. 27c
Copy in NFTVA 999

Nos. 5623 to 5628 Eugene Sandow Series
For description of each film consult the reference

Ref: WTC catalogue (April 1901), pp. 145–146

5629   TROOPS, ARTILLERY, AND CAVALRY TO THE FRONT (N) 150 ft

'The Royal Dublin Fusiliers, Royal Horse Artillery, and the Natal Carbineers marching through Adderley-street, Cape Town, on their way to the front. A fine contrast of Foot Soldiers and their Mounted Comrades passing between a double file of enthusiastic crowds, while the decorations on the buildings, in honour of the Troops, consist principally of waving Union Jacks and the Stars and Stripes. Beautifully defined, sharp and clear.'

Ref: *The Era*, 7 April 1900, p. 27d

5630   A BIT OF NATAL SCENERY (N) 150 ft

'Between Mooi River and Escourt. Panoramic view taken from a projecting platform of a fast-moving transport train, showing the character of country our troops are fighting in. Most interesting.'

Ref: *The Era*, 7 April 1900, p. 27d

5631   FROM NAAUPOORT TO DE AAR (N) 100 ft

'A characteristic bit of South African scenery, taken from a projecting platform of an armoured train. Aside from the interesting panorama of the country, this subject shows the engine and tender of the train swerving from side to side as it passes around some of the sharp corners, through cuttings, over veldt, &c. Can be joined to No 5630, making a most striking subject.'

Ref: *The Era*, 7 April 1900, p. 27d

5632   PANORAMA OF MODDER RIVER (N) 100 ft

'This subject was photographed in a similar manner to the preceding films— namely, from a projecting platform on the side of a moving transport train. A splendid idea of the lower section of this now famous river can be gained by viewing the panorama spread out before the spectator as the train proceeds on its way. Several passengers are seen looking out of the windows of the carriage, a section of which, together with the engine and tender, is shown in this picture.'

Ref: *The Era*, 7 April 1900, p. 27d

5633   OFF TO THE FRONT BY ARMOURED TRAIN (N) 100 ft

'Panoramic view between Belmont and Modder River. This subject has created a sensation at the London Hippodrome, where it was first exhibited. The views include several kopjes, a section of the veldt with a herd of cattle grazing within close view, and as the train rounds a curve it comes to a stop, allowing an up train, which is seen approaching, to pass the siding before it again proceeds on its way. The spilling of the water from the tender, the swaying of the engine, &c., all of which is constantly in view, come to an interesting close, depicting the engineer stepping from the cab, oiling the machine and blowing off steam, then mounting and away. Something new and novel, never portrayed in the many panoramic views hithertofore published. Steady, sharp, clear.'

Ref: *The Era*, 7 April 1900, p. 27d

5634   (No title available).

5635   THE 'HANDY MAN' AT DURBAN (N) 125 ft

'A cutlass and physical drill is proceeded with on a field before Durban, after which the marines salute the Union Jack, dissemble, reform ranks, and march off. This is a favourite subject with the public, especially since the brave stand of our Bluejackets at Colenso, and shows Jack putting the finishing touches to his training before his transfer to the front, there to apply his weapons in dead earnest. A large Union Jack in the hands of a stalwart sailor forms a prominent feature of this picture as it flutters briskly in the breeze. Sharp and clear.'

Ref: *The Era*, 7 April 1900, p. 27d

5636   BLUEJACKETS' FIELD GUN DRILL AT DURBAN (N) 125 ft

'Before transporting the "Handy Man" to the front he is put through a series of drills and manoeuvres in order to perfect his training in the handling of the landing guns when operating on terra firma. This subject portrays a gun squad arriving, firing, dismantling the gun and hurriedly retreating from the scene, taking the wheels and coupling with them so as to make the guns absolutely useless to an enemy should they capture same. They again put in appearance and assemble the gun and limber in the incredible time of six seconds, fire another round, and retire. Full of action, clear, and sharp.'

Ref: *The Era*, 7 April 1900, p. 27d

5637   THE UNIVERSITY BOAT RACE (31 March) (N) 100 ft

'The beginning of the film shows numerous boats and yachts, laden with spectators plying up and down the river, getting into position to view the race. The film then changes to a panoramic view of the race from Barnes and shows the river road lined with people and enormous traffic. The camera is gradually turned so as to include the crowds lining the river, barges, &c., and allows the Cambridge crew to pass the field of view. Upon the arrival of the Oxford crew and Press boats, the camera is again slowly revolved gradually, following the crew up the river with an ever-changing panorama as a background, until the Oxfords pass out of sight under Barnes Bridge. Most interesting film of the Boat Race yet photographed.'

Ref: *The Era*, 7 April 1900, p. 27d

5638   THE GRAND NATIONAL (31 March) (N)

'Showing four views of this famous course at Aintree, Liverpool, during the Grand National Race, taken from as many different points of view. The FIRST section depicts the horses coming down the straight track the first time around; SECOND, the horses taking the last hurdle; THIRD, a curve of the track, showing the horses going into the country for the second time around, and the last section shows the finishing spurt down the straight near the Grand Stand. The end of the film shows the people closing in on the track after the race to see the Prince of Wales leading off the winner.'

Ref: *The Era*, 7 April 1900, p. 27d

5639   RETURN OF EARL CADOGAN, LORD LIEUTENANT OF IRELAND, after attending the Ceremony of presenting Her Majesty with the keys of the City (4 April) (N)

'His Lordship is preceding the Royal Procession passing up Dame Street, surrounded by his body guards, and is cheered by the thousands who crowd both sides of the street.'

Ref: WTC catalogue (April 1901), p. 147

5640   THE ROYAL PROCESSION PASSING THROUGH DUBLIN (4 April) (N)

'Showing the entire Royal Procession from start to finish.
The point of view commands both sides of Dame-street as far as the eye can reach, and shows to advantage the decorated buildings and tremendous crowds held in check by the Dublin Volunteers, who present arms as the head of the procession comes to view. First the Body Guard, then the carriages in the following order: in the first carriage were Lord Denbigh, Sir Fleetwood Edwards, and Sir James Reid. In the next were the Countess of Antrim, the Hon. Harriet Phipps, and Sir Matthew White Ridley. Next came the Duchess of Connaught, Prince Arthur, and the young Princesses, and then the Queen, with Princess Christian and Princess Beatrice. The Duke of Connaught is seen riding beside the Queen's carriage. As the cavalcade passes close to the camera very fine portraits were secured, and her Majesty is distinctly seen bowing to the people, who cheer lustily, waving flags, hats, and handkerchiefs, giving the royal guests a right royal welcome. The crowds follow the mounted troops who bring up the rear of the procession, and a finer film of an enthusiastic fast-moving mass of people was never photographed.'

Ref: *The Era*, 14 April 1900, p. 24b

5641   THE 21st LANCERS MARCHING THROUGH DUBLIN (4 April) (N)

'This is a separate section of the Royal Procession, and can be joined to the preceding number. These mounted troopers look very smart in their new uniforms, and as they pass between the ranks of spectators receive their share of cheering, for Omdurman was remembered without the aid of the Soudan medals most of them wore.'

Ref: *The Era*, 14 April 1900, p. 24b

5642   LANCERS, GUARDS, AND VOLUNTEERS WINDING THEIR WAY THROUGH THE CROWDED STREETS AFTER THE PROCESSION (4 April) (N) 75 ft

'A novel aspect is had in this film showing several companies of troops passing in opposite directions to the moving crowds. The entire picture is one moving mass of humanity.'

NOTICE. All the above subjects were photographed from one point of view, and can, therefore, be joined, making a grand series of this historical event

Ref: *The Era*, 14 April 1900, p. 24b

5643   THE SHARPSHOOTERS OF THE IMPERIAL YEOMANRY BIDDING
           FAREWELL TO THEIR FRIENDS, WHO MINGLE IN THE RANKS (N)

'The troops are seen leaving the barracks on their way to South Africa.'

Ref: *The Era*, 14 April 1900, p. 24b

5644   SCOTTISH SHARPSHOOTERS LEAVING EDINBURGH (N)

'This splendid subject was taken by courtesy of the Caledonian Railway
Company, and shows a crowd of people on the station platform bidding goodbye
to the troops, who are seen leaning out of the carriage windows waving flags and
handkerchiefs. The train is seen puffing out of the station, and rapidly passing
out of view. One of the best subjects yet taken of the departure of troops for the
front.'

Ref: *The Era*, 14 April 1900, p. 24b

5645   TRAVELLING TWO HUNDRED MILES AN HOUR (N-F) 75 ft

'Showing a section of an experimental line of the "Halford Gradient Railway"
which is the fastest railway system in the world. The only motive power is in the
track, which creates, by hydraulic power and in sections, a continuous gradient
down which the cars run at an ever increasing speed.'

Ref: WTC catalogue (September 1900), p. 137

5646   PONTOONS AND GUNS EN ROUTE FOR ORANGE RIVER (N) 75 ft

'An exceedingly fine film, showing a transport train laden with pontoons which
was used by General Clement's army in crossing the Orange River. The second
section shows another train with guns and troops passing a station en route for
the front. Excellent subject.'

Ref: *The Era*, 14 April 1900, p. 24b

5647   WASH DAY IN CAMP (N)

'Showing Tommy Atkins turning washerwoman, at the same time taking the
opportunity of giving himself and his comrades a scrub-down. One of the
humorous and interesting incidents of camp life near the front. Splendid
definition.'

Ref: *The Era*, 14 April 1900, p. 24b

RETURN OF THE HEROES OF LADYSMITH. ARRIVAL OF H.M.S. 'POWERFUL'
NAVAL BRIGADE AT PORTSMOUTH:

5648   PORTSMOUTH PREPARING TO WELCOME THE HEROES (April) (N)
           150 ft

'Scenes of H.M. Dockyard. This is a most interesting series, showing numerous
battleships of all descriptions, with other moving craft plying past the camera in
every direction. First is seen H.M.S. *Trafalgar* anchored off the jetty; then a
gunboat laden with Bluejackets (the cheering party) followed by a steam dredger,
showing H.M.S. *Hero* in the background. A broadside view of the training ship

Vincent, with marines climbing up the mast to the Crow's Nest is next depicted, while several barges pass in the foreground. The Isle of Wight boat is also steaming past, followed by two torpedo boats and the Admiral's launch rushing by the camera. This most interesting naval film is brought to a close by a view of H.M.S. *Vincent*, dressing the ship, showing hundreds of flags strung from stem to stern fluttering in the breeze. Nelson's flagship the *Victory*, of which a splendid view is included, is an appropriate ending to the subject.'

Ref: *The Era*, 28 April 1900, p. 27e

5649   ARRIVAL OF H.M.S. 'POWERFUL' AT PORTSMOUTH (11 April) (N) 150 ft

'The *Powerful*, after an absence of two years (including six months at the Cape), is seen slowly steaming up the harbour after passing the fort. A closer view is then obtained, and as the ship approaches the South Railway Jetty a broadside view is shown, depicting the details of the armament and the gallant bridge on board, who receive a most enthusiastic reception by those in waiting at the dock where the *Powerful* finally ties up. The gangway is raised and the ship is boarded by Sir M. Culme Seymour, Commander-in-Chief, Flag Captain Bridgeman, Mr Goschen, First Lord of the Admiralty, the Earl of Durham, Messrs Fred, George, William and Francis Lambton, Lord and Lady Hamilton, Lady Anne Lambton, and others of the assemblage there to welcome the return of the heroes.

   Capt. Lambton, the officers and some of the marines, are walking on the decks, greeting their friends on shore. Although it rained at the time, a remarkably fine and the only complete set of pictures was obtained by us. Most interesting.'

Ref: *The Era*, 28 April 1900, p. 27e

5650   SIR GEORGE WHITE'S RETURN FROM LADYSMITH (14 April) (N) 50 ft

'One of the first heroes to return from the seat of war is the central figure of this picture, showing Sir George White, who so gallantly commanded the garrison at besieged Ladysmith for 119 days, and since the relief of the town, by H.M.S. *Powerful* Naval Brigade and General Buller's army, has been invalided home. This film shows the arrival of the *Dunvegan Castle* with Sir George White standing on the captain's bridge, acknowledging the cheers and good wishes of the crowds lining the docks, who give him an enthusiastic reception. He is greeted by Colonel Stackpool, who gives three cheers for Sir George and Lady White. As soon as the gangway is in place, Lady White, with Colonel Stackpool, the mayor, and corporation of Southampton are seen going aboard. General White is accompanied ashore and while on the gangway raises his hat to the multitudes, who give him a veritable ovation. He is then seen coming directly towards our camera, surrounded by his friends and accompanied by Lady White, we obtaining magnificent likenesses of all the distinguished personages. Beautifully sharp and clear. By courtesy of Messrs Donald Currie and Co., Managers of the Union-Castle Mail Steamship Company, Limited.'

Ref: *The Era*, 28 April 1900, p. 27e

5651   THE QUEEN'S VISIT TO DUBLIN (4 April) (N) 100 ft

Production company J. Lizars (Belfast)

'This is the best view taken of Her Majesty entering the city gates at Dublin, and shows the royal carriage with body guard passing beneath the castelated tower, erected in honour of the Queen's visit. Enormous crowds follow the procession, and as a slight shower was falling at the time, hundreds of umbrellas are being raised, giving a most novel and interesting effect. This subject is technically perfect, and superior in every respect to other similar films in the market. By courtesy of J. Lizars, Belfast.'

Ref: *The Era*, 28 April 1900, p. 27e

5652   WAR SUPPLIES AND STORES DRAWN OVER THE PONTOON BRIDGE, ORANGE RIVER, BY MULE TEAMS (N) 125 ft

Photographed by Edgar M. Hyman

'This view is photographed from the Cape Colony side, and shows the steep wooded banks of the Orange Free State in the back ground. The pontoon bridge is crossed by mule teams drawing war supplies, each followed by armed guards. A depression of the pontoons into the water as the heavy loads are drawn over them is distinctly depicted. The first person seen crossing the bridge and walking towards the camera is Mr Rosenthal, of our War Staff, he having just completed a series of pictures on the opposite side of the river, and is returning, carrying the Bioscope camera and tripod. Splendid definition. Photographed by Edgar M. Hyman, of our War Staff.'

Ref: *The Era*, 28 April 1900, p. 27e

5653   THE SOUTH AUSTRALIANS CROSSING OVER THE PONTOON BRIDGE AND ENTERING THE ORANGE FREE STATE (N)

Photographed by Joseph Rosenthal

'This bridge was constructed in the record time of forty hours, considering its length. Over it are seen passing a detachment of General Clement's troopers on their way to Bloemfontein. As the scene was photographed from the Orange Free State side by Mr Rosenthal, of our War Staff, the troopers are entering the enemy's country the moment they step off the bridge.'

Ref: *The Era*, 28 April 1900, p. 27e

5654   TOMMY ATKINS CUTTING ROADS THROUGH THE BRUSH (N) 75 ft

Photographed by Joseph Rosenthal

'The Orange River is seen through the trees in the background, which forms a most picturesque setting to the action in this picture. The scene shows the troopers armed with pick and shovel, accompanied by mule teams making roads by spreading twigs and brushwood over the sandy soil on the Orange Free State side. Colonel Hoad and Staff are seen galloping over this road, having just crossed the Pontoon Bridge. The clear South African atmosphere enables us to practically produce stereoscopic effects and clear, sharp photography. Photographed by J. Rosenthal, now with Lord Roberts's Army.'

Ref: *The Era*, 28 April 1900, p. 27e

5655   SIR GEORGE WHITE LEAVING THE LONDON HIPPODROME (9 April) (N)

'Showing the entrance of this famous amusement resort lined with thousands of spectators anxious to catch a glimpse of the defender of Ladysmith as he leaves the theatre. He emerges in company of Mr Cook, the genial manager of the Hippodrome, and as soon as the crowds catch sight of him they literally mob them in their eagerness to possibly shake hands or get as close as the crush would permit. Surely General White was more at ease in Ladysmith than in the midst of a surging enthusiastic crowd. By kindness of the management of the London Hippodrome.'

Ref: *The Era*, 28 April 1900, p. 27e
    Copy in NFTVA (N.76)

5656   THE RECEPTION OF SIR GEORGE WHITE AND THE H.M.S. 'POWERFUL' NAVAL BRIGADE AT THE PORTSMOUTH CITY HALL (24 April) (N) 100 ft

'This superb view was taken from the top of the Portsmouth City Hall steps, and shows the street thronged with thousands of spectators greeting the arrival of Captain Lambton and the "handy men" of Ladysmith fame, who march down the street, then ascend the City Hall steps, passing closely by the camera. The picture is a most comprehensive one, including the Guards of Honour, the band, the enormous crowds, street decorations, and the entire squad of Marines as they wind along like some huge serpent. Another section shows the arrival of Sir George White, the gallant defender of Ladysmith, who drives up with Sir Baker Russell (the Commander-in-Chief of the Forces in Portsmouth). They are received by the mayor and corporation amid the cheering and waving of thousands of flags, &c. A splendid film, sharp and clear.'

Ref: *The Era*, 5 May 1900, p. 28c

5657   SAILORS OF THE QUEEN (2 May) (N) 100 ft

'This magnificent film shows the arrival of the *Powerful*'s "handy men" at Windsor, Marching towards Windsor Castle previous to their inspections by Her Majesty. The procession is headed by the Life Guards' band, with Capt. Lambton leading the heroes of Ladysmith, followed by the marines, two Maxims, and a 12-Pounder Gun, painted a khaki colour, these guns being the identical ones used at Ladysmith. The men make a gallant show as they sturdily step the music of the band, being lustily cheered by the multitudes crowding both sides of the street.'

Ref: *The Era*, 5 May 1900, p. 28c

5658   THE HEROES OF LADYSMITH MARCHING THROUGH LONDON (7 May) (N) 100 ft

'Previous to the review at the Horse Guards' Parade by H.R.H. Prince of Wales. Capital film.'

Ref: *The Era*, 19 May 1900, p. 27e
    Copy in NFTVA

5659   THE CAMERON HIGHLANDERS ENTERING BLOEMFONTEIN (N)
          75 ft

          'One of the very best South African war subjects.'

          Ref: *The Era*, 19 May 1900, p. 27e

5660   REVIEW OF THE H.M.S. 'POWERFUL' NAVAL BRIGADE AT THE
          HORSE GUARDS' PARADE, LONDON BY H.R.H. THE PRINCE OF
          WALES (7 May) (N) 75 ft

          Ref: *The Era*, 19 May 1900, p. 27e
             Copy in NFTVA

5661   MARCH PAST OF THE NAVAL BRIGADE (7 May) (N) 50 ft

          'A splendid film, showing these famous marines marching in squad before
          H.R.H. Prince of Wales.'

          Ref: *The Era*, 19 May 1900, p. 27e

5662   MORE AMMUNITION WANTED (N) 75 ft

          'An interesting view of troopers hurrying their teams, drawing ammunition across
          a drift to their comrades fighting at Pardeberg.'

          Ref: *The Era*, 19 May 1900, p. 27e

5663   THE COLDSTREAM GUARDS LEAVING BLOEMFONTEIN (N) 75 ft

          'Showing this detachment of General French's Column, both Infirmary [sic] and
          Cavalry, on the march to Kroonstad. One of the prominent troopers passing
          before the camera is Mr Burnham, "The American Scout".'

          Ref: *The Era*, 16 June 1900, p. 28d

5664   THE C.I.V.S MARCH ON JOHANNESBURG (N) 75 ft

          'Showing this gallant regiment (who has cut a most prominent figure in the
          capture of Johannesburg) leaving Kroonstad for the march across the Veldt. A
          magnificent picture.'

          Ref: *The Era*, 16 June 1900, p. 28d

5665   THE COLDSTREAM GUARDS CLEANING THEIR RIFLES IN CAMP
          (N)

          'Having just reached their camp at Bloemfontein after an engagement, these
          troops are seen busily engaged cleaning the dust and smoke from their guns. The
          tents and camp in the background make this a most interesting picture of the
          camp life of our troops in South Africa.'

          Ref: *The Era*, 16 June 1900, p. 28d

5666   AN INTERRUPTED GAME OF NAP IN CAMP (N)

          'Another one of the series of sidelights of our troops in South Africa, showing a
          group of players seated on the ground in front of a tent, evidently reaching a
          most exciting period of the game, when they are interrupted by the appearance of

an officer who commands them to stop the game and disperse the crowd of onlookers.'

Ref: *The Era*, 16 June 1900, p. 28d

5667   ON THE ROAD TO THE RACES (30 May) (N)

'A companion picture to the famous "Epsom Town" film. Showing brakes, vans, tally-hos and vehicles of every description, including the coster's cart, the people all loaded with enthusiasm, and otherwise, blowing horns, waving flags, &c., passing in rapid procession down the road midst picturesque surroundings, forming a splendid picture.'

Ref: *The Era*, 16 June 1900, p. 28d

Nos. 5668 to 5670   PANORAMA OF THE PARIS EXHIBITION (N) 625 ft

Taken from a moving vehicle. In three sections:

Section 1 The Champs Elysees and Esplanade des Invalides (175 ft)
Section 2 The Seine (250 ft)
Section 3 The Trocadero and Champs de Mars (200 ft)

For descriptions of each film consult the reference.

Ref: *The Era*, 16 June 1900, p. 28d

5671   THE CHATEAU D'EAU AND PALACE OF ELECTRICITY (N)

'A close panoramic view of the buildings radiating from both sides of the Palace of Electricity in front of which is seen the Chateau d'Eau, built in the form of a gigantic grotto from the top of which falls a series of cascades into basins further supplied with many fountains which play incessantly.'

Ref: WTC catalogue (April 1901), p. 153

5672   THE ESPLANADE DES INVALIDES (N) 75 ft

'A circular panoramic view giving a closer view of the grand group of Palaces lining both sides of this avenue, with the Hotel des Invalides in the background. As the camera is slowly revolved a splendid view of the Alexandre Bridge with its monuments and bronze statues is obtained.'

Ref: WTC catalogue (April 1901), p. 153

5673   CIRCULAR PANORAMA OF THE PLACE DE LA CONCORDE (N)

'Showing a most comprehensive view of many fine buildings, surrounding the finest square in the world with its obelisque, fountains and statues, vehicular traffic and many pedestrians all hurrying past the camera, the picture finally including a splendid view of the monumental gateway or main entrance to the Exposition.'

Ref: WTC catalogue (April 1901), p. 153

5674   NAVAL GUN CROSSING THE VET RIVER DRIFT (N) 100 ft

'One of the most interesting of all the South African War Series, showing a 4.7-inch naval gun and transport being drawn across the drift by ox teams, which splash through the water and tug at the heavy gun in crossing. As the gun descends the steep embankment of the river it is held back by ropes in the hands of scores of troops. A fine film, photographically perfect.'

Ref: *The Era*, 23 June 1900, p. 27d

5675   A SIEGE GUN AND TRANSPORT (N)

'This subject shows a 5-inch Howitzer Siege Gun and Transport (which played such havoc with Cronje's army) being drawn up a hill by ox teams, which are urged on by the dextrous handling of the long whips in the hands of native drivers. A splendid subject, full of action.'

Ref: *The Era*, 23 June 1900, p. 27d

5676   BOER PRISONERS UNDER ESCORT (N) 75 ft

'The prisoners shown in this subject were captured by Lord Roberts's army during their march on Kroonstad. They are seen leaving the camp, being conducted by a mounted escort, on their way to Bloemfontein. The two prisoners in the carts are Field Cornets; as they all pass closely by the camera every face is recognisable, all of them wearing a most dejected look. An interesting picture.'

Ref: *The Era*, 23 June 1900, p. 27d

5677   A SPANISH BULL FIGHT (24 May) (N) 500 ft

'Having secured special facilities by courtesy of the management of the Gran Plaza de Toros de Bordeaux, with apparatus specially built for the purpose of following the quick movements of the bull and fighters, we herewith place on the market the only complete bull fight ever published . . . Total length 500 feet. Price £25. Only furnished in the complete length.'

Ref: *The Era*, 16 June 1900, p. 28d

5678   THE SURRENDER OF KROONSTAD TO LORD ROBERTS (12 May) 150 ft

Photographed by Joseph Rosenthal
Showing Lords Roberts and Kitchener, with Staff Officers, entering Kroonstad at the head of the mounted column of foreign attaché's bodyguard, waggonette, in which are seated the Landrost and other officials who went out to surrender the town to Lord Roberts. As the column slowly files into the town and by our camera magnificent portraits of all were secured. This picture is a most valuable one, as it is the first, showing Lord Roberts in campaign uniform, and also includes a fine likeness of Lord Kitchener, the first ever produced by a cinematograph. The other only existing animated pictures, wherein Lord Roberts forms the central figure were taken by us—namely, Lord Roberts leaving Southampton, and the arrival of the Field Marshall at Cape Town. Photographed by Mr J. Rosenthal, of our War Staff, now with Lord Roberts's army in South Africa.'

Ref: *The Era*, 23 June 1900, p. 27d
Copy in NFTVA

5679   'THE RATS' OFF ON A PICNIC (N) 75 ft

'This scene shows a road through Mitcham, down which is seen approaching the cavalcade of four-in-hand coaches, cyclists, &c., &c., occupied by the members of the London Music Hall Society, bent on one of their annual outings. An interesting coaching subject.'

Ref: WTC catalogue (April 1901), p. 154

5680   'THE RATS' AT PLAY (N) 100 ft

'The leading members of the Music Hall Society, known as "the Rats", comprised of such artistes as Messrs. Dan Leno, Herbert Campbell, Joe Elvin, Will Evans, George Robey, T. Dunville, Harry Randall, &c., are seen in this picture enjoying themselves with the skipping rope and performing other antics, much to the amusement of the spectators. Many of the gentler sex of music hall fame join in the fun. Full of life and humour.'

Ref: WTC catalogue (April 1901), p. 154

5681   'THE RATS' AT DINNER (N) 100 ft

'The table cloths and covers are spread on the grass under the shade of sturdy oaks. These are surrounded by "Rats" members, all doing full justice to the edibles before them. Mr. Herbert Campbell presides, and the fun commences.
This subject will be thoroughly enjoyed by all music hall audiences familiar with the principal participants in the picture, all of whom are famous in the theatrical world.'

Ref: WTC catalogue (April 1901), p. 155

5682   THE KHEDIVE OF EGYPT AT WINDSOR (28 June) (N) 75 ft

'A splendid view of High Street, showing the entire procession of Band Guards of Honour, carriages occupied by the Khedive of Egypt, his favourite wives and suite all in Oriental costume, &c., &c., on their way to Windsor Castle to pay a visit to Her Majesty. A splendid portrait of this Oriental Ruler.'

Ref: WTC catalogue (April 1901), p. 155

5683   MERRY SCHOOLDAYS (N-F)

'This picture shows the exterior of a school house, the first section depicting a class of school boys, entering, many doing so rather reluctantly, according to the expressions on their face. The other section showing the boys and girls leaving school by rushing pell mell from the entrance, even falling over one another in their eagerness to get away to the playground. Splendid film.'

Ref: WTC catalogue (April 1901), p. 155

5684   THE PLEASURES OF PHOTOGRAPHY (N)

'Showing the arrival of the fire brigade in a field. After bringing the apparatus to a halt they unhitch the horses and commence to pump the engine. An energetic photographer wishing to take a snapshot of the proceedings has the stream of water directed upon himself and his camera by the fire laddies who enjoy a good laugh at his expenses. He retires more hurriedly than gracefully from the scene. Very funny.'

Ref: WTC catalogue (April 1901), p. 155

5685   THE GUARDS' BRIGADE OF GENERAL POLE-CAREW'S COMMAND
        CROSSING A SPRUIT BEFORE ENTERING KROONSTAD (12 May) (N)
        75 ft

        'The Brigade of General Pole-Carew is shown fording the drift on the outskirts of
        Kroonstad. Many of the troops look tired, dusty and foot-sore after their long
        march from Bloemfontein.'

        Ref: WTC catalogue (April 1901), p. 155

5686   LORD ROBERTS'S ARMY ENTERING KROONSTAD (12 May) (N)

        'A similar view as the preceding picture showing another section of the army
        entering the late Free State temporary capital. A splendid marching subject.'

        Ref: WTC catalogue (April 1901), p. 155

Nos. 5687 to 5700.   THE MUSIC HALL SPORTS AT HERNE HILL (10 July) (N)

5687   FIVE MILE BICYCLE HANDICAP RACE

5688   THE COLONIAL FLAG RACE

5689   THE EXECUTIVE CLUB CUP CYCLE OBSTACLE RACE

5690   THE LADIES' RUNNING RACE

5691   THE OBSTACLE SACK RACE

5692   LADIES, HURDLE, AND BOYS' AND GIRLS' RACES

5693   ONE MILE CHAMPION BELT RACE

5694   COMIC COSTUME SCRAMBLE

5695   OBSTACLE AND RUNNING RACES FOR ARTISTES

5696   ONE MILE WALKING HANDICAP

5697   BURLESQUE INDIAN ATTACK ON SETTLERS' CABIN

5698   CYCLE RACE OVER PLANKS AND DITCHES

5699   DAN LENO'S ATTEMPT TO MASTER THE WHEEL

5700   BURLESQUE FOX HUNT

        For descriptions of each film consult the reference.
        Ref: WTC catalogue (April 1901), pp. 155–156

5701   THE 'NATIONAL' TEAM CYCLE POLO MATCH (N) 75 ft

'Whoever has witnessed the Cycle Polo Matches at the Empire and Alhambra between the American and National Cycle Polo Teams will appreciate this view of an exciting match played for the benefit of being photographically recorded by us. Shows several collisions and spills with much furious riding and splendid play.'

Ref: WTC catalogue (April 1901), p. 157

5702   THE TUG OF WAR (N)

'Between two sets of heavy men, each team pulling at the rope as if their very lives depended on gaining the victory over their opponents, who fight hard for every inch of ground. They are seen to gradually lose. After the first victory the teams change about and have another try at it with a similar result. A blind man (who is led by his companions) seems to be the most enthusiastic one of the lot as far as pulling is concerned.'

Ref: WTC catalogue (April 1901), p. 157

5703   LIFE IN A PROVINCIAL TOWN (N-F)

'Life in a provincial town on a Sunday is anything but monotonous. The entire populace flocks to the streets and promenade up and down, others stopping in little knots, discussing with each other the events of the week with all the gossip of the village, &c. Truly a study of humanity. The young and old, feeble and strong, fat and lean, short and tall, all mingle together, clad in their best, making a most interesting picture.'

Ref: WTC catalogue (April 1901), p. 157

5704   THE MAYOR LEAVING CHURCH (N)

'Showing the exterior of the church entrance, from which emerges the Mayor and Mayoress, his dignitary appearing in his state robes. They both enter a carriage in waiting and drive off, amid the admiration of the crowds who throng around the church. Another study of humanity as we find it in the smaller towns.'

Ref: WTC catalogue (April 1901), p. 157

5705   CHURCH PARADE IN A PROVINCIAL TOWN (N-F)

'A splendid view of a fine wide street, both sides of which are lined with rows of trees. Under the cooling shades are seen promenading thousands of well dressed people. Still another study from a different standpoint.'

Ref: WTC catalogue (April 1901), p. 157

5706   SUNDAY IN A PROVINCIAL TOWN (N-F)

'The surprise with which some of the villagers regard the camera as they pass before it is plainly depicted in the countenances, and is of a most amusing character.
While this subject is of a similar nature to the preceding ones it nevertheless differs therefrom, showing another class of people we meet in outlying hamlets.'

Ref: WTC catalogue (April 1901), p. 157

5707   ONE SORT OF SUNDAY CROWD AT HYDE PARK (N-F)

'Shows a section of Hyde Park much frequented by disciples of anarchy, social-
ism, and other freaky and fanatical dogmas, with its usual crowds of listeners, all
eager, however, of appearing in the picture as soon as it was learned that the
"Bioscope man was out for the business that day". Here's where you get
expression of countenances and can study human nature as you will find nowhere
else on earth. Exceedingly interesting.'

Ref: WTC catalogue (April 1901), p. 157

5708   MARCH PAST OF THE QUEEN'S OWN CAMERONS (N)

'A splendid marching film showing the parade of this famous company of
Cameron Highlanders in their picturesque native uniform, passing by the camera
at close quarters, so that each face is recognizable. The troops are preceded by a
kilted band and pipers.'

Ref: WTC catalogue (April 1901), p. 157

5709   FEEDING THE HOG AND ITS YOUNG (N-F)

'A hog is a hog always, showing its hoggish nature to best advantage at feeding
time.
This scene shows a farmer filling a trough for the benefit of a score of little pigs
which crowd each other in their eagerness to get their share. Their feed is
suddenly cut short as an old sow breaks through the pailing and proceeds to
monopolize the trough and its remaining contents. The little fellows, however,
make a good fight for it.'

Ref: WTC catalogue (April 1901), pp. 157–158

5710   UNVEILING THE STATUE OF FLORA MACDONALD (N)

'Scene at the recent unveiling of the statue to the Jacobite heroine at Inverness,
showing the statue enveloped by a white cloth which at the proper moment opens
up and falls to the ground disclosing the beautiful white marble monument. The
large crowd is seen raising their hats and cheering.'

Ref: WTC catalogue (April 1901), p. 158

5711   WORKMEN LEAVING THE FACTORY (N-F)

'Between six and seven hundred workmen leaving the factory, emerging at a
narrow doorway. The picture is beautifully sharp and clear, and shows the facial
expressions of the men to good advantage.'

Ref: WTC catalogue (April 1901), p. 158

5712   PARADE OF PRIZE CART HORSES AT THE AGRICULTURAL SHOW
            (N)

'A picture such as Rosa Bonheur delighted in portraying, showing a parade of
prize Clydesdale horses (the finest draught horses in the world) before the
spectators at the Highland Society Agricultural Show. A splendid subject.'

Ref: WTC catalogue (April 1901), p. 158

5713   SIR GEORGE WHITE'S PRESENTATION OF A CHARGER (16 June) (N)

'A subscription list was opened in the North of Ireland to make a presentation from the people of the district to Sir George White. The subscriptions were generally from the working people, and it was decided to let the presentation take the form of an Irish bred charger. The charger was bought and presented at the N.E. Show Grounds, Balmoral, Belfast, on Saturday, June 16th, in the presence of some twenty or thirty thousand of the inhabitants of this district. After the presentation, the horse was taken charge of by a trooper who had served through the siege of Ladysmith. The film shows the charger passing the stand with this trooper on its back. It also shows the gentleman who made the presentation handing the charger over to Sir George White, and winds up with an excellent portrait of Sir George White standing at the charger's head.'

Ref: *The Era*, 4 August 1900, p. 24a

5714   THE TROCODERA FOUNTAINS AND CASCADE (N)

'The Trocodera Cascades are world famed, and a splendid picture of same was procured showing two different views, the first from the side, giving a good view of the Russian section of the Paris Exposition in the background. The other section was taken from the front of the Trocodera, and shows the entire series of tumbling sheets of water. Fine.'

Ref: WTC catalogue (April 1901), p. 158

5715   THE BOIS DE BOULOGNE, PARIS (N-F)

'A splendid view of this famous Parisian drive with its numerous gorgeous equipages going in both directions. The Arc de Triumph looms up in fine proportions in the background while the people sauntering beneath the shade of the trees which line this boulevard lends further action to this picture.'

Ref: WTC catalogue (April 1901), p. 158

5716   THE CASCADES OF THE BOIS DE BOULOGNE (N-F)

'But very few visitors to Paris miss the opportunity of viewing this beautiful waterfall in its most picturesque natural setting of rocks, trees and ferns and its placid, miniature lake. There is not much excitement of turbulent action to this subject—it is simply a delightful and refreshing depicture of nature.'

Ref: WTC catalogue (April 1901), p. 158

5717   T.R.H. DUKE AND DUCHESS OF YORK AT A GARDEN PARTY (N)

'Showing splendid portraits of TRH the Duke and Duchess of York with the Duke of Cambridge and other royal guests at the garden party given in honour of the Duke of Cambridge at Richmond. The surrounding scenery, pavilions, tents and shrubbery of the beautiful grounds make a splendid setting to the picture.'

Ref: WTC catalogue (April 1901), p. 158

Nos. 5718 to 5720   SPANISH BULL FIGHT IN MADRID (N) 400 ft

5718   ENTRY OF THE BULL AND FIGHT WITH PICADORS (175 ft)

5719   FIGHT WITH BANDERILLEROS (125 ft)

5720   THE MATADOR'S SWORD THRUSTS AND DEATH OF BULL (100 ft)

Nos. 5718 to 5720 are from one continuous negative and can be supplied in one strip.

For a description of each film consult the reference.

Ref: WTC catalogue (April 1901), p. 159

5721   THE ESSEX REGIMENT GOING INTO ACTION (June) (N)

Photographed by Joseph Rosenthal

'Showing men of this regiment walking cautiously to the line of action, some going right on, others looking for cover from which to fire their guns, while in the background is seen a line of soldiers advancing to the front. A naval gun in action is also seen in the far distance. One of the few subjects which Mr Rosenthal (of our S.A. War Staff) found possible to photograph during action.'

Ref: *The Era*, 4 August 1900, p. 24a

5722   THE 4.7-INCH GUN IN ACTION AT THE BATTLE OF PRETORIA (4 June) (N)

Photographed by Joseph Rosenthal

'This and the following films are the only subjects yet photographed while the guns were in action (not prearranged for the occasion). It shows a 4.7-inch gun firing at the Boers outside Pretoria on June 4th, 1900. Mr Rosenthal photographed this incident in company with Mr Bennett Burleigh, war correspondent of the "Daily Telegraph", while bullets fell thick and fast, and both gentlemen were almost smothered twice by the dirt thrown up by bursting shells, which fell in rather too close proximity for comfort. One of the officials, within 30 ft of our photographer, was wounded in this battle, and several horses and mules were killed.'

Ref: *The Era*, 4 August 1900, p. 24a

5723   THE 5-INCH SIEGE GUNS IN ACTION AT THE BATTLE OF PRETORIA (4 June) (N) 100 ft

Photographed by Joseph Rosenthal

'This photograph was secured in another section of the battlefield, showing a 5-inch siege gun firing two rounds, while much smoke from firing of other guns in close proximity is also seen. After the recoil from the firing the guns are again drawn into position by the gunners. Little clouds of dust are thrown up constantly by the enemy's bullets striking the ground. Our photographer's horse was shot in this battle. Mr. Rosenthal, referring to the taking of the film, writes that Boer shells were bursting all around and overhead, and that but very few of the thousands of people who will see the reproductions of these films "will think of the poor devil who turned the handle of the camera".'

Ref: WTC catalogue (April 1900), p. 160

5724   ENTRY OF LORD ROBERTS INTO PRETORIA (5 June) (N) 75 ft

Photographed by Edgar M. Hyman

'Showing Church-square, Pretoria, with a view down Market-street. The Grand Hotel, with its verandahs packed with spectators, is seen on the right hand side, while a splendid view of the Raadzaal (Houses of Parliament) is shown on the left corner of Church-square. Lords Roberts and Kitchener with Staff, Guard, Attachés &c., are seen approaching down from Market-street, preparatory to taking their positions for the hoisting of the Union Jack over the Government Buildings. Photographed June 5th, 1900, by E. M. Hyman, of our War Staff in South Africa.'

Ref: *The Era*, 4 August 1900, p. 24a

5725   ENTRY OF TROOPS INTO PRETORIA (5 June) (N) 75 ft

Photographed by Edgar M. Hyman

'This film is taken from same position as the preceding one, showing the arrival of the troops in Church-square, previous to the review before Lord Roberts and Staff. Thousands of soldiers are seen marching down Market-street. The troops passing the camera during this photograph series are the Suffolk Regiment.'

Ref: *The Era*, 4 August 1900, p. 24a

5726   LORD ROBERTS HOISTING THE UNION JACK AT PRETORIA (5 June) (N) 125 ft

Photographed by Joseph Rosenthal

'This film is composed of three views of incidents as follows: the first section shows the hoisting of the Union Jack over the Raadzaal (the flag used is very small, similar to the one used at Johannesburg, and is only just visible in the picture), while many in the crowds cheer. Section two shows Lord Roberts, Staff, and Troops giving three cheers for the Queen, and in the third is seen the Review of the troops before the Commander-in-Chief, Staff, Guards of Honour, &c. A splendid film of an interesting historic event. Photographed by J. Rosenthal, of our South African War Staff.'

Ref: *The Era*, 4 August 1900, p. 24a

5727   RAZING A FACTORY CHIMNEY (14 July) (N) 100 ft

'This film shows the interesting operation of razing the 150 ft chimney which stood for eighty years on the property of Messrs Lee at Hooley Bridge, Heywood, and was successfully felled by Mr T. Smith, of Rochdale, the "Lancashire Steeple-Jack", on July 14th, 1900

The first section comprises a close view of the base of chimney, showing the lighting of the fire for burning the props which support the column. Next is shown a view from a distance, showing the fierce burning of the props, with Mr Smith pouring pails of kerosene to feed the flames. Then is seen the buckling of the supports, and the corresponding leaning of the tall stack, until the supports give way and the chimney falls (apparently towards the camera), telescoping while descending, and reaches the ground amid dense clouds of smoke and dust.

The operator was dangerously close in order to secure a successful and interesting picture, in both of which he succeeded admirably.'

Ref: WTC catalogue (April 1901), p. 160

5728   CHURCH PARADE ON NORTH PIER, BLACKPOOL (N) 75 ft

'Showing hundreds of people leaving the Pavilion, wherein Church Service was held. Also a general view of the Pier with its thousands of visitors on church parade. The sea breaking on the beach with its sailing yachts and bathing machines, and a view of Blackpool in the background make this one of the most interesting of sea-shore pictures.'

Ref: WTC catalogue (April 1901), p. 160

Nos. 5729 and 5730 allocated to films by G. A. Smith, q.v.

For a description of each film consult the reference.

Ref: WTC catalogue (September 1900), p. 149

5731   ARTILLERY FORDING THE VAAL RIVER (N)

'A detachment of artillery of Lord Roberts's army crossing the Drift while on their march on Johannesburg. The men mount horses, guns, and ammunition waggons while crossing, but dismount as soon as dry land is reached. The horses are seen splashing and lingering in the water as though loth to leave the pleasantly cooling bath.'

Ref: *The Era*, 4 August 1900, p. 24a

5732   THE ESSEX REGIMENT CROSSING VAAL RIVER ON THE WAGGON PUNT (N) 100 ft

'This film is unique, showing about 200 men of the Essex Regiment crossing the Vaal River on a waggon punt, which was used at this point to transport a good proportion of the army from bank to bank. It is drawn back and forth by ropes in the hands of the men on shore. As soon as the punt touches the bank the front men jump ashore, while the others all closely packed together, disembark in a hurry. An exceedingly interesting film.'

Ref: *The Era*, 4 August 1900, p. 24a

5733   WAR BALLOON AND TRANSPORT CROSSING THE VAAL RIVER (27 May) (N) 100 ft

Photographed by Joseph Rosenthal

'Much has been written regarding the war balloon, which is shown in this picture, with the basket or car attached to the balloon waggon while crossing the Vaal River at Viljohn's Drift. Hundreds of transport waggons, carts, mule and ox teams belonging to this convoy, lend much life to this picture, which aside from the interesting nature of the subject, is a fine example of animated photography. Vereeniging Station is about two days' march from Johannesburg, and was reached on May 27th, 1900. Photographed by J. Rosenthal, of our S. A. War Staff.'

Ref: WTC catalogue (April 1901), p. 161
Copy in NFTVA

5734   HOISTING THE UNION JACK AT JOHANNESBURG (31 May) (N)

'This film is of great importance, as it shows the ceremony of hauling down the Boer flag and hoisting the Union Jack in front of the Government Building at Johannesburg, May 31st, 1900. Lord Roberts arrives with his Staff Officers, and after the formation of a square by the troops, the ceremony is proceeded with while the 30,000 spectators groan and cheer in turn as their respective flags appear on the staff in the foreground. Dr Krause, the town commandant under Boer government, is seen astride a horse between Lords Roberts and Kitchener gloomily watching the scene. (Note. The Union Jack used is a very small one, the silk flag made by Lady Roberts, which Lord Roberts promised her to raise over every town he occupied).'

Ref: *The Era*, 4 August 1900, p. 24a

5735   TERRIBLE ROW IN A BARNYARD (N-F) 100 ft

'Showing several pigs rutting about amongst the chickens in a corner of the barnyard. Two roosters start fighting, and after waging the battle fiercely for a time, they are joined by a third and finally a fourth game cock, all of which take turns at fighting with one another, two fights going on at the same time. The very best film of a cock fight ever taken.'

Ref: WTC catalogue Supplement no. 1 (Nov/Dec 1900)

5736   THE CLOWN AND ENCHANTED CANDLE (F)

Producer: unknown

'A good subject for the pantomime season, showing a clown seated at a table reading by the light of two candles. One of the candles grows higher and higher when it recedes into the candlestick. The other candle also commences to play pranks, and in his confusion and surprise the paper catches fire and the clown flees from the scene in dismay.'

Ref: WTC catalogue Supplement no. 1 (Nov/Dec 1900)

5737   THE 5-INCH SIEGE GUNS CROSSING VAAL RIVER (N)

'Showing a general view of the Vaal River, the stream which is the dividing line between the Transvaal and Orange Free State, the 60,000 men of General Roberts' army were compelled to cross this river by no other means than fording same. This view shows the siege guns being drawn across the stream by ox teams, urged on by native drivers with long whips. Lots of action. A splendid subject.'

Ref: WTC catalogue Supplement no. 1 (Nov/Dec 1900)
Copy in NFTVA

5738   FIELD AMBULANCES CROSSING THE VAAL RIVER (N)

'Another section of the convoy crossing the river at the same point of view as the preceding picture, showing scores of field hospital and ambulance waggons drawn by mule teams. The fluttering of the Red Cross flags on each waggon with the plunging of the mules and the gesticulations of the drivers and members of the Corps lend much life and action to this splendid picture.'

Ref: WTC catalogue Supplement no. 1 (Nov/Dec 1900)

  Copy in NFTVA

5739   TRANSPORTS AND WATER CARTS CROSSING VAAL RIVER (N)

'Hundreds of waggons and carts of every description are depicted in this view crossing the river, all bent on reaching the opposite shore (the Transvaal) as quickly as possible. At this point the army was only three days march from Johannesburg, which city surrendered on May 31st. All three subjects 5737 to 5739 can be joined into one long strip, 150 feet, thereby conveying some idea of the enormous number of waggons, horses and oxen required to carry the supplies of an invading army and look after its sick and wounded. The preceding three films were photographed by our War Staff with Lord Roberts' Army in South Africa.'

Ref: WTC catalogue Supplement no. 1 (Nov/Dec 1900)

5740   TUG OF WAR AT THE POLICE SPORTS (N)

'This is a splendid representation of a contest of strength between two teams of athletes of the Scotch Police Force. After one team triumphs over the other, they change places, when there is further opportunity of denoting the winning team.'

Ref: WTC catalogue Supplement no. 1 (Nov/Dec 1900)

5741   BICYCLE RACE—WITH BAD SPILL (N)

'This picture shows a crowded course and grand stand at the bicycle races. The beginning of the film shows the start of some dozen entries. After spinning around the track three laps, the contestants becoming fewer each time, the final lap photographically recorded shows a bad spill among five of the foremost cyclists. A splendid film, with an exciting ending.'

Ref: *The Era*, 22 September 1900, p. 27e

5742   ASSOCIATION FOOTBALL GAME BETWEEN PROMINENT ENGLISH TEAMS (N) 150 ft

'Showing mid-field play, kicks, interrupted goals, and a few accidents. One of the liveliest as well as the most successful football games ever recorded cinematographically.'

Ref: *The Era*, 22 September 1900, p. 27e

5743   THE CLOUTCHAM STAG HUNT (September) (N) 150 ft

'A series of nine scenes at the opening meeting of the Devon and Somerset Hounds. The various scenes portray some of the most magnificent views of land and sea, hill and dale, barren moor and fertile fields, that even the West Country can show. The film begins with a view of the hunters going to the meet at Dunkerry Beacon. Arrival of the hounds. The Master of the Hunt (M. R. Sanders) arrives, and greets the riders. Kennelling the pack. The hunters awaiting the announcement of the beginning of the hunt. The Master of the hunt returning with the tufters, and unkennelling the pack. Off to the hunt, showing the hunters, hounds, and riders, to the number of several hundred, galloping over the moors.

Note. For completion of this series it would be advisable to add thereto subject "Hounds Following the Stag Across Stream" and "Feeding the Pack after Break-up of the Stag'.' (Nos. 70002 and 7004).

Ref: *The Era*, 22 September 1900, p. 27e

5744   BADGER DIGGING IN WEST SOMERSET WITH THE PORLOCK TERRIER PACK AT ISON NEAR QUARME (September) (N) 200 ft

'Showing incidents connected with the badger hunt, as follows: The Meet. The Arrival of the Pack. Climbing the Hills. Locating the badger, and putting the terriers into the hole. Digging for the badger. The badger escapes. The hunters, with terriers, chase, and return with the badger bagged. Killing and skinning the badger (the badger in this instance was an old one, weighing 22 lbs.) Holding up the carcase [sic] and skin, giving the former to the terriers. Distribution of trophies of the hunt, consisting of head and the pads. Return from the hunt. The above is one of the most interesting sporting pictures. This is the first instance where a subject of this nature was successfully cinematographed, owing to the many difficulties encountered in securing photographs of a badger digging, which generally takes place in an almost inaccessible country, privately controlled, and for the photographing of which we have only secured permission and facilities with considerable trouble.'

Ref: *The Era*, 22 September 1900, p. 27e

5745   YACHTING OFF CARNARVON ON THE MENAI STRAITS (N)

'Showing many yachts sailing by in a good breeze, preparatory to entering the races of the Regatta. A splendid subject, sharp and clear.'

Ref: WTC catalogue (April 1901), p. 163

5746   THE S.S. 'ST. TUDNO' LEAVING LLANDUDNO (N-F)

'Photographed from the Pier. Showing the S.S. *St. Tudno* crowded with passengers, all waving their caps and handkerchiefs after the steamer as it proceeds on its way towards the Menai Straits. Also shows the arrival of the S.S. *St. Elvies* approaching the Pier at full speed. An interesting shipping subject.

By courtesy of the Liverpool & North Wales Steamship Co.'

Ref: WTC catalogue (April 1901), p. 163

5747   PANORAMIC VIEWS OF MENAI STRAITS (N-F) 100 ft

'From Puffin Island to Menai Bridge. Showing successive views of the foreland and lighthouse approaching Bangor Pier, the scenery along the shores, panoramic view of Menai Bridge, arrival at the landing stage, &c. This subject includes some of the most interesting and picturesque views to be found in North Wales.

By courtesy of the Liverpool & North Wales Steamship Co.'

Ref: WTC catalogue (April 1901), p. 164

5748   LAUNCH OF THE S.S. 'SALAMIS' (N)

'View from the ways showing the prow of the vessel, with its heavy cables, chains and anchors, which are dropped with a splash into the water as the ship leaves the ways. A splendid photograph.'

Ref: WTC catalogue (April 1901), p. 164

5749   LAUNCH OF THE S.S. 'SALAMIS' (N)

'Seen from Mathews' Quay, showing the stern of the vessel entering the water. Further interest is attached to this and the preceding picture from the fact that S.S. *Salamis* was chartered by the Government as a transport for conveying troops to China.'

Ref: WTC catalogue (April 1901), p. 164

5750   THE S.S. 'SALAMIS' OUTWARD BOUND (N)

'Showing the splendid lines of this ship, leaving the docks under fair headway.'

Ref: WTC catalogue (April 1901), p. 164

Nos. 5751 to 5766   THE NAVAL MANOEUVRES (N-F)

The following is a series of photographs taken by special permission of the Admiralty.

Photographed from the decks of H.M.S. *Gibraltar*

5751   THE ATTACKING FLEET OFF IRELAND (150 ft)

5752   THE DEFENDING FLEET AT BEREHAVEN (125 ft)

5753   MANNING AND LOWERING SHIP'S BOAT FROM THE DECK OF H.M.S. 'GIBRALTAR'

5754   ARRIVAL OF THE SMALL BOAT—RAISING SAME WITH CREW ON BOARD SHIP

5755   OFF FOR A LAND ATTACK

5756   JACK AT PLAY (75 ft)

5757   JACK'S GAME OF CRICKET ON BOARD H.M.S. 'GIBRALTAR'

5758   JACK AT WORK (75 ft)

5759   JACK SCRUBS HIS HAMMOCK

5760   SERVING OUT THE GROG

5761   HOISTING GUNS INTO POSITION

5762   JACK AT THE GUNS

5763   MARINES DRILL WITH QUICK-FIRING GUNS (75 ft)

5764   BLUEJACKETS' DRILL WITH HEAVY GUNS

5765   FIRING HEAVY GUNS FROM A CRUISER (100 ft)

            For fuller particulars consult the reference.
            Ref: WTC catalogue (April 1901), p. 165

5766   FIRING GUNS FROM A FORT (N-F) 125 ft

            'It is but seldom that a photographer is allowed to take views for public exhi-
            bition inside a fort, but as our operators are ever alive, they readily overcame this
            slight obstacle, the Commander evidently being convinced of the interest with
            which these pictures would be received by the public, thus showing the manner in
            which our coast is defended from land. The view includes a section of the
            fortifications with a battery of three heavy guns firing several rounds each in
            rapid succession, further showing the high efficiency and training of the gunners
            and officers. Full of action.'

            Ref: WTC catalogue (April 1901), p. 165

Nos. 5767 to 5771   THE ROYAL NORTHERN AGRICULTURAL SHOW (N)

5767   PARADE OF THE QUEEN'S ENTRIES OF SHORT HORN CATTLE

5768   PARADE OF THE POLLED CATTLE

5769   THE PONY PARADE

5770   THE HORSE PARADE

5771   THE HORSE PARADE No. 2

            (For fuller particulars see the reference).
            Ref: WTC catalogue (April 1901), p. 166

5772   SHEEP ON THE MOORS (N-F)

            'A flock of Exmoor sheep being driven over a road on their native heath by a
            mounted sheep farmer and his dog. The timidity of hundreds of the sheep as they
            approach the camera, towards which they are driven, and their sudden dash by
            the instrument lends much action and interest to the picture. This and the
            following subject are entirely different from the usual sheep driving pictures
            already on the market.'

            Ref: WTC catalogue (April 1901), p. 166

5773   DRIVING A THOUSAND EXMOOR SHEEP OVER A MOUNTAIN ROAD
            (N-F) 75 ft

'A flock of a thousand sheep is difficult to control on a narrow road, and in order to make progress they are driven in sections of about one hundred each. Several occupants of a carriage driving by get out and try their hand at the game. They and the sheep dog have a lively time of it in keeping the sheep from scattering in different directions over the moors.

The rolling hills and typical highland scenery in the background lend much beauty to this picturesque subject.'

Ref: WTC catalogue (April 1901), p. 166

5774   BORDEAUX TRAFFIC DURING A RAIN STORM (N-F)

'A street scene in Bordeaux, showing much vehicular traffic and thousands of pedestrians making their way through a driving rain storm. The splashing of the rain in the puddles in the street, the dripping from the hundreds of umbrellas, &c., make this a most unique subject, sharp and clear. One of but very few pictures taken during the rain.'

Ref: WTC catalogue (April 1901), p. 166

5775   A PARISIAN BOULEVARD ON A RAINY DAY (N-F)

'The success of the preceding picture induced us to have another try under similar conditions on one of the Parisian Boulevards. In this we were likewise successful, and offer this subject to our patrons as one we can conscientiously recommend as being different from the ordinary street scenes which are usually photographed on a bright day. It is sharp, clear and full of life and interest.'

Ref: WTC catalogue (April 1901), pp. 166–167

5776   PANORAMA OF BAUCHORY, SCOTLAND (N-F) 75 ft

'Taken from an express train on the Deeside Railway. A splendid panoramic view of this picturesque town, perched on the side of a Scotch hill, like a gem in a setting. The hundreds of cottages, surrounded by gardens, the village church, the stately trees, and a distant view of the mountains in the background, make this one of the most interesting and refreshing subjects included in our list.

A characteristic bit of scenery in the vicinity of the Queen's Highland home.'

Ref: WTC catalogue (April 1901), p. 167

Nos. 5777 to 5788 allocated to films made by G. A. Smith

For full particulars consult the reference or the Smith filmography above.

Refs: *The Era*, 22 September 1900, p. 27e
   WTC catalogue (April 1901), pp. 167–168

5789   SANGER'S CIRCUS PASSING THROUGH INVERNESS (N) 75 ft

'A circus procession is always viewed with interest by young and old alike. As it was raining at the time this circus passed through the streets of Inverness, further life is lent to the picture by the hurry of the caravan of riders, chariots, cages, camels and elephants, the latter extending their trunks towards the crowds in the hope of receiving some dainty on the way. Always takes well with an audience.'

Refs: *The Era*, 20 October 1900, p. 30e
    WTC catalogue (April 1901), p. 169

5790   SCOTCH LASSIES' INDIAN CLUB EXERCISES (N) 75 ft

'About a score of little girls exercising with Indian clubs at a prize drill during a Highland gathering. The precision and adeptness with which these lassies handle the clubs speaks well for their training and the assurance that they can well "hold their own" in after life. A very pretty scene, full of action, sharp and clear.'

Refs: *The Era*, 20 October 1900, p. 30e
    WTC catalogue (April 1901), p. 169

5791   LORD LOVETT'S SCOUTS PASSING OVER THE HIGHLANDS / SCOTCH LIGHT HORSE CROSSING THE HIGHLANDS (N) 50 ft

'This volunteer company here shown riding over a Highland road in civilian dress, who were mobilised at the commencement of the South African war, form a body of stalwart men who have since distinguished themselves by their daring and adroitness. This fine company of horsemen have been much discussed and written about, and this picture would be well received by any British or Colonial audience.'

Refs: *The Era*, 20 October 1900, p. 30e
    WTC catalogue (April 1901), p. 169

5792   THE ISLE OF MAN BOAT, 'EMPRESS QUEEN', LEAVING PRINCE'S DOCK, LIVERPOOL / THE 'EMPRESS QUEEN' LEAVING PRINCE'S DOCK (N-F) 50 ft

'This is a fine picture of the departure of a favourite Isle of Man steamer, with hundreds of pleasure seekers on board going to the gay town of Douglas. The dock is crowded with thousands of people who are witnessing the embarkation of passengers and the departure of the boat. A splendid subject. Full of action. By courtesy of the Mersey Docks and Harbour Board.'

Refs: *The Era*, 20 October 1900, p. 30e
    WTC catalogue (April 1901), p. 169

5793   THE S.S. 'ST. TUDNO' AT PRINCE'S DOCK / THE 'ST. TUDNO' AT LIVERPOOL AND MENAI STRAITS (N-F) 50 ft

'The S.S. *St. Tudno* is the largest steamer of the Liverpool and North Wales Steamship Co.'s fleet, and is seen lying alongside Prince's Dock taking aboard hundreds of passengers. The second section shows a panoramic view of the picturesque Menai Straits, through which the steamer passes, while the third section reproduces a scene of the arrival of the steamer at the landing stage.'

Refs: *The Era*, 20 October 1900, p. 30e
    WTC catalogue (April 1901), p. 169

5794   PANORAMA OF THE DECKS OF 'ST. TUDNO' / 'ST. TUDNO'S' OFFICERS AND PASSENGERS (N-F) 50 ft

'While moored at the Menai Bridge landing stage a panoramic view of the decks of the S.S. *St. Tudno* and the S.S. *St. Elvies* was procured, showing splendid portraits of the smart captains and officers of the two vessels, besides hundreds of the passengers. An interesting picture.'

Refs: *The Era*, 20 October 1900, p. 30e
　　WTC catalogue (April 1901), p. 169

5795   APPROACHING AND LANDING AT BANGOR PIER / THE 'ST TUDNO' ARRIVING AT BEAUMARIS PIER (N-F) 50 ft

'As the steamer approaches the pier a panoramic view was procured from the deck of the ship, which as it draws nearer shows hundreds of expectant faces crowding against the railing of the landing stage welcoming their friends, who are furthermore seen disembarking.'

Refs: *The Era*, 20 October 1900, p. 30e
　　WTC catalogue (April 1901), p. 169

5796   THE LIVERPOOL AND NORTH WALES STEAMSHIP COMPANY'S S.S. 'ST. TUDNO' AND 'ST. ELVIES' LEAVING MENAI BRIDGE / THE 'ST. TUDNO' AND 'ST. ELVIES' LEAVING MENAI BRIDGE (N-F) 50 ft

'The first section of this picture shows the S.S. *St. Tudno* under full headway leaving Menai Bridge, the second view shows the same vessel meeting the S.S. *St. Elvies*, which is on her way to Menai Bridge to collect her passengers for the return trip to Liverpool, when the third view shows her passing the camera under full headway, her decks crowded with people waving a good-bye to their friends left ashore.

The preceding four pictures were secured by courtesy of management of the Liverpool and North Wales Steamship Co.'

Refs: *The Era*, 20 October 1900, p. 30e
　　WTC catalogue (April 1901), p. 169

5797   A HIGHLAND WATERFALL (N-F) 50 ft

'A waterfall is always a subject of interest and fascination. The one portrayed in this picture is located near Inverness, and its large volume of tumbling waters, from which the spray and mists arise in clouds as it falls on the rugged rocks below, makes this one of the finest pictures of animated photography it has been our good fortune to secure.'

Refs: *The Era*, 20 October 1900, p. 30e
　　WTC catalogue (September 1900), p. 165

5798   THE SWALLOW FALLS NEAR BETWS-Y-COED (N-F) 50 ft

'These falls are considered by many to be the finest in Wales, and in order to gain a better idea of the whole scene (it being an impossibility to portray the entire falls in one picture owing to the inaccessible and dangerous rocks which separate torrents and miniature falls until they meet again in one vast volume of water, a closer view of which is shown in the second picture, while in the third section the falls are seen from another point of view, the fourth shows the lower falls with its turbulent waters rushing away, finally being lost to view between the high rocks and trees.'

Refs: *The Era*, 20 October 1900, p. 30e

WTC catalogue Supplement no. 1 (Nov/Dec 1900), pp. 165–166

5799   THE ROCKS AND FALLS OF PONT-Y-PAIR (N-F) 50 ft

'This most picturesque bridge with its surrounding scenery has been often
painted, and makes a lovely picture. The Llugwy River, which, crossed by Pont-y-
Pair (the bridge of the Cauldron), is evidently so termed on account of its rocky
bed, among which the seething waters rush, forming many falls and pools. A
further panoramic view of this rugged section, with its woodland glades, forms a
favourite spot for all visitors, and produces a most soothing and peaceful effect
when projected on the screen.'

Refs: *The Era*, 20 October 1900, p. 30e

WTC catalogue Supplement no. 1 (Nov/Dec 1900), p. 166

5800   PANORAMA OF CHURCH ISLAND, MENAI BRIDGE. Two views (N-F)
            50 ft

'The first view is taken from a distance, while the second is a complete panorama,
taking in the churchyard, showing its many quaint tombstones and monuments.
The former are made use of by the majority of visitors, as shown in the picture.'

Refs: *The Era*, 20 October 1900, p. 30e

WTC catalogue Supplement no. 1 (Nov/Dec 1900), p. 166

5801   GLIMPSES ON THE LIVERPOOL OVERHEAD RAILWAY (N-F) 100 ft

'The picture represented here . . . was photographed from the front of an electric
train, running at full speed over this structure, until it reaches Dingle, after
crossing the Girder Bridge, it enters the tunnel at its southern terminus. Further
action is lent to the picture by meeting many trains running in the opposite
direction.'

Refs: *The Era*, 20 October 1900, p. 30e

WTC catalogue Supplement no. 1 (Nov/Dec 1900), p. 166

5802   THE ELECTRIC TRAINS OF THE LIVERPOOL OVERHEAD RAILWAY
            (N-F) 75 ft

'This picture shows the arrival at the station of several trains, which discharge
their passengers and quickly depart for the next station. A further view is had of
several trains on the overhead structure, rounding the sharp curves at
Hurculaneum Docks, crossing the bridge, and rushing in and out of the Dingle
tunnel.

This and the preceding picture were photographed by courtesy of the Liverpool
Overhead Railway Co.'

Refs: *The Era*, 20 October 1900, p. 30e

WTC catalogue Supplement no. 1 (Nov/Dec 1900), p. 166

5803   PANORAMA OF CONWAY CASTLE (N-F) 50 ft

'Photographed from the rising ground at the south side of the North Western
Railway, including a portion of the Conway River, the North Western Tubular

Bridge, the Castle, its embattlements, as well as a view of the town. A decidedly picturesque view.'

Refs: *The Era*, 20 October 1900, p. 30e
    WTC catalogue Supplement no. 1 (Nov/Dec 1900), p. 166

5804   PANORAMA OF CONWAY CASTLE FROM CONWAY RIVER (N-F) 50 ft

'Another most interesting panoramic picture taken from the opposite shore of the Conway River, from which is obtained another most graceful view of the Castle, embattled towers and walls, besides the traffic over the Chain Bridge. Sharp and clear.'

Refs: *The Era*, 20 October 1900, p. 30e
    WTC catalogue Supplement no. 1 (Nov/Dec 1900), p. 166

5805   NORTH WESTERN TRAINS ENTERING CONWAY TUBULAR BRIDGE (N-F) 50 ft

'This subject starts with a panoramic view embracing the Conway Chain Bridge, a section of the Castle, and halting long enough at the entrance of the . . . picturesque arches of the structure. When the panoramic turn table of the camera was again brought into play, disclosing a view of the fields and hills in the background.'

Refs: *The Era*, 20 October 1900, p. 30e
    WTC catalogue Supplement no. 1 (Nov/Dec 1900), pp. 166–67

5806   PANORAMIC GLIMPSES OF CONWAY/PANORAMIC VIEWS OF PICTURESQUE CONWAY Five Views (N-F) 125 ft

'An aggregate of five different views make up this interesting series. The first shows a more complete panoramic view than described under No. 5803, considerable interest being depicted of a Holyhead express, the progress of which gives further action to the picture until it passes from view under one of the ancient arches. The second section gives a panoramic view of the interior Castle ruins taken from the top of a tower, showing many visitors edging along the walls. In the third section is given a view similar to that described under 5805, and depicts the Holyhead Mail (Wild Irishman) rushing through the arches. A splendid view of the Chain Bridge with the Castle for background, with much traffic crossing the former structure; while the last section shows a bit of domesticity along the shore with its quaint cottages, shipping and surroundings. A most interesting and beautiful subject.'

Refs: *The Era*, 20 October 1900, p. 30e
    WTC catalogue Supplement no. 1 (Nov/Dec 1900), p. 167

5807   PANORAMA OF CARNARVON CASTLE (N-F) 50 ft

'Carnarvon . . . occupies a commanding situation on the banks of the River Sciout, from the opposite bank of which this photograph was taken, starting with the old town walls opposite Menai Straits, the esplanade and river front, the recently built swinging bridge, the Castle, and the shipping of the River Sciout, with Carnarvon town in the background.'

Refs: *The Era*, 20 October 1900, p. 30e
  WTC catalogue Supplement no. 1 (Nov/Dec 1900), p. 167

5808   CARNARVON CASTLE INTERIOR AND EXTERIOR, Three Panoramic
        Views (N-F) 100 ft

        'A similar view of this fine Castle to the preceding picture, although photo-
        graphed opposite the slate quarry, affording a better view of the walls and towers
        of the Castle, as well as the shipping along the river front. The second section
        contains two panoramic views of the interior ruins of the Castle as seen from the
        top of a tower on the south side and from the terrace, showing the Eagle Tower .
        . . and entrance. A most interesting picture. Sharp and clear.'

        Refs: *The Era*, 20 October 1900, p. 30e
          WTC catalogue Supplement no. 1 (Nov/Dec 1900), p. 167

Nos. 5809 to 5813   EXHIBITIONS AT CRYSTAL PALACE:

5809   EXHIBITION OF QUICK HARNESSING BY THE KANSAS FIRE
        DEPARTMENT (N) 75 ft

5810   THE KANSAS CITY FIRE DEPARTMENT DRILL AT CRYSTAL PALACE
        (N) 100FT

        'Another section of preceding subject. By courtesy of Chief Officer Hale and the
        Crystal Palace Co.'

        [Chief Officer Hale (George C. Hale) of 'Hale's Tours' fame].

5811   PANORAMA OF CRYSTAL PALACE LAKE (N-F) 50 ft

5812   PANORAMIC VIEW OF THE CRYSTAL PALACE. TERRACES, STATUES,
        AND FIREWORK STATION (N-F) 100 ft

5813   PANORAMIC VIEW OF THE PREHISTORIC MONSTERS AT THE
        CRYSTAL PALACE (N-F) 100 ft

        For particulars of all the above consult the references.

        Refs: *The Era*, 20 October 1900, p. 30e
          WTC catalogue Supplement no. 1 (Nov/Dec 1900), pp. 167–8

5814   COALING A BATTLESHIP AT SEA (N-F) 75 ft

        'This is another of the Naval Manoeuvres Series, showing a tender steaming
        alongside a battleship for coaling purposes. As soon as the tender is in position,
        the operations of transferring the cargo of coal to the bunkers of the battleship
        proceeds, steam cranes and "buckets" being employed for the purpose. A sight
        seldom witnessed by the "land lubber".'

        Refs: *The Era*, 20 October 1900, p. 30e
        WTC catalogue Supplement no. 1 (Nov/Dec 1900), p. 168

Nos. 5815 to 5846   WITH THE BIOSCOPE THROUGH IRELAND (N-F):

5815   TRANSPORT OF THE AMERICAN MAIL AT QUEENSTOWN (75 ft)

5816   PANORAMIC VIEW OF QUEENSTOWN, IRELAND, FROM THE RIVER
            (125 ft)

5817   PANORAMA OF SEASHORE AND PROMENADE AT YOUGHALL

5818   FROM QUEENSTOWN TO CORK (75 ft)

5819   PATRICK STREET, CORK

5820   APPROACHING CORK—PANORAMA FROM ENGINE FRONT (75 ft)

5821   THE PRINCE OF WALES' ROUTE BETWEEN CORK AND BANTRY
            (100 ft)

5822   PASSENGERS GETTING ON COACHES AT BANTRY

5823   PANORAMIC VIEW OF GLENGARIFF

5824   COACHING THROUGH THE KEIM-AN-EIGH PASS (75 ft)

5825   THE SHRINE OF GOUGANE BARRA

5826   PANORAMA FROM ENGINE FRONT BETWEEN MACROOM AND
            CORK (150 ft)

5827   COACHING THROUGH THE TUNNEL ON THE KENMERE ROAD

5828   PANORAMA OF PARKNASILLA AND ITS HOTEL

5829   COACHES LEAVING GT. SOUTHERN HOTEL AT KILLARNEY

5830   ON HORSEBACK THROUGH THE GAP OF DUNLOE, KILLARNEY
            (150 ft)

5831   SHOOTING THE RAPIDS AT KILLARNEY

5832   THE RIVER SHANNON AT KILLALOE (100 ft)

5833   PANORAMA OF COLLEGE GREEN, DUBLIN (40 ft)

5834   ROYAL AVENUE, BELFAST

5835   HIGH STREET, BELFAST (75 ft)

5836   FROM BELFAST TO THE ANTRIM COAST (175 ft)

5837   THREE WATERFALLS NEAR THE ANTRIM COAST (125 ft)

5838   THE GIANT'S CAUSEWAY, IRELAND (75ft)

5839   ROUGH SEA AT PORT STEWART

5840   DOWNHILL TO CASTLE ROCK BY RAIL (100 ft)

5841   PANORAMA OF SEA SHORE AT BUNDORAN

5842   LONDONDERRY TO BALLYKELLY (PANORAMA) (125 ft)

5843   PANORAMIC VIEWS BETWEEN PETTIGO AND BALLYSHANNON
              (125 ft)

              For particulars of all the above consult reference.

              Refs: *The Era*, 20 October 1900, p. 30e
                 WTC catalogue Supplement no. 1 (Nov/Dec 1900), pp. 168–171

5844   THE UNFORTUNATE EGG MERCHANT (F) 175 ft

              Producer: G.A. Smith

              Ref: WTC catalogue Supplement no. 1 (Nov/Dec 1900), p. 171
                 For description see under G.A. Smith, p. xxx

5845   THE FLYING SCOTS (F) 175 ft

              'One of the funniest acrobatic films taken, showing the "Three Missouries" (the
              well-known and famous comic acrobats) in their side-splitting creation, entitled
              "More Rosin", in which most marvellous tumbling and difficult feats are
              performed, combined with studied awkwardness and funny situations. This is a
              subject which is highly appreciated, and well received wherever exhibited.'

              Ref: WTC catalogue Supplement no. 1 (Nov/Dec 1900), p. 171

Nos. 5846 to 5854   FOLKESTONE MILITARY TOURNAMENT
(11–13 September) (N)

5846   FOUR SCENES AT THE TOURNAMENT (100 ft)

5847   DUELS WITH SWORDS AND BAYONETS (75 ft)

5848   WRESTLING ON HORSEBACK

5849   SEVENTH DRAGOONS MUSICAL RIDE (75 ft)

5850   MILITARY DISPLAY OF THE SEVENTH ROYAL DRAGOONS (75 ft)

5851   MILITARY CYCLISTS' DISPLAY AND BARE-BACK RIDING (75 ft)

5852   MILITARY GYMNASTICS—VAULTING

5853   MILITARY GYMNASTICS—PARALLEL BARS (75 ft)

5854   PANORAMA OF FOLKESTONE SEA FRONT AND PIER

For particulars consult the reference.

Ref: WTC catalogue Supplement no. 1 (Nov/Dec 1900), pp. 171–172

5855   THE YOKELS DINNER—Reversing (F) 75 ft

Producer: G.A. Smith

Ref: WTC catalogue Supplement no. 1 (Nov/Dec 1900), p. 172
   For description see under G.A. Smith, p. xxx

5856   THE NOTTINGHAM GOOSE FAIR (N) 75 ft

'The fair held once a year is far famed throughout England. The market place is turned over to showmen, who reign supreme during the three days, attracting tens of thousands of visitors from all parts to behold its wonders. Many round-abouts, swings, whirligigs, switchbacks, and other paraphernalia of *The Showman* in full swing gives a splendid idea of this vast concourse of people occupying themselves each in their own way, is most amusing. As the camera photo-graphically records this event panoramawise a continuous view of the entire market place is had.'

Ref: WTC catalogue Supplement no. 1 (Nov/Dec 1900), pp. 172–173

5857   GLIMPSES OF THE EMERALD ISLE (8 views) (N-F) 125 ft

'1. Panoramic View of the Coast near the Giant's Causeway
2. Kenmere and the Southern Hotel, including circular panorama of its picturesque surroundings
3. Coaches leaving Vickers Hotel, Bantry
4. Panoramic View of Queenstown, taken from a moving steamer
5. High Street, Belfast, full of life and interest
6. Panoramic View of Ross Castle, Killarney, and its surroundings
7. Panoramic View of Waterville, including the Southern Hotel
8. River Erne at Ballyshannon, a very effective view of the River Erne, and salmon leap at Ballyshannon, showing the water rushing over the rocks with terrific force, and the salmon leaping from rock to rock with seagulls passing in front of the camera.'

Ref: WTC catalogue Supplement no. 1 (Nov/Dec 1900), p. 173

5858   (No title available).

5859   (No title available).

5860   LAUNCH OF BRIGHTON LIFEBOAT FROM PIER (N) 100 ft

'An interesting series of photographs, showing the christening and lowering of the lifeboat from the Brighton pier. After the boat reaches the water, the crew are seen to rapidly slide down the ropes into the boat, taking their oars. They row off, and are next seen sailing their boat. After cruising about, they lower the sail. After again reaching the pier, a view is shown in which the crew are seen hoisting their lifeboat to the top of the davits on the pier. Very interesting exhibition.'

Ref: WTC catalogue Supplement no. 1 (Nov/Dec 1900), p. 173

5861   CIRCULAR PANORAMA OF SINGAPORE AND LANDING STAGE (N-F)

'This film shows a splendid view of one of the principal streets in Singapore with its grand commercial buildings contrasting with the abutting huts and shanties of the natives, while the scene is further enlivened by the many rickshaws drawn by coolies. Contrast this latter with a single sleepy cab horse plodding along drawing a dilapidated four-wheeler and you gain a good idea of the mode of "rapid" transit in China. As the camera sweeps around a good view of the landing stage is had.'

Ref: *The Era*, 10 November 1900, p. 30d

5862   PANORAMA OF SINGAPORE SEA FRONT (N-F)

'Another circular panoramic view of life in one of Singapore's principal streets fronting the sea, showing the Hongkong and Shanghai Banking Corporation's magnificent buildings, besides many others of different architecture. Much running to and fro by coolies and Europeans. A splendid picture, full of life.'

Ref: *The Era*, 10 November 1900, p. 30d

5863   COOLIE BOYS DIVING FOR COINS (N-F) 75 ft

'When the ship left Singapore our photographer had an opportunity of taking an interesting view of coolie boys diving from the boats, which crowd around the steamer, and pick up the coins thrown to them by the passengers, before the same can sink to the bottom. The dexterity with which these boys again enter their boats and paddle about is wonderful, and bespeaks of long practice of these beggar urchins.'

Ref: *The Era*, 10 November 1900, p. 30d

5864   SHANGHAI'S SHOPS AND OPIUM DENS (N-F)

'A circular panorama taken at a street crossing in one of the worst sections of Shanghai, showing numerous vile dens and shops, while hundreds of Chinamen are seen pulling their carts and carrying bundles, many appearing in a semi-nude state all eyeing the camera operated by the "foreign devil" with suspicion. The police generally patrol this section in squads, not trusting themselves alone and the particular squad shown in this picture formed the body-guard of our photographer.'

Ref: *The Era*, 10 November 1900, p. 30d

5865   THE DIVER (N-F)

'This scene takes place near a breakwater, showing a small boat at anchor, from which a diver, in his diving dress, is seen descending into the water several times, until at last he goes down for some minutes to examine a wreck on the bottom of the sea, while the men on the boat are manning the air-pump and gradually paying out the life-line and air-pipe.

NOTE. This film, when joined to 4147 (the diver examining the wreck under water) makes a splendid series, and meets with the approval of all audiences, wherever shown.'

Ref: WTC catalogue Supplement no. 1 (Nov/Dec 1900), p. 174

THE ARRIVAL AND MARCH OF THE CITY IMPERIAL VOLUNTEERS

From Paddington Station, London, October 29th, 1900.

The complete Procession is portrayed in the following four sections, which, when joined in the order named, will make one continuous film.

5866   THE C.I.V.S' HOME COMING—No. 1 (29 October) (N) 100 ft

'The view is a most picturesque one, depicting the troops marching up the private roadway from Paddington, further enlivened by numerous mottoes, viz.: "Defenders of the Empire", "Welcome C.I.V.s" and "Soldiers of the Queen", stretched across the road, midst garlands, flags, and other decorations, while crowds line the walls and roadways. First in line is an escort of mounted police, followed by Major-General Trotter, Colonel Ricardo and Home District Staff, Colonel Makinnon, commanding the C.I.V.s, the Artillery or Battery of the C.I.V.s with the khaki painted guns used in South Africa, and an Orange Free State Flag captured by the C.I.V.s being proudly born as a trophy along the line of march.'

5867   THE C.I.V.S' HOME COMING—No. 2 (29 October) (N) 125 ft

'This is a continuation of the preceding film, and shows a portion of the Battery of the C.I.V.s, Companies A and B Infantry Battalion C.I.V., and Mounted Infantry C.I.V.'

5868   THE C.I.V.S' HOME COMING—No. 3 (29 October) (N) 100 ft

'This, the third section of the procession is perhaps the most interesting, showing the Cycle Corps of the C.I.V. A captured Boer flag carried as a trophy, companies C and D of the C.I.V. Infantry Battalion, &c.'

5869   THE C.I.V.S' HOME COMING—No. 4 (29 October) (N) 150 ft

'The remainder of the Infantry Battalion of the C.I.V.s is depicted in this the last section of the procession followed by the Machine Gun Section, C.I.V., the Ambulance Corps, and the C.I.V. Invalides carried in brakes, with crowds following and closing in on the procession. As the last of the procession turns the corner the crowds in Praed Street are seen breaking through the line of police who are almost swept off their feet in the rush.

A film of the entire procession can be furnished in one continuous length 475 feet, duration of exhibit about 10 minutes. Price £23 15s.'

Ref: *The Era*, 3 November 1900, p. 31e

5870   THE CITY IMPERIAL VOLUNTEERS DISEMBARKING FROM THE 'AURANIA' AT SOUTHAMPTON (29 October) (N) 50 ft

'Showing the speed with which these gallant Volunteers left the good ship which carried them from South Africa, walking rapidly down the gang plank to the trains in waiting to whirl them on to London. Splendid portraits of the men.'

Ref: *The Era*, 3 November 1900, p. 31e

5871   THE SPECIAL C.I.V. TRAIN LEAVING SOUTHAMPTON (29 October) (N) 50 ft

'Showing the departure of the troop train for London on the morning of October 29th, 1900. The soldiers are seen leaning from the windows of the coaches answering the cheers and waving of the people on the platform as the train slowly moves out of the station.'

Ref: *The Era*, 3 November 1900, p. 31e

5872   THE JOLLY OLD FELLOWS / THEY ARE JOLLY GOOD FELLOWS (November) (F) 100 ft

Production: G. A. Smith

Refs: *The Era*, 17 November 1900, p. 30b
     WTC catalogue Supplement no. 1 (Nov/Dec 1900), p. 175
     For synopsis see under G.A. Smith.

5873   THE WORLD CONGRESS OF BEAUTIES (N) 100 ft

'By special arrangement with Mr Imre Kiralfy, we are enabled herewith to reproduce a review of the women of different nationalities as they march in sections past the camera at the Women's Exhibition, Earl's Court . . . A very unique procession, beautifully sharp and clear, every face a portrait.'
For fuller particulars see reference.

Ref: *The Era*, 17 November 1900, p. 30b

5874   A BUSY STREET SCENE IN SHANGHAI (N-F)

'An interesting view of the traffic and bustling of the Chinese population in one of Shanghai's busiest thoroughfares. The native method of carrying bundles and bulky burdens, while passengers are whirled about in the two-wheeled rickshaws drawn by coolies, lends much variety and action to the picture.'

Ref: *The Era*, 17 November 1900, p. 30b

5875   THE SIKHS CAMP AT SHANGHAI (N) 100 ft

'Anything portraying active scenes connected with any of the Allied Troops now stationed in China is of great interest to the public, especially as in this case when the scene includes a panoramic view of an encampment of our Indian fighters, all of whom appear in their picturesque native costumes, busying themselves with preparing their meals, cleaning their accoutrements, while the regimental band of Pipers (all Indian) are parading up and down before the camera to the air of the pipes and drums. A splendid subject.'

Ref: *The Era*, 17 November 1900, p. 30b

5876   THE CHINESE JUNKS IN HONG KONG HARBOUR (N-F) 75 ft

'A circular panorama of that section of Hong Kong Harbour showing thousands
of native boats moored along the shore . . . The steamers and moving boats in the
harbour give further variety to the picture, while the hills on the opposite shore
with its quaint buildings form a most appropriate background.'

Ref: *The Era*, 17 November 1900, p. 30b

5877   CIRCULAR PANORAMA OF HONG KONG HARBOUR (N-F) 100 ft

'This circular panoramic view includes many of the palatial-looking buildings
lining the seafront, as well as a number of battleships (including several British)
and transports at anchor, also many large ocean-going steamers, whilst a multi-
tude of junks, steam launches and other craft are moored in all directions. This
scene is very impressive.'

Ref: *The Era*, 17 November 1900, p. 30b

5878   THE CHINATOWN BAZAARS, HONG KONG (N-F)

'This scene was secured in the midst of the native quarters of Hong Kong and
shows a panoramic view of the many picturesque better-class Chinese shops, its
native merchants and patrons, and varied merchandise displayed for sale.'

Ref: *The Era*, 17 November 1900, p. 30b

5879   A RIDE ON 'THE PEAK' TRAMWAY, HONG KONG (N-F) 150 ft

'This panoramic view was taken from the front of a car on "the Peak" Tramway
(the steepest tramway on earth), and is without exception the finest example of
animated photography ever procured, in which the stereoscopic effects, so
famous in our panoramic pictures, is seen to exceptional advantage. As the car
descends from the peak, a fine view of the city of Hong Kong and its harbour
with shipping is shown, while the beautiful scenery and Chinese houses, with
viaducts, bridges, and an ascending car is met with on the down trip, lending
much variety and charm to this splendid subject.'

Ref: *The Era*, 17 November 1900, p. 30b

5880   GUY FAWKES DAY INCIDENT (5 November) (N) 75 ft

'A procession of boys and men carrying an effigy of Kruger. After jabbing at it
for some time with their wooden swords, they set it on fire. A very few minutes
sees the "End of Kruger", as the dummy is rapidly consumed by the flames, the
boys dancing around and jeering at the blazing figure meanwhile. Lots of fun for
the boys.'

Ref: WTC catalogue (April 1901), p. 181

5881   SOLDIERS OF THE CENTURY (November) (N) 75 ft

'The most interesting section of the Lord Mayor's procession was the portion
portraying the Soldiers of the Century from 1800 to 1900 in their picturesque and
varying uniforms and old-pattern firearms. The film concludes with a Company
of Bluejackets and car, representing a 4.7-inch gun at Ladysmith. According to

the vast crowd which lines both sides of the line of march, this latter show is heartily cheered, and is evidently pleasing.'

Ref: WTC catalogue (April 1901), p. 181

5882   THE LORD MAYOR'S PROCESSION (November) (N) 75 ft

'This is a continuation of the preceding subject, and shows the elaborately carved coaches of the Lord Mayor and Suit, drawn by gaily caparisoned horses, while the coachmen and footmen, in their old world costumes, are famous, having performed similar functions for many years.

The Lord Mayor's Procession was photographed at Ludgate Circus by courtesy of Messrs, Thos. Cook & Son.'

Ref: WTC catalogue (April 1901), p. 181

5883   GENERAL BULLER'S RETURN FROM SOUTH AFRICA. HIS RECEPTION AT SOUTHAMPTON AND ALDERSHOT (24 October) (N) 75 ft

Ref: *The Era*, 24 November 1900, p. 27a; 1 December 1900, p. 31e

5884   THE ANNEXATION OF THE TWO SOUTH AFRICAN REPUBLICS (25 October) (N) 100 ft

Photographed by Sydney Goldman

The commencement of this historic subject shows the hoisting of the Royal Standard in front of the Government Buildings at Pretoria during the formal annexation ceremony by Lord Roberts, October 25th, 1900. The troops give "Three Cheers for their Queen" as the flag is raised. This scene followed by Lord Roberts decorating several heroes with the much coveted Victoria Cross, finishing which, a review of the troops is held. While the infantry and mounted troops line the square on every side, the cavalry and artillery is seen marching by. Lack of space forbids a further detailed description, but for an inspiring and patriotic subject, this one, aside from its historical interest, would be hard to beat.

Photographed by Mr. Goldman, of our War Staff in South Africa.'

Ref: WTC catalogue (April 1901), p. 181

5885   REVIEW OF TROOPS BY LORD ROBERTS (25 October) (N) 75 ft

Photographed by Edgar M. Hyman

'This is a continuation of the preceding picture, showing the march past of the Lincoln Regiment and the Gordon Highlanders during the review of the troops before Lord Roberts after the annexation ceremony at Pretoria, October 25th, 1900.

Photographed by Mr. Edgar Hyman, of our War Staff in South Africa.'

Ref: WTC catalogue (April 1901), p. 181

SHANGHAI, PORT ARTHUR, TAKU AND TEINTSIN

Photographed by our Mr. J. Rosenthal, now operating in China.

5886   THE BOULEVARD AT SHANGHAI / LIVELY STREET SCENE IN
        SHANGHAI (N-F)

5887   A CURIOUS CROWD AT SHANGHAI / CURIOUS NATIVES ON
        SHANGHAI'S STREETS (N-F)

5888   CIRCULAR PANORAMA OF CROSS STREETS IN THE NATIVE
        QUARTERS   OF   SHANGHAI / CIRCULAR   PANORAMA   OF
        SHANGHAI'S NATIVE QUARTERS (N-F)

5889   PANORAMA OF THE BUND AND ENGLISH BATTLESHIPS AT
        SHANGHAI / FOREIGN WARSHIPS OFF THE BUND AT SHANGHAI

5890   CIRCULAR PANORAMA OF THE BUND AND RIVER AT SHANGHAI
        (N-F) 75 ft

5891   LIFE IN THE NATIVE QUARTERS OF SHANGHAI, ON THE CANAL
        AND MARKET / CHINESE MARKET AND CANAL AT SHANGHAI
        (N-F) 75 ft

5892   THE RUSSIAN STRONGHOLD IN THE FAR EAST PORT ARTHUR (N)
        60 ft

5893   PORT ARTHUR AND ITS FORTS (N-F) 75 ft

5894   SCENE AT TAKU / TRANSPORTS AND BATTLESHIPS AT TAKU (N)

5895   THE STREETS OF TIENTSIN AFTER THE TOWN'S CAPTURE BY THE
        BOXERS / A STREET IN TEINTSIN AFTER OCCUPATION BY THE
        ALLIED TROOPS (N)

5896   TIENTSIN IN RUINS / THE STREETS AND RUINS OF TIENTSIN (N) 75 ft

5897   THE NATIVE QUARTERS OF TIENTSIN (N) 75 ft
        Refs: *The Era*, 24 November 1900, p. 27b; 1 December 1900, p. 31e
          .WTC catalogue (April 1901), pp. 182–183

OUR EASTERN EMPIRE: AN INTERESTING SERIES OF SCENES IN INDIA (N-F)
Taken by F.B. Steward, our Special Photographer, now in India.

5898   ARRIVAL OF A TRAIN AT POONA

5899   DRILL OF CYCLE CORPS IN INDIA

5900   A MID-DAY SIESTA IN CALCUTTA

5901   CHURCH GATE STREET, BOMBAY

5902   PYOOWINE, BOMBAY

5903   STREET SCENE IN POONA

5904   A FIRE BRIGADE TURNOUT IN BOMBAY

5905   A NATIVE STREET SCENE, CALCUTTA

5906   DIFFICULTIES OF A SHAVE IN INDIA

5907   THE 16th FIELD BATTERY, BOMBAY—in Action

5908   REGIMENTAL PIPERS, CALCUTTA

5909   INDIAN LABOURERS LEAVING A BOMBAY FACTORY

5910   THE GIMPATI PROCESSION AND OBSTINATE BULLOCKS

5911   THE TWO-PENNY TUBE IN INDIA

5912   A PRACTICAL JOKE FROM AN INDIAN STANDPOINT

5913   THE INDIAN DHOBIE

5914   CHARGE OF THE BOMBAY LANCERS

5915   PLAGUE INOCULATION AT BOMBAY, 1900 (N)

5916   RACE FOR THE GOVERNOR'S CUP, BOMBAY (N) 150 ft
            For descriptions of each film, consult the reference.
            Ref: WTC catalogue (April 1901), pp. 184–186

IMPORTANT SUBJECTS FROM PEKIN, &C
Photographed by our staff now operating in China and Japan

5917   PANORAMA OF TEINTSIN FROM THE RIVER (N-F)

5918   STREET LIFE IN THE TARTAR CITY, PEKIN (N-F) 100 ft

5919   PANORAMA OF PEKIN FROM THE TARTAR GATE (N-F)

5920   CAMEL TRANSPORT ENTERING PEKIN (N-F) 75 ft

5921   AMERICAN TRANSPORT ENTERING PEKIN (N-F) 100 ft

5922   ENTRY INTO THE SACRED CITY, PEKIN, OF COUNT VON
            WALDERSEE (17 October) (N) 100 ft

For descriptions of each film consult the reference.

Ref: *The Era*, 29 December 1900, p. 31a
   WTC catalogue (April 1901), pp. 186–187

G. WEST & SON ('OUR NAVY')

The films of G. West & Son were made exclusively for presentation in the firm's own shows known as 'Our Navy', and were never intended to be sold on the open market. Consequently no catalogue of films was published for our period, and any filmography has to rely on printed programmes or press reviews. The present list is therefore far from complete. The length of the individual films is nowhere stated and there is very little description of the content of each film available. As far as is known, all the films were photographed by Alfred J. West.

NAVAL GUNS IN ACTION (N-F)

'As used at Ladysmith.'

Ref: Portsmouth Evening News, 28 March, 1900

ON BOARD H.M.S. 'JUPITER' (August) (N-F)

Several scenes 'By permission of the Lords of the Admiralty'
(a) The crew on the quarter-deck summoned to 'general quarters'
(b) Heaving the lead in a heavy sea
(c) Manning the cutter to rescue a drowning man
Ref: Portsmouth Evening News, 21 August, 1900

YACHT RACING SCENES (N-F)

Ref: Portsmouth Evening News, 21 August, 1900

THE TURBINE BOAT 'VIPER' (N-F)

Ref: Portsmouth Evening News 21 August, 1900

SOUTHSEA REGATTA (24 August) (N)

(a) All Comers' Race
(b) Walking the Greasy Pole
Ref: Portsmouth Evening News, 28 August, 1900

SOUTHSEA GYMKHANA (August) (N)

Ref: Portsmouth Evening News, 4 September, 1900

JAMES A. WILLIAMSON

Towards the end of 1900, Williamson was just getting into his stride as a serious filmmaker. His first really important film from the point of view of film technique was *Attack on a China Mission*, which can be said to mark a turning point in his career. The films that followed are already fairly well documented and several of them survive. They have also received expert attention from a new generation of film historians. But what of the preceding films? An exact filmography is difficult to compile as very little contemporary material describing them survives. Of the lists issued by Williamson himself, historian Frank Gray has located two catalogues at George Eastman House, Rochester, N.Y., one dated September 1899 and the other September 1902. Both incidentally, are photocopies. Ronald Grant of the Cinema Museum, Kennington, also has two incomplete photocopies of the same catalogues. A Supplementary List, issued in December 1903, is in the Barnes Collection. Twelve 'Old Favorites' are listed at the end, among which is *Attack on a China Mission*. Rachael Low, in *The History of the British Film* (vol. 1) lists the two Williamson catalogues for the years 1899 and 1902, but fails to state their whereabouts. Descriptions of other Williamson films are scattered about in the catalogues of WTC and Charles Urban as well as in the local press.

1   THE JOVIAL MONKS, No. 1 (F) 72 ft

'Monk reading comic paper and laughing, hearing someone coming hides paper and pretends to be studying, and bears himself very devoutly while attendant monk brings in fruit and wine. Attendant evidently has a joke of his own; retires leaving monk to enjoy his refreshment, which he does most expressively. Helping himself to a second glass of wine out of another bottle, he discovers that it is nauseous, and looking at it finds he has been tricked into drinking black draught. Mons. D. Philippe has a most expressive face, and tells his story in an irresistibly funny way.'

Refs: Williamson catalogue (September 1902), p. 3, no. 14
    Hove Echo, 24 November 1900

2   THE JOVIAL MONKS, No. 2 Tit for Tat. (F) 54 ft

'Monk and attendant reading comic paper; monk asks attendant to drink, and on the second occasion he fills the glasses from black draught bottle, empties his own over his shoulder, and enjoys the chagrin of his companion discovering that his little joke has come back to him.'

Ref: Williamson catalogue (September 1902), p. 3, no. 15

3   COURTSHIP UNDER DIFFICULTIES (F) 67 ft

'Young lady in garden evidently expecting someone; hearing whistle, looks round and sees young man getting over hedge; greets him effusively and they sit down together. While engaged in spooning, the little sister comes in and slyly ties the young man to the chair by the coat waistband; this rather handicaps the young man in his tussle with the old gentleman who next appears on the scene, but he manages to reach the hedge, old gentleman hanging on to chair; however something gives way releasing the young man and upsetting the old gentleman.'

Ref: Williamson catalogue (September 1902), p. 4, no. 20

4   THE SLEEPING LOVERS (F) 60 ft

'A practical joke. Two lovers asleep on chairs in garden; friend arrives, carries off the lady and sits in her place without waking the gentleman, who continues to embrace his friend, unaware of the change. After some laughable situations, the lover awakes, and extinguishes his jocular friend with a chair.'

Ref: Williamson catalogue (September 1902), p. 4, no. 21

5   CRICKET (N) 100 ft

' "Ranji" and others of the Sussex Eleven coming out of Pavilion to field, Lord Hawke following to bat.
"Ranji" and Grace batting at the nets.'

Refs: Williamson catalogue (September 1902), p. 4, no. 21a
      Hove Echo, 24 November 1900

6   FIRE BRIGADE SPORTS (N) 72 ft

'Dressing Competition. The men scramble into boots, coat, helmet, &c., and hurry away to Manual Engine.'

Ref: Williamson catalogue (September 1902), p. 5, no. 41

7   FIRE BRIGADE SPORTS (N) 50 ft

'Tilting the bucket.'

Ref: Williamson catalogue (September 1902), p. 5, no. 42

8   FIRE BRIGADE SPORTS (N) 65 ft

'Life-saving demonstration, life line and jumping sheet.'

Ref: Williamson catalogue (September 1902), p. 5, no. 44

9   LAWN TENNIS (N-F) 60 ft

Ref: Williamson catalogue (September 1902), p. 5, no. 44

10   CLEVER AND COMIC CYCLE ACT (N) 100 ft

'By Messrs. Lotto, Lilo, and Otto.'

Ref: Williamson catalogue (September 1902), p. 6, no. 45

11   CYCLE PARADE (N) 70 ft

'Which finishes with a disastrous collision between a carrier-tricycle and a motor-tricycle; the latter collapses, policeman comes to the assistance of the victim, followed by gaping crowd.'

Refs: Williamson catalogue (September 1902), p. 6, no. 46
      Hove Echo, 24 November 1900

12   QUEEN VICTORIA IN IRELAND (4 April) (N) 75 ft

'H.M. the Queen and escort of Life Guards leaving the Vice-Regal Lodge to review the troops in Phoenix Park.'

Refs: Williamson catalogue (September 1902), p. 8, no. 87
      Hove Echo, 24 November 1900

13   REVIEW IN PHOENIX PARK, DUBLIN (4 April) (N) 150 ft

'The March Past.'

Refs: Williamson catalogue (September 1902), p. 8, no. 88
      Hove Echo, 24 November 1900

14   THE 'BRIGHTON QUEEN' (N-F) 200 ft

'Splendid steam-boat subject. Arrival at Brighton West Pier, Brighton; passengers disembarking; departure; full steam ahead.'

Refs: Williamson catalogue (September 1902), p. 8, no. 93
Hove Echo, 24 November 1900

15   CIRCULAR PANORAMA OF BRIGHTON FRONT (N-F) 52 ft

'From Band Stand on Parade.'

Refs: Williamson catalogue (September 1902), p. 8, no. 94
Hove Echo, 24 November 1900

16   VOLK'S ELECTRIC RAILWAY, BRIGHTON (N-F) 44 ft

'Car starting full of passengers; another arriving and passengers alighting.'

Ref: Williamson catalogue (September 1902), p. 8, no. 95

17   THREE NOVEL RAILWAYS (N-F) 75 ft

'The steep-grade railway, and the aerial railways at the Dyke, and the sea-going car at Brighton (each 25 ft).'

Refs: Williamson catalogue (September 1902), p. 8, no. 98
Hove Echo, 24 November 1900

18   THE SEA-GOING CAR AT BRIGHTON (N-F) 75 ft

'A charming effect of rolling waves, showing the car passing through.'

Refs: Williamson catalogue (September 1902), p. 8, no. 102
Hove Echo, 24 November 1900

19   CIRCULAR PANORAMA OF WINDSOR CASTLE (N-F) 30 ft

'A charming picture of this magnificent pile. Makes a good opening picture.'

Refs: Williamson catalogue (September 1902), p. 8, no. 104
Hove Echo, 24 November 1900

20   'LA MARGUERITE.'

'The Margate Steamboat.'

Ref: Williamson catalogue (September 1902), p. 8, no. 105

21   GREAT GLOVE FIGHT (N) 150 ft

'Between Frank Lewis, champion of South of England, and Fred Gausden, champion of Sussex. Gausden beaten in three rounds.'
'Continuation, showing the two combatants receiving the attention of their seconds, and a bookmaker paying up his calls. 80 ft'

Ref: Williamson catalogue (September 1902), p. 9, no. 106

22   MILITARY TOURNAMENT (N) 800 ft

107. Quarter-staff Display 60 ft

108. Wrestling on Horseback 45 ft
109. Heads and Posts 30 ft
110. Gymnastic Exercise on Chairs 70 ft
111. Bayonet Exercise 41 ft
113. Bare-back Riding 50 ft
114. Vaulting-horse Display 75 ft
115. Tug-of-War 50 ft

Ref: Williamson catalogue (September 1902), p. 9

23   PANORAMA OF FOLKESTONE FROM THE PIER (N-F) 60 ft
         Ref: Williamson catalogue (September 1902), p. 9, no. 117

24   PANORAMA OF DOVER HARBOUR (N-F) 50 ft
         Ref: Williamson catalogue (September 1902), p. 9, no. 118

25   THE DISABLED MOTOR (N) 70 ft
         'Several smart traps pass, the last one stopping to look behind for someone
         lagging; a horse is seen approaching, dragging a motor car, one of the occupants
         limping alongside, the other sitting inside with his leg bandaged up.'
         Ref: Williamson catalogue (September 1902), p. 9, no. 121

26   RECEPTION OF THE CREW OF THE 'POWERFUL' (24 April) (N)
         'Preceded by a picture of the vessel in Portsmouth Harbour.'
         Ref: *Hove Echo*, 24 November 1900

27   C.I.V. PROCESSION IN LONDON (29 October) (N)
         Ref: *Hove Echo*, 24 November 1900

28   ATTACK ON A CHINA MISSION—BLUEJACKETS TO THE RESCUE (F)
         230 ft
         'The scene opens with the outer gate of the premises; a Chinaman with
         flourishing sword approaches and tries the gate. Finding it fastened, he calls the
         others who come rushing up; one leaps over the gate, and the combined attack
         results in forcing it open; nine Boxers in Chinese costumes of varied character
         now swarm in, stopping occasionally to fire in the direction of the house.
            The second scene shows the front of the house—the missionary walking in
         front with a young lady; wife and child are seated a little further off. At the first
         alarm, the missionary drops his book and sends the young lady into the house to
         fetch rifle and pistols; he then rushes to his wife and child, and sees them safely
         into the house; takes cover behind some bushes, discharges his revolver at the
         Boxers advancing in different directions, kills one, then picks up rifle and
         discharges it at another; his ammunition exhausted, he comes to close quarters
         with another Boxer armed with a sword, and, after an exciting fight, is overcome,
         and left presumably killed. Meanwhile, others of the attacking party have closed
         round the young lady and followed her, retreating into the house.
            Missionary's wife now appears waving handkerchief on the balcony; the scene

changes and shows party of bluejackets advancing from the distance, leaping over a fence, coming through the gate, kneeling and firing in fours, and running forward to the rescue, under command of a mounted officer.

The fourth scene is a continuation of the second. The Boxers are dragging the young lady out of the house, which they have set on fire, at the moment the bluejackets appear; a struggle takes place with the Boxers; mounted officer rides up and carries off the young lady out of the melee.

The missionary's wife now rushes out of the house pointing to the balcony, where she has left her child; a bluejacket has secured it, but his passage down the stairs being blocked, three sailors mount on each other's shoulders and land the child safely in the mother's arms.

The struggle with the Boxers continues, but they are finally overcome and taken prisoners.

This sensational subject is full of interest and excitement from start to finish, and is everywhere received with great applause.'

Refs: *Hove Echo*, 24 November 1900

Williamson catalogue (September 1902), p. 22, no. 123

Williamson's Supplementary List, December 1903, p. 15, no. 123 (Barnes Collection)

Charles Urban Trading Co. cat 1903/1904, pp. 113–114, no. 4123 (Science Museum, London, Urban Collection), 6 frame illustrations.

PHILIPP WOLFF

1   DEPARTURE AND EMBARKATION OF THE CITY OF LONDON VOLUNTEERS (13 January) (N)

Ref: *The Era*, 13 January 1900, p. 27

2   CRONJE'S SURRENDER (27 February) (N) 60 ft

Ref: *The Era*, 7 April 1900, p. 27(e)

3   PRINCE OF WALES INSPECTING YEOMANRY (March) (N)

Ref: *The Era*, 17 March 1900, p. 27

4   PRINCE OF WALES SHAKING HANDS WITH OFFICERS (March) (N)

Taken at the same ceremony as no. 3 above

Ref: *The Era*, 17 March 1900, p. 27

5   NAVAL BRIGADE IN LONDON (7 May) (N) 80 ft

Ref: *The Era*, 26 May 1900, p. 28(b)

6   NAVAL BRIGADE WITH THEIR 4.7 GUN (12 May) (N) 80 ft

Ref: *The Era*, 26 May 1900, p. 28(b)

7   VIEWS OF CHINA AND JAPAN (N-F) Each 50 ft

Shanghai Police
Hong Kong Wharf Scene
Street Scene in Hong Kong
Government House in Hong Kong
Canton Steamboat Landing Chinese Passengers
Chinese Procession
Arrest of a Chinaman
Street Scene in Yokahama
Japanese Sampans
Shanghai Street Scene
Canton River Scene
Parade of Chinese
Opium Den
Ref: *The Era*, 1900, p. 24c

JOHN WRENCH & SON

1   SIR ALFRED MILNER ARRIVING AT THE PRESIDENCY AT
       BLOEMFONTEIN (N)
       Ref: *The Optician*, vol. 18 (18 May 1900), p. 347

2   CHANGE OF GUARD OUTSIDE THE PRESIDENCY AT
       BLOEMFONTEIN (N)
       Ref: *The Optician*, vol. 18 (18 May 1900), p. 347

3   WOUNDED BEING CARRIED ON STRETCHERS (N) (Two scenes)
       'The wounded being carried on stretchers out of the hospital into the ambulance
       waggon, the scene changing to the driving off of the waggon.'
       Ref: *The Optician*, vol. 18 (18 May 1900), p. 347

The above three films photographed by A. Underwood, Wrench's representative with Lord
Roberts in South Africa.

4   WASHING BOER PRISONERS (N)
       Photographed by A. Underwood (?)
       Ref: *The Optician*, vol. 18 (18 May 1900), p. 347

5   THE MILITARY TRAIN (N)
       Photographed by A. Underwood (?)
       Ref: *The Optician*, vol. 18 (18 May 1900), p. 347

6   THE VOLUNTEER PARADE (N)
       Probably a parade by City Imperial Volunteers
       Ref: *The Optician*, vol. 18 (18 May 1900), p. 347

7   DISCHARGING WOUNDED AT NETLEY HOSPITAL (N)

         Ref: *The Optician*, vol. 18 (18 May 1900), p. 347

8   WINNING THE VICTORIA CROSS (May) (F)

9   THE WHITE FLAG TREACHERY (May) (F)

10   THE NURSE'S BROTHER (May) (F)

11   SHELLING THE RED CROSS (May) (F)

12   THE DISPATCH BEARER (May) (F)

         Nos. 8–12

         Ref: *The Optician* (18 May 1900), p. 347
         According to Denis Gifford these films were produced by Mitchell & Kenyon.

'The following films of the departure of the transport *Jelunga* for China were taken by special permission of the Admiralty, granted to us only, and are therefore unique:

13   30A. OFF TO THE EAST (July) (N) 100 ft

         'Showing the Bluejackets and Marines marching with their kit bags on board the *Jelunga*, bound for China. The photograph is taken from the deck of the vessel looking towards the gangway, over which the men are passing, laden with their kits. Having deposited their bags they return ashore.'

14   31A. BLUEJACKETS FOR CHINA (July) 75 ft

         'This is a somewhat similar subject to the last, but taken from the quay in such a position that the men are seen crossing the gangway, while in the background is seen a huge man-of-war, with colours flying. The glistening water between the vessel and the quay, and the men constantly crossing and recrossing, make up a picture which, apart from its association, is full of intrinsic interest.'

15   32A. DEPARTURE OF THE 'JELUNGA' (July) (N) 50 ft

         'This is a very fine photograph, showing the transport *Jelunga*, for the present known as No. 7, leaving Portsmouth Harbour for the China Station. Every available inch of space on the decks and in the rigging is occupied by the men, who are crowding together waving farewell to their friends on the quay. As the whole vessel passes panorama-wise in front of the camera a splendid view of this brave vessel is obtained, and the whole forms a most interesting and exciting picture.'

         The three films joined together make a most magnificent up-to-date show.'

         Ref: *The Era*, 7 July 1900, p. 24e

'FAKED WAR FILMS'
(CHINA CRISIS)

A series of four highly sensational and stirring scenes of the Chinese crisis, showing Boxer barbarity, as follows:

16   181 ATTACK ON A MISSION STATION (July) (F) 87 ft

Production: Mitchell & Kenyon (?)

'A missionary is seen seated in front of his house reading his book. His wife and daughter come out of the house to go for a walk. They proceed and the missionary continues his studies. Presently, however, he starts up in alarm on perceiving his wife and child running screaming towards him, pursued by a number of Chinese, who are rapidly overtaking them. As they reach the house the missionary quickly gets them inside and turns just in time to snatch the chair upon which he has been sitting and fell the foremost of the mob The rest seeing the fate of their comrade, are momentarily checked, and the missionary takes advantage of this to form a rough barricade with odd articles of furniture in front of the doorway. Upon this several ugly rushes are made by the Boxers, who eventually carry all before them, and drag the household forth to murder them. Just at this juncture, however, when all is apparently hopeless, a party of marines is seen rapidly approaching, a volley is fired into the mob, which scatters in all directions, some of them being killed and others captured. One of the latter makes frantic efforts to escape but is finally overcome and bound.'

Ref: *The Era*, 14 July 1900, p. 24e

17   191 ATTEMPTED CAPTURE OF AN ENGLISH NURSE AND CHILDREN (July) (F) 60 ft

Production: Mitchell & Kenyon (?)

'A little girl is sitting in the fields, and the nurse is seen walking towards her with the baby in her arms. An English officer approaches and teases the little girl by brushing her face as he passes. The nurse places the baby by her side and begins to sew a garment, the baby meanwhile playing about. Whilst the nurse is intent on her work a Boxer, concealed in the vegetation, crawls stealthily up, and, snatching the baby, raises it high above his head, and flings it crash [sic] on the ground at the nurse's feet, who starts up in terror, and reaches for the child, only to be roughly dragged to the ground by the Boxer, who at this moment is reinforced by a number of other Chinese, one of whom makes off with the baby whilst the rest are maltreating the nurse and little girl, preparatory to making them captive. The screams of the nurse, however, have caught the ear of the British officer, who is now some distance up the hillside. He fires his revolver to give alarm, and a party of British soldiers are quickly on the scene, upon which the Boxers drop their captives and fly, the soldiers pursuing them and firing as they run. The officer has fortunately observed the Boxer who is making off with the child, and, giving chase, manages to capture him, and saves the child, which is restored to the arms of the nurse, who passionately clasps it to her breast.'

Ref: *The Era*, 14 July 1900, p. 24e

18   201 ASSASSINATION OF A BRITISH SENTRY (July) (F) 91 ft

Production: Mitchell & Kenyon (?)

'A British marine is seen on sentry duty. As he strides along a Chinaman creeps through the grass behind him, and suddenly springing upon him, stabs him fatally in the back. As the sentry falls his gun goes off, and this gives the alarm. The Chinaman gleefully dances round the body of his victim, and then makes off pursued by a distant sentry, who stops to fire. The wily heathen, perceiving this, throws himself flat on the ground and escapes the shot, but is chased by two other marines, who eventually capture him and bring him back just as the body of the dead sentry has been respectfully carried away. He is brought before an officer, who orders him to be shot, when the assassin grovels at the feet of his captors and prays them to release him, but to no purpose. A bandage is placed over his eyes, and he is stood with his back against a building. A firing party is formed up and the wretch is executed. The officer examines the body, and the party leaves.'

Ref: *The Era*, 14 July 1900, p. 24e

19   211 THE CLEVER CORRESPONDENT (July) (F) 54 ft

Production: Mitchell & Kenyon (?)

'This picture shows how a clever correspondent escapes capture at the hands of the Boxers. He is sketching a scene when two Boxers creep up behind, and are just about to seize him when he perceives one of them behind him. Pretending not to have seen him, he cautiously peers around and sees that he has two enemies to deal with. He makes several moves in various directions, every move-ment being intently followed by the two Boxers, whose antics are very funny. He at length manages to get within reach of one foot of each of the Chinamen, and by a dextrous movement throws them both head over heels simultaneously. He then dashes off, leaving the astonished Boxers to collect their wits, which they quickly do, and start in pursuit. However, the Briton manages to dispose of them singly in a neat manner as they come up. He then leisurely returns, and, gathering up his impedimenta, leaves the scene.'

Ref: *The Era*, 14 July 190, p. 24e

Appendix 2

Revised List of Biograph Films for the Year 1899

This supersedes the list of Biograph films published in volume 4, pp. 188–192.

1 LAUNCH OF THE S.S. 'OCEANIC' (14 January) (N)
'Largest ship in the world.'
Refs: Palace Theatre programme, 6 March 1899 (M & M)
  The Penny Pictorial Magazine, vol. 1, no. 8 (29 July 1899), p. 348 (2 frame illus.)

2 'THE LANE' ON SUNDAY MORNING (February) (N-F)
[Petticoat Lane Market, Middlesex Street, London]
Ref: Palace Theatre programme, 6 March 1899 (M & M)

3 AN IRISH PEASANT SCENE—FEEDING PIGS (February/March) (N-F)
Ref: Palace Theatre programme, 13 March 1899 (T.M.)

4 GRAND MILITARY STEEPLECHASE AT SANDOWN (3 March) (N)
Ref: Palace Theatre programme, 13 March 1899

5 LANDING OF LORD CHAS. BERESFORD FROM S.S. 'ST LOUIS' AT
SOUTHAMPTON ON HIS RETURN FROM HIS MISSION IN CHINA
(8 March) (N)
Ref: Palace Theatre programme, 20 March 1899 (M & M)

6 DEPARTURE FROM FOLKESTONE OF THE QUEEN (March) (N)
Ref: Palace Theatre programme, 20 March 1899 (M & M)

7 GRAND NATIONAL STEEPLECHASE (24 March) (N)
Directed and photographed by W.K.-L. Dickson: assisted by George W. Jones
Refs: Palace Theatre programme, 3 April 1899 (B.C. photocopy)
  Photography, vol. 11, no. 546 (27 April 1899), p. 284 (1 frame illus.)
  The Golden Penny (May 1899) p. 391 (2 frame illus. + 4 sketches)

8 OXFORD & CAMBRIDGE UNIVERSITY BOAT RACE (25 March) (N)
Taken from the umpire's boat.
Directed and photographed by W.K.-L. Dickson; assisted by George W. Jones
Refs: Palace Theatre programme, 3 April 1899 (B.C. photocopy)
  Photography, vol. 11, no. 546 (27 April 1899), p. 284 (2 frame illus.)

9 Ditto. CREWS LEAVING THE WATER
Ref: Palace Theatre programme, 10 April 1899 (T.M.)

10 LORD WOLSELEY REVIEWING SCOTS GREYS AND GORDON
    HIGHLANDERS AT EDINBURGH (April) (N)
    Refs: Palace Theatre programme, 27 April 1899 (B.C.)
       Palace Theatre programme, 1 May 1899 (T.M.)
       War by Biograph, 19.3.1900 (2 frame illus.) (R.B.)

11 THE MARRIAGE OF THE EARL OF CREWE AND LADY 'PEGGY' PRIMROSE
    AT WESTMINSTER ABBEY (April) (N)
    Ref: Palace Theatre programme, 27 April 1899 (B.C.)
       Palace Theatre programme, 1 May 1899 (T.M.)

12 THE LANDING OF 'SAVAGE SOUTH AFRICA' AT SOUTHAMPTON (April) (N)
    Ref: Palace Theatre programme, 27 April 1899 (B.C.)
       Palace Theatre programme, 1 May 1899 (T.M.)
       Copy in the NFTVA
       (Plate 114)

13 BUMPING RACE (CAMBRIDGE MAY RACES) (May) (N)
    Ref: Palace Theatre programme, 26 June 1899 (M & M)

14 HER MAJESTY THE QUEEN ARRIVING AT SOUTH KENSINGTON ON THE
    OCCASION OF THE LAYING OF THE FOUNDATION STONE OF THE
    VICTORIA AND ALBERT MUSEUM (17 May) (N)
    Refs: *Photo. News*, vol. 43, no. 178 (26 May 1899), p. 322
       Palace Theatre programme, 12 June 1899 (T.M.)

15 THE RIGHT HON. CECIL RHODES IN HYDE PARK (19 May) (N)
    Riding in Rotten Row.
    Ref: Palace Theatre programme, 30 May 1899 (D.F.)

16 RECEPTION OF THE DUCHESS OF YORK AT TENBY (May) (N)
    Ref: Crystal Palace programme, 30 May 1899 (D.F.)

17 TRH THE DUKE AND DUCHESS OF CONNAUGHT OPENING THE ARTICLE
    CLUB INDUSTRIAL EXHIBITION (30 May) (N)
    Ref: Crystal Palace programme, 30 May 1899 (D.F.)

18 THE DERBY (31 May) (N)
    (a) The Race
    (b) The Paddock (Epsom)
    (c) Members Enclosure (Epsom)
    Ref: Palace Theatre programme, 26 June 1899 (M & M)

19 LONDON FIRE BRIGADE (June) (N-F)
    (a) Alarm
    (b) Rescue Drill
    Ref: Palace Theatre programme, 12 June 1899 (T.M.)

20 MEADOWBROOK HUNT (June) (N)*
    Ref: Palace Theatre programme, 26 June 1899 (M & M.)
    *Since identified by Barry Anthony as an American production

21 HENLEY ROYAL REGATTA (7 July) (N)
    (a) The Race
    (b) After the Race
    Refs: *The Era*, 15 July 1899, p. 17
        Palace Theatre programme, 21 August 1899 (M & M)

22 CRICKET MATCH AT THE OVAL (16 August) (N)
    Ref: Palace Theatre programme, 21 August 1899 (M & M)

23 HONOURABLE ARTILLERY COMPANY REVIEW, QUEEN IN CARRIAGE
    (August) (N)
    Ref: Palace Theatre programme, 21 August 1899 (M & M)

24 POLO AT HURLINGHAM (August) (N)
    Ref: Palace Theatre programme, 21 August 1899 (M & M)

25 PANORAMA OF LAKE WINDEMERE (August) (N-F)
    Ref: Palace Theatre programme, 21 August 1899 (M & M)

26 PANORAMA OF BOWNESS LANDING (August) (N-F)
    Ref: Palace Theatre programme, 21 August 1899 (M & M)

27 INTERNATIONAL SPORTS, QUEEN'S CLUB (August) (N)
    (a) Finish of One Mile
    (b) 100 Yards Race
    (c) Hurdle Race
    Ref: Palace Theatre programme, 21 August 1899 (M & M)

28 FURNESS RAILWAY (August) (N-F)
    Ref: Palace Theatre programme, 21 August 1899 (M & M)

29 SHAMROCK UNDER SAIL (September) (N)
    This may have been made by the American company.
    Ref: Palace Theatre programme, 25 September 1899 (T.M.)

30 EMBARKATION OF THE 1ST BATTALION NORTHUMBERLAND FUSILIERS
    (THE FIGHTING FIFTH) (18 September) (N) (3 shots)
    The first troops to leave for the Transvaal embarking at Southampton on S.S. *Gaul*
    Refs: *The Era*, 23 September 1899, p. 19
        Palace Theatre programme, 25 September 1899 (T.M.)
        To-Day, 23 November 1899, Supplement p. 5 (5 frame illus.)
        War by Biograph, (2 frame illus.) (R.B.)

31 KING JOHN (20 September) (F)
'A scene—"King John" now playing at Her Majesty's Theatre.'
Refs: *The Era*, 23 September 1899, p. 19
   Palace Theatre programme, 25 September 1899 (T.M.)
   Luke McKernan, 'Further News on Tree's *King John* in *Shakespeare Bulletin*, Spring
   1993, pp. 49–50.
   (Plate 111)

32 ADMIRAL DEWEY (September) (N)
Photographed by W.K.-L. Dickson at Gibraltar for the American company
Refs: Palace Theatre programme, 25 September 1899 (T.M.)
   Boston Herald, 24 September 1899 (cited in Charles Musser, *The Emergence of Cinema*
   (N.Y., 1990), p. 264

33 GENERAL BULLER LEAVING THE CARLTON CLUB / HOTEL (14 October) (N)
Refs: Palace Theatre programme, 19 October 1899 (S.M.)
   The War by Biograph, (1 frame illus.) (R.B.)

34 GENERAL BULLER AT SOUTHAMPTON WITH PRESS REPRESENTATIVES
(14 October) (N)
Ref: Palace Theatre programme, 19 October 1899 (S.M.)

35 GENERAL BULLER EMBARKING AT SOUTHAMPTON (14 October) (N)
'General Sir Redvers Buller going on board *Dunottar Castle* at Southampton.'
(medium close-up)
Refs: Palace Theatre programme, 19 October 1899 (S.M.)
   The War by Biograph, (1 frame illus.) (R.B.)

36 MADEIRA: BOYS DIVING FOR PENNIES (18 October) (N-F)
'Boys diving for pennies, and boats crowding in to get their share.'
Ref: W.K.-L. Dickson, *The Biograph in Battle* (London, 1901), p. 4

37 LORD WOLSELEY ASCENDING COMPANION LADDER OF THE 'ROSLYN
CASTLE' TO BID FAREWELL TO TROOPS (20 October) (N)
Refs: *To-Day*, 26 October 1899, p. 403.
   Ibid, 23 November 1899, Supplement p. 5 (1 frame illus.)

38 SCHOOL OF PORPOISE (21 October) (N-F)
Ref: Dickson, p. 7

39 CROSSING THE LINE (23 October) (N)
'Sports on board ship.'
Ref: Dickson, p. 12

40 GENERAL BULLER ON DECK GAZING AT A PASSING VESSEL
(29 October) (N)
Ref: Dickson, p. 17

Nos. 38, 39 and 40 taken on the voyage to South Africa.

41 LANDING OF GENERAL BULLER AT CAPETOWN (31 October) (N)
'General Buller and Staff disembarking at Capetown.'
Refs: Palace Theatre programme, 21 November 1899 (M & M)
    Dickson, p. 18
    The War by Biograph, (1 frame illus.) (R.B.)

42 LANDING OF THE NEW SOUTH WALES LANCERS AT CAPE TOWN
(1 November) (N)
'The New South Wales Lancers landing at Capetown.'
Refs: Dickson, p. 23
    The War by Biograph, (1 frame illus.) (R.B.)

43 THE NEW SOUTH WALES LANCERS MARCHING UP THE QUAY AT
CAPETOWN EN ROUTE FOR THE FRONT (1 November) (N)
Ref: *The War by Biograph*, (1 frame illus.) (R.B.)

44 PANORAMIC VIEW OF SIMONSTOWN [?] SHOWING H.M.S. 'TERRIBLE' AND
ALSO 'PENELOPE' NOW USED AS A BOER PRISON SHIP (1 November) (N)
Ref: *The War by Biograph*, (2 frame illus.) (R.B.)

45 PANORAMIC VIEW OF THE BAY OF CAPE TOWN (3 November) (N-F)
Ref: Dickson, p. 24

46 COALING SCENE, CAPE TOWN (3 November) (N-F)
Ref: Dickson, p. 24

47 THE 'DAILY MAIL' WAR EXPRESS LEAVING GRAND CENTRAL STATION,
LONDON (November) (N)
Ref: Palace Theatre programme, 6 November 1899 (B.C.)

48 QUEEN REVIEWING HOUSEHOLD CAVALRY (11 November) (N) (two shots)
(a) Her Majesty the Queen Reviewing the Household Cavalry at Spital Barracks,
Windsor.
(b) Three Cheers for the Queen. After the Review the officers gave several cheers for the
queen placing their khaki helmets on their carbines.
Refs: *British Journal of Photography* vol. 46, no. 2063 (17 November 1899), p. 722.
    Palace Theatre programme, 21 November 1899
    To-Day, 23 November 1899, Supplement p. 5 (3 frame illus.)
    The War by Biograph (2 frame illus.) (R.B.)

49 GORDON HIGHLANDERS ON BOARD THE TRANSPORT (November) (N)
Ref: Palace Theatre programme, 21 November 1899 (M & M)

50 LANDING TROOPS FROM THE 'ROSLYN CASTLE' AT DURBAN
(12 November) (N)
Ref: Dickson, p. 34

51 DEPARTURE OF BRITISH TROOPS FOR THE FRONT BY TRAIN FROM
    DURBAN (12 November) (N)
    Ref: Dickson, p. 36

52 STRETCHER BEARERS EN ROUTE FOR THE FRONT (12 November) (N)
    Ref: *The War by Biograph* (1 frame illus.) (R.B.)

53 HOSPITAL STAFF EN ROUTE FOR THE FRONT (12 November) (N)
    Ref: *The War by Biograph* (1 frame illus.) (R.B.)

54 TRAIN LOAD OF GUNS ENROUTE FOR ESCOURT (16 November) (N)
    Ref: Dickson, p. 39

55 AN ARMOURED TRAIN LEAVING DURBAN FOR ESCOURT (17 November) (N)
    Refs: Dickson, p. 39
        The War by Biograph (2 frame illus.) (R.B.)

56 TRAIN LOAD OF TROOPS ON WAY TO THE MOOI RIVER (21 November) (N)
    Ref: Dickson, p. 49

57 HIGHLAND STATION AFTER BOER ATTACK WITH WRECKED SAFE LYING
    ON THE PLATFORM (27 November) (N)
    Ref: Dickson, p. 50

58 PANORAMA OF THE ARMY CAMP AT FRERE TAKEN FROM A RAILWAY
    TRUCK (28 November) (N)
    Refs: Dickson, p. 52
        The War by Biograph (2 frame illus.) (R.B.)

59 REPAIRING THE BROKEN BRIDGE AT FRERE (29 November) (N)
    'Royal Engineers bridging the River Tugela at Frere, showing the old bridge wrecked
    by Boers.'
    Ref: *The War by Biograph* (1 frame illus.) (R.B.)
        Copy in the NFTVA

60 RIFLE HILL SIGNAL STATION NEAR FRERE CAMP (7 December) (N)
    Refs: Dickson, p. 62
        The War by Biograph (1 frame illus.) (R.B.)
        Copy in the NFTVA

61 NAVAL BRIGADE PITCHING CAMP AT AN OUTPOST NEAR FRERE
    (8 December) (N)
    Refs: Dickson, p. 65
        The War by Biograph (1 frame illus.) (R.B.)

62 BOYS OF H.M.S. 'TERRIBLE' GETTING THEIR GUNS INTO POSITION (12
    December) (N)
    Ref: *The War by Biograph* (1 frame illus.) (R.B.)
        Copy in the NFTVA

63 NAVAL GUNS FIRING AT COLENSO (13–14 December) (N)
    (Several scenes)
    Refs: Dickson, pp. 70–71
        Black & White Budget, vol. 5, no. 86 (1 June 1901), p. 294 (1 frame illus.).
        The War by Biograph (1 frame illus.) (R.B.)
        Copy in the NFTVA

64 STANDING BY THE SIDE OF OUR NAVAL FRIENDS SHOWING THE
    BIOGRAPH CAMERA (15 December) (N)
    Ref: *The War by Biograph* (1 frame illus.) (R.B.)

65 ADVANCING IN EXTENDED ORDER (15 December) (N)
    Ref: *The War by Biograph* (1 frame illus.) (R.B.)

66. LORD ROBERTS EMBARKING ON THE S.S. 'DUNOTTAR CASTLE' AT
    SOUTHAMPTON (23 December) (N)
    Ref: *The War by Biograph* (1 frame illus.) (R.B.)

67 A RECONNOITRE IN FORCE (23 December) (N)
    'Troops taking up positions on a Kopje near Colenso.'
    'Lord Dundonald and Major Mackenzie leading a reconnaissance near Spion Kop.'
    Refs: Dickson, p. 90
        The War by Biograph (1 frame illus.) (R.B.)

68 Ditto
    'The cavalry dismount, the horses are led round under cover of the hill and the men
    proceed to advance taking advantage of the ground for shelter.'
    Ref: *The War by Biograph* (2 frame illus.) (R.B.)

69 PANORAMA VIEW OF THE ARTILLERY, CAVALRY, NAVAL AND IRISH
    FUSILIER CAMPS (23 December) (N)
    Ref: Dickson, p. 91

70 13TH HUSSARS EN ROUTE TO A PICKET (24 December) (N)
    Ref: Dickson, p. 92.

71 CHRISTMAS FESTIVITIES TUG-OF-WAR WITH JOHN BULL AND KRUGER
    (24 December) (N)
    Ref: Dickson, p. 95

72 FIGHT BETWEEN A TARANTULA AND SCORPION (30 December) (N)
    Refs: Dickson, p. 101
    The Music Hall, 16 February 1900, p. 101b

Appendix 3

Amendments and Additions to Volume 4

ERRATA

Page 38, line 6: *for* Apolostick *read* Apostolic
Page 78, line 1 (caption): *for* 1951 *read* 1961
Page 88, line 14: *delete* in Bournemouth (?) and *add* at Westcliff-on-Sea, near
   Southend-on-Sea
Page 117, line 13: *for* week, *read* weeks
Page 133, second line from bottom: *for* new *read* news
Page 134, line 2: *for* Neysy *read* Veysy
Page 165, line 2: after Cape Town'. *add raised index number* 90
Page 188, film no. 12 *for* 1990 *read* 1900
Page 200, film no. 14: *for* cat.1901 *read* cat.1903
Page 226, line 27: *for* Hasooks *read* Hassocks
Page 236, film no. 5182: *for* (N-F) *read* (N)
Page 238, film no. 5197: *for* (N-F) *read* (F)
Page 238, film no. 5198: *for* (N-F) *read* (F)
Page 239, films nos. 5205/6/7: *for* (N-F) *read* (N)
Page 246, film no. 5251: *for* (N-F) *read* (N)
Page 248, film no. 5262: *for* (F) *read* (N-F)
Page 255, film nos. 5306/8/9/10: *for* (N-F) *read* (N)
Page 303, line 33: *for* Sutherland *read* Sunderland
Page 318, note 34: *for* Birmingham *read* Manchester

ADDENDA

Page 45: *The Kiss in the Tunnel.* I am informed by John Huntley, of the Huntley Film Archives, Islington, that the footage of the 'phantom ride' used in the film, is taken from Hepworth's *View From an Engine Front, Shilla Mill Tunnel* (cat. no. 50). The tunnel itself can be identified from the number 669 visible on the stone plaque on the right-hand side of the tunnel entrance. Shilla Mill Tunnel is situated between Plymouth and Tavistock on the old London & South Western Railway. *Kiss in the Tunnel* is one of the films depicted in a special video produced by John Huntley called *Victorian Steam Railways 1895–1901* (VHS Pal video, 1987). The Bamforth version of the tunnel kiss was later issued as a picture postcard (Plate 107).

Page 52: Edgar M. Hyman. *The Variety Stage*, 8 August 1896, p. 6, carries an interview with Hyman written whilst on a trip to London where he had been visiting the London music halls. The article in question is illustrated with a portrait, which we reproduce here (Plate 108). A contemporary photograph of Hyman in his Boer War uniform is reproduced in Thelma Gutsche's *The History and Social Significance of Motion Pictures in South Africa 1895–1940* (Cape Town, 1972), facing page 39. An interview with Hyman is also to be found in *The Sunday Times*, 3 December 1903 (page no. not known).

Plate 107   *In the Tunnel*. A picture postcard published by Bamforth & Co., Holmfirth, circa 1904. Based on Bamforth's film *Kiss in the Tunnel* (*Barnes Collection*)

Plate 108   Edgar M. Hyman (18??–1936). South African impresario and manager of the Empire Palace Theatre of Varieties, Johannesburg. With a camera supplied by WTC he filmed many incidents during the Boer War (*Barnes Collection*)

Plate 109   John Benett-Stanford, the noted Boer War cinematographer, circa 1898 (*Copyright Royal Pavilion, Art Gallery and Museums, Preston Park*)

Page 53: Portrait of John Benett-Stanford. I am pleased to be able to reproduce here a more evocative photograph taken in about 1898, when he was a temporary major in the Royal Dragoons. The photograph comes courtesy of Mr David Beevers, Keeper of Preston Manor, who apologizes for the quality of the photograph which was copied from a poor original (Plate 109).

Page 85: Irving Bosco. For information on this showman and his later career, see Ned Williams, *Cinemas in the Black Country* (Uralia Press, Wolverhampton, 1982). This book also contains a photographic portrait of Bosco. See also C. & R. Clegg, *Dream Palaces of Birmingham* (Chris & Rosemary Clegg, Birmingham, 1983).

Page 97: G. West & Son. In a recently acquired programme leaflet of about 1911, a claim is made that the first Royal command film performance before Queen Victoria at Osborne, took place in 1896. I have found no contemporary evidence to support such a claim, but we do know that West gave a show at Osborne House on 27 August 1898 (see vol. 3, p. 46). The same leaflet also states that since that date, Alfred West photographed 100,000 feet of film of naval and military subjects. However, a catalogue of 1912 lists some 529 films amounting to a total length of 56,000 feet.

Page 134: Mutoscopes. According to a document kindly brought to my attention by R. Brown, Mutoscopes were not sold but leased and thus remained the property of the Mutoscope & Biograph Co. (Biograph prospectus, 1899).

(b)

(a)

Plate 110   (a) Scenes from 'King John'. Photographs by the British Mutoscope and Biograph Co. Frame illustrations from actual films taken of the play. *The Sketch*, 17 September 1900, p. 413 (*Barry Anthony*). (b) Portrait of Beerbohm Tree as King John. Postcard published by The Biograph Studio, 107 Regent St., London (*Barnes Collection*)

Pages 142–143: Dreyfus. There is an interesting account of how the Mutoscope & Biograph Company obtained a film of Captain Dreyfus in the prison yard at Rennes, to be found in *The Penny Magazine*, 23 September 1899, pp. 101–104 (4 Illus.). I am indebted to R. Brown for kindly bringing this article to my attention.

Page 143: King John. In *The Sketch* of 20 September 1899, p. 388, there is an account of Beerbohm Tree and his Company of Players hurrying off in full dress and make-up to the vicinity of the Hotel Cecil in the Strand, where they were to be filmed in selected scenes from the play. After the filming, the actors returned to Her Majesty's Theatre for a full dress rehearsal in readiness for the opening performance that night. Meanwhile, the Biograph films were developed and printed and ready to receive their première at the Palace Theatre at the same time as the opening night of the play.

A review of the play appeared in a subsequent issue of *The Sketch*, 27 September 1899, p. 413, where it was accompanied by four illustrations supplied by the British Mutoscope & Biograph Co. Ltd (Plate 110), which probably show frames from actual films.

The American publication, edited by Kemp Niver, *The Biograph Bulletins*, vol. 1, p. 40, gives one of the scenes filmed as *The King's Death at Winstead*. A copy of this film is preserved at the Nederlands Filmmuseum's archives at Overeen, Holland.

For this additional information on the filming of 'King John', I wish to thank Barry Anthony, Richard Brown and Van den Tempel. For a detailed study of the Biograph films of Tree's *King John*, see Luke McKernan, 'Shakespeare on Film' in *Shakespeare Bulletin* (Spring 1993), pp. 49–50.

Page 144: *Hearts are Trumps*. A drawing by Fred Pegram of Act II, Scene III, shows two characters in the play, the Earl of Burford (John Tresahar) and Miss Maude St Trevor (Beatrice Ferrar), dancing before the 'Cinematograph', but the camera depicted does not resemble any known machine (Plate 111). The play includes a spectacular scene representing the auditorium and stage of the 'Frivolity Music-Hall'. During the course of this scene, a screen is lowered and films are shown by means of the American Biograph, just as in a real music hall (programme 7 November 1899, Barnes Collection).

Page 157: Canovascopes. So named after the Italian artist, Roberto Canova (1757–1822) famed for his sculptures of the female form, which the stereo-views of nude models, as seen in the Canovascopes, were supposed to resemble.

Page 163: Crystal Palace. Joseph Paxton's great glass and steel structure, erected for the Great Exhibition of 1851 in Hyde Park, had been removed to Sydenham to serve as a sporting and entertainment complex. As well as sports facilities and exhibition galleries, it contained indoor and outdoor theatres (Plate 112). The latter proved a useful venue for filming various stage productions in the open air, such as the ballet and pantomime extravaganzas filmed in 1899 by WTC (cat. nos. 5349–5355). The indoor facilities provided space for cinematograph displays. The Theatre Café Chantant, for instance, included films among its variety programmes; a programme for 4 August 1900, in the Barnes Collection, records 'The Royal Biorama' with all the latest war pictures. Cinematograph entertainments were also given in the Music Court, South Nave (Programme dated 10 March 1900, Theatre Museum). In the 'Egyptian Court' and 'Biograph Court' a number of Mutoscopes were permanently on display (Programme & Guide, 4 August 1900, p. 4, Barnes Collection).

Plate 111   Hearts are Trumps, in which two of the characters in the play dance for the cinematograph camera. Illustration in *Black and White*, 20 September 1900, p. 388

Plate 112   The Open-air Theatre, Crystal Palace which provided an ideal locale for filming theatrical events. Illustration in *Black and White*, 22 July 1899, p. 119

Plate 113   *The Landing of 'Savage South Africa'* (M&B, 1899). The Africans were to appear at Earl's Court in a show of that name. Frame illustration from a contemporary print in National Television and Film Archive

Films had been associated with the Crystal Palace for several years and the Cinématographe-Lumière, under Trewey, had been presented here as long ago as 25 May 1896.

Olympia, Addison Road, Kensington, was another huge complex where films were regularly shown. Paul had presented his Theatrograph in the 'Palmarium' here on 21 March 1896. In June of that year, Banks & Greaves presented the Vivaceographe in the same venue (Programme for 16 June 1896, Douglas-Jewell Collection). Banks & Greaves of 366 Clapham Road, London, were opticians and dealers in all kinds of photographic equipment, including optical magic lanterns and accessories (*Magic Lantern Journal Annual 1896–7*) (London, 1896), p. lxxiii, advert. At Earl's Court, close by, films were also presented; in 1899, the Royal Bioscope held sway (Official Guide 1899, p. 68, Barnes Collection). It was at this venue that the spectacular show 'Savage South Africa' was filmed (Plate 113).

Pages 188–192: Biograph Filmography. Since compiling this list, I have had access to many more sources which has resulted in additional titles and more accurate dating of those already listed. Rather than amend the matter here, I have deemed it more fitting to entirely recast the filmography for 1899 and include it as Appendix 2.

Pages 225–226: Riley Bros. and Bamforth (RAB). The only reference I have been able to find to Riley's film production for the whole of the period covered by this history, occurs in the journal *Photography* for 18 August 1898, p. 548a, where it is stated that the firm 'has issued a number of kinematographic slides' i.e. films. It seems more than likely that the films listed by me on p. 225–226 relate to this quotation and should therefore be backdated to 1898. The films in question are: *The Honeymoon*; *Kiss in the Tunnel*; *Fox Hounds*; *The Biter Bit*; and *The Tramp and the Baby's Bottle*. For the latest study of early Bamforth films see Richard Brown, *Notes on the Nomenclature and Dating of Some Early Bamforth Films* (privately distributed, 1994).

Page 300: Pope Leo XIII. One evening in December 1898, Dickson's Biograph films of the Pope were given a special showing at the Archbishop's Palace, Carlisle Street, Westminster, for Cardinal Vaughan and a few of his invited guests. *Black and White*, 31 December 1898, pp. 835–836, published an account of the exhibition, together with four frame illustrations from the films.

Pages 303 and 304 (illustrations 108a and b): It now seems that the performances billed at the Palace and Empire theatres as the 'Cinématographe', were not in fact given by the Lumière machine. The début of the genuine Cinématographe-Lumière did not take place in Newcastle until 15 June, when it was exclusive to the Empire.

MATERIAL RELATING TO PREVIOUS VOLUMES

I listed R.W. Paul's film *Sisters Hengler* among his 1897 productions (vol. 2, p. 229), but the summer of 1896 seems a more likely date. In June that year, the sisters were sharing the bill at the Alhambra Theatre with Paul's Animatographe (Theatograph) and it is most likely that Paul took this opportunity to film the sisters on the roof of the theatre, a locale which he had previously used in April to film *The Soldier's Courtship*. Both these Alhambra subjects came to be used in Short's Filoscope, along with other films taken by Paul in 1896. An Alhambra Theatre programme for June 1896, listing May and Fiora Hengler and the Animatographe as items 8 and 10 on the bill, can be seen displayed (in reproduction) at the Museum of the Moving Image, London.

   We have further information on Williamson's chemist shop at 144 Western Road, Hove. The premises were previously occupied by two photographers who traded under the names Wells & Grey. With the departure of one partner, the business continued as S. Grey. The Barnes Collection has *carte-de-visite* photographs with the insignia of both firms. Our illustration (Plate 114) shows the shop as it appeared on 16 August 1886 after it had been acquired by James Williamson. Four years later, the shop-front was altered; a photograph of the shop in its altered state is reproduced in vol. 2, p. 93, illustration 47. During September 1898, Williamson moved his pharmaceutical business to 55 Western Road, Hove (see vol. 4, p. 41, illustration 23). His next move was to Wilbury Road, where in 1902 he built his famous glasshouse studio. The architect's drawings for this studio can be seen at the Hove Museum & Art Gallery, where a permanent exhibition of the Brighton film pioneers has been set up by the curator Timothy Wilcox, with the assistance of Frank Gray of the South East Film & Video Archive.

   The Williamson filmography can be much enlarged since the discovery by Frank Gray, of two photocopied catalogues for 1899 and 1902 in George Eastman House. These two catalogues also provide fuller synopses than I was able to provide in my previous volumes. Besides George Eastman House, photocopies can also be consulted at the South East Film Archive, Brighton; the Barnes Collection, St Ives; and the Cinema Museum, London.

   We are able to give here a fuller synopsis of some G.A. Smith films for the years 1897 and 1898, by referring to Warwick Trading Co.'s catalogue of April 1901 (copy in Science Museum Library, London).

Plate 114   J. Willimason's chemist shop, at 144 Western Road, Hove, as it appeared in 1886 (*British Film Institute*)

1897, vol. 2, pp. 232–236:

1 FOOTBALL/GAME OF FOOTBALL
   An association game and scrimmage. Lively scene. One of the best football films.'
   WTC no. 5597b

7 MOHAWK MINSTRELS/AN INCIDENT ON BRIGHTON PIER
   'Showing an audience leaving the Pier Pavilion, following Messrs. Danvers and Schofield, of the Mohawk Minstrels, who, in full costume, amuse the surrounding crowds by cutting many funny capers.'
   WTC no. 5615b

9 MISS ELLEN TERRY AT HOME
   'A charming half-length portrait of the popular actress. She appears at the casement window of her country cottage, kisses her hand, throws a flower, &c. Beautifully sharp and clear.'
   WTC no. 5591b
   MISS ELLEN TERRY IN HER GARDEN
   'Showing this famous actress slowly walking down the garden path towards the camera, gathering roses, while her pet dog scampers about around the bushes.'
   WTC no. 5592

TEA WITH MISS ELLEN TERRY
'Seated at a table in a garden in the company of a lady friend, Miss Terry is seen reading and partaking of an afternoon tea. Splendid face and profile portrait.'
WTC no. 5593b

10 PIERROT TROUPE/MINSTRELS AT THE SEA-SIDE
'A pierrot troupe performing before a large crowd of spectators on the sands at Margate. One of the sights at seaside resorts.'
WTC no. 5608b

12 BRIGHTON SEA-GOING ELECTRIC CAR/THE SEA-GOING CAR IN A ROUGH SEA
'A curious structure of iron in the shape of a tower topped by a platform for passengers propelled by electricity, slowly moving along over rails laid under the sea, while the waves break against the girders and break on the sands. A novelty in animated pictures.'
WTC no. 5605b

14 WALKING GREASY POLE/WALKING A GREASY POLE
'A scene at a regatta, showing a spar projecting from the side of a yacht, along which several competitors attempt to reach the prize hung at the end, but the greasy condition of the pole precipitates several in the water. The pig is finally won.'
WTC no. 5600b

15 PADDLING/PADDLING AT THE SEA-SIDE
'An amusing scene at the seashore. Little tots are led to the edge of the water where they gingerly place their tiny feet into the lopping waves. Their elder sisters are also seen paddling to their hearts content.'
WTC no. 5601b

16 HANGING OUT THE CLOTHES/THE MAID IN THE GARDEN HANGING OUT CLOTHES
'The busy maiden hanging out the clothes is tickled by the master who entices her behind a sheet. 'Missus' returns from shopping, looks for maid, sees the pair of feet beneath the hanging sheet, tears it down—tableau. Maid flies, master 'faces the music' and doubtless makes rapid progress towards baldness in consequence.'
WTC no. 5573b

17 THE LADY BARBER
'Her want of skill is atoned for by her dexterity as a surgeon. Her customer's face is finally covered with sticking plaster, yet he seems to thoroughly enjoy the innovation.'
WTC no. 5581b

18 THE MILLER AND THE SWEEP
'The original rendering of this subject. A windmill is at work in the background. The Miller emerges, advances to the front, and comes into collision with a Sweep. Indignation leads to blows, developing into a lively soot and flour fight, which is only stopped by the arrival of a number of excited villagers.'
WTC no. 5576b

20 WEARIE WILLIE/WEARY WILLIE
'Tramp, engaged to beat carpets, beats employer by mistake, and sits down to smoke. Carelessness and laziness punished by pail of water.'
WTC no. 5583b

21 WAVES AND SPRAY/A STORM AT HASTINGS PIER
'One of the best films, showing enormous waves dashing against the stone sea wall, the spray being thrown in great height and volume over the top.'
WTC no. 5602

23 FOOTBALL AND CRICKET
'Half of the film shows a lot of boys playing football, which is followed by the other section of a game of cricket. Sharp and clear. Section of blank spacing between the two sections.'
WTC no. 5598b

24 PASSENGER TRAIN/ARRIVAL AND DEPARTURE OF TRAIN AT HOVE
'Arrival at station. Passengers bustle and change, train moves off. A capital example of this popular subject. Fine definition, full of action.'
WTC no. 5590b

25 LOVE ON THE PIER/LIVELY SCENES ON HASTINGS PIER
'A lady is seen flirting with a young man both seated on the pier bench, when the husband puts in an unexpected appearance with a resulting climax.'
WTC no. 5607b

26 THE X RAYS/THE X RAY FIEND
'A pair of lovers on a seat are approached by professor with X Ray apparatus. *He reveals their bones*, and, having satisfied his scientific curiosity, retreats as quietly as he came, leaving the lovers to continue their spooning, quite unconscious of the grotesque figures they have cut. Very funny.'
WTC no. 5582b

28 TRAFALGAR DAY/TRAFALGAR SQUARE ON NELSON DAY
'Tremendous crowds gathering around the decorated Nelson Monument while the traffic slowly wends its way through the multitudes.'
WTC no. 5595b

29 MAKING SAUSAGES/THE END OF ALL THINGS—MAKING SAUSAGES
'Four men cooks at work in the kitchen. Live cats and dogs are put into the machine and come out as sausages. Incidentally a duck and an old boot is added to give flavour to the "string". Always goes well.'
WTC no. 5574b

30 TIPSY, TOPSY, TURVEY (REVERSAL)/TIPSY, TOPSY TURVEY (REVERSING)
'Somewhat similar to the above *Ally Sloper*, [WTC no. 5587b]. A reveller comes home from his club, and throws down his hat, stick and other garments. The articles all return to him, and he goes out of the room backwards.'
WTC no. 5588b

31 YACHTING/SAILING YACHTS AT HASTINGS 50ft
    'A pretty scene, showing many outgoing yachts leaving the shore and riding the waves after
    being launched.'
    WTC no. 5603b

1898 Vol. 3, pp. 190–192:

 2 GYMNASTICS/HORIZONTAL BAR ACROBATIC FEATS
    'By two prize winners at an acrobatic tournament, many difficult feats are performed by
    these inteprid [sic] acrobats.'
    WTC no. 5611b

 5 CYCLE BOAT/THE WATER CYCLE AT SEA
    'A novel method of propulsion over the water. The water cycle is ridden over the waves
    breaking on the shore, goes out to sea, and returns, passing the camera very closely,
    thereby disclosing the details of construction of this unique craft.'
    WTC no. 5613b

 8 THE BAKER AND THE SWEEP/RIVALS IN BLACK AND WHITE
    'Another soot and flour fight outside the house where the baker is delivering his goods.
    The servant of the establishment puts a damper on the fury of the combatants by means
    of a pail of water.'
    WTC no. 5577b

 9 COMIC COSTUME RACE/COSTUME RACE
    'An amusing scene at some out-door sports. One competitor dresses in a ballet skirt.'
    WTC no. 5584b

10 GARDENER WITH HOSE/A JOKE ON THE GARDENER
    'Boy secretly treads on the hose pipe, and suddenly releases it. Finale: A general "mix up",
    in which the boy gets a sound trouncing.'
    WTC no. 5585b

12 THE SIGN WRITER/THE AWKWARD SIGN WRITER (REVERSING) 75ft
    'Writes the words, "This house to let", and then accidentally knocked off his ladder by a
    passing hawker. When reversed, he "falls up" on to his ladder again, and "paints out" his
    previous work letter by letter.'
    WTC no. 5589b

13 THE POLICEMAN AND COOK; OR, THE 'COPPER' IN THE COPPER 75ft
    'Servant, unfortunately, conceals her Bobby in the copper a few minutes before "Missus"
    decides to commence washing. From the farce "Area Belle".'
    WTC no. 5580b

    THE RUNAWAY KNOCK (Date uncertain) (F)
    Not previously listed.
    'Several urchins knock at an old lady's front door and run away. A tiny child anxious to
    "have a go" at the knocker, is too short to reach it. A kindly old gentleman who happens

to pass lifts the little one up, and is rewarded for his pains by the irated [sic] householder, who suddenly emerges and deluges him with a pail of water.'
WTC no. 5579b

COMIC FACE/ANIMATED CLOWN PORTRAIT (1898) (F)
Not previously listed.
'A portrait of a clown, just finished by the artist, gradually becomes animated, and the extraordinary grimaces produced scare the artist almost out of his wits.'
WTC 5614b
Ronald Smith catalogue 1898, no. 23A (copy in Ronald Grant Collection)

A typed copy of a catalogue of films issued by G.A. Smith in 1898, which emanates from the Graham Head Collection, now in the Cinema Museum, Kennington,* lists three films not previously included in my filmography for 1897/8. These are:

COMIC FACE (F) (Date uncertain) Approx: 75 ft
'Clown's portrait in frame comes to life.'
May be the same as film no. 21 in my list for 1898 (vol. 3, p. 192)
ALLY SLOPER (F) (Date uncertain) 75 ft or 50 ft
'Ally Sloper as the quick-change artiste (Behind the scenes) Reversing.'
YACHTING (N) (Date uncertain) Approx: 75 ft
'Continuous procession of small yachts at regatta pass and repass very close to camera.'
May be contemporary with film no. 8 in my list for 1897 (vol. 2, p. 233)

I was very pleased to receive a communication from Tony Tester, who had vital information and documents relating to his grandfather and great-grandfather, two film pioneers who had connections with Birt Acres and Esmé Collings. Tony kindly supplied me with copies of valuable material from his great-aunt's scrapbook and put me in touch with his father, who was kind enough to send me a brief history of the Tester family (letter to the author from R.D. Tester, dated 26 February 1991).

John Tester senior, who was born in Brighton, Sussex, in 1844 and died in Fulham, London, in 1916, was a travelling salesman with a wide interest in contemporary mechanical devices such as sewing machines, phonographs, and metal toys produced in Germany. He became the managing director of the British Toy and Novelty Company, Limited, 29 Ludgate Hill, London, E.C. An advertisement for this firm is illustrated in my first volume (p. 73) in connection with the Kineopticon of Birt Acres, for which the firm was appointed the sole wholesale agents. Previously, in 1895, this firm was trading under the name of the Electro-Magnetic Toy Company at the same address. Evidently it had been formed expressly for the purpose of exploiting a new magnetic toy called 'The Patent Magic Box', the invention of John Tester's eldest son, John Frederick Tester, A.I.E.E. According to a report in the *Hardwareman* of 31 August 1895, 'this toy is practically a means of giving small fancy figures a life-like and fascinating motion, which charms the young and raises the curiosity of the old.' The same paper gives a brief description of the toy:

The box is placed on a level surface, and held with the left hand. A brass bar projecting

* I am grateful to Ronald Grant, of the Cinema Museum, Kennington, for kindly making this list available to me.

Plate 115   John Frederick Tester, A.M.I.E.E. (1869–1926) early cinematographer and projectionist. His father, John Tester, was Managing Director of the British Toy & Novelty Co., which promoted the Kineopticon, or Royal Cinematoscope, of Birt Acres (*Tester Collection*)

from it is slowly withdrawn to its full extent, and then returned smartly to its former position by the first or second finger of the right hand, which action sets the mechanism in motion. One of a number of wires or small tin pieces, with a dancing figure attached to it, is then placed on the surface of the box so that it touches the side of a small pivot projecting through the centre of the lid, and the toy operates, the figure going through all sorts of motions, and moving over the polished surface of the box in a most pleasing manner. The neatest device is a pair of waltzers who circle round the pivot. This should be a good thing for ironmongers to display on their counters.

The price of the toy was 2s 6d post free.

Its inventor, J.F. Tester (Plate 115) was born in Oldham, Manchester, on 28 December 1869, and when the family settled in London, he was apprenticed to Messrs Woodhouse and Rawson, electrical engineers, at what is now known as Cadby Hall, Hammersmith Road, Kensington. He qualified as an electrical engineer and later worked with his father as a cinematographer and projectionist. According to his son, he left the film business when he got married and moved to East Dereham, Norfolk in 1898, where incidentally, my correspondent Ron Tester was born in 1902.

In October 1896, the British Toy & Novelty Company exhibited a programme of films at the Polytechnic Institute, Regent Street, which was given a favourable review in the *Daily Telegraph* on the 28th:

Although 'animated photographs' have grown very much into popular favour they have one blemish, the constant vibration, which must be removed before they can be pronounced perfect. This is, however, in a fair way of being done at the Polytechnic Institute, Regent Street, where there is at the present moment a capital series of 'living pictures' on view. It is a great boon to find that in most instances the scenes depicted are comparatively free from this photographical defect, furthermore, satisfaction is likely to be expressed when it is known that the machine used is an English one. The representations, which are offered at popular prices, and last about twenty-five minutes, are given every half-hour in the afternoon, and include some excellent views of Brighton, notably one of the King's-road; a scene from a play; the march-past of the Royal Horse Artillery at Aldershot, and the Prince and Princess of Wales visiting the Cardiff Exhibition. Members of the fair sex, as well as others, whilst engaged in the arduous pastime of shopping in the neighbourhood, would do well to look in at the institute and watch the 'latest wonder of the nineteenth century', as exhibited there.

The above quotation is printed on a handbill in the Tester Collection, with the added rider:

'The Machine referred to is being Exhibited by the British Toy & Novelty Co., Limited,.
29 Ludgate Hill, London, E.C.
    Arrangements can be made for Exhibiting at Bazaars, At Homes, Private and Public Entertainments. For Terms apply to the Manager.

The make of the machine is not revealed, but the review states that 'the machine is an English one.' It seems probable, therefore, that it referred to the Birt Acres Kineopticon, or Royal Cinematoscope which the company had exhibited in the East End of London, at the People's Palace during August and October, just prior to the Polytechnic show. Notice of this particular show has already been given in my first volume (p. 77). Here the apparatus is named as the Kineopticon and was introduced by T.C. Hayward. Among testimonials printed on a leaflet issued in 1897 by J.F. Tester, from an address at 83 St Dunstan's Road, Hammersmith, is one referring to this East London exhibition:

'Originally it was intended that the East London Exhibition at the People's Palace should be closed next week. So successful has it been of late that it has been definitely decided to keep it open until the end of October. The attendances have been fully up to the average of the past month. The great attraction has undoubtedly been the re-engagement of the "Animated Photographs".'

East London Advertiser, Aug. 29th, 1896.

Among other documents in the Tester scrapbook is a stock list of films held by the British Toy & Novelty Co. in December 1896. This is perhaps the most important of all the Tester papers as it provides the titles of a number of films made by Birt Acres and Esmé Collings, some of which have not been previously recorded. The titles are handwritten on two pages from a ledger extracted and pasted into the scrapbook. The list is headed, 'Complete List of Films', and the films are numbered from 1 to 43. Against each title is the price paid for the film and the name of the photographer. Apparently, the films were held at three different repositories, namely at Bristol, Kensington Stores, and Ludgate Hill. The titles of the films deposited at each of these three locations are listed on separate pages extracted from the same ledger and pasted into the same scrapbook. The three pages are dated 7th, 14th and 8th December, respectively. All the films entered on these pages are also to be found on the complete list, which is here transcribed:

COMPLETE LIST OF FILMS

		Purchase price	Photographer
1.	Prince of Wales, Cardiff	£10.	Acres
2.	Crowd at Law Court	£3.10.	Collings
3.	Lord Mayor	£3.10.	Ditto
4.	West St, Brighton	£3.10.	Ditto
5.	Rough Sea	£3.10.	Ditto
5a.	Ditto (2nd. copy)	£3.10.	Ditto
6.	King's Rd, Brighton	£3.10.	Ditto
6a.	Ditto (2nd. copy)	£3.10.	Ditto
7.	Boys Under Pier	£3.10.	Ditto
8.	Children Paddling	£3.10.	Ditto
9.	Ditto Yarmouth	£2.15.	Acres
10.	Arrest of Pickpocket	£2.15.	Ditto
11.	Bryant & May	£2.15.	Ditto
12.	Tom Merry. Gladstone	£2.15.	Ditto
13.	Ditto. Salisbury	£2.15.	Ditto
14.	Haymaker	£3.2.	Edison
15.	Children in Garden	£2.15.	Acres
16.	Carpenter's Shop	£2.15.	Ditto
17.	Road Sprinkler	£3.2.	Edison
18.	Steamer & Smack	£2.15.	Acres
19.	Golfing Extraordinary	£2.15.	Ditto
20.	Highgate Tunnel	£2.15.	Ditto
20a.	Ditto (2nd copy)	£2.15.	Ditto
21.	French Ry Station	£3.	De Bedts (Hough)
22.	Finsbury Pk [Park] Stn.	£2.15.	Acres
23.	Dyke Station	£3.10.	Collings
24.	Soldiers Landing	£3.10.	Ditto
25.	Czar in Paris	£4.4.	Ditto
26.	German Emperor	£2.15.	
Carr'd to folio 25		£97.13	
Brought ford.		£97.13	
27.	Boxing Match	£2.15.	Acres
28.	Julian, Butterfly Dance	£2.15.	Ditto
29.	Broadway, N.Y.	£2.15.	Ditto
30.	Ilfracombe, Capstone [Parade]	£2.15.	Ditto
31.	Musical Party, Van Biene	£3.10.	Collings
32.	Broken Melody	£3.10.	Ditto
32a.	Ditto (2nd copy)	£3.10.	Ditto
33.	Boxing Kangaroo	£2.15.	Acres
34.	Feeding Tiger	£2.15.	Ditto
34a.	Ditto (2nd copy)	£2.15.	Ditto
35.	Niagara	£2.15.	Ditto

36.	Derby	£2.15.	Ditto
37.	Hose Scene	£3.10.	Collings
38.	Going for Sail	£2.15.	Acres
39.	Donkey Riding	£3.10.	Collings
40.	Sailors Gun Drill	£3.10.	Ditto
41.	Ditto [?] Cavalry	£3.10.	Ditto
42.	Policeman & Cook	£3.10.	Ditto
43.	Shoe Black	£2.15.	Acres

£155.18.0.

The small amount of material on the British Toy & Novelty Co. in the Tester scrapbook leads me to believe that its existence was of very short duration and that by the end of 1896 it had already ceased to exist. The presence instead of a number of documents relating to the Scientific Exhibits Co., which had its address at 'The Parlour', 445 Strand, suggests that this was another Tester enterprise, set up to replace the former concern. Its period of activity seems to date from early January 1897, but it too appears to have been short lived, perhaps no more than a few months.

'Animated photographs' were exhibited at 'The Parlour', along with Roentgen X Rays and Edison's latest 'New Motor Phonograph.' The machine used at 'The Parlour' to project the films was the Pholimeograph (Heinze's patent), which has been mentioned already in previous volumes of this history. Two handbills in the Tester Collection, give a list of the films to be exhibited there. Neither handbill is dated, but the year 1897 has been added by hand. One bill is pink and the other white. The films listed on the pink handbill are:

1. Roman Wrestlers.
2. Paddle Dance.
3. Military Manoeuvres.
4. Feeding an Elephant.
5. Women Washing.
6. Hat Manipulator.
7. Lord Mayor at Law Courts.
8. Rough Sea Breaking Against the Admiralty Pier, Dover.
9. Cartoonist Sketching Celebrities.
10. Fan Dance (in Colours).
11. The Vanishing Lady.
12. TRH The Prince and Princess of Wales at Cardiff Exhibition.

Among the filmmakers represented we can recognize Acres (nos. 8, 9, and 12); Collings (no. 7); and Méliès (no. 11). The rest are possibly Lumière films. The following films are listed on the white handbill:

1. Roman Wrestlers.
2. Paddle Dance.
3. Military Manoeuvres.
4. Feeding the Elephant.
5. Loïe Fuller.
6. Women Washing.

Scientfic Entertainments,

Provided by ~~JOHN~~ TESTER. *and J.F.* *in conjunction with the*

Bioscenagraph Co —

~~83, ST. DUNSTAN'S ROAD~~,

~~HAMMERSMITH~~,

~~LONDON, W.~~

Messrs J and J.F. Tester

Majesty the King ~~Mr. John Tester has~~ had the distinguished honour of Entertaining *(by command)* T.R.H. The Prince and Princess of Wales and other members of the Royal Family at the Yachting and Fisheries Exhibition, Imperial Institute (*Diploma awarded*). ~~He has~~ *and* also Exhibited at the People's Palace, Mile End Road, with unbounded success for 13 weeks in succession ; also at the Polytechnic, Regent Street, for several weeks, besides many Public Institutions throughout London and the Provinces, including Westbourne Park Institute, (~~see testimonial from Dr. Clifford~~), The Battersea and the Woolwich Polytechnics, &c., and at Drawing Room Entertainments, Schools, " At Homes " ~~and~~ and Private Parties.

A High Class and Unique Entertainment

illustrating

The Marvels of SIGHT and SOUND.

as exemplified by the

CINEMATOGRAPH (ANIMATED PHOTOGRAPHS)

Of the latest and best kind

AND THE

NEW "GRAND CONCERT" PHONOGRAPH,

by means of which

SONGS, BANDS, SPEECHES, INSTRUMENTAL SOLOS, &c.,

can be reproduced LOUD and CLEAR and DISTINCT enough

to be heard in the LARGEST HALLS.

Plate 116   Leaflet for John Tester's Scientific Entertainments, circa 1899, with revised text written in by hand by his son J.F. Tester (*Tester Collection*)

SECTION OF THE ORIGINAL FILM

His Majesty the King

taken by special permission of H.R.H. the Prince of Wales, on the deck of his yacht, "The Britannia," at Nice, for reproduction at the Yachting and Fisheries Exhibition, Imperial Institute.

A selection of 350 Animated Photograph Subjects
to choose from, amongst the most popular being the following :—

A Heavy Load. The Fraudulent Beggar. The Sleeping Coachman. Santa Claus. Gladstone's Funeral. The Procession. Weary Willie in the Park. Joe Darby in his various Jumps. A Switchback Railway. Feeding the Swans. Rich and Poor (pathetic, with Snow Effects). The Steeplechase. The Big Fire!—The Alarm (Brigade leaving the Station—The Run to the Fire—Arriving at the Scene of Action.) Jerusalem (near Railway Station). Baby's First Steps. Gale at Sea. The Bloodless Encounter. View from an Engine front (Barnstaple Station). Arrival of an Excursion Train. Camel Corps crossing Desert into Cairo. Scottish Highlanders return to Cairo after the fall of Omdurman and Khartoum. Defence of the Colours. Scots Guards in Hyde Park. Change of Guards at St. James' Palace. The Gordon Highlanders. Skirmish at Glencoe. Lord Roberts leaving England. Crossing Modder River. Red Cross Waggons. Nurses attending Wounded, &c. &c.

The New Grand Concert Phonograph
may be hired either with or without the CINEMATOGRAPH.

The two combined produce one of the finest Entertainments ever placed before the public—Interesting, Instructive and Amusing, always delighting an audience whether composed of young or old.

Terms :—

CINEMATOGRAPH alone	*and travelling expenses*	£3 3 0	*for one evening.*	
CONCERT PHONOGRAPH	,,	,,	£2 2 0	,, ,,
THE TWO TOGETHER	,,	,,	£4 4 0	,, ,,

A reduction for a series.

7. Steamers on the Seine.
8. Lord Mayor at Law Courts.
9. Rough Sea at Brighton.
10. Shrimpers at Work.
11. Fan Dance.
12. Leap Frog.
13. TRH The Prince and Princess of Wales at Cardiff Exhibition.

Once again we can recognize films by Acres (no. 13) and Collings (nos. 8, and 9). Among several press reviews preserved in the scrapbook, this is a typical example from *The Evening News*, of 19 January 1897:

NEW SHOW IN THE STRAND

The Scientific Exhibits Company have added another place of entertainment to the numerous shows in the Strand by opening a Hall at No. 445, where an exhibition of the latest scientific discoveries is on view.

These include the X Rays apparatus, which enables visitors to see portions of their anatomy denuded of flesh, and the Edison Improved Phonograph, which emits selections of popular and operatic music at intervals. Another attraction is the Pholimeograph, which has been brought to a high state of perfection, and exhibits genuine coloured photographs.

The pictures thrown on the screen are all new and very effective. The feeding of the huge elephant at the Jardin des Plantes is especially good and free from vibration, and that of Miss Loïe Fuller doing a skirt dance is an extremely pretty coloured reproduction of the little lady's performance.

The entertainment is unique of its kind, and ought to draw plenty of visitors to the comfortably fitted up hall opposite Charing Cross Station.'

J.F. Tester was still in business well after 1898, the year when he is supposed to have retired, as is evident from an examination of a four-page leaflet to be found among the Tester papers. This document is headed 'Scientific Entertainment, Provided by John Tester' and contains a list of films, among which are some Boer War scenes known to have been taken in 1899, which is also likely to be the year when the leaflet was printed. The document also bears numerous alterations to the text, written in ink, indicating that it was being prepared for a reprint (Plate 116). Where HRH the Prince of Wales is mentioned, this is crossed through and 'His Majesty the King' is substituted, indicating that these alterations were penned some time after the death of Queen Victoria in January 1901.

The leaflet has a double interest because it was originally issued under the sole name of John Tester and sets out the nature of the entertainment then currently on offer. In the amended version however, the name of the son is added to that of the father's, so that the leaflet now reads, 'Scientific Entertainments, Provided by John and J.F. Tester.' Also added in the same hand, are the words, 'in conjunction with the Biosenagraph.' The leaflet bears the Hammersmith address mentioned above, but this has been crossed out, indicating a change of residence had taken place since then, or was imminent.

Prominence is given in the leaflet to a film showing HRH the Prince of Wales (Edward VII) on the deck of his yacht *Britannia* at Nice. A strip of about eight consecutive frames from the film are reproduced, and a statement says that the film was exhibited by John Tester in a programme of 'Animated Photographs' at the Imperial Institute: Yachting & Fisheries Exhibition, 1897. A contemporary print of a section of this film is still owned by the Tester family (Plate 117).

According to R.D. Tester (in a letter to the author, dated 10 March 1991), the Royal film was photographed by his father, J.F. Tester, and that, 'the gentleman in the foreground trying to keep out of the picture is [his] grandfather, John Tester'. (Plate 118) However, there is another claim to the authorship of this film, which has kindly been brought to my attention by Dr Nicholas Hiley. In an article by the collector and historian Will Day in *The Photographic Annual* (December 1931, p. 462), he writes:

> Undoubtedly the first film of a Royal Personage ever taken was the one of King Edward VII, when he was Prince of Wales, in June, 1896. This rare film of a great king and a fine English gentleman was secured by the early kinematographer, Mr. Monti Williams (the son of Mr. Randall Williams, the famous showman) on board the royal yacht *Britannia* as she lay in Cannes Harbour.

Will Day's account is wrong on at least four counts. Firstly, this was not the first film taken of a royal personage. Secondly, Dr Hiley has found out that the Prince was not in Cannes in 1896, but in March, 1897. Thirdly, Randall Williams did not have any sons. The Monti Williams referred to is obviously Richard Monte, Randall Williams's son-in-law (see my vol. 2, p. 241). Fourthly, according to the near contemporary document in the Tester Collection, the royal yacht was not at Cannes, but at Nice. Day also states that the gentleman seen with the Prince on deck is Sir Simon Fortescue. He also adds that the film was taken with an improvised Eragraph camera produced by Haydon & Urry, of Islington, with whom Williams [sic] was at that time associated.

The film is listed in my filmography under Edisonia Ltd. (vol. 2, p. 225). We know that Tester was an exhibitor of the Edison Phonograph, and it seems probable that he made arrangements with Edisonia to market the film. There is no question of there being two films of the same subject, because the frame illustrations accompanying both accounts reveal they are taken from the same film. The problem remains; whose testimony are we to accept? A copy of the film is preserved in the National Film and Television Archive. Clips from three other films attributed to J.F. Tester are in the Tester Collection (Plate 119).

An advertisement for a performance of the Royal Cinématographe at the Agricultural Hall, Norwich, on 11 January 1897, lists a number of films known to have been made by Birt Acres (Plate 120). The advertisement states that the Royal Cinématographe is 'the first machine that was shown in England, and also the only one that has been before HRH the Prince of Wales by special command.' But it seems most unlikely that this was indeed the original Kineoptikon first exhibited by Birt Acres. Although his name does not actually appear on the bill, it is obvious from the internal evidence that he was connected with the show. The illustration was first published in Stephen Peart's *The Picture House in East Anglia* (Lavenham, Suffolk, 1980) p. xii; and also appears in David Cleveland, *East Anglia on Film* (North Walsham, Norfolk, 1987) p. 7.

Mr Richard Brown of Bury, Lancs, has uncovered a most revealing document which confirms my suspicion that the Birt Acres projector being exhibited in 1896–1897, as the Royal Cinematoscope was not of his own design. I wrote in vol. 1, p. 73:

> No details or illustration of the Kineopticon [re-named the Royal Cinematoscope after its command film performance] ever appear to have been published, as if Birt Acres

Plate 117   HRH The Prince of Wales [Edward VII] on board the royal yacht *Britannia* in Nice harbour (Edisonia, 1897). Photographed by J.H. Tester under the direction of his father, John Tester (seen here in the foreground). Frame illustration from a contemporary print in the Tester Collection

Plate 118   John Tester (1844–1916) Managing Director of The British Toy & Novelty Co., in 1896. He is to be seen in the film of the Prince of Wales on board Britannia at Nice (*Tester Collection*)

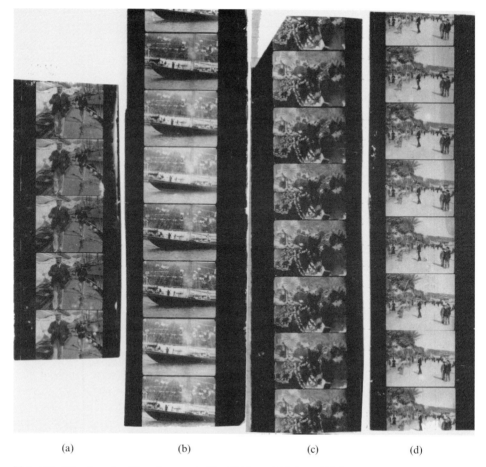

(a)   (b)   (c)   (d)

Plate 119   Clips from four films photographed by J.F. Tester (a) Prince of Wales on board *Britannia* (b) The *Britannia* (c) Carnival at Nice (?) (d) Baie des Anges (?) (*Tester Collection*)

deliberately intended to keep the details of its mechanism secret. In fact, he had stubbornly ignored requests by the photographic press for such information.[*] The suspicion naturally arises that perhaps the apparatus was not entirely of his own design.

Amateur Photographer, vol. 26, no. 678 (1 October 1897) p. 277.

Since writing this passage nearly twenty years ago, my suspicions have been vindicated by the document Mr Brown has recently unearthed at the Public Record Office. It is a letter from R.W. Paul, dated 7 September 1896, addressed to 'The Secretary, The Lord Great Chamberlain's Office, Royal Court, House of Lords, S.W.' (PRO ref.: LO1/642) The letter reads:

'I have the honour to draw your attention to the fact that an apparatus is being exhibited at a London Music Hall, (advertisement of which I enclose), under the title of the "Royal Cinematescope" sic . I have authoritative information that the machine used is not the one exhibited at Marlborough House, but is of French construction.

ONE OF MR. GILBERT'S

SURPRISE PROGRAMMES

COMMENCING TO-NIGHT, JAN. 11TH, 1897.

Something to Astonish the Amusement World at

Gilbert's Modern Circus

AGRICULTURAL HALL, NORWICH.

First Appearance of the

ROYAL
CINEMATOGRAPHE,

THE ANIMATED PHOTOGRAPHS,

Representing with Marvellous Accuracy Scenes of Everyday Life.

This is the first machine that was shown in England, and also the only one that has been before H.R.H. the

PRINCE OF WALES,

by special command. The Royal Films were taken direct at Marlborough House by the Prince's own request.

Selections will be made from the following :—

THE DERBY. BOXING KANGAROO.
THE SOUTH WESTERN RAILWAY AT DOVER.
A PRIZE FIGHT BY JEM MACE AND BURKE.
TOM MERRY, LIGHTNING CARICOONIST.
HIGHGATE TUNNEL : THE GOODS TRAIN.

YARMOUTH BEACH,

THE DANCING DOGS.

THE ROYAL FILMS.

1. Arrival of the Royal Party at Marlborough House.
2. Departure of the Royal Party from Marlborough House.
3. Garden Party on the Lawn at Marlborough House.
4. Arrival of the Prince and Suite.

Plate 120   Handbill announcing the Royal Cinematographe at the Agricultural Hall, Norwich, 11 January 1897 (*East Anglian Film Archive*)

As the public is liable to be misled, I beg you to inform me if permission has been given for the use of the word "Royal" in this case, and for the use of the arms of H.R.H. the Prince of Wales, which are used in this connection. I am, Sir,.

Your obedient Servant,

Robt. W. Paul.

The advertisement referred to in Paul's letter is for the Metropolitan Music Hall, Edgware Road, where the 'Royal Cinematoscope' was being exhibited by Lewis Sealy (see also my vol. 1, p. 75).

Paul, who had fallen out with Acres after the latter had patented the Paul-Acres Camera in his own name, had tumbled that the apparatus being exhibited at the Metropolitan as the 'Royal Cinematoscope' was indeed of French construction. In order to expose the fraud, Paul wrote the letter to the Lord Chamberlain, just quoted.

There is no difficulty in linking Acres' name with the show at the Metropolitan, for a statement to that effect was published in the *Photographic News*, 4 September 1896 p. 561:

> The Cinematoscope. This is the distinctive title given by Mr. Birt Acres to his system of projecting animated photographs that now forms part of the entertainment of a London music-hall.

The only London music hall to which this statement could refer is the Metropolitan since it is the only one that fits the bill. All the others where films were being presented at that time were supplied by Lumière and Paul. It is little wonder that Birt Acres refused to give particulars of his apparatus when pressed to do so by both Cecil M. Hepworth and the editor of the *Amateur Photographer*, when the former was preparing his article for the magazine under the title 'A Review of Some Present Day Machines', published on 24 September 1896 (pp. 264–268). Referring to the matter in his journal, the editor wrote: 'neither the writer [Hepworth] nor ourselves were able to obtain a reply in response to requests for particulars', (*Amateur Photographer*, 1 October 1897, p. 277). It is now quite understandable why the information was not forthcoming, the simple reason being that Birt Acres had nothing of his own to contribute, for the apparatus masquerading as the 'first machine which was shown in England' (*The Era*, 2 January 1897, p. 34) was in actual fact of French origin!

If there is still any doubt that Birt Acres was connected with the apparatus being exhibited at the Metropolitan, one has only to read the Music Hall Gossip column in *The Era* for 15 August 1896, p. 16:

> Mr. Lewis Sealy's cinematoscope, which was exhibited at Northumberland House [sic] on July 21st, before the Prince and Princess of Wales and other royalties [sic], will be on view at the Metropolitan on the 24th inst. The exhibition will be a distinct novelty in this part of London.

Other references in *The Era* to the Royal Cinematoscope and Lewis Sealy occur on 5 and 12 September, p. 18, but here the name of the royal residence is correctly given as Marlborough House.

Thus believing he had been tumbled, Birt Acres set about covering over his tracks. A statement in *The Era* for 15 August 1896 announced that 'no person or firm has any authority to advertise themselves as my agents.' The only firm doing so when this statement appeared was The British Toy and Novelty Co. Ltd, which shortly thereafter went out of business, not so much because of Acres' statement, but because there was no Kineopticon or Royal Cinematoscope to sell. Be this as it may, another agent soon announced itself. In the music hall gossip column of *The Era* for 26 December 1896, p. 16, the following appeared:

> 'A very interesting picture of His Royal Highness has been taken by Mr. Birt Acres for his Royal Cinematographe [sic], showing the Prince drawing up and alighting from his carriage and bowing to the spectators. The Dramatic and Musical Syndicate has taken this machine up, and it is attracting large houses in the provinces.

It is hardly surprising that this enterprise, too, quickly disappeared. From that day to this, there has never been published a description or illustration of the Birt Acres machine. Does not Paul's letter to the Lord Chamberlain's Office tell us the reason why?.

Among the list of films in Tester's inventory, transcribed above, is one by de Bedts. All the other films listed are by Birt Acres or Esmé Collings, with the exception of two Edison films. It will be recalled that the Kinetographe de Bedts was one of the very first machines available for sale in France (see vol. 1, pp. 173–175). I suspect that the projector being exhibited in England as the Royal Cinematoscope was the Kinetographe de Bedts, and that the only film by this firm in Tester's list, came to this country along with the French machine.

Presumably as an excuse for not having published particulars of his Kineopticon, or Royal Cinematoscope, Birt Acres sent a letter to the editors of the *British Journal of Photography* (18 September 1896) in which he wrote:

> After an inventor has obtained an English patent, he finds that he has published his ideas to the world through the Patent Office, and all he has gained is the privilege to enter an expensive law suit against infringers.

Yet, when he comes up with the idea for the Birtac, Birt Acres does not hesitate to apply for a patent (Pat. No. 12,939, 9th June 1898) even though the apparatus was original in only one respect, its use of a sub-standard gauge film. There was nothing original about the mechanism. It served as a camera/projector (à la Lumière); employed the 'dog' or beater *movement* patented by the Frenchman Georges Demeny and made use of standard 35mm film stock, which he split down the middle to form the 17.5 mm film. This he perforated down one side with two perforations per frame.

Birt Acres will be best remembered as Paul's collaborator on the invention of the first ciné camera to be made in England, and as the photographer of the first English films. But his lasting fame will probably rest on being the first person in England to project films on a screen. As Richard Brown has revealed, his first recorded screen performance took place, not as is commonly supposed on 14 January 1896 at the Royal Photographic Society, but on 10 January at the Lyonsdown Photographic Society (ref: *The Barnet Press*, 18 January 1896, p. 5, column 2).

Referring to the Cinématographe-Lumière Model B (vol. 2, pp. 124–125), a special attachment could be had which allowed the projector to be used with much greater lengths of film. A free standing arm supporting a film spool of about 500 foot capacity, was coupled to the main drive of the projector in lieu of the regular crank handle. The projector was then driven by a handle at the side of the attachment which also worked the sprockets that fed the film from the spool. An attachment of this kind, called a *Défileur* and made by Carpentier, came up for auction at Christie's, South Kensington on 18 August 1992 (Plate 121). The Model B Cinématographe, with the increased film capacity provided by the *défileur*, was henceforth exhibited as Lumière's Triograph (Plate 122).

Plate 121   Cinématographe-Lumière's. The apparatus on the right is the Model B coupled with the special extension arm which allows the projector to be used with greater lengths of film (*Christie's, South Kensington*)

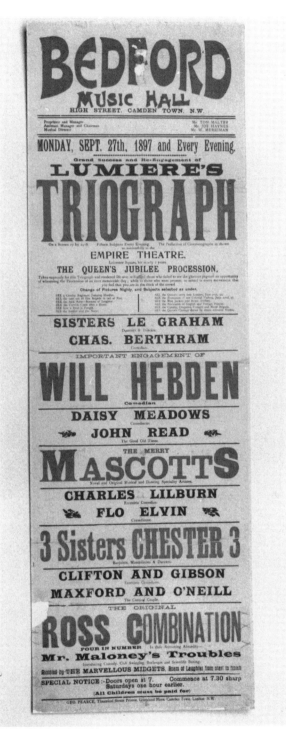

Plate 122   Poster advertising Lumière's Triograph at the Bedford Music Hall, London, 27 September 1897. This was an updated version of the Cinématographe. Equipped with the *Defileur* attachment (shown in illustration 122), it had a film capacity of 500ft (*Barnes Collection*)

Epilogue and Acknowledgements

On 22 January 1901, Queen Victoria died, signalling the end of an era. At the time of her death, the cinema as a public spectacle was barely five years old. Yet during that short period, it had become a major attraction at music halls, fairgrounds, pleasure parks, seaside piers and pavilions, town halls, assembly rooms and penny gaffs. Before it could be given a permanent home of its own in a cinema theatre, a way had to be found by which the film could tell its own story without having to rely on a lecturer or a written text presented as lantern slides. It had also to become a marketable commodity that could be leased out or exchanged instead of being sold at so much per foot. All these requirements were not to come about in Britain until 1907.

The history of the early cinema seems to fall into three distinct periods of development. The years from its birth to the end of 1900, which are covered by the five volumes that constitute this history of the beginnings of the cinema in England, may be said to constitute the first of these periods, and may aptly be termed the 'Victorian Cinema'.

These years saw remarkable developments in film technique, which were only possible in tandem with the technological progress being made in cinematographic equipment. We have only to compare the films taken of Queen Victoria's Jubilee Procession 1897 with those of her funeral cortège in 1901 to see the striking changes that had taken place in cinematography in so short a period (Plate 123). Indeed, many of the innovations in film technique had first been applied to the non-fiction film, and it was only at the turn of the century that the photoplay or 'made-up' film, as it came to be termed, began to adapt to the techniques pioneered in the field of actuality.

The Victorian Cinema was characterized by the short single-shot film, the overall length of which was restricted to the footage capacity of the camera, usually about 40 to 75 feet. At the same time, the majority of machines for projecting the films were also restricted to these short lengths. Only when projectors were designed to hold longer lengths of film were producers induced to make longer films, either by increasing the capacity of the camera, or by joining two or more shots together. Films of the non-fiction class were the first to benefit in this way, whereas dramatic and comic films before 1901 would seldom exceed 100 feet in length.

The second period of the cinema's development spanned the years 1901 to 1907, when the story-film began to take precedence over the non-fiction film. Films increased in length and multi-shot films, making occasional use of camera movement and découpage, became more frequent leading to a form of discontinuous narrative which was mostly dependent on a commentator for elucidation. In turn, this gave way to the one reel (1,000 feet) period, when a satisfactory narrative technique, supported by explanatory inter-titles which did away with the need for a commentator, had evolved. These developments ushered in the third period of early cinema, the era of the 'nickelodeon', which lasted until 1914, when D.W. Griffith's *The Birth of a Nation* signalled the end of the primitive phase of the cinema's history.

(a)

(b)

Plate 123 *Queen Victoria's Diamond Jubilee Procession*, 1897 and *Funeral Cortège*, 1901. Note the cinematic composition of the funeral film compared with the rather dull frontal aspect of the Jubilee film. By the turn of the century, a new cinematic approach to film making had begun (*National Film and Television Archive*)

It is to be hoped that some future historian of the British cinema will continue my present survey to include the second phase of its history, that is to say, the years from 1900 to 1907. Thereafter, British cinema had little to contribute to world cinema. Those first twelve years of its development will be remembered as the most inventive and creative period in the history of British cinematography.

Although acknowledged in the text, I would like to list here the names of all those who have so generously given me their help in the preparation of this volume: Barry Anthony, David Beevers, Stephen Bottomore, Richard Brown, A. S. Clover, Roland Cosandey, Graeme Cruickshank, Geoffrey Donaldson, Bill Douglas, Tony Fletcher, David Francis, Denis Gifford, Ronald Grant, Frank Gray, Stephen Herbert, Nicholas Hiley, John Huntley, Peter Jewell, Laurence Kamm, Francis Lacassin, Lester Smith, Martin Sopocy, Mark Van den Temple, John and Tony Tester, John Townsend, Anthony Ward. I wish to thank too, Professor Richard Maltby for his fine Introduction and his overall support, and I particularly wish to thank my collaborator William Barnes, whose help has been immeasurable.

Notes

Introduction

1 John Fell, review of John Barnes, *Pioneers of the British Film*, *Film Quarterly*, vol. 42 no. 4 (Summer 1989), p. 47.
2 Quoted in G.J. Mellor, *The Northern Music Hall* (Newcastle upon Tyne: Frank Graham, 1970), pp. 131–2.
3 Theatres and Music Halls Committee of the London County Council Palace Theatre of Varieties, 1880–1903, attached to report of licensing discussion, 28 November, 1902, quoted in Susan Pennybacker, 'It Was Not What She Said but the Way in which She Said It: The London County Council and the Music Halls' in *Music Hall: The Business of Pleasure*, edited by Peter Bailey (Milton Keynes: Open University Press, 1986), p. 118.
4 André Bazin, 'The Myth of Total Cinema' in *What Is Cinema? Volume 1*, trans. Hugh Gray (Berkeley, University of California Press, 1967), p. 21.
5 Deac Rossell, 'Double Think: The Cinema and Magic Lantern Culture', paper given at the *Celebrating 1895* conference, Bradford, 1995.
6 Michael R. Booth, *Victorian Spectacular Theatre, 1850–1910* (London: Routledge, 1981), pp. 72, 74, 14.
7 John Cher, 'Who is the Father of the Trade?' in *The Bioscope*, October 17, 1912, p. 187, quoted in Joost Hunningher, 'Première on Regent Street' in *Cinema: The Beginnings and the Future*, edited by Christopher Williams (London: University of Westminster Press, 1996), p. 49.
8 John Stokes, *In the Nineties* (Chicago: University of Chicago Press, 1989), p. 56.
9 Max Beerbohm, quoted in Stokes, p. 93.
10 Gustav Doré and Blanchard Jerrold, *London: A Pilgrimage* (1872), quoted in James Walvin, *Leisure and Society, 1830–1950* (London: Longman, 1978), p. 118; Hyppolyte Taine, *Notes on England* (1876), quoted in Hugh Cunningham, *Leisure in the Industrial Revolution* (London: Croom Helm, 1980), p. 124; Peter Bailey, *Leisure and Class in Victorian England: Rational Recreation and the Contest for Control, 1830–1885* (London: Methuen, 1978), p. 98.
11 R.W. Paul, *Proceedings* of the British Kinematograph Society, no. 38, 3 February, 1936, p. 4.
12 Dave Russell, *Popular Music in England, 1840–1914: A Social History* (Manchester: Manchester University Press, 1987), p. 73.
13 Bailey, p. 162.
14 Henry Pelling, *Popular Politics and Society in Late Victorian Britain* (2nd edn., London: Macmillan, 1979) p. 54; Walvin, p. 63; Hugh Cunningham, 'Leisure' in John Benson (ed) *The Working Class in England, 1875–1914* (London, Croom Helm, 1985), p. 137.
15 Jose Harris, *Private Lives, Public Spirit: Britain 1870–1914* (Harmondsworth: Penguin, 1994), p. 210.
16 Walvin, p. 65.
17 Harris, p. 10.
18 *Jones' Parlour Floor*, quoted in Jane Traies, 'Jones and the Working Girl: Class Marginality in Music Hall Song 1860–1900' in J.S. Bratton (ed) *Music Hall: Performance and Style* (Milton Keynes: Open University Press, 1982), p. 30.
19 Bailey, *Leisure*, p.171
20 Chris Waters, 'Manchester Morality and London Capital: The Battle over the Palace of Varieties' in *Music Hall: The Business of Pleasure*, p. 150.
21 Charles Masterman, *The Heart of the Empire* (London, 1901), pp. 7–8. Quoted in Gareth Stedman Jones, 'Working Class Culture and Working Class Politics in London, 1870–1900: Notes on the Remaking of a Working Class' in Bernard Waites, Tony Bennett and Graham Martin (eds) *Popular Culture: Past and Present* (London: Croom Helm 1982), p. 92.
22 *The Outlook*, 14 July 1900, p. 757a. See Chapter 3 for a more extended quotation.
23 *McGlennon's Star Song Book* (1888), no. 8, p. 2; quoted in Stedman Jones, p. 113.
24 *The Era*, 28 November, 1885, quoted in Russell, p. 126.
25 Quoted in Richard Price, *An Imperial War and the British Working Class: Working-Class Attitudes and Reactions to the Boer War 1899–1902* (London: Routledge and Kegan Paul, 1972), p. 67.
26 Martin Pugh, *State and Society: British Political and Social History, 1870–1992* (London: Arnold, 1994), p. 102.
27 Norman McCord, *British History 1815–1906* (Oxford: Oxford University Press, 1991), p. 465; J.F.C. Harrison, *Late Victorian Britain* (London: Fontana, 1990), p.155.

28 Jan Morris, *The Spectacle of Empire: Style, Effect and the Pax Britannica* (London: Faber, 1982), p. 187.
29 Lawrence Senelick, 'Politics as Entertainment: Victorian Music-Hall Songs', *Victorian Studies* Vol. 19, December 1975, p. 174.
30 Quoted in Price, p. 175.
31 John M. MacKenzie, *Propaganda and Empire: The Manipulation of British Public Opinion 1880–1960* (Manchester University Press, 1984), p. 40.
32 Mellor, p. 134; Bailey, p. 171.
33 Quoted in Bailey, p. 157.
34 Dagmar Höher, 'The Composition of Music Hall Audiences 1850–1900' in *Music Hall: The Business of Pleasure*, p. 86; Jeremy Crump, 'Provincial Music Hall: Promoters and Public in Leicester, 1863–1929' in *Music Hall: The Business of Pleasure*, p. 65.
35 Peter Bailey, 'A Community of Friends: Business and Good Fellowship in London Music Hall Management c.1860–1885' in *Music Hall: The Business of Pleasure*, p. 46.
36 Quoted in Penelope Summerfield, 'The Effingham Arms and the Empire: Deliberate Selection in the Evolution of Music Hall in London' in Eileen and Stephen Yeo (eds) *Popular Culture and Class Conflict 1590–1914: Explorations in the History of Labour and Leisure* (Brighton: Harvester Press, 1981), p. 226.
37 Peter Bailey, 'Introduction' in *Music Hall: The Business of Pleasure*, p. x.
38 Quoted in Summerfield, p. 227.
39 Summerfield, pp. 221, 234.
40 Bailey, *Leisure*, p.171.
41 James Williamson catalogue, September 1899, quoted in Rachel Low and Roger Manvell, *The History of the British Film, 1896–1906* (London: Allen & Unwin, 1948), p. 88.
42 Low and Manvell, p. 50.
43 Lois Rutherford, '"Harmless Nonsense": The Comic Sketch and the Development of Music Hall Entertainment' in *Music Hall: Performance and Style*, p. 137.
44 *Optical Magic Lantern Journal*, vol. 9, no. 112 (September 1898), p. 127, quoted in John Barnes, *The Beginnings of the Cinema in England, 1894–1901, Volume Three: 1898* (London, Bishopsgate, 1988), p. 1.
45 Vanessa Toulmin, 'Telling the Tale: The Story of the Fairground Bioscope Shows and the Showmen who Operated Them', *Film History* vol. 6 no. 2 (Summer 1994), p. 221.
46 *British Journal of Photography*, vol. 45, Monthly Supplement (7 January 1898), p. 1, quoted in John Barnes, *The Beginnings of the Cinema in England, 1894–1901, Volume Three: 1898* (London, Bishopsgate, 1988), p. 74.
47 Austin, quoted in Morris, *The Spectacle of Empire*, p. 156.
48 *British Journal of Photography*, vol. 45, Supplement (6 May 1898), p. 40, quoted in *The Beginnings of the Cinema in England, 1894–1901, Volume Three: 1898* (London, Bishopsgate, 1988), p. 157.
49 Charles Musser, *The Emergence of Cinema: the American Screen to 1907* (New York: Scribner's, 1990), p. 161.
50 *The Era*, 8 October, 1898, p. 19a, quoted in *The Beginnings of the Cinema in England, 1894–1901, Volume Three: 1898* (London, Bishopsgate, 1988), p. 157.
51 *Photograms of '97*, p. 38 quoted in John Barnes, *The Beginnings of the Cinema in England, 1894–1901, Volume Two: 1897* (London, Bishopsgate, 1983), p. 117.
52 Stephen Bottomore, 'Dreyfus and Documentary', *Sight and Sound* vol. 53 no. 4 (Autumn 1980), p. 293; *The Beginnings of the Cinema in England, 1894–1901, Volume Four: 1899* (London, Bishopsgate, 1992), pp. 69–74.
53 Crump, p. 66.
54 Morris, *The Spectacle of Empire*, p. 187.
55 Quoted in James Curran and Jean Seaton, *Power Without Responsibility: The Press and Broadcasting in Britain* (London: Fontana, 1981), p. 52.
56 Morris, *The Spectacle of Empire*, p. 156.
57 Liberal imperialist Lord Rosebery, who had been Prime Minister from 1894 to 1895 in *The Times*, 1900. Quoted in Bernard Porter, *The Lion's Share: A Short History of British Imperialism, 1850–1970* (London: Longman, 1975), p. 130.
58 Quoted in Porter, p. 134.
59 John MacKenzie, 'Introduction' in John Mackenzie (ed) *Imperialism and Popular Culture* (Manchester: Manchester University Press, 1986), p. 4.
60 Ben Shephard, 'Showbiz Imperialism: The Case of Peter Lobengula' in *Imperialism and Popular Culture*, p. 94.
61 Rudyard Kipling, *The Light that Failed* (Harmondsworth: Penguin, 1980; 1st pub 1890), p. 51.
62 *Westminster Gazette*, 1898, quoted in Philip Knightley, *The First Casualty: From the Crimea to Vietnam: The War Correspondent as Hero, Propagandist and Myth Maker* (London: André Deutsch, 1975), p. 41.

63 Knightley, pp. 62, 66.
64 Sir Charles Callwell, *Small Wars: Their Principles and Practice* (London: War Office, 1896). Quoted in John MacKenzie (ed) 'Introduction' in *Popular Imperialism and the Military, 1850–1950* (Manchester: Manchester University Press, 1992), p. 7.
65 Iain R. Smith, *The Origins of the South African War, 1899–1902* (London: Longman, 1996), p. 2.
66 Smith, p. 2.
67 P.B. Bull, *God and Our Soldiers*, (3rd edn. London, 1914), p. 39, quoted in Price, p. 226.
68 The *Era* obituary for Charles Morton, 1904, quoted in Raymond Mander and Joe Mitchenson, *British Music Hall* (2nd edn. London: Gentry Books, 1974), p. 27.
69 Edgar Sanderson, *The Fight for the Flag in South Africa: A History of the War from the Boer Ultimatum to the Advance of Lord Roberts* (London: Hutchinson, 1900), p. 90.
70 Sanderson, p. 92.
71 M.D. Blanch, 'British Society and the War' in Peter Warwick (ed) *The South African War: The Anglo-Boer War 1899–1902* (London: Longman, 1980), p. 229; Price, p. 195.
72 James Morris, *Farewell the Trumpets* (Harmondsworth: Penguin, 1979), pp. 88–9.
73 Porter, p. 178.
74 Price, p. 1.
75 John Montgomery, *1900: The End of an Era* (London: Allen and Unwin, 1968), pp. 48, 58
76 Morris, *Farewell to Trumpets*, p. 86.
77 *Daily Express*, May 19, quoted in Rebecca West, *1900* (London: Weidenfeld and Nicholson, 1982), p. 69
78 Morris, *Farewell the Trumpets*, p. 79
79 Pelling, p. 89
80 The *Handsworth Herald*, quoted in Blanch, p. 218.
81 Blanch, p. 235.
82 Quoted in Elizabeth Grottle Strebel, 'Primitive Propaganda: The Boer War Films', *Sight and Sound*, vol. 46, no. 1 (Winter 1976/77), p. 46.
83 Charles Urban, 'Notes', *Optical Magic Lantern Journal* vol. 11, no. 139 (December 1900), pp. 153–4.
84 Knightley, p. 75.
85 Dave Russell, '"We Carved our Way to Glory": The British Soldier in Music Hall Song and Sketch, c.1800–1914' in John M. Mackenzie (ed) *Popular Imperialism and the Military, 1850–1950* (Manchester: Manchester University Press, 1992), p. 64; Jeffrey Richards, 'Popular Imperialism and the Image of the Army in Juvenile Literature', in *Popular Imperialism and the Military*, p. 64.
86 Blanch, p. 232; MacKenzie, *Propaganda and Empire*, p.148.
87 Shephard, p. 98; David Mayer, 'The World on Fire 8 Pyrodramas at Belle Vue Gardens, Manchester, c.1850–1950', in *Popular Imperialism and the Military*, p. 192.
88 Roger T. Stearn, 'War Correspondents and Colonial War, c1870–1900', in *Popular Imperialism and the Military*, p. 139.
89 Charlie Keil, 'Steel Engines and Cardboard Rockets: The Status of Fiction and Nonfiction in Early Cinema', *Persistence of Vision*, no. 9 (1991), pp. 37–45.
90 *Photographic News*, 8 December 1899, quoted in Bottomore, p. 293
91 'Notes', *Optical Magic Lantern Journal*, vol. 11, no. 130 (March 1900), p. 30.
92 Warwick Trading Company Catalogue, 1901, quoted in Strebel, p. 45.
93 Paul, *Proceedings* of the British Kinematograph Society, no. 38 (3 February, 1936), p. 5, quoted in Barnes, *The Beginnings of the Cinema in England, 1894–1901, Volume Four: 1899* (London, Bishopsgate, 1992), p. 21.
94 The pose can be seen, for example, in the painting by R. Caton Woodville used as the frontispiece in H.W. Wilson, *With the Flag to Pretoria* (London: 1900).
95 *The Era* obituary for Charles Morton, 1904, quoted in Mander and Mitchenson, p. 27.
96 Quoted in Montgomery, p. 196.
97 Low and Manvell, pp. 58–9.
98 Pugh, p. 102.
99 *Music Hall and Theatre Review*, 20 December 1900, quoted in Russell, 'We Carved Our Way to Glory', p. 53; MacKenzie, *Propaganda and Empire*, p. 212.

1 Three Pioneers—Paul, Acres and Hepworth

1 John Barnes, *The Beginnings of the Cinema in England, 1894–1901, Volume Three: 1898* (London, Bishopsgate, 1988), p. 11, illustration 2. This photograph was first published in *The Optician*, 5 October 1900, p. 74, fig. 18, with the following description: 'Fig. 18 will give an idea of his combination studio-theatre; perfect with traps and scenery and all those little accessories necessary

for the animated stories which are so popular. It will be seen that the front of the studio can be closed when using the building for rehearsals; for photographing, the front opens, the camera being placed on a running stage outside. This enables long-focus lenses to be used to considerable advantage.'

2 R.W. Paul, lecture delivered to a meeting of the British Kinematograph Society (BKS) on 3 February 1936, *Proceedings*, p. 5.

3 Frederick A. Talbot, *Moving Pictures: How They are Made and Worked* (London, 1912), pp. 77–8.

4 BKS *Proceedings*, 3 February 1936, p. 5.

5 Rachel Low, *The History of the British Film 1906–1914* (London, 1949), p. 106.

6 R.W. Paul, *Important Notice of Removal*. Single sheet circular. Copy in the British Film Institute. See also *Amateur Photographer*, vol. 32, no. 826 (3 August 1900), p. 96.

7 *The Optician*, 5 October 1900, p. 76. For a fuller description of the New Century Animatographe see pp. 73–6 of the same journal.

8 *The Era*, 26 May 1900, p. 28.

9 *The Era*, 14 April 1900, p. 24.

10 *The Era*, 21 July 1900, p. 24.

11 BKS *Proceedings*, 3 February 1936, pp. 5–6.

12 See Denis Gifford, *The British Film Catalogue 1895–1970* (Newton Abbot, 1973); and Erik Barnouw, *The Magician and the Cinema* (New York, 1981), pp. 66–7.

13 Barnow, pp. 66–7.

14 Talbot, pp. 200–21.

15 *The Era*, 2 November, 1901, p. 32.

16 *The Era*, 21 July, 1900, p. 24.

17 Talbot, pp. 198–99.

18 Geoffrey Lamb, *Victorian Magic* (London, 1976), p. 67.

19 Talbot, p. 205.

20 BKS *Proceedings*, 3 February 1936, p. 5.

21 Frank S. Mottershaw, 'Early Days', *The Picturegoer*, August, 1927, pp. 51 and 55. See also 'The Movie Stars of Muswell Hill', *The Evening News* (London, 1 October 1929). This article was kindly brought to my attention by Dr Nicholas Hiley.

22 BKS *Proceedings*, 3 February 1936, p. 6.

23 *British Journal of Photography*, 13 July 1900, p. 447.

24 BKS *Proceedings*, 3 February 1936, p. 5.

25 *The Era*, 15 September, 1900, p. 21.

26 *The Era*, 15 September 1900, p. 21.

27 *The Era*, 15 September 1900, p. 27.

28 *The Era*, 22 September, 1900, p. 18.

29 Paul catalogue, June 1903 (Copy in the Barnes Collection).

30 *The Era*, 13 October 1900, p. 19c. See also *British Journal of Photography*, 21 September 1900, p. 603.

31 Copies of this brochure are located in the British Film Institute, and the Will Day Collection at the Cinémathèque Française, Paris (C 86/1098).

32 *The Era*, 14 April 1900, p. 24.

33 The illustration on page 22 of my book *The Beginnings of the Cinema in England, 1894–1901, Volume Four: 1899* (London, Bishopsgate, 1992) shows the photograph from which this slide was taken.

34 *The Era*, 24 February 1900, p. 27.

35 BKS *Proceedings*, 3 February 1936, p. 5.

36 *The Era*, 28 July 1900, p. 16c.

37 Letter from R.W. Paul to Thelma Gutsche, dated 20 September 1937, now in the South African State Archives. Copy kindly supplied by Dr Nicholas Hiley.

38 *The Optician*, 5 October 1900, p. 76.

39 John Barnes, *The Beginnings of the Cinema in England, 1894–1901, Volume Four: 1899* (London, Bishopsgate, 1992), illustration on p. 22.

40 Lewin Fitzhamon (1869–1961) was reputed to have directed more than 600 British films, including *Rescued by Rover* and *Tillie the Tomboy*. He retired from the film industry in 1920.

41 *Amateur Photographer*, vol. 31, no. 812 (27 April 1900), p. 337.

42 *Amateur Photographer*, vol. 32, no. 846 (21 December 1900), p. 489.

43 Rollo Appleyard, *The History of the Institution of Electrical Engineers (1871–1931)* (London, 1939), p. 182.

44 Appleyard, p. 182.

45 *The Photogram*, vol. 7, no. 76 (April 1900), p. 125.

46 *The Optician*, vol. 18 (1 June 1900), p. 401. See also *The Photogram*, August 1900, p. 268: 'Birt Acres has fitted up works at Whetstone for the manufacture of kinetograph films.'

47 *The Era*, 10 January 1901, p. 22d.

48 *The Era*, 14 July 1900, p. 24c.

49 H. Tummel, 'Birt Acres—ein englischer Kinopionier filmte in Deutschland' in *Kine-Technik*, no. 12, 1962, p. 299. English translation in *Cinema Studies*, vol. 1, no. 7 (June 1963), p. 157.

50 Address given on Pat. No. 18,689, 21 November 1889.

51 Address given on Pat. No. 10,474, 27 February 1896.

52 Address given on Pat. No. 10,603, 28 April 1897.

53 Address given on a photograph dated 1918; see illustration (Plate 20).

54 *British Journal of Photography*, 14 May 1909, p. 389. I am indebted to Richard Brown for kindly bringing this matter to my attention.

55 Letters from Peter Jewell to the author, dated 20 and 22 May 1994.

56 Hauke Lange-Fuchs, *Birt Acres* (Kiel, Germany, 1987, p. 63).

57 Cecil Hepworth, *Came the Dawn* (London, 1951), p. 31.

58 Hepworth, pp. 44–5.

59 Hepworth, pp. 44–5.

60 Hepworth, pp. 48–9.

61 Hepworth, pp. 53 and 56.

62 NFTVA F181 and F652. Twelve frame illustrations from *How it Feels to be Run Over* are reproduced in Emmanuelle Toulet, *Cinématographe, invention du siecle* (Paris, 1988), pp. 162–63. The films are also discussed in *Cinema 1900–1906: An* Analytical Study (Brussels, 1982).

63 BKS *Proceedings*, 3 February 1936, pp. 10–1.

64 Hepworth, p. 51.

65 Hepworth, p. 55.

66 *Amateur Photographer*, vol. 32, no. 836 (12 October 1900), p. 295.

67 Hepworth, p. 51.

68 Hepworth, p. 55.

69 *The Photogram*, vol. 7, no. 75 (March 1900), p. 96.

70 *Amateur Photographer* (12 October 1900), p. 295.

71 *The Photogram*, vol. 7, no. 82 (October 1900), p. 330; *Photographic News* (6 July 1900), p. 425; *Amateur Photographer* (12 October 1900), p. 295.

72 *The Photogram*, February 1900, p. 62.

73 *Photographic News*, 2 February 1900, p. 69; *British Journal of Photography*, 2 February 1900, 78; *Amateur Photographer*, 2 February 1900, p. 96.

74 *British Journal of Photography*, 13 April 1900, p. 230.

75 *British Journal of Photography*, 20 April 1900, pp. 255–6.

76 *The Music Hall and Theatre Review*, 10 April 1896. This reference was kindly supplied by Richard Brown.

77 *Optical Magic Lantern Journal* vol. 11, no. 132 (May 1900), p. 58, see also *Amateur Photographer* 16 April 1900, p. 297; *The Photogram* June 1900, pp. 192–94; *Photographic News*, 4 May 1900, p. 284.

78 *Optical Magic Lantern Journal* (August 1900), p. 93; see also *Amateur Photographer*, 6 July 1900, p. 5.

79 Cecil M. Hepworth, *Animated Photography: the ABC of the Cinematograph* (2nd edn.). Revised and brought up to date by Hector Maclean. The Amateur Photographer's Library, No. 14 (London, 1900).

2 The South Coast Filmmakers—Smith Williamson and West

1 Denis Gifford, *The British Film Catalogue 1895–1970* (Newton Abbot, 1973), film nos 00322 and 00333.

2 Warwick Trading Co catalogue, suppl no 1, p. 164, film no. 5784.

3 Picture postcards in the Barnes Collection reveal that, at some time, this building underwent considerable structural alteration. It is necessary to point out here that the illustration of the lodge, or gate-house, shown in my previous volume *The Beginnings of the Cinema in England 1894–1901, Volume 4: 1899* p. 44, illustration 23, shows what the building looked like after it had been altered in about 1910, and not, as stated, as it appeared during Smith's tenancy. The present illustration (Plate 29) shows how the building looked when Smith leased the Gardens.

4 For a graphic description of this film, see Maurice Bessy and Lo Duca, *Georges Méliès Mage* (Paris, 1945), p. 62.

5 A shorter version of this film was also issued at the same time, called *The Sick Kitten* (50ft).

6 Barry Salt, *Film Style and Technology: History and Analysis* (London, 1983), p. 60; (2nd ed., 1992), p. 49.

7 The lady in the carnival hat in the first scene, also plays Mary Jane in *Mary Jane's Mishap* (1903), and has been identified as G.A. Smith's wife.

8 The effect was admirably demonstrated by reversing the Lumière film *Bain de Diane à Milan* (no. 277). See Barnes, vol. 2, pp. 86–7. In 1897 Smith used *reverse motion* in his film *Tipsy, Topsy, Turvey*.

9 Barnes, vol. 3, p. 36, illustration 21.

10 This is an obvious reference to the Lumière film (no. 295), photographed by Promio.

11 *The Brighton Herald* (14 October 1899), p. 2c, anon. [Victor W. Cook] 'A Brighton Kinematograph Factory. Its Wonders and Humours.'

12 *Brighton Herald*, (14 October 1899), p. 2c. *The Herald* article also appeared, in a modified form, in *Chamber's Journal*, pp. 486–90, under the title, 'The Humours of "Living Picture" Making', where the author's name appears as Victor W. Cook.

13 *Brighton Herald*, 6 January 1900, p. 5f. Benett-Stanford's war films are also mentioned in *The Photogram*, February 1900, p. 62; and *The British Journal of Photography*, 19 January 1900, p. 44.

14 See, for example, the Charles Urban Trading Company's catalogue for 1903–4, a copy of which is in the Science Museum Library, London.

15 WTC catalogue, September 1900, p. 72 (copy in the Museum of Modern Art, New York).

16 WTC catalogue, September 1900, p. 72.

17 *The Photogram*, February 1900, p. 62.

18 WTC catalogue, September 1900, p. 75.

19 Brighton Aquarium programmes (Brighton Reference Library, ref.: R64,275). The original building was erected in 1869, purchased by the Corporation of Brighton in 1901, and reconstructed in 1928–9 (Ref.: County Borough of Brighton Commemoration plaque).

20 Brighton Aquarium programme, 16 March 1896 (Brighton Reference Library, R64,275). This was a re-engagement. It has not been determined when Smith first gave his performance at the Aquarium.

21 Brighton Aquarium programme, 29 March 1897 (Brighton Reference Library, R64,276).

22 Brighton Aquarium programme, 26 December 1896 (Brighton Reference Library, R64,276).

23 *Hove Echo* (10 November 1900), p. 14d.

24 Gifford, The British Film Catalogue, no. 00365.

25 Hove Museum & Art Gallery, *Film Locations in Hove* (brochure), 1989. Williamson was to use the house again in his film *Fire!*.

26 Williamson catalogue, Revised to September 1902. p. 3 (cat. nos. 14 and 15). Gifford gives the date of this film as October 1899. Gifford, no. 00238.

27 *The Optician*, 6 April 1900, p. 80; see also *Hove Echo*, 6 January 1900, p. 2c.

28 Williamson's Popular Entertainments were held at Hove Town Hall on 13, 20 and 27 January; 3, 10, and 17 February; 17 and 24 November; and 1 and 8 December, 1900.

29 *Hove Echo*, 3 February 1900, p. 11b.

30 *Hove Echo*, 1 December 1900.

31 *Hove Echo*, 24 November 1900.

32 *Hove Echo*, 8 December 1900, p. 13c.

33 *Hove Echo*, 3 February 1900, p. 11b.

34 For a full list of films see Denis Gifford, *The Illustrated Who's Who in British Films (London, 1978)*. For an appreciation of Williamson as film maker, see Martin Sopocy, 'A Narrated Cinema: The Pioneer Story Films of James A. Williamson', in *Cinema Journal*, vol. 18, no. 1 (Fall 1978), pp. 1–28.

35 However, this was not the case in later years, when West became quite a prolific filmmaker. In 1912, an 81-page illustrated catalogue *Life in Our Navy and Our Army* by Alfred West, FRGS, was published, listing some 529 films comprising a total of 56,000 feet. As far as can be ascertained, none of the films listed in the catalogue can be definitely ascribed to the years covered by our history, except perhaps for the film of the *Turbinia*. The only known example of this catalogue is in the British Library (8829 K34), but a photocopy has been very kindly presented to the Barnes Archives by the grandson Mr A.S. Clover'.

36 *Hove Echo*, (17 February 1900), p. 5(b).

37 *Portsmouth Evening News*, 26 March, 1900. I am most grateful to Mr A.S. Clover for kindly sending me photocopies of his press clippings file on 'Our Navy', which has largely provided the source material for this section'.

38 *Portsmouth Evening News*, 27 March, 1900.

39 *Portsmouth Evening News*, 28 March, 1900.

40 *Portsmouth Evening News*, 3 April, 1900.

41 *Portsmouth Evening News*, 10 April, 1900.

42 *Portsmouth Evening News*, 21 August, 1900; 11 September, 1900.

43 *Portsmouth Evening News*, 21 August, 1900, advert.

44 *Portsmouth Evening News*, 21 August, 1900.

45 *Portsmouth Evening News*, 28 August, 1900.

46 *Portsmouth Evening News*, 4 September, 1900.

47 *Portsmouth Evening News*, 4 September, 1900.

48 *The Globe*, 28 November; and *The Referee*, 23 October, 1900.

49 *Birmingham Mail*; and *Birmingham Gazette*, 30 October, 1900.

50 *Manchester News*; and *Manchester Evening Mail*, 6 November, 1900.

51 *The Stage*, 15 November, 1900.
52 *Cambridge Express*, 17 November, 1900; and *Cambridge Daily News*, 27 November, 1900.
53 *Peterborough Evening News*, 20 November, 1900.
54 Unidentified clipping.
55 *Black and White*, 17 March, 1900, p. 422.
56 *British Journal of Photography*, 6 July 1900, p. 50.
57 *The Era*, 17 November 1900, p. 30e.
58 *British Journal of Photography*, 31 August 1900, p. 557.

3 American and French connections

1 *The Era*, 5 February 1898, p. 18. Another music hall manager who made a brief appearance on the screen, was Dundas Slater of the Empire Theatre, Leicester Square. He appears in a Lumière film where he is in the scene taken outside the theatre (250. *Londres, entrée du Cinématographe/Entrance to the Cinematograph Exhibition*) see *The Era*, 1 August 1896, p. 16.
2 'A Novel War Correspondent', in *To-Day*, 26 October 1899, p. 403.
3 For further details of Dickson and the Biograph the reader is referred to the following: Gordon Hendricks, *The Edison Motion Picture Myth* (Los Angeles, 1961); Gordon Hendricks, *The Beginnings of the Biograph* (New York, 1964); and Gordon Hendricks, *The Kintoscope* (New York, 1966). See also, 'Quick Work with the Biograph', in *The Golden Penny* (6 May 1899), p. 391; R.H. Mere, 'The Wonders of the Biograph', in *Pearson's Magazine*, vol. 7, 1899, pp. 194–9; 'A Novel War Correspondent', *To-Day*, 26 October 1899, pp. 402–3; 'Our Future King at Play', *The Harmsworth Magazine*, vol. 5, no. 27 (October 1900), pp. 194–200; H.L. Adam, 'Round the World for the Biograph' in *The Royal Magazine*, vol. 6, (1901), pp. 120–8; Pat Brooklyn, 'Biograph Operators. Some of the Risks they Run', in *Black and White Budget*, vol. 5, no. 86 (1 June 1901), pp. 297–300; *Black and White,* 31 December 1898, pp. 835–6 (Pope Leo XIII); *Black and White*, 3 February 1900, p. 186 (illustrations showing the Mutagraph camera at the Battle of Colenso); W.K.-L. Dickson, *The Biograph in Battle* (London, 1901).
4 His exploits during these first two months have been noted in Volume 4 of this Series.
5 Thelma Gutsche, *The History and Social Significance of Motion Pictures in South Africa 1895–1940* (Cape Town, 1972), pp. 42–3.
6 *The Era*, 17 February 1900, p. 18a.
7 *The Optician*, 10 August 1900, p. 721.
8 *British Journal of Photography*, 16 February 1900, p. 98.
9 W.K.-L. Dickson, *The Biograph in Battle* (London, 1901), p. 116.
10 Dickson, p. 172.
11 Dickson, pp. 181–2.
12 Dickson, pp. 145–6.
13 Dickson, p. 237.
14 Gutsche, p. 44; here the author quotes correspondence in the *Natal Mercury*, 19 November 1900.
15 Dickson, p. 237.
16 *The Era*, 6 January 1900, p. 19a.
17 *The Era*, 10 March 1900, p. 18c.
18 *The Era*, 24 March 1900, p. 18c.
19 *The Era*, 21 April 1900, p. 18.
20 *The Era*, 28 July 1900, p. 17a.
21 *The War by Biograp*h, London: The British Mutoscope and Biograph Co. Ltd, 18 & 19 Great Windmill Street, W. 1900. Front cover printed in gilt lettering against white ground, with engraving top left of Palace Theatre; text reads: 'The Palace Theatre Shaftesbury Avenue Manager Mr. Chas. Morton Souvenir Presented by the Palace Theatre to commemorate the third Anniversary of the Biograph March 19th, 1900.' Very few copies of the souvenir publication are known to exist and I am most grateful to Richard Brown for kindly sending me a photocopy of the one in his own collection. Copies are also to be found at the British Film Institute, the South African Film Archive and the Mander & Mitchenson Collection. This publication has also provided us with more precise dates for some of the films in our 1899 filmography as well as providing additional Biograph titles (see Appendix 2).
22 Dickson, p. 256.
23 Whilst in Italy, Dickson also filmed in Venice, which resulted in the following views: *Panoramic View of the Vegetable Market*; *Panoramic View of the Prisons, Palace of the Doges and Royal Palaces*; *The Grand Canal*; and *Boys Bathing* (Palace Theatre programme, 26 December 1898). He also made a trip to Gibraltar to film the American Admiral Dewey (Palace Theatre programme, 25 September 1899).

24 South African National Film Archives, Pretoria, File 24, Gutsche Collection. I am very grateful to Dr Nicholas Hiley for kindly bringing this matter to my attention. The original film illustrations in America cannot now be traced.

25 S.A. Notes of Film Archives, File 24, Gutsche Collection.

26 English newspaper clipping in the Barnes Collection.

27 In a letter to the author dated 3 December 1991.

28 From a list supplied by Mark van den Tempel of the Nederlands Filmmuseum, Amsterdam.

29 *The Era*, 28 July 1900, p. 17a.

30 *The Era*, 3 November 1900, p. 20a. *The Pathé Journal* was first introduced in 1909 or 1910 and is reputed to have been the first regular news reel.

31 Anonymous letter, dated 10 July 1900, in *The Outlook*, 14 July 1900, p. 757a; kindly brought to my notice by Dr Hiley.

32 *Exhibition of the Biograph (Proprietors, The British Mutoscope and Biograph Co., Ltd., London) Under the Direction of Mr. E. B. Koopman, at Sandringham, by Command of HRH the Prince of Wales, Friday, June 29th, 1900*. Printed programme in the Charles Urban Collection (URB 12/6–2), at the Science Museum Library, London.

33 'Peepshow' by John Wiggins, in *The Cine-Technician*, September-October 1938, pp. 76–7.

34 I am indebted to Dr Nicholas Hiley for kindly sending me details of these sailings. He writes: 'The passenger lists in the Public Record Office show that John Benett-Stanford was the first British cameraman to leave for the war. BT27/312 (Southampton Outward—Sept./Oct. 1899) shows that he left on the steamer *Mexican* on 7 October 1899, whilst W.K.-L. Dickson left only on 14 October, and Walter Beevor on 21 October. The War Office file WO32/7137 shows that Stanford had been issued with his official Press Pass as early as 29 September 1899, as a reporter for the *Western Morning News*.

35 *The Jewish World*, 3 August 1900, p. 292. I am grateful to Dr Hiley for kindly bringing this reference source to my attention. Stephen Bottomore, 'Joseph Rosenthal: The Most Glorious Profession' in *Sight & Sound*, vol. 52, no. 4 (Autumn 1983), p. 261, states that Rosenthal was born on 7 April 1864 into a Jewish family living in Whitechapel, East London.

36 *The Jewish World*, 3 August 1900, p. 292. See also note 35 above.

37 *The Showman*, September 1900, p. 11.

38 Plate 60 is also reproduced in Albert E. Smith's autobiography, *Two Reels and a Crank* (New York, 1952), where the man at the camera is incorrectly stated to be Mr Smith.

39 *The Era*, 20 January 1900, p. 27a.

40 *The Era*, 10 February 1900, p. 27c.

41 Stephen Bottomore, 'Joseph Rosenthal: The Most Glorious Profession', in *Sight & Sound* (Autumn 1983), p. 261.

42 The *Daily Mail*, 22 January 1900, p. 7, columns 4 and 5. This reference has kindly been brought to my attention by Dr Nicholas Hiley. The incidents mentioned in this article all took place in 1899 and accordingly have been described in the previous volume.

43 *The Era*, 4 August 1900, p. 24a.

44 *The Daily Mail*, 22 January 1900, p. 7, columns 4 and 5.

45 *The Jewish World*, 3 August 1900, p. 293.

46 *The Era*, 4 August 1900, p. 24a.

47 *The Era*, 4 August 1900, p. 24a.

48 WTC catalogue (April 1900), p. 181, film no. 5884.

49 R.W. Paul had devised a revolving tripod-head as early as 1897 for the express purpose of filming the Diamond Jubilee Procession. But it has never been established whether this was used for a panning shot, or merely for facilitating the positioning of the camera. From the evidence available, G.A. Smith must be credited for the first panning shot in the modern use of the term.

50 See, for example, WTC films nos. 5672–5673.

51 *The Era*, 10 November 1900, p. 30d.

52 The films of Port Arthur suffered climatic damage and WTC were obliged to add a note to this effect: 'Owing to climatic changes during transport of the negative to England, this and the following film 5892 and 5893 were found slightly 'spotty', but on account of their otherwise fine photographic quality and the scarcity of accurate pictures of Port Arthur, the negatives are most valuable and very interesting.' *The Era*, 22 December 1900, p. 26e.

53 *The Bioscope*, 17 December 1908, p. 22.

54 *The Era*, 1 December 1900, p. 31e.

55 WTC catalogue 1900. Copy in the Urban Collection, Science Museum, London.

56 Information obtained from Biokam film cans in the Barnes Collection.

57 WTC catalogue 1903–4. Copy in the Urban Collection, Science Museum, London (URB 10/1–19, Box One).

58 *The Optician*, 14 September 1900, p. 883.

59 *The Optician*, 5 October 1900, pp. 71–2.
60 Terry Ramsaye, *A Million and One Nights* (New York, 1926), vol. 1, p. 363.
61 *The Optician*, 5 October 1900, p. 72.
62 *Photographic News*, 5 October 1900, p. 641.
63 *British Journal of Photography*, 16 March 1900, p. 187.
64 *The Era*, 3 November 1900, p. 30e.
65 *Amateur Photographer*, vol. 31, no. 803 (23 February 1900), p. 156. See also *Optical Magic Lantern Journal*, vol. 11, no. 130 (March 1900), p. 30.
66 *Amateur Photographer*. vol. 32, no. 840 (9 November 1900), p. 376.
67 *British Journal Photographic Almanac for 1901* (November 1900), pp. 26–7.
68 *The Era*, 10 November 1900, p. 30c; 17 November 1900, p. 30c; 24 November 1900, p. 27c.
69 The details in French are taken from the filmography of Alice Guy by Francis Lacassin, published in Guy's autobiography (Edition Denoel/Gonthier, Paris, 1976), pp. 174–5.
70 Guy, pp. 174–5.
71 *The Era*, 10 November 1900, p. 30c.
72 *The Era*, 1 December 1900, p. 32c.
73 *The Era*, 1 December 1900, p. 32c.
74 John Barnes, *Filming the Boer War* (London, 1992), p. 127.
75 *The Era*, 22 December 1900, p. 27d. See also 'A Chat With Mr. Bromhead' in *The Era*, 12 January 1901, p. 22c, 22d.
76 *British Journal Photographic Almanac for 1901* (November 1901), pp. 1482–3.
77 *Pioneers of the British Film* (London, 1988), pp. 131–32.

4 Manufacturers and Dealers

1 *The Photogram*, vol. 7, no. 81 (September 1900), p. 299.
2 *The Photogram*, vol. 7, no. 82 (October 1900), p. 328.
3 'A Model Workshop' in *The Optical Magic Lantern Journal*, vol. 11, no. 137 (October 1900), p. 131.
4 John Barnes, *The Beginnings of the Cinema in England, 1894–1901, Volume Four: 1899* (London, Bishopsgate, 1992), (p 121).
5 *The Photogram*, vol. 7, no. 73 (January 1900), p. 31; *British Journal Photographic Almanac for 1901*, p. 258.
6 *Optical Magic Lantern Journal*, vol. 11, no. 139 (December 1900), p. 155; *The Photogram*, vol. 7, no. 82 (October 1900), p. 330. For a fuller description of the 'Primus' Matagraph see *The Optician* (October 1900), pp. 76–8.
7 *British Journal of Photography Almanac for 1901*, p. 258;. S.J. Levi & Co., *Nett Price List of Optical Lanterns, Electrical Apparatus, Model Engines and Microscopes 1893–4*. Copy in the Mike Simkin Collection.
8 *The Photogram*, vol. 7, no. 83 (November 1900), p. 362; *The Optician*, 15 February 1901, p. 662; John Barnes, *The Beginnings of the Cinema in England, 1894–1901, Volume Three: 1898* (London, Bishopsgate, 1988), pp. 105–6.
9 *Amateur Photographer*, 5 January 1900, p. 16.
10 *Amateur Photographer*, 19 January 1900, p. 43.
11 *The Era*, 25 August 1900, p. 24b.
12 *The Era*, 15 December 1900, p. 32b.
13 *The Era*, 25 August 1900, p. 24b.
14 *The Era*, 1 September 1900, p. 28b.
15 *The Era*, 22 September 1900, p. 27d.
16 *The Era*, 15 December 1900, p. 32b.
17 *The Era*, 11 August 1900, p. 27e; 6 October 1900, p. 28c.
18 *The Era*, 11 August 1900, p. 27e; 14 July 1900, p. 24e.
19 *The Era*, 6 January 1900, p. 7a; 20 January, p. 27b; 3 February, p. 27d; 10 February, p. 27d.
20 *The Era*, 3 March 1900, p. 27d.
21 *The Optician*, vol. 18 (30 March 1900), p. 36.
22 *The Era*, 26 January, 1901, p. 26c.
23 *The Era*, 20 January 1900, p. 27b; and 26 January 1901, p. 31c; to quote only two of many advertisements appearing in *The Era* for the period spanned by the two references.
24 *The Era*, 6 January 1900, p. 7a.
25 *The Era*, 7 April 1900, p. 27e.
26 *The Era*, 3 February 1900, p. 27d.
27 *The Era*, 17 November 1900, p. 30e.

28 *Optical Magic Lantern Journal*, vol. 11, no. 137 (October 1900), pp. 132–3 (illus.). This apparatus is identical to the Prestwich projector illustrated in my vol. 3, p. 114.

29 *The Era*, 13 October 1900, p. 27e.

30 *The Era*, 15 December 1900, p. 32b.

31 *The Era*, 22 September 1900, p. 27d.

32 *The Optician*, 5 October 1900, p. 79.

33 Cecil M. Hepworth, *Animated Photography: the ABC of the Cinematograph* (London, 2nd edn. 1900), p. i, advert.

34 *Optical Magic Lantern Journal*, vol. 11, no. 132 (May 1900), p. 66 (Adjustable Sprocket).

35 *Photograms of the Year 1900* (November 1900), p. lxxi advert.

36 *Optical Magic Lantern Journal*, vol. 11, no. 139 (December 1900), pp. 165–6. For a fuller description of this projector see *The Optician*, 5 October 1900, p. 78.

37 *The Photogram*, vol. 7, no. 82 (October 1900), p. 330.

38 *The Optician*, 5 October 1900, p. 78.

39 *Optical Magic Lantern Journal*, vol. 11, no. 137 (October 1900), p. 134.

40 *The Era*, 6 January 1900, p. 7a.

41 *The Era*, 16 June 1900, p. 28e.

42 This title was also released by Philipp Wolff.

43 *The Era*, 16 June 1900, p. 28e.

44 *The Optician*, 5 October 1900, p. 74.

45 *The Era*, 7 July 1900, p. 24e; 14 July 1900, p. 24c.

46 *The Era*, 7 July 1900, p. 24e.

47 *The Era*, 4 August 1900, p. 24c.

48 *The Photogram*, vol. 7, no. 74 (February 1900), p. 62.

49 *The Era*, 28 April 1900, p. 27d.

50 *The Optician*, 16 February 1900, p. 804.

51 *The Era*, 24 September 1900, p. 27e.

52 *The Era*, 14 July 1900, p. 24e.

53 *The Era*, 21 July 1900, p. 24e.

54 Denis Gifford, *The British Film Catalogue 1895–1970* (Newton Abbot, 1973), films 00309–00312.

55 *The Optician*, vol. 18 (18 May 1900), p. 347.

56 NFTVA Catalogue Part 2, p. 26, film no. 223.

57 NFTVA Catalogue Part 2, p. 25, film no. 214.

58 NFTVA Catalogue Part 2, p. 25, film no. 215.

59 NFTVA Catalogue Part 2, p. 27, film no. 233 Britain's National Film & Television Archive follows a bibliographical method of classification and these 'fake newsfilms' are classified as non-fiction. This is absurd. Films are not books. In the graphic arts for instance, it is the medium (drawing, water colour, oil, etc.) that is specified, not the subject matter. Films too should have their own special system of classification. In *The Beginnings of the Cinema in England*, Vol 1 (Newton Abbot, 1976), I have suggested just such a system and this has been followed throughout the filmographies that appear in each volume of this history.

60 *The Era*, 23 June 1900, p. 27e.

61 *The Era*, 10 February 1900, p. 27a.

62 *The Era*, 14 July 1900, p. 24e.

63 *The Era*, 23 June 1900, p. 27e.

64 *The Era*, 24 November 1900, p. 27d.

65 *The Optician*, vol. 18 (11 May 1900), pp. 324 and 327.

5   Exhibitors

1 John Barnes, *The Beginnings of the Cinema in England, 1894–1901, Volume Four: 1899* (London, Bishopsgate, 1992), p. 77.

2 'The latest war films are daily reproduced by Gibbons' Bio-Tableaux at the London Hippodrome, where we invite our patrons to view them.' (WTC advertisement in *The Era*, 24 March 1900, p. 28b. See also, *British Journal of Photography*, 14 September 1900, p. 582.

3 *The Era*, 15 September 1900, p. 28b.

4 Printed programme of the London Hippodrome, 16 April 1900 (Barnes Collection).

5 *The Era*, 4 August 1900, p. 19.

6 *The Era*, 27 October 1900, p. 26e.

7 *The Era*, 17 November 1900, p. 30d.

8 *The Era*, 22 September 1900, p. 28a. A full-page advertisement listing dozens of films available, was published in *The Era*, 8 December 1900, p. 23.
9 *The Era*, 10 November 1900, p. 30b.
10 *Photographic News*, 23 November 1900, p. 775.
11 *The Era*, 26 December 1900, p. 27e.
12 *The Era*, 26 December 1900, p. 27e.
13 *The Era*, 29 December 1900, p. 31b.
14 George Eglin, 'Mr Lever, the Film Pioneer' in *The Liverpool Echo*, 7 March 1957. I am indebted to Dr Nicholas Hiley for kindly bringing this article to my attention.
15 For information regarding Lavanchy-Clarke (1848–1922), see Rosalind Cosandey and Jean-Marie Pastor, 'Lavanchy-Clarke: Sunlight & Lumieère, ou les debuts du Cinématographe en Suisse', *Equinoxe*, no. 7 (Spring 1992), pp.8–27.
16 *The Era*, 13 January 1900, p. 18b.
17 Poster (25.5375.5 cms) in the Barnes Collection.
18 *Black and White*, vol. 19, no. 481 (21 April 1900), p. 614.
19 *The Era*, 21 April 1900, p. 18.
20 *The Era*, 18 August 1900, p. 14c.
21 Printed programme in the Charles Urban Collection, Science Museum, London (URB 12/1–3).
22 *Histoire d'un crime* was directed by Ferdinand Zecca and based on a series of wax tableaux exhibited at the Musée Grevin, Paris, in 1899. See Claude Cezan, *Le Musée Grevin* (Toulouse, 1954), p. 124; and Roger Baschet, *Le monde fantastique du Musée Grevin* (Paris, 1982), p. 55, four ills. The film contains eleven shots, including the three scenes staged as flashbacks in the dream sequence.
23 Brighton Alhambra programme, 19 February 1900 (Brighton Public Reference Library Box SB 792 BR1).
24 Handbill: Alhambra Theatre, Attercliffe, 29 October 1900 (photocopy supplied by Tony Fletcher).
25 *The Era*, 6 January 1900, p. 7a.
26 *The Era*, 15 September 1900, p. 28c; 27 October, 1900, p. 26d.
27 *The Era*, 16 June, 1900, p. 28e; 23 June 1900, p. 27e.
28 *The Era*, 16 June 1900, p. 28e.
29 Printed programme in the collection of Judith A. Norton of Quebec, Canada.
30 *British Journal of Photography*, 2 November 1900, p. 86.
31 *The Era*, 6 October 1900, p. 28c.
32 *Optical Magic Lantern Journal*, vol. 11, no 135 (August 1900), p. 94.

6   Home Movies

1 Henry V. Hopwood, 'Cinematography for All' in *The Optician* (29 March 1901), pp. 66–74.
2 For a comprehensive account of toy cinematographs the reader is referred to Stephen Herbert, 'German Home and Toy Magic Lantern-Cinematographs' in *The New Magic Lantern Journal*, vol. 5, no. 2 (August 1987), pp. 11–15.
3 *Optical Magic Lantern Journal*, vol. 11, no. 132 (May 1900), pp. 66–7.
4 *Optical Magic Lantern Journal* vol. 11, no. 132 (May 1900), p. 67.
5 W.C. Hughes, *'La Petite' Living Picture Camera and Projector*. Four-page leaflet in the collection of La Cinémathèque Française.
6 *La Nature*, 22 September 1900 (No page no. ref).
7 *La Nature* 15 December 1900, pp. 43–4. See also *Amateur Photographer*, vol. 32, no. 829 (24 August 1900), p. 144. An example of this apparatus, in an incomplete state, is in the Barnes Collection.
8 *The Kammatograph; Accessories & Specialities*. Catalogue published by L. Kamm & Co. (London, N. D., 1900. Copy in the Fox Talbot Museum, Lacock. The museum also has on loan a Kammatograph apparatus and instruction manual.
9 Fifteen miscellaneous negative and positive Kammatograph glass discs, in their original box, are in the Barnes Collection.
10 Date of application, 17 March 1898; Complete specification left 1 September 1898; Accepted 3 December 1898.
11 An example of the 1918 model is in the Barnes Collection.
12 *The Optician*, 5 October 1900, p. 157.
13 See Herbert, 'German Home and Toy Magic Lantern-Cinematographs', pp. 11–5.
14 *The Photogram*, vol. 7, no. 73 (January 1900), p. 30.
15 British Patent No. 925, 18 March 1868. The subjects of two Kineographs in the Barnes Collection are, *The Windmill*; and *Paganni*.

16 The Filoscope is described and illustrated in John Barnes, *The Beginnings of the Cinema in England*, Vol. 1 (Newton Abbot, 1976), pp. 107–8.

17 I am grateful to Peter Jewell for kindly bringing my attention to this catalogue, a copy of which is in the Jewell-Douglas Collection.

18 Barnes, *The Beginnings of the Cinema in England*, Vol. 1, pp. 107–8.

19 Examples in the Barnes Collection and in the collection of Lester & Stephenie Smith and the Jewell-Douglas Collection.

20 I am grateful to Lester Smith for kindly bringing this document to my attention, a copy of which is in the Smith Collection.

21 I wish to acknowledge Peter Jewell for kindly supplying the complete text which was previously quoted in an incomplete state in my book *The Beginnings of the Cinema in England*, Vol. 1, p. 108.

22 Five examples in the Barnes Collection are rubber stamped: 'Manufactured by license from the Mutoscope and Biograph Syndicate Ltd for the United Kingdom'. Two other examples have printed marks: 'Manufactured by licence from the British Mutoscope & Biograph Co. Ltd.' Obviously H.W. Short's patent of 1898 was in conflict with Casler's original patent of 1895.

23 The example in the Barnes Collection states: 'Sole Licensee under patents of American Mutoscope and Biograph Company. US patent no. 838,610. Other patents applied for.' A list of thirteen Winthrop Moving Picture Books, offered for sale by the London dealer Jilliana, is in the Barnes Collection.

24 Barnes, *The Beginnings of the Cinema in England*, Vol. 3, pp. 161–64.

25 'Our Future King at Play', in *The Harmsworth Magazine*, vol. 5, no. 27 (October, 1900), pp. 194–200. The photographs appearing in the article are credited to the Biograph Studio, Regent St.

26 *Amateur Photographer*, vol. 31, no. 812 (27 April, 1900), p. 321.

27 *La Nature*, 18 August, 1900, p. 192.

28 Reproduced in Daniel Brochard, *Photo-Compilation* (Theleme, 1978), p. 41.

29 Examples of both models are in the Barnes Collection.

30 For a detailed study of the Kinora, see Stephen Herbert, *Kinora Living Pictures* (London, 1984), a privately published paper; and Barry Anthony, *The Kinora: Motion Pictures for the Home 1896–1914* (The Projection Box, 66 Culverden Road, London SW12 9LS) 1966.

Index of Film Titles

General Index